THE DICTIONARY OF MAINE PLACE-NAMES

by

Phillip R. Rutherford

Professor of English
University of Maine at Portland-Gorham, Gorham Campus

The Bond Wheelwright Company
Publishers
Freeport, Maine

For Lou, Phil, and Kris

PREFACE

One of the more fascinating aspects of Maine history is that relating to the origin of the many varied and picturesque place-names. Some names are quickly identified with persons of local, state or national distinction; others are associated with English, Scottish, Irish or French towns or Massachusetts or New Hampshire communities; and still others have obvious Indian origin. Many, however, are hard to assign authoritatively and must be researched extensively.

Dr. Phillip Rutherford, professor of language and linguistics at the Gorham campus of the University of Maine at Portland-Gorham, has contributed a valuable addition to our literature, for he goes far beyond the previous work by Dr. Ava Chadbourne. Especially noteworthy is the identification of place-names within the boundaries of the individual towns. Students of local history will find this work an interesting and useful index to the study of Maine towns and their various neighborhoods.

Robert M. York
State Historian

August 1970

ACKNOWLEDGMENT

I wish to thank the people who have assisted me in the compilation of this dictionary. Located at the end of the county entries is a list of those Maine citizens who have given of their time so that this book could become a reality. Also included there are the names of students at the Gorham State College Campus of the University of Maine at Portland-Gorham to whom I express special gratitude. I especially thank my secretary, Kerry Sue Wallace, who did so many different and monotonous jobs. To Lou, my wife, I express my most sincere appreciation for her encouragement and aid in preparation of the final manuscript. In addition, I thank all those people who have helped me in any manner in the research for this book and whom I may have failed to include in the list of sources.

CONTENTS

MAINE

MAINE: It is easier to find the positive derivation of an insignificant stream in Aroostook County than it is to say for certain just how the state of Maine received its name. There are at least three possibilities: it could have been named for the province of Maine in France; it could have been named for its being the "main" land (frequently spelled "maine") which lay beyond the many coastal islands; or it could have been named for being the land on the "main," or ocean.

THE NAMING OF NAMES

Names. What causes man to give names to cities, towns, brooks, rivers? It might be an attempt to grasp a little immortality when the name is the name of the man who bestows it. It might be to do honor to some benefactor when all the people have to give is the vow not to forget his name. It might simply be a term of reference so that people can talk and know the place of which they speak. Why does man give names? Everywhere man has traveled, in the mountains, in the plains, in the desert, in the forests, he has left a part of himself, a name. Some are monuments to his fame: Bingham, Hancock, Wayne; some are signs of his failures: Emery's Misery, Folly Pond, Wreck Island; some are displays of his patriotism: Freedom, Washington, Columbia; some are remembrances of former homes: New Sweden, York, Portland; some are attempts at humor: Death Valley, Butter Hill, The Promised Land; most are there for countless other reasons.

This investigation of Maine place-names has been initiated and completed about twenty-five years too late. Time and time again the author has been told that he should have talked to Aunt Shirley or Uncle Ralph or Old Man Schleh, who would have known all the information, but alas, has been dead since the 1940's. A significant number of people have advised against a place-name study due to the paucity of written information, lack of adequate town records, and impossibility of verification of many of the derivations. All of these objections are valid; however, the longer such an investigation is delayed, the more information disappears. The last of the settlers have been dead for many years. Now, most of the people who had at least dim recollections of them are gone. If the information, which lies as much in the area of folklore as history, is not recorded now, it will soon be as irretrievably lost as the history of Celtic England.

Although there are numerous obstacles a researcher faces when attempting a place-name study, the first is determining just what are the place-names of a given locality. The names which man gives to the familiar landmarks around him are not stable like the bedrock or even as long-lived as an oak; they are as nebulous and changeable as the summer wind and as fleeting as the snows of April. As one man settles on an ocean point, it may be named for him, "Cooper's Point." When he dies, or sells to someone else, the name will frequently change to reflect the new ownership, "Perry's Point." Over a period of three hundred years, the point may have a dozen names, the latest of which denoting only its last, or present, occupant. By the same token, a particular landmark, such as a hill, may be known by three or four names simultaneously. One family may call it "Julian Hill" for James Julian, who first settled on its crest. Another may call it "Huckeba's Knob," for Grandpa Huckeba, who bought it from Julian. Yet another person may know it as "Zachery's Leap" for Zachery Phillips, who stumbled over a cliff there one night while drunk.

In addition to the multiplicity of names for one geographical feature, another problem lies in attempting to collect all the place-names of even a small area. The names which occur on a map are recorded, supposedly, because they are important or reflect general usage, but it frequently happens that some are there by accident; for instance, the surveyor asks someone the name of a small brook, and the person gives his private name for it, ignoring the name by which it is usually known. Compounded with this problem is another: any area will have a great many names known only in that immediate locality and never recorded on a map because of their comparative insignificance.

Considering the difficulties in simply collecting the names to be investigated, this researcher limited those that are listed in this book—approximately twenty thousand—to those that appear on the latest set of United States National Geological Survey maps. This, of course, limits the scope of the work to names that are still in existence. (The derivation of these past place-names is a complete and needed study in itself, outside the scope of this investigation.) The maps, while probably the most complete, are frequently inaccurate, placing streams in the wrong locations, recording names that were used fifty years ago but have now changed, grossly misspelling many names, and depending too much on previous maps for information instead of original research. Although these two hundred and seventy-seven maps were combed meticulously three times for names, there is little doubt that some have been overlooked.

Maine itself presents certain obstacles to the onomastics scholar that exist in only a few other places in the United States. Much of the coastal and southern area has been settled for three hundred and fifty years, with correspondingly aged place-names.

Naturally many of the names in these areas are totally covered by the dust of history. The derivations that exist are frequently interlaced with folklore and tradition, and cannot be proved accurate at this late date. If, then, it is true that old place-names present difficulties, it might seem, conversely, that the derivation of newer place-names should be easy to find. Sadly enough, such is not the case. If place-names are of a relatively recent origin, they are frequently unknown to a great many inhabitants, who may call them by names differing from those that are found on the map. In other words, the name for a particular geographical feature may not be old enough for it to have stabilized. An informant may know for whom or what a feature was named, as he knows the name, but may not have ever heard of the name used on the map.

The primary difficulty in investigating Maine place-names, however, does not lie in the very old or the very new names, but in finding the derivations of the names in the unorganized areas. These places frequently have more names located within their boundaries than the heavily populated southern area, but there are relatively few people who live there or are familiar with the history of the region. For this reason, it will be noticed that those counties with large, unorganized areas, such as Somerset, Aroostook, and Piscataquis, have many place-names with unknown derivations.

Still another problem encountered in this study was with the Indian place-names. These names have been recorded numerous times over the years by whites who were not familiar with the local Indian languages and were something less than adept at spelling their own language (as the frequent variation between the spelling of the place-names and family names clearly shows in this study); consequently, their spelling of the Indian words, which contained sounds that did not even exist in English and French, varied greatly—so much, in fact, that it is even difficult for the experts to ascertain just what the original words were. Together with this problem were two others. The principal Indian languages in Maine, Micmac, Malecite, and Abnaki, are quite similar in vocabulary, structure, and phonology. Cognate words which may have had approximately the same pronunciation in the three languages, frequently have different meanings. For instance, Mattawamkeag means "fishing place beyond the gravel bar" if it is Abnaki; "rapids at the mouth" if it is Malecite; or "on a sand bar" if it is Micmac. The other problem is that the

Indian word will frequently have one meaning in the older form of the particular language and another in the more recent form; therefore Mousam may mean "grandfather" in late Abnaki and "snare" in Old Abnaki.

Maine is quite fortunate in having at least three good sources for its Indian place-names. The derivations listed in this dictionary have been taken, with only a few exceptions, from *Indian Place Names of New England* by John C. Huden (Hey Foundation, New York, 1962), "Indian Place Names on the Penobscot and St. John Rivers in Maine" by Moses Greenleaf (DeBurian Club, Bangor, Maine, 1904), and *Indian Place Names of the Penobscot Valley and the Maine Coast* by Fannie H. Eckstorm (University Press, Orono, Maine, 1941).

The information contained in this book comes essentially from two sources—inhabitants of the state and printed material. While there is a considerable amount of written matter on the older, organized townships, there have been few histories written on the newer townships and almost nothing on the unorganized areas. Nevertheless, what town histories, county histories, and maps were available were investigated. Of particular value was Ava H. Chadbourne's *Maine Place Names* (The Bond Wheelwright Company, Portland, Maine, 1955), which deals with the settling of the organized townships and how they were named. The primary deviation in the use of her approximately four hundred place-name derivations has been to omit many of the "forced" reasons why some of the towns were given classical names, foreign place-names, names of famous personages, and Massachusetts place-names. The main reason why these first three categories of names were bestowed is simply because it was a custom of the time, primarily the early nineteenth century, both in Maine and across the United States. While it is true that many names in the last category were bestowed by settlers from Massachusetts in remembrance of their old homes, some were given for no reason except that it was customary.

Although written information was helpful in preparing this work, it could not compare in value to the information received from the inhabitants of the various areas. Naturally, much of it is folklore and cannot be verified, except possibly by other inhabitants, who might themselves cling to conflicting stories. And since so much of it is folklore, it is not possible, in most cases, to pronounce a particular opinion as correct and another as untrue. It will be observed that when two or more conflicting derivations of a place-name exist, all are recorded with, usually, little editorial comment. About the only derivations that were rejected outright by the author were the patently folk etymological derivations of Indian names, such as "My gal away" for Magalloway; "Scow, he gone" for Skowhegan; "See Bay go" for Sebago; "Moose, look, me gun tick," for Mooselookmeguntic; etc. A few of these, however, for various reasons have been included.

The author apologizes for the large number of place-names in the following listings that have only the explanation, "for the so-and-so family." The reader may feel that it is perfectly obvious that Penny Hill was named for the Penny family; however, it should be remembered that in many cases this is all that is known about how a certain place was named. The family which left its name might have lived there for only a brief time and left no other records in their short sojourn. This type of entry, however, has only been recorded when the information was obtained from an informant: it has not been used indiscriminately by the author.

If someone finds what he considers an error in the *Dictionary,* there are a number of possible explanations for it. One, there may be a difference of opinion as to what the correct derivation is, and in some cases, where there are no records, one opinion may be as valid as another, for they may both be based on tradition.

Two, there may be a difference in interpretation of the available information. The reader may feel that the name stemmed from another member of the family rather than the person to whom it is attributed. Wilson Hill, for instance, may be said to be named for John Wilson, whereas one reader may feel it was named for John's father, Joel Wilson, and another reader, for his grandson Rosen Wilson. It is usually impossible to draw any definite conclusions as for whom it was actually named. Although the name might appear first on a map at the time Rosen Wilson was living there, it might have actually gained its name for all the members of the Wilson family who lived here for three generations; therefore, it could reasonably be said to be named for any or all of them. Sometimes, therefore, when it was impossible to say a name was given for a certain member of the family, the author has attributed it to the family's earliest member in the area.

Three, the reader may be confusing a different, non-recorded name with the one listed. For example, the explanation for Devine Hill may be "for Jim Devine," whereas the reader knows conclusively that a Devine Hill in the same county was named for Kenneth Wayne Devine. Upon checking the National Geological Survey map, if he finds that the hill he was thinking of is not shown, the listed explanation for the hill can be assumed to be correct.

Four, the given derivation of a name may be an outright error. Pope once said,

> Whoever thinks a faultless piece to see
> Thinks what ne'er was, nor is, nor e'er shall be.

While he was speaking of poetry, the same may be applied to this or any other place-name dictionary. In dealing with approximately twenty thousand place-names, considerable error is bound to creep in, whether it be from accidental or intentional misinformation on the part of the informant or misunderstanding or ignorance on the part of the author. It is hoped that the reader, when he discovers an error, has a difference of opinion, or knows the derivation of a place-name listed as unknown, will contact the author so that it can be corrected, and another small bit of Maine heritage be preserved for posterity.

GENERAL EXPLANATION

Sample entry:

REUTER: BRIDGE (settlement), HILL (2), NORTH-CORNER, settlement, -VILLE, WEST-. Bridge, for J. Reuter, settler, 1869. Settlement, Hill, North-Corner, and West- in Roxton Township, for Rath Reuter, local woodsman. Hill and -ville in Belle Mead Township, for L.C. Reuter.

1. The place-names within the counties, and the counties, are in alphabetical order, except when it has been necessary to violate it for clarity.

2. The place-names are in capital letters; for instance, in the sample entry, "Reuter" should be read with all the words in capitals after the colon: Reuter Bridge, Reuter Hill.

3. If a dash follows a part of a place-name after the colon, the name preceding the colon should be read in the place of the dash: North Reuter Corner, West Reuter.

4. If a dash precedes a part of a place-name after the colon, the name preceding the colon should be read in place of it: Reuterville.

5. If a word in the main entry is not in capitals (or not in capitals and in parenthesis), it means that the word is just an explanation of the main entry: "Reuter" and "Reuter Bridge" are settlements.

6. A number in parenthesis following any name signifies the number of places within a county with that particular name: there are two Reuter Hills in this county. If both Reuter Hills are in the same township, the name of the township is not mentioned. If they are in different townships, the townships' names are given. If both Reuter Hills are named for the same reason—such as "for the respective Reuter families"—even though they are in different townships, the names of the townships are not given.

The term "township" has been used in the entries whether the body be a township, plantation, or unorganized territory, for the status of these frequently changes. Likewise the term "settlement" is used to designate a collection of houses, whether that collection be two empty houses or a group as large as Portland.

The place-names are recorded in the *Dictionary* as they appear on the Survey maps, even if the spellings are obviously in error. Since the maps do not make use of the apostrophe in such names as Cooper's Point, this style is also followed here.

The derivation of a waterway should be searched for in adjoining counties if it is not to be found in the county one thinks it should be, as some run over county lines.

When a place-name is made up of separate words, such as West Robbers Cove, one may have to look up each word until the name is found.

ANDROSCOGGIN COUNTY

ABRAMS POINT. For Abram Edwards, resident, 1858.

ALLEN: POND, STREAM. For John Allen, Revolutionary War veteran, settler, 1790.

ANDROSCOGGIN: COUNTY, LITTLE-RIVER, RIVER. Abnaki: "the place where fish are cured."

APPLE SASS HILL. The Davis family owned an apple orchard here, and the wife made and sold apple sauce, sometimes pronounced "apple sass" in the Maine dialect.

AUBURN: EAST-, LAKE-, NEW-, NORTH-, PLAINS, TOWNSHIP, WEST-. Some say the name is taken from Goldsmith's poem "Sweet Auburn, loveliest village of the plains." Others say for Aubourn, Lincolnshire, England.

BAILEY HILL. For Thomas Bailey, settler, 1794.

BARKER BROOK. For Jacob Barker, owner of a saw and gristmill, 1774.

BARTLETT POND. For Asa Bartlett, settler, before 1800.

BASIN, THE. Descriptive.

BEALS BROOK. For Samuel Beals, early settler.

BERRY POND. For George Berry, settler, about 1775.

BILLINGTON BROOK. For F. N. Billington, living on the banks in 1873.

BISHOP HILL. For Zadock Bishop, who settled here in 1783 after nearly getting flooded out in Monmouth. He chose the hill for his home, vowing never to be in a flood again.

BLACK CAT MOUNTAIN. For a huge black wildcat cornered there by hunters.

BLACK: ISLAND, POND. Descriptive.

BLAKES CORNER. For I. Blake, resident, 1858.

BOG BROOK. Descriptive.

BONNEY POND. Possibly for being a pretty ("bonny") pond.

BOOTHBY HILL. For Stephen Boothby, early landowner.

BOWIE HILL. Probably for George Bowie, early settler.

BRADFORD BROOK. For William Bradford, nearby in 1877.

BRETTUNS: MILLS, POND. For William H. Brettun, mill owner, early 19th century.

BUTTER HILL. About 1820 the area farmers used to gather in the general store to talk, and among them was a man who lived on this hill. As he was always stealing from the store, the owner decided to lay a trap for him by placing some fresh butter so that it was accessible and told a number of the other men of his plan. As this man started to leave the store, he slipped the butter under his cap. Being hemmed in by the other men and not wanting to look suspicious, he continued sitting next to the stove, where the storekeeper had a hot fire burning. Before long the butter began to stream down his face as it melted under his heavy cap. From then on his home was called Butter Hill.

CHASE HILL. For the Thomas Chase family, prominent early settlers.

CHASE MILLS. For Isaac Chase, settler, 1820, sawmill owner.

CHRISTIAN HILL. For the pious people living there.

CLARK MOUNTAIN. For Joseph Clark, veteran, War of 1812.

COOL BROOK. Descriptive.

COUSINS BROOK. Possibly for John Cousens, settler, about 1800.

CROSSMAN CORNER. For David Crossman, early settler.

CRYSTAL POND. Descriptive.

CURTIS: BOG, BROOK. For the early Curtis family who lived near.

CURTIS CORNER. For William Curtis, settler, 1800.

CUSTER POINT. Named by Mrs. Henry S. Marr for no known reason.

DAGGETT BOG. For Captain John Daggett, who settled here in 1786.

DANVILLE: CORNER, settlement. Probably for Danville, Vermont.

DAVIS BROOK. For a Captain Davis, who settled between 1768-95.

DEAD: RIVER, flagstation. Description of flowage.

DEANE POND. For Cyrus Deane, settler, 1790.

DEATH VALLEY. For a joking conversation between two men. One said that he did not want to live down in "Death Valley" where the other lived. That man replied he wouldn't want to live on "Poor Man's Hill." The first name survived; the second did not.

DILLINGHAM HILL. For the Dillingham family, settlers, 1798.

DRINKWATER CORNER. For Captain Edward Drinkwater and his son Abijah, prominent early settlers.

DURHAM: SOUTH-, SOUTHWEST BEND, TOWNSHIP, WEST-. For Durham, England, former home of the proprietor, Colonel Royal of Medford, Massachusetts.

DYER BROOK. For David Dyer, early settler.

EAST HEBRON. For Hebron Township.

EMPIRE. Named by Joshua Dunn for its fancied greatness and its influence on state politics.

ESTES BOG. Possibly for William Estes, local farmer.

FAIRVIEW HILL. Descriptive.

FISHER STREAM. For S. Fisher, who lived there in 1873, or his ancestors.

FISH MEADOW BROOK. For Major Thomas Fish, Revolutionary War soldier, settler of 1779.

FOGGS CORNER. For the Walter Fogg family, settlers, 1804-1805.

FORD BROOK. In 1790-1800, the only general store in the area was at Brettuns Mills. All the settlers living east of Bartlett Pond had to cross this stream to get to the store. As there was no bridge here, they found a shallow place to "ford."

FORD HILL. For a number of Ford families in the area.

FROG POND. For frogs.

GARCELON BOG. For James Garcelon, settler, 1776.

GARDNER BROOK. For John Gardiner, Revolutionary War veteran.

GENERAL TURNER HILL. For Colonel William Turner, son of the namesake of Turner Township.

GERRISH BROOK. For the William Gerrish family, early settlers.

GLENROCK SPRING. Selected only because it was a "pretty name."

GOFF LEDGE. For James Goff, Revolutionary Was veteran, settler about 1785.

GREENE CORNER, TOWNSHIP. For General Greene of Revolutionary War fame.

GRISWOLD ISLAND. For E. Griswold, who lived there in 1873.

GULF ISLAND POND. Formed by the building of a dam across a natural depression or "gulf."

HACKETT HILL. Probably a cartographer's mistake and named for E. Haggett, who lived there in 1873.

HACKETT MILLS. For Levi Hackett, mill owner for 40 years.

HAINES CORNER. For the Captain Peter Haines family, settlers, 1796.

HARMONS CORNER. For many Harmons living there, 1873.

HARRIS HILL. For William and David Harris, settlers about 1845.

HASKELL CORNER. For the Nathan Haskell family, settlers before 1800.

HEDGEHOG HILL. (2). The dialect name for porcupines, which inhabit the area.

HERSEY HILL. For James, Noah, and Amos Hersey, settlers before 1800.

HIGGINS CORNER. For Captain Jeremiah Higgins, a settler, the early 1800's.

HIGHLAND SPRINGS. Descriptive.

HILL RIDGE. For Nathaniel Hill, settler of 1808.

HODGE HILL. For John Hodge, farmer, settler before 1800.

HODGKINS BROOK. For the early Hogkins family.

HODGMAN HILL. For L. Hodgman, resident, 1873.

HOOPER BROOK. For Captain David Hooper, settler, 1807.

HOUSE BROOK. (2). In Turner Township, for the Caleb House family, settlers before 1793. In Auburn Township, for Elisha House, who bought the land at its head and later drowned in the brook.

HOWES CORNER. For Dr. Timothy Howe, settler about 1804.

HUNTON BROOK. For W. Hunton, merchant, 1800's.

INDIAN BROOK. For the area Indians.

ISLAND POND. Descriptive of an island located in it.

JEPSON BROOK. For the many Jepsons in the area in 1873.

JOCK STREAM. For an old hunter and trapper who lived there, John Munyaw, possibly an Indian. The stream was first called Jocmunyaw, and later shortened.

JOHNSON HILL. For Joseph Johnson, early settler.

JUG HILL. Named by an early trader because the inhabitants of the area brought their jugs to him every Saturday night to be filled with rum.

KEENES CORNER. For G. Keene, resident, 1858.

KEENS MILLS. For Hanover Keen, settler, 1805, gristmill owner.

KEITH BROOK. For Ebenezer Keith, settler, late 1700's.

LAPHAM BROOK. For Abiel Lapham, settler, 1798.

LARD POND. During a timber operation in the woods of Turner Township, a logging crew sat down for lunch on the banks of this pond. One of the men opened his lunch bucket to discover that he had picked up his wife's lard bucket that morning by mistake. The loggers thought that this was so funny they named it for the incident.

LAURAFFE RIDGE. Probably named for D. Larrabee, who lived there in 1873. More than likely "Lauraffe" is a cartographical error.

LEAVITT BROOK. For Captain Leavitt, farmer and settler, early 1820's.

LEEDS: JUNCTION, NORTH-, settlement, SOUTH-, Township, WEST-. For Leeds, England the home of John Stinchfield, the father of the first settlers, Thomas and Roger.

LEWISTON: JUNCTION, settlement, SOUTH-, TOWNSHIP. According to folklore, a drunk Indian named Lewis drowned at the falls in the present settlement and the falls were named for him. The township was named for the falls.

LIBBY HILL. Probably for Jonathon Libby, settler, 1804.

LIBBY PIT. For T.F. Libby, who operated a quarry there in 1873.

LILY POND. For lilies.

LISBON: CENTER, FALLS, RIDGE, settlement, TOWNSHIP. For Lisbon, Portugal. In the 1800's it was popular in Maine to name townships after foreign cities.

LITTLEFIELD CORNER. For Colonel Thomas Littlefield.

LITTLE WILSON POND. For the former name of Lake Auburn, Wilson Pond.

LIVELY BROOK. Descriptive.

LIVERMORE: CENTER, EAST-(settlement), EAST-TOWNSHIP, FALLS, NORTH-, SOUTH-, TOWNSHIP. For Deacon Elijah Livermore, proprietor and first settler.

LONG POND. Descriptive.

LOON POND. For loons.

LOTHROP ISLAND. For the family of Colonel Daniel Lothrop, Revolutionary war soldier, settler, 1785.

MANN HILL. For J. Mann, resident, 1858.

MARR POINT. For the Daniel and Rufus Marr families, settlers about 1809.

MARSTON CORNER. For the owner of Marston Tavern.

MARTIN STREAM. For the early Martin family.

MAXWELL BROOK. For James Maxwell, settler, late 1700's.

MAXWELL SWAMP. For Joseph Maxwell, settler about 1800.

MEADOW BROOK. (4). Descriptive.

MECHANIC FALLS: settlement, TOWNSHIP. For the early local industry and the "mechanics" who operated it.

MEGUIER: HILL, ISLAND. For Edmund Meguier, settler, 1790.

MERRILL HILL. (3). In Auburn Township, for Elias Merrill, settler, 1791. In Turner Township, for Jabez Merrill, settler, 1776. In Greene Township, for the Benjamin Merrill family, first permanent settlers.

MINOT: CENTER-, settlement, TOWNSHIP, WEST- For Judge Minot, member of the General Court of Massachusetts.

MOODY BROOK. Probably for Robert Moody, settler, early 1800's.

MOOSE: BROOK, HILL, HILL POND. For moose in the area. Moose Hill was named specifically for a moose killed there by Deacon Elijah Livermore in the 1790's.

MORGAN BROOK. For Samuel Morgan, settler, 1784.

MOUNT APATITE. For apatite, a mineral mined there.

MOUNT DAVID. For David Davis, owner.

MOUNT GILE. For Edwin T. Gile, who attempted to create a recreational area there.

MOUNT HUNGER. Named by the early settlers because they could barely make a living farming the rocky ground.

MOUNT PROSPECT. Descriptive of the view.

MOUSSAM. If Abnaki, it means "grandfather"; if Old Abnaki, "a snare."

MUD POND. (3). Descriptive.

NASON BEACH. For C.F. Nason who lived there in 1873.

NELSON POND. Probably for Lot P. Nelson, early trader.

NEWELL BROOK. For Ebenezer Newell, early settler.

NEZINSCOT RIVER. Abnaki: "place of descent."

NO NAME: BROOK, POND. When the area was surveyed the cartographers could discover no name for the pond or brook.

OAK: HILL (3), HILL (settlement). For oak trees.

PENLEYS CORNER. For Captain John Penley, settler before 1850.

PICKEREL POND. For pickerel fish.

PIGEON HILL. For the pigeons which roosted there.

PINE POINT. For pine trees.

PINKHAM BROOK. For Andrew Pinkham, early settler.

PLAINS, THE. Descriptive.

PLEASANT POND. Descriptive.

PLUMMER MILL. For Henry Plummer who ran a saw and gristmill there before 1835.

POLAND: EAST-, settlement, SPRING, SPRING STATION, SOUTH-, TOWNSHIP,WEST-. One source says for the old hymn "Poland," a favorite of Moses Emery, an agent of the General Court of Massachusetts. Another says for the Indian Chief Polan. Yet another says for the nation of Poland.

POPLAR HILL. For poplar trees.

POTASH: BROOK, COVE. For potash made here by Captain Waite, about 1800.

POTTER BROOK. Probably for Benjamin R. Potter, settler, 1817.

POTTLE HILL. For William Pottle, settler, 1782-83.

PRIDE HILL. For Nathan Pride, farmer and early settler.

PROMISED LAND. This land was held in trust for many years for the Emerson heirs, and anyone who squatted on it could not get a clear title. Disappointed settlers claimed that it must be promised to the children of Israel.

QUAKER HILL. For members of the Quaker Church who lived there.

RACK POND. Unknown.

RANGE: BROOK, HILL, LOWER-POND, UPPER-POND. "Range" is a surveying term meaning a primary surveying line.

RASPBERRY HILL. For raspberries growing there.

RED WATER BROOK. Descriptive.

RICHS MOUNTAIN. For Thomas and David Rich, settlers about 1800.

RICKER HILL. (2). In Poland Township, for Jabez Ricker and his sons, developers of Poland Spring. In Turner Township, for the Ricker family, there by 1843.

ROBINSON CORNER. For the Benjamin Robinson family, settlers about 1800.

ROBINSON MOUNTAIN. For Deacon and Willard Robinson, who had a carriage house at its foot.

ROUND POND. (4). Descriptive.

ROWES CORNER. For the Jonathon Rowe family, settlers before 1800.

RUMFORD JUNCTION. A junction on the Maine Central Railroad which goes to Rumford, Maine.

RUNAROUND POND. Descriptive of its irregular shore line.

SABATTUS: LITTLE-MOUNTAIN, LITTLE-RIVER, MOUNTAIN, POND, RIVER, settlement. For Sabattus, chief of the Anasagunticooks, who was killed in the area. "Sabattus" is said to be the Indian pronunciation of the common French name "Jean Baptiste."

SALMON BROOK. For salmon fish.

SAND HILL. Descriptive.

SANDY BOTTOM POND. Descriptive.

SCOTT BROOK. For a man of that name who was the first white settler in the area.

SHACKLEY HILL. For M. Shackley, in the area by 1873.

SHAKER: BOG, HILL. For a nearby Shaker community.

SHAW HILL. For Samuel Shaw, settler, 1776-77.

SHILOH. For the Shiloh Religious Colony, founded by Frank W. Sanford, a member of the Holy Ghost and Us Society.

SHY CORNER. The Kennebec Indians would always abandon their camp when approached by members of the Roccomeka tribe. The Roccomekas called them "the shy Indians."

SKILLINGS CORNER. For S.B. Skillings, who lived there in 1873.

SNELL HILL. For Thomas Snell, one of the proprietors of Turner Township.

SOPER MILL BROOK. For H. Soper, there in 1873, or his ancestors.

SPRAGUE MILL. For Colonel William Sprague, Revolutionary War veteran, settler, 1779.

STETSON BROOK. For E. Stutson, who lived near in 1873.

STEVENS MILL. For Jacob Stevens, settler, 1789.

STRICKLAND. For Hastings Strickland, farmer and settler of 1798.

SUMMIT SPRING. Descriptive.

SUTHERLAND POND. For the early Sutherland family.

TAYLOR: BROOK, POND. For Thomas and Joshua Taylor, settlers, 1795.

TEAGUE HILL. For the Bani Teague family, settlers before 1796.

THORNCRAG HILL. For A.D. Thorne, who lived there in 1873.

TRIPP POND. For Richard Tripp, settler before 1800.

TURNER: CENTER, EAST-, NORTH-, NORTH-BRIDGE (settlement), settlement, SOUTH-, TOWNSHIP. For the Reverend Charles Turner, state senator of Massachusetts and resident of the area before 1786.

TURNER POND. For a man who drowned there in the 1800's.

TURTLE ISLAND. For turtles.

WALES: CENTER, CORNER, EAST- , TOWNSHIP. For the Wales area of England, home of the ancestors of John Welch, one of the prominent early settlers.

WEBSTER: CORNER, TOWNSHIP. For the renowned Daniel Webster.

WHITES HILL. For the first area settler, White, who owned the hill before1800.

WINDSOR SPRING. For the Windsor family who bottled and sold water from the spring.

WOODBURY HILL. For True Woodbury, settler before 1800.

WOODMAN HILL. For True Woodman, settler, 1785.

WORTHLEY: BROOK, POND. Unknown.

YOUNG CORNER. For Christopher Young, settler, 1798.

AROOSTOOK COUNTY

ABRAHAM POINT. Unknown.

ACADIA. For French-Acadians in the area.

ADALINE. For Adeline Bugbee Crouse.

ADAMS MOUNTAIN. Probably for the Edward Adams family.

ADVENT: BROOK, SWAMP. Unknown.

AEGAN BROOK. Unknown.

AGNES POND BROOK. For Agnes, wife of a lumberman, who traveled with him as a cook. She got her water here.

AKER BROOK. Unknown.

ALDER: BROOK (5), LAKE. For alder trees.

ALEC BROOK. For Alex Paradis, an old trapper.

ALERTON LAKE. For R.F. Alterton, Civil War veteran.

ALEXANDER BROOK. Unknown.

ALLAGASH: FALLS, RIVER, TOWNSHIP. Abnaki: "bark cabin."

AMITY: NORTH-, TOWNSHIP. For the friendliness that existed among the early inhabitants.

AMSDEN BROOK. For Thomas Amsden, settler, 1836.

ANDERSON BOG. For Robert Anderson, settler, early 1800's.

ANDERSON BROOK. For the Anderson family, who bought it from the Alley family.

ANGUS BROOK. Unknown.

ARBO BROOK. For the early Arbo family.

ARBO FLATS. For Miles D. Arbo, who lived and did business here.

ARMSTRONG BROOK. For Armstrong, a logger.

ARNOLD BROOK. Reportedly for Benedict Arnold.

AROOSTOOK: COUNTY, RIVER. Micmac: "beautiful" or "shining river."

ASHLAND: settlement, TOWNSHIP. For Ashland, Henry Clay's estate.

ATWELL BROOK. Unknown.

AUDIBERT BROOK. For Willette Audibert, who had a farm there.

BABCOCK BROOK. Unknown.

BACK SETTLEMENT. For two families of lumbermen who settled here, back from the St. Francis River.

BAKER BROOK. Unknown.

BALD MOUNTAIN. Descriptive.

BALDY. Descriptive.

BANCROFT: NORTH-, settlement, SOUTH-, TOWNSHIP. For George Bancroft, the historian, whose brother was historian of the town.

BARKER RIDGE. For Cyrus Barker, settler, 1853.

BARLEY LAKE. Unknown.

BARRETTS. For the Barrett family, who had holdings in the Caribou area.

BARSTOW: BROOK, POINT. For Barstow, a logger.

BASKAHEGAN STREAM. Abnaki: "branch downstream" or "branch stream that turns down current."

BASS BROOK. (2). For bass fish.

BASTE RIPS. Unknown.

BASTON BROOK. For Joseph Baston, settler, 1840.

BATES RIDGE. For Jake and Howard Bates, uncles of Rosmari Hill's husband.

BATESVILLE. For the numerous Bates who lived here in the last half of the 19th century.

BATTLE: BROOK (2), LITTLE-BROOK. In Bancroft Township, for, as legend tells, a battle between two tribes of Indians. In Dyer Brook Township, unknown.

BAXTER BROOK. Unknown.

BEAN: BROOK, POND. For a soldier of the Aroostook War, who settled after the "hostilities."

BEAR: BROOK (6), ISLAND, MOUNTAIN, MOUNTAIN POND, RIDGE. For bears.

BEARSLEY BROOK. For Beardsley, a surveyor or lumberman.

BEAU LAKE. Descriptive. French: "beautiful."

BEAULIEU: BROOK, LOWER-BROOK. For Benoit Beaulieu, who owned an area farm.

BEAVER: BRANCH, BROOK (5), BROOK LAKE, -DAM POINT, EAST BRANCH-BROOK, LITTLE-BROOK, POND (3), POND BROOK, WEST BRANCH-BROOK. For beavers.

BEAVER TAIL POND. Descriptive of shape.

BEECH HILL. (2). For beech trees.

BELANGER SETTLEMENT. For Antoine Belanger, who first settled in the area.

BELLANGER POINT. For Baptiste Bellanger, who owned the point.

BELL BROOK. Unknown.

BENEDICTA: settlement, TOWNSHIP. For Bishop Benedict Fenwick, who held title to the land.

BEN GLAZIER: BROOK, WEST BRANCH-BROOK. For Benjamin Glazier of the famous logging Glazier brothers.

BEN LAKE. Probably for Ben Soucier, farmer, 1877.

BENNETT. Unknown.

BENNETT LAKE. For J. Bennett, area landholder, 1877.

BEN THOMAS SIDING. For Benjamin F. Thomas, a farmer here in 1859.

BIBLE POINT. Unknown.

BIG: BROOK (4), BROOK LAKE, COVE (2), ISLAND, RAPIDS. Descriptive.

BILLINGS: BROOK, POND. Unknown.

BILLY JACK BROOK. For Billy Jack Noble, a logger.

BIRCH: BROOK, NORTH BRANCH-BROOK (2), POINT (3), RIVER (2). For birch trees.

BISHOP. For William Bishop.

BISHOP BROOK. For the local Bishop family.

BISHOP: MOUNTAIN, POND (2), POND STREAM. Pond in Fort Fairfield Township, named for the William and Amos Bishop families, settlers in 1831. Mountain, Pond, and Pond Stream in the T13R7 area, named for Butler, a soldier who settled in the area after the Aroostook War.

BITHER BROOK. For Benjamin Bither, one of the surveyors of the town.

BLACK: BIG-BROOK LAKE, BIG-RAPIDS, BIG-RIVER, BROOK (7), LAKE (2), LEFT FORK-BROOK, LITTLE-BROOK, LITTLE-BROOK LAKE, LITTLE-PONDS, LITTLE-RIVER, MOUNTAIN, NORTH BRANCH-WATER RIVER, POINT, POND (2), RIGHT FORK-BROOK, RIVER, SOUTH BRANCH-WATER RIVER, -WATER RIVER, WEST BRANCH LITTLE-RIVER. Descriptive.

BLACKSMITH BROOK. Unknown.

BLACKSTONE. For the descendants of Hartson Blackstone, settlers in nearby Perham Township.

BLAINE: settlement, TOWNSHIP. For James G. Blaine, unsuccessful Republican candidate for President of the United States.

BLAKE BROOK. For the Josiah H. Blake family, early settlers.

B: LAKE, RIDGE, STREAM, For the former designation of Letter B Townships.

BLIND BROOK. Descriptive of its emptying into Mooseleuk Lake in a cove.

BLOOD LAKE. Unknown.

BLUEBERRY ISLAND. For blueberries.

BLUE: BROOK, POND. Descriptive of the color of the water.

BOARS HEAD FALLS. Fanciful description of a projecting rock.

BOAT LANDING MOUNTAIN. For a boat landing at its foot on the Black River.

BOGAN BROOK. (2). A variation of "logan," a stretch of slow water.

BOG: BROOK (2), LAKE. Descriptive.

BOLES BROOK. For W. Boles, who had a farm there in 1877.

BONEY BROOK. For Oliver (Boney) Lapointe, who lived nearby.

BOODY: BROOK, COVE. For R. Boody, who ran a hotel there in 1877.

BOOM BRANCH. For a log boom.

BOOT SWAMP. For one of the men on a surveying crew who lost his boot in this swamp about 1869.

BOSSY MOUNTAIN. For James Bossy.

BOTTING POND. For William Bottin, a settler about 1843.

BOUCHER BROOK. Unknown.

BOYLES POINT. For J. Boyles, landowner, 1877.

BOYTON BROOK. Probably for Warren L. Boynton, prominent farmer, 1859.

BRACKETT LAKE. For James Brackett, settler, 1830.

BRADBURY. For the location of a mill owned by Ward Bradbury, Incorporated, about World War One.

BRADBURY LAKE. (2). In Ludlow Township, possibly for the Cyrus Bradbury family. In New Limerick Township, for Christopher and True Bradbury, settlers about 1820.

BRADFORD: BROOK, POND. For Calvin Bradford, farmer, 1844.

BRAGG BROOK. For Columbus Bragg, settler, about 1840.

BRALEY BROOK. Unknown.

BRANDY: BROOK (3), POND, WEST BRANCH-BROOK. For the amber color of the water.

BRAN LAKE. For Ira or Ruben Bran.

BRAWN: BIG-, LITTLE-. Probably descriptive of an imposing hill.

BRIDGEWATER: settlement, TOWNSHIP. For Bridgewater, Massachusetts.

BRISHLOTTE LAKE. French nickname: "broken pants." No known reason for its application.

BRITTON LAKE. For Britton, who ran a nearby tannery.

BROWN: BROOK (5), POINT. Brook in Ashland Township, for Solomon Brown, a farmer in 1840. Brook and Point in Eagle Lake Township, for John Brown, an early farmer. The others, unknown.

BROWN CORNER. For Gilbert Brown.

BRULEAU POND. Unknown.

BRUSHY HILL. Descriptive.

BRYANT POND. For the Charles Bryant family.

BUFFALO. One source says that during the Aroostook War, when troops were on their way to Fort Kent, groups from certain sections of the country would march together. The men who came through here were from Buffalo, New York. Another source says for men who let their hair and beards get shaggy in cold weather for warmth and were called "buffalo" by the storekeeper at the store where they traded.

BUGBEE. For Samuel Bugbee, farmer, 1843.

BUGBEE BROOK. For the local Bugbee family.

BUGGY BROOK. (2). In Wallagrass Township, for Edward (Buggy) Michaud. In Winterville Township, for the bugs and insects which infested it in summer.

BUG'ISLAND. For the insects which infested it.

BULL: BRANCH, HILL, RIDGE. A quick-flowing stream frequently is named "Bull"; however, these names could have derived from the lumbermen's use of oxen to drag logs.

BULLS BROOK. For Peter Bull, settler, 1836.

BUNKER HILL. For the Bunker family.

BUREPO BROOK. For Baptiste Durepo, who operated a starch factory there. The spelling discrepancy is a cartographical error.

BURGOIN BROOK. For Josephell Bourgoin, an Acadian.

BURNHAM BROOK. For John Burnham, settler, 1868.

BURNT: BROOK, DAM RIDGE, ISLAND, -LAND BROOK (2), LAND BROOK, LANDING, -LAND LAKE, LAND RIDGE, LAND STREAM, LITTLE-LAND STREAM, MILL, POND. Descriptive.

BURPEE BROOK. For Burpee, a logger.

BUSH BOG. Descriptive.

BUTLER BROOK. Unknown.

BUTTERFIELD: BROOK, LAKE. For A.J. Butterfield, farmer, 1877.

BUTTERFIELD LANDING. For William Butterfield, area surveyor about 1827 and justice of the peace.

BYRON MOUNTAIN. For Josiah B. Byron, who lived on it, and a number of other Byron families in 1870.

CALDWELL BROOK. For Wesley Caldwell, settler, 1841.

CALIFORNIA: BROOK, LITTLE-POND, POND, settlement. Probably for the California Road south of there, which cut across the northern reaches of Maine.

CAMEL BROOK. For Israel Camel, who lived near the brook.

CAMERON BOG. For J. Cameron, farmer here in 1877.

CAMPBELL. Unknown.

CAMPBELL: BRANCH, BROOK (4). Brook in Allagash Township, for the Campbell family. The others, unknown.

CANIBA BROOK. For Camiba Violette, Acadian, who weighed 300 pounds and was 7 feet tall.

CAPITOL HILL. For a large two-story building erected by the state for the Swedish colonists, which was called the "Capitol."

CARIBOU: BROOK, LAKE (2), POINT, POND, ROAD (settlement), settlement, STREAM, TOWNSHIP, WEST BRANCH-STREAM. For caribou which were once plentiful in Maine. Stream specifically for a caribou shot there in 1829 by John Cochrane.

CARLISLE: BROOK, POND. Unknown.

CARLSON POND. Possibly for Charles Carlton, settler, 1859.

CARLTON: BOG, BROOK. Unknown.

CARLYSLE BROOK. Unknown.

CARMICHAEL RIDGE. Unknown.

CARON BROOK. Unknown.

CARPENTER RIDGE. For the local Carpenter family.

CARRIE: BOGAN, BOGAN BROOK. Unknown.

CARRIVEAU MILL. For the Carriveau family, owners.

CARR: POND, STREAM. Unknown.

CARRY: BROOK (3), EAST BRANCH-BROOK, LAKE, POND (2), THE-, WEST BRANCH-BRANCH. For various areas where canoes had to be carried overland from one body of water to another or around rapids or falls.

CARSON. For the Carson family, who lived there about 1912.

CARSON POND. For the early Carson family.

CARTER BROOK. (2). In Allagash Township, for the local Carter family. In St. John Township, unknown.

CARYS MILLS. For Shepard Cary, who built a gristmill there, 1840.

CARY TOWNSHIP. For Shepard Cary, one of the leading lumbermen of Aroostook County.

CASEY: BROOK, RAPIDS. For the early Casey family.

CASTLE HILL TOWNSHIP. For a large log building which stood on a hill and resembled a castle.

CASWELL TOWNSHIP For the Caswell family, who lived on the first farm in the township after crossing the townline from Limestone Township.

CATON ISLAND. For Richard Caton, Canadian.

CEDAR: BROOK (3), EAST BRANCH-BROOK. For cedar trees.

CENTER BROOK. It rises in the center of T11R15.

CENTER LINE BROOK. It cuts the town line between T4R3 and Oakfield Township in half.

CENTER: MOUNTAIN, POND. Descriptive of location in the township.

CHAMPION POND. Unknown.

CHANDLER: DEADWATER, LAKE, MOUNTAIN (2), STREAM. Mountain in Chapman Township, for Mark Chandler, who had a camp and small farm at its foot. The rest, for Chandler, a logger.

CHANDLER RIDGE. For the Cyrus Chandler family.

CHAPMAN: settlement, TOWNSHIP. For Cyrus Chapman, surveyor of the town, who carved his name on the four corner posts marking the township.

CHARLES POND. Unknown.

CHARLEY ANDERSON POND. Unknown.

CHASE: BROOK (3), BROOK RIDGE, POND, WEST BRANCH-BROOK. For Chase, a lumberman.

CHEMQUASABAMTICOOK: LAKE, STREAM. Abnaki: "where there is a large lake together with a river."

CHIMENTICOOK STREAM. Abnaki: "principal islands in river."

CHIPUTNETICOOK LAKES. Abnaki: "at the place of the big hill stream."

CHISHOLM BROOK. For Walter Chism, a logger.

CHURCHILL LAKE. For the Nathaniel Churchill family, settlers about 1829.

CITY CAMP LANDING. For a moderate size camp located there.

CLARK BROOK. (3). In Amity Township, for William Clark, settler, 1828. In Wallagrass Township, for the J. Clark family. In Westfield Township, for John Clark, early settler.

CLARK POND. For J.D.B. Clark, blacksmith, 1866.

CLAY BLUFF. Descriptive.

CLAYTON BROOK. (2). In Ashland Township, for C.W. Clayton, early mill owner. In Washburn Township for Clair Clayton, owner of the farm traversed by the brook.

CLAYTON: LAKE (2), LAKE (settlement), STREAM. Unknown.

CLEVELAND: settlement, SIDING. For an Acadian family who anglicized their name to Cleveland.

CODFISH RIDGE. Unknown.

COFFIN: BOG, BROOK. Unknown.

COLBROTH BROOK. For C. Colbroth, nearby farmer, 1877.

COLBY. For Colby Buzzell, there in 1912.

COLD: BROOK (4), BROOK LAKE, MOUNTAIN, SPRING BROOK. Descriptive.

COLLICUT BROOK. Abnaki: "at place of flames."

COLLINS RIDGE. Possibly for the family of George Collins, mill owner in Bridgewater, the 1860's

COLLINS SIDING. Unknown.

COLLIS BROOK. Unknown.

COLLISION BROOK. A cartographical error for Gallerson Brook, named for Randall Gallerson, resident farm owner, 1830's.

COLONEY BROOK. For E. Cloney , who lived there in 1877.

CONANT BROOK. For the Isaac Conant family, settlers in 1845.

CONNERLY BROOK. For the Connely family.

CONNOR TOWNSHIP. For Selden Connor, a governor of Maine.

CONNORS: BROOK (4), COVE. Brook in T11R9, for John Connors, logger. The rest, for Robert Connors, logger.

CONROY LAKE. For J.W. Conroy, who owned it in 1877.

COOK BROOK. For the Samuel Cook family, settlers in 1807.

COOMBS: BROOK, COVE. Unknown.

CORDUROYS, THE. Fanciful name for three brooks running into the main brook like ripples in corduroy cloth.

CORNER BROOK. Runs through northwest corner of township.

COTE CORNER. For F. Cote, who lived there in 1877.

COUNTY ROAD LAKE. For a county road which runs to it.

COX PATENT. Unknown.

CRANBERRY: BROOK, POINT, POND (2). For cranberries.

CROPERLY TURN. The Croperly family lived at this fork in the road.

CROQUE BROOK. Unknown.

CROSS LAKE. (2). In T18R10. One had to cross a projection of land to get quickly to its south end from the St. Francis River. In T17R5, one had to cross to get from Mud Lake to Square Lake.

CROTON RIDGE. Probably for J. Crudden, who lived on it in 1877.

CROUSEVILLE. For Gould Crouse and his sons, who lived there.

CROW HILL. For crows.

CRYSTAL: BROOK, LAKE, settlement, STREAM, TOWNSHIP. Descriptive of clearness of water.

CULLING POND. For Frank Cullins.

CUNLIFFE: BROOK, ISLANDS, LAKE, POND. For Will Cunliffe, famous river driver.

CUT: POND, POND BROOK. For a log channel cut there.

CYR MOUNTAIN. For Maxime Cyr, early Acadian settler.

CYR TOWNSHIP. Unknown.

DAAQUAM RIVER. Abnaki: "thy beaver."

DAGGETT. For Henry Daggett, who lived near the foot.

DAGGETT BROOK. (2). In Amity Township, for James Daggett, settler, 1838. In Caswell Township, for the early Daggett family.

DAGGETT HILL. Probably for Major James Daggett, settler, 1828. By 1877, there were many Daggetts in the area.

DAIGLE: BROOK (3), MILL, POND, settlement. Brook in Fort Kent Township, for Daigle, who had a farm on it. Brook and Mill in Grand Isle Township, for Joseph Daigle, early settler. Brook, Pond, and settlement in the New Canada Township area, for Vital Daigle, early settler.

DARK COVE. A mariner's word for a protected, hard-to-spot cove.

DAVENPORT: COVE, POINT. For John Davenport, settler, 1820.

DAVIS: BROOK, BROOK BOG. For Israel Davis, who built a sawmill there about 1836.

DEAD: BROOK (9), LOWER-WATER (2), LOWER-WATER POND, STREAM, -WATER BROOK (2). Descriptive of the flow of the water.

DEADHORSE GULCH. Where a horse was thrown after it died while working on a logging team.

DEADMANS CORNER. Unknown.

DEBOULLIE: MOUNTAIN, POND. For Deboullie, French Canadian lumberman.

DEEP: BROOK. LAKE. Descriptive.

DEER: LAKE, POND. For deer.

DELANO LAKE. For Delano, who owned it, 1877.

DE LETTE RIDGE. Unknown.

DELIGHT RIDGE. For the anglicized French "de lette."

DEMARCHANT BROOK. For Jonathon De Merchant, who had a farm here in 1877.

DENNITT BROOK. For N. Dennett, who had a farm here in 1877.

DENNY POND. Unknown.

DEPOT: LAKE, MOUNTAIN, STREAM. For woods depots, or supply camps.

DEVILS WALL. A fanciful name for a natural wall.

DEVOE BROOK. For V. and B. Devon, who owned land traversed by the brook.

DICKEY: BROOK (2), EAST FORK-BROOK, POND, settlement, WEST FORK-BROOK. Brook and West Fork-Brook in Frenchville Township, for William H. Dickey, early settler. The others, unknown.

DICKWOOD LAKE. For Dickwood, early settler and lumberman.

DILLING LAKE. For J. Dilling, resident, 1877.

DIMOCK BROOK. Unknown.

DINAH POINT. Unknown.

DINGEY POND. For J.H. Dingee, landholder, 1877.

DINSMORE COVE. For Francis, Joshua, and Eben Dinsmore, who settled here briefly in the 1860's.

DIONNE CORNER. For Eloie and Joseph Dionne, who lived here.

DOCKENDORFF BROOK. Unknown.

DOG BROOK. Unknown.

DONNELLY: BROOK, ISLAND. Unknown.

DOW. For the local Dow family.

DOYLE RIDGE. Unknown.

DRAKE: BROOK (2). WEST BRANCH-BROOK. Brook in Wallagrass Township, for Melzer Drake. The others, unknown.

DREW HILL. For Moses Drew, who lived there in 1877.

DRISCOLL BROOK. For the early Driscoll family.

DRY: POINT, POND. Descriptive.

DUBAY LAKE. Unknown.

DUBAY POINT. For Clement Dubay, who owned the point.

DUCK: POINT, POND (3), POND OUTLET. For ducks.

DUDLEY: BROOK (2), BROOK RIDGE, NORTH BRANCH-BROOK, SWAMP (2). Brook and Swamp in Castle Hill Township, for Micajah Dudley, farmer in 1851. The others, unknown.

DUG BROOK. Unknown.

DUNN BROOK. (4). In Smyrna Township, for Dunn, who owned a mill in 1841. The others, unknown.

DURRELL BROOK. Unknown.

DYER: BROOK, BROOK (settlement), BROOK TOWNSHIP. Unknown.

EAGLE: LAKE, LAKE (settlement), LAKE TOWNSHIP. Named by Major Hastings Strickland, 1839, while encamped on his way to a military outpost on the Maine border, for bald eagles seen there.

EAST: BRANCH PINNACLES, BROOK, INLET, LAKE, LITTLE-LAKE. Descriptive.

EASTON: CENTER, settlement, STATION, TOWNSHIP. Because it lies on the east line of Aroostook County and of Maine.

EAST ROAD: (crossing). For the easternmost road in the township where it crosses the Bangor and Aroostook Railroad.

ECHO LAKE. Descriptive and fanciful.

ED JONES POND. Unknown.

EDMUNDS HILL. For the early Edmunds family.

ELEVENMILE LAKE. For location eleven miles from Mattawamkeag Lake.

ELIZA HOLE RAPIDS. Unknown.

ELLIOT BROOK. For John Elliot, farmer here in 1877.

EMERSON: RIDGE, SIDING. Unknown.

ESTABROOK HILL. For Wilson Estabrook, Canadian settler and farmer, 1880.

ESTABROOK LAKE. For John W. Estabrook, who owned a farm and sold ice from the pond in the early 1900's.

ESTABROOK SETTLEMENT. For Horace and Hammond Estabrook, who had farms there.

ESTCOURT: settlement, STATION. For Estcourt, Canada.

EVANS BROOK. For J. Evans, farmer, 1877.

EVERETT BROOK. Probably for Job or William Everett, settlers, 1835.

EYELET POND. Descriptive of a pond with an island in it that looks like the eye of a needle.

FACTORY BROOK (5). In Saint Agatha Township, for a starch factory owned by Michael Michaud. In Woodland Township, for Colby Cook's starch factory on nearby Caribou Stream, 1860.

FAIRMOUNT. Descriptive: "fair" and "mount."

FALL BROOK. For falls.

FALLS: BROOK, LITTLE-POND, LOWER-, POND. For falls.

FARM BROOK. Because it ran through the Michaud farm.

FARM CAMP BROOK. For a farm camp located there.

FARRAR: BROOK, LEFT FORK-BROOK, POND, RIGHT FORK -BROOK. Unknown.

FAULKNER LAKE. For Patrick Faulkner, settler from Ireland, 1835.

FERGUSON: BROOK, MOUNTAIN, POND. Unknown.

FIFTH LAKE BROOK. For Fifth Negro Brook Lake.

FINLEY BOGAN. Unknown.

FINN BROOK. Unknown.

FIRST: BROOK (3), LAKE (3). Descriptive.

FISHER LAKE. Probably for the Joseph Fisher family, the head of which was a soldier who remained after the Aroostook War.

FISHING BROOK. Because people fished there.

FISH POND. For fish.

FISH: RIVER, RIVER FALLS (2), RIVER ISLAND, RIVER LAKE. For Ira Fish, explorer in the early 1800's.

FISH STREAM. For Fish, who had a mill there.

FIVE FINGER BROOK. Because it was fed by five smaller brooks like fingers.

FIVE ISLANDS. Descriptive.

FIVEMILE: BRANCH OF-BROOK, BROOK (2). Brook in T14R8 for location five miles from High Landing on the Fish River. Branch of-Brook and Brook in T15R14 area, for its entry into the Big Black River 5 miles from where the Big Black River enters the St. John River.

FLING BROOK. For Alex, D., and F. Fling, whose land it traversed in 1877.

FLINN: POND, POND BROOK. Unknown.

FLINT BROOK. For a type of rock that looks like flint.

FLYING HILL. Unknown.

FOG BROOK. Unknown.

FOGELIN: HILL, POND. For A. G. Fogelin, who settled from Sweden, 1810.

FOOL BROOK. Unknown.

FORK BROOK. For being a fork of B Stream.

FORKSTOWN TOWNSHIP. For its location near the two forks of the Mattawamkeag River.

FORT FAIRFIELD: settlement, TOWNSHIP. For a fort built there that was named for John Fairfield, a governor of Maine.

FORT KENT: MILLS, PIT, settlement, TOWNSHIP, VILLAGE. For a fort named for Edward Kent, a governor of Maine.

FOSS BROOK. Unknown.

FOSTER-RAND BROOK. For Foster and Rand, major lumber proprietors in the area.

FOUR CORNERS. Descriptive of an intersection of roads forming four corners.

FOURMILE BROOK. (5). In T9R7, for location four miles from Oxbow. In T1R5, for location about four miles from Molunkus. In Garfield Township, because the brook runs into the Machias River four miles from where the Machias meets the Aroostook River. In T13R5, because the brook is about four miles from Seven Islands. In T14R8, because the brook is about one mile from Fivemile Brook.

FOURNIER. For Lawrence Fournier, Acadian settler.

FOURTH LAKE. Descriptive.

FOWLER: BROOK (2), LITTLE-POND. Unknown.

FOX: BROOK (2), BROOK RAPIDS, NORTH BRANCH-BROOK, POND, SOUTH BRANCH-BROOK. For foxes.

FRAZIER BROOK. For Frazier, a logger.

FREEMAN RIDGE. Unknown.

FREEZE BROOK. Descriptive of cold water.

FRENCHVILLE: settlement (2), TOWNSHIP, UPPER-. For the large French-Canadian population.

FROST AND ADAMS RIDGE. For Frost and Adams, woodland proprietors.

GAGNON BROOK. For Hypolite Gagnon, who owned a lumbermill here.

GAGNON HILL. For Horace and Donat Gagnon, Acadians.

GALILEE POND. Unknown.

GARDINER RIDGE. Probably for Andrew Gardner, settler, 1870's.

GARDNER: BROOK (3), MOUNTAIN, POND. Brook in Ashland Township, for William and I. Gardner, whose land it traversed. The others, unknown.

GARDNER ISLAND. For the Gardner family, who left New Brunswick in 1812 to escape persecution.

GARFIELD TOWNSHIP. For James A. Garfield, President of the U.S.

GARLAND HILL. Unknown.

GELOT: HILL, POND. For C. Gelott, Swedish immigrant.

GENTLE LAKE. For Herbert Gentle.

GERALD BROOK. For Gerald, local lumberman.

GERARD POND. For E. Girard, who owned it in 1877.

GERMAIN LAKE. For Germain Souci, Acadian settler.

GETCHELL BROOK. For I. Getchell, whose land it crossed in 1877.

GHOST LANDING BAR. In the 1800's during a lumbering operation, a pine that a logger was cutting fell on him and killed him. When it was finally taken to the water to be floated to the mill, it was found to have a rotten heart and was left on the bank. Passersby see a ghost there beseeching them to put the log in the river so that his soul can rest.

GIGGEY HILL. For Brinard and Edward Guiggey, settlers, 1840.

GILBERT: BROOK (2), LITTLE-BROOK, PONDS. Brook and Ponds in Saint John Township, for Edward Gilbert. Another source says for Zeno Jalbert. The others, unknown.

GILMAN BEACH. Unknown.

GILMAN POND. For Smith Gilman, mill owner.

GILMAN SIDING. Unknown.

GILMORE BROOK. For Gilmore, lumberman and settler.

GIN BROOK. (2). In Bridgewater Township, for men who used to buy gin and come here to "split" or dilute it. It is sometimes called Split Brook. In TER2, unknown.

GINN BROOK. For E. Ginn, who lived nearby.

GIZOQUIT: BROOK, LAKE. If Indian, Abnaki: possibly "eel weir place."

GLANCY LAKE. For J. Glancey, who farmed nearby in 1877.

GLASS HILL. Unknown.

GLAZIER: BROOK (2), BROOK MOUNTAIN, LAKE, NORTH BRANCH-BROOK, POND, POND BROOK. For any of the famous Glazier logging family—Benjamin, John, etc.

GLEASON BROOK. Unknown.

GLENDENNING BROOK. For the early settling Glendenning family.

GLENWOOD: settlement, TOWNSHIP. Probably descriptive.

GLIDDEN BROOK. Because the brook rose on the H.C. Glidden farm in 1877.

GODDARD: BROOK, COVE, LITTLE-BROOK, LITTLE-RIDGE, RIDGE. For Colonel John Goddard, timberman, who owned much area land, had agreed to relinquish it for settlement, and then refused. This started the "Goddard War," which the settlers finally won.

GODFREY BROOK. For Godfrey, old French lumberman.

GOLDEN RAPIDS. For the Golden family, who settled nearby.

GOLDEN RIDGE. Descriptive of the good farming land.

GONYA BROOK. Unknown.

GOOD BROOK. Unknown.

GOODRICH: BROOK, settlement. For Noah Goodrich, farmer in the area, 1877.

GOODWIN. For the early Goodwin family.

GOULD BROOK. Unknown.

GOULD POND. For the Oliver Gould family, settlers before 1837.

GRAND ISLE; settlement, TOWNSHIP. For a large island in the St. John River.

GRAND LAKE. (2). Descriptive.

GRASS CORNER. Possibly descriptive.

GRASS POND. Descriptive.

GRASSY LANDING. Descriptive.

GRAY BROOK. Probably for Justin Gray, settler, 1836.

GREENLAW BROOK. For H. Greenlaw, who lived nearby in 1877.

GREENLAW COVE. Unknown.

GREENLAW: CROSSING, MOUNTAIN, POND, STREAM. For Greenlaw, local lumberman.

GREENLEAF BROOK. For Jonathon Greenleaf, settler, 1828.

GREEN: MOUNTAIN, POND (2). Possibly descriptive.

GRENDELL HILL. For Sylveneous Grendell, settler, after 1870.

GREY: BROOK, BROOK MOUNTAIN, POND. Unknown.

GRIFFIN RIDGE. For J.G. Griffin, farmer, 1877.

GRIMES MILL. For E.P. Grimes, mill owner and shingle manufacturer.

GRINDSTONE. Where river drivers sharpened their axes.

GRISWOLD. Unknown.

GROSS BROOK. Unknown.

GROVE HILL. For the grove of trees there.

GUERETTE. For the local Guerette family.

GULCH BROOK. Descriptive.

GULLIVER BROOK. Descriptive of size, relating to Swift's Gulliver.

HACKER BROOK. Probably for the Isaac Hacker family, settlers about 1860.

HAFEY: BROOK, LITTLE-BROOK, MOUNTAIN, POND. Unknown.

HAFFORD BROOK. (2). For the Hafford family who came to the area from New Brunswick in 1812 to escape persecution.

HAINES HILL. For Peter Haines, who lived in the area in 1877.

HALE BROOK. (2). In Hersey Township, for Timothy Hale, a settler in 1839. In T7R3, unknown.

HALE POND. For John Hale, settler, 1839.

HALEY BROOK. Unknown.

HALEY ISLAND. For W. Haley, a farmer in 1877.

HALF: -MOON ISLAND, -MOON POND. Descriptive of shape.

HALFWAY BROOK (4). In Stockholm Township, for where it meets Little Madawaska River halfway between where the Little Madawaska River runs into the Madawaska River and Stockholm. In T16R12, for halfway between Poplar Island Rapids and Fox Brook Rapids. In T16R6, for halfway between Eagle Lake and Cross Lake. In T11R11, because it runs into Musquacook Stream halfway between Second and Third Musquacook lakes.

HALL: BROOK, POND. Unknown.

HALLS CORNER. For a Hall who lived at the corner, mid 1800's.

HAMILTONS MISTAKE. For a lumberman named Hamilton who drove his logs into a nearby cove thinking it was the West Branch Mattawamkeag River.

HAMLIN: settlement, TOWNSHIP. For Hannibal Hamlin, Vice-President of the U.S.

HAMMOND: BROOK, BROOK LAKE. For W.C. Hammond, who owned the land where the stream emptied.

HAMMOND TOWNSHIP. Unknown.

HANEY BROOK. For Alexander Haney, settler, 1868.

HANFORD. For Hanford Carr, lumberman, who lived near the siding in 1910.

HANNIGAN POND. For E. Hannigan, farmer, there in 1877.

HANSON BROOK. Unknown.

HARDING: BROOK, BROOK RIDGE. Unknown.

HARDWOOD BROOK. For hardwood trees.

HARPER BROOK. Unknown.

HARRIS BROOK. Unknown.

HARVEY. For Len "Strong Man" Harvey.

HARVEY: BROOK (2), POND. Brook, in Allagash Township, for the local Harvey family. Brook and Pond in T12R13, for the Harvey family who ran a farm on the bank.

HASTINGS: BROOK, EAST-BROOK, WEST-BROOK. Unknown.

HAWKINS BROOK. For the Hawkins family.

HAWKINS STATION. Unknown.

HAYDEN BROOK. For Elias and Samuel Hayden, settlers, 1839.

HAYNESVILLE: settlement, TOWNSHIP. For Alvin Haynes, local storekeeper, 1835.

HAY SHED BEND. Because it was the site of an old hay shed.

HAYSTACK MOUNTAIN. Descriptive.

HAYWIRE POND. For a lumbering operation where everything went "haywire," or wrong.

HEDGEHOG MOUNTAIN. (2). For hedgehogs (porcupines).

HEMORE BROOK. Unknown.

HENDERSON: BROOK (2), LOWER-BROOK. Brook in T13R12, for Henderson, a man who logged in the area. The others, unknown.

HENDERSON HILL. For J.V. Henderson, farmer, 1877.

HERSEY BROOK. Unknown.

HERSEY TOWNSHIP. For General Samuel Hersey, candidate for governor of Maine on the Prohibition ticket, 1894.

HERSOM LAKE. For S. Hersom, who farmed nearby in 1877.

HESSE BROOK. Unknown.

HEWES: BROOK, BROOK POND. Unknown.

HICKS BROOK. For Z. Hicks, nearby farmer, 1877.

HIDDEN POND. Descriptive of isolation.

HIGGINS BROOK. For Benjamin F. Higgins, who had a mill there about 1867.

HIGH LANDING. Descriptive of a landing on Fish River.

HILL. For I. Hill, who lived there in 1877.

HILL BROOK. Unknown.

HILLMAN. Unknown.

HILT BROOK. For William Hilt, farmer, 1877.

HITCHING POST POINT. Unknown.

HOBART HILL. For Hobart, who lived there.

HOCKENHILL BROOK. For the Hockenhill family, who owned a sawmill on it.

HODGDON: CORNERS, EAST-, settlement, TOWNSHIP. For John Hodgdon, proprietor.

HOG ISLAND. For its use as a hog pen.

HOLMES BROOK. Unknown.

HOOK POINT. Descriptive of shape.

HORSE BROOK. For a horse that was drowned above a log driving dam built by a lumberman named Trafton.

HORSE MOUNTAIN. Unknown.

HORSE RACE: LOWER-RAPIDS, RAPIDS. Descriptive of fast water.

HORSESHOE: MOUNTAIN, POND (2). Descriptive of shape.

HOUGHTONVILLE. Probably for E.L. Houghton.

HOULTON: BROOK (3), POND. Unknown.

HOULTON: settlement, TOWNSHIP. For Joseph Houlton, one of the proprietors and a settler about 1810.

HOUSTON BROOK. Possibly for Samuel Hustin, settler, 1839.

HOVEY: BROOK, MOUNTAIN, SWAMP. Unknown.

HOVEY HILL. For the W. Hovey family, farmers, 1877.

HOWARD: BROOK (2), LITTLE-BROOK. In Easton Township, for H. Howard, whose land it traversed, 1877. The others, unknown.

HOWE: BROOK, BROOK (settlement), BROOK MOUNTAIN, EAST BRANCH-BROOK. Unknown.

HOYT BROOK. For Winslow Hoyt.

HUGHES BROOK. For James Hughes, farmer, 1877.

HUNNEWELL: ISLAND, LAKE. For Barnabas Hunnewell, who received a soldier's grant for the island.

HUNTER POND. Unknown.

HUNTLEY: BROOK, MILL POND. For the I. Huntley family, who had a mill on the pond.

HUNTLEY LAKE. For Joe Huntley, who cut logs there.

HUNT RIDGE. Unknown.

HURD. For the local Hurd family.

HURRICANE RIDGE. For a hurricane that knocked down timber here, 1879.

HUSON: BROOK, LANDING. For Huson, lumberman in the area.

IKES BROOK. Unknown.

INDIAN: BROOK, POINT. For Indians.

INGALLS BROOK. Unknown.

INNES BEAVER POND. Unknown.

IRISH RIDGE. For a settlement of people of Irish extraction.

ISIE LAKE. For Isie Dube.

ISLAND FALLS: settlement, TOWNSHIP. Descriptive.

ISLAND: POND (2), POND STREAM. For islands in the middle of ponds.

JACK AIKER BROOK. Unknown.

JACKINS SETTLEMENT. For L.E., P., and K. Jackins, who lived here, 1877.

JACK MOUNTAIN. Unknown.

JACKSON SLUICE. Unknown.

JACOBS. For the Jacobs family, who lived there about 1914.

JACOBSON HILL. For Per J. Jacobson, Swedish settler, 1870.

JAMESON RIDGE. Unknown.

JAY BROOK. Unknown.

JEMTLAND: settlement, STATION. Named by the Hedman, Jacobson, and Peterson families, for their former home province of Jamtland in Sweden.

JEWELL LAKE. For J.B. Jewell, farmer, 1877.

JEWELLS CORNER. For Jacob Jewell, who lived there, 1877.

JIMMY: BROOK, BROOK BOG. Unknown.

JIMSON BROOK. Possibly for the Jamison family.

JOE CORO BROOK. For Joseph Coro, settler from near the Canadian border.

JOE DUBAY BROOK. For Joe Dubay, Aroostook logger.

JOHNSON: BROOK (4), BROOK MOUNTAIN, POND. Brook and Brook Mountain in Allagash Township, for the local Johnson family. The others, unknown.

JONES: BROOK (2), MILL (2), POND. Brook in Saint Francis Township, for a Jones family from Quebec, Canada. The others, unknown.

JUNIPER BROOK. (2). For juniper trees.

JUNKINS ISLAND. For Julius J. Junkins, farmer, the 1880's.

KEEGAN. For Peter Charles Keegan.

KELLY: BROOK (4), BROOK MOUNTAIN. Brook in Saint Francis Township, for James Kelly. Brook and Brook Mountain in Allagash Township, for the Kelly family, who settled from New

Brunswick to escape persecution in 1812. The others, unknown.

KELLYS RAPIDS. Unknown.

KENNARD BROOK. For George Kennard, who cleared the land and settled there.

KENNISON HILL. For I.W. Kennison.

KETCHAM BOG. Unknown.

KETCH POND. Probably for Hazen Keech, a settler by 1859.

KETCHUM LAKE. For the Joseph Ketchum family, settlers, 1829.

KING ISLAND. For the King family who lived on it.

KINNEY HILL. For the J. Kenny family.

KNIGHTS BROOK. Unknown.

KNOWLAND BROOK. Unknown.

KNOWLES CORNER. For Henry T. Knowles, settler, 1843.

LABBE BROOK. Unknown.

LABBE POND. For Johnny Labbe, owner.

LABBY MICHAUD POST OFFICE. For Labby Michaud, local resident.

LAC FRONTIERE. (settlement). French: "frontier lake."

LAGASSE BROOK. For G., F., and R. Lagasse, Acadian farmers.

LA GRANDE ISLAND. French: "big island."

LAKE BROOK. Because the brook drains Faulkner Lake.

LAKE MOUNTAIN. For Long Lake.

LAMB BROOK. For Henry Lamb, resident.

LAMSON BROOK. Because it rose on the Lamson farm in 1877.

LANIGAN MOUNTAIN. For Jim Lanigan, who lived at its foot.

LA POMKEAG: LAKE, LOWER-LAKE, STREAM. Abnaki: "the place of rocks." The "La" is French.

LARRY BROOK. Unknown.

LA SEPTIEME ISLAND. French: "the seventh," for being the largest of seven islands.

LAST BROOK. Descriptive.

LAVELS LAKE. Unknown.

LAVOIE BROOK. For Joseph Lavoie, Sr., resident.

LAYTON LAKE. Unknown.

LEDGE: FALLS, THE-. Descriptive.

LEDGES. Descriptive.

LEFT FORK BROOK. Descriptive.

LES TROIS. Cartographical error for "Les Etroits." French: "the narrows," of the St. John River.

LEVESQUE ISLAND. For Damase Levesque, owner.

LEWIS BROOK. For the local Lewis family.

LIBBY BROOK. (2). In Fort Fairfield, possibly for Ephraim and Daniel Libby, who operated mills in Limestone Township. In Castle Hill Township, unknown.

LILLE. French: "island," for an island in the St. John River.

LIMESTONE: BROOK, settlement, STREAM, TOWNSHIP. For limestone deposits.

LINDSAY LAKE. For Dan Lindsay, owner.

LINNEUS: settlement, TOWNSHIP. The land was granted to Harvard to endow the Swedish botanist Linnaeus.

LINSCOTT POND. Unknown.

LITTLE BROOK. Descriptive.

LITTLE CANADA. For many residents of Canadian extraction.

LITTLE: RIVER, RIVER COVE, RIVER POINT. Descriptive.

LITTLE ST. ROCH RIVER. For the St. Roch River in Canada.

LITTLETON: RIDGE, settlement, STATION, TOWNSHIP. For Josiah Littleton of Portland, proprietor.

LIZOTTE BROOK. Unknown.

LOGAN BROOK. For Logan family who settled in the 1860's-70's.

LONG: BROOK, BROOK RIDGE, LAKE (4), POND (2). Descriptive.

LONGFELLOW LAKE. Unknown.

LONGLEY LAKE. For Abram Longley, settler, about 1830.

LONGS RAPIDS. Unknown.

LOON LEDGE. For loons.

LOST POND. (9). Descriptive of isolation.

LOVEJOY: BROOK, RIDGE. Unknown.

LOWELL HILL. For the Peter Lowell family, early settlers.

LUCIFEE POND. For the local pronunciation of the French name of the Canadian lynx: "Loup-cervier."

LUDLOW: settlement, TOWNSHIP. For Ludlow, Massachusetts.

LUFMAN BROOK. Unknown.

LUNKSOOS: LAKE, MOUNTAIN, STREAM. Abnaki: "a cata mount."

LYMAN. Unknown.

LYNDON: EAST-, NORTH-. For the former name of Caribou Township.

MacALLISTER COVE. For William H. McAllister, local farmer.

MACHIAS: BIG-LAKE, FORKS OF-, LITTLE-LAKE, RIVER SOUTH BRANCH-RIVER. Abnaki: "bad little falls."

MACK BROOK. For McNally Ridge.

MACWAHOC: LAKE, LOWER-LAKE, RIDGE, settlement STREAM, TOWNSHIP. Abnaki: "wet ground, bog."

MADAWASKA: LAKE, LITTLE-RIVER, RIVER, settlement (2) TOWNSHIP. Micmac: "where one river runs into another," or "where there is much hay," or "having its outlet among reeds."

MADDUSKEAG STREAM. Malecite: "falls or rapids at mouth."

MAINE. For the State of Maine.

MALCOLM BRANCH. Unknown.

MANSUR BROOK. Unknown.

MAPLE: GROVE, MOUNTAIN. For maple trees.

MAPLETON: settlement, TOWNSHIP. For maple trees.

MARCIAL LAKE. Unknown.

MARCUM POND. For Marcum Ouellette, owner.

MARGISON. For W.A. Margison, selectman of Woodland Township, 1912.

MARLEY BROOK. For John Marley, settler from England, 1831.

MARS: HILL, HILL (settlement), HILL TOWNSHIP. For a verse in the Bible which mentions a Mars Hill where Paul preached. In 1790, a British army chaplain read this verse to a survey crew in a service here.

MARTIN BOG. Unknown.

MARTIN: BROOK (3), LAKE. Lake and Brook in the Caswell Township area, for the Martin family, who ran a small sawmill there. Brook in Madawaska Township, for Pea Martin, who owned an area farm. Brook in Wallagrass Township, for the local Martin family.

MARTINS SIDING. For Joseph Martin, who owned land bought by the Bangor & Aroostook Railroad in 1900.

MASARDIS: settlement, TOWNSHIP. Abnaki: "place of white clay."

MASTERS BROOK. For Masters, who lived nearby.

MATHERSON: BROOK, POND. Unknown.

MATRIMONY POINT. Unknown.

MATTASEUNK LAKE. Abnaki: "furtherest rapid stream."

MATTAWAMKEAG: EAST BRANCH-RIVER, HILL, LAKE, RIVER, UPPER-LAKE, WEST BRANCH-RIVER. If Abnaki: "fishing place beyond gravel bar." If Malecite: "rapids at mouth." If Micmac: "on a sandbar."

MATTIGAN POINT. If Indian, possibly Abnaki: "far on the other side."

MAY MOUNTAIN. For Levi H. May, settler, 1861

MAYSVILLE. Unknown.

McAVOY POND. For Fenton McAvoy, a relatively early settler.

McCLUSKY: BROOK (3), LAKE. For the John McCluskey family, loggers.

McCONNELL BROOK. For McConnell, logger.

McDONALD BROOK. (2). In Fort Fairfield Township, for F. McDonald, whose land it crossed. In Hodgdon Township, unknown.

McDONALD MOUNTAIN. For Daniel McDonald, farmer here in 1877.

McGARGLE ROCKS. For McGargle, a river driver who was killed attempting to pick loose a jam.

McGOWAN POND. Unknown.

McGRAW. For the local McGraw family.

McKEEN: BROOK, CROSSING, LAKE. Unknown.

McKINNON BROOK. Unknown.

McLEAN: BROOK (2), LAKE, MOUNTAIN, NORTH FORK-BROOK, RIDGE, WEST FORK-BROOK. Brook, Mountain, and Lake in St. Francis Township, for McLean, a lumberman. The others, unknown.

McNALLY: BROOK, DEADWATER, flagstation, RIDGE, UPPER-POND. Unknown.

McPHERSON LAKE. For Clarence McPherson, who cleared the land.

McSHEA. For P. McShea, who had a farm there, 1877.

MEADOW: BRANCH, BROOK (4), -BROOK POND, LITTLE-BROOK. Descriptive.

MEDUXNEKEAG: LAKE, MILL STREAM, NORTH BRANCH-RIVER, NORTH BRANCH-STREAM, RIVER, SOUTH

BRANCH-RIVER, SOUTH BRANCH-STREAM. Malecite: "falls or rapids at mouth."

MEETINGHOUSE; COVE, POINT. For a meetinghouse there.

MELVILLE HILL. For the early Melville family.

MERRILL BROOK. Unknown.

MERRILL TOWNSHIP. For Captain William Merrill, proprietor about 1840.

MICHAUD HILL. For Damus Michaud, Acadian resident.

MICHAUD ISLAND. For Romain Michaud, a captain during the Aroostook War.

MICHAUD MILL. For the Michaud family, owners.

MICHAUD SIDING. For Labby Michaud Post Office.

MICHIGAN SETTLEMENT. For a group of people who started a knitting business here and branded their merchandise "Michigan."

MIDDLE BROOK. For location between First and Last brooks.

MIDDLE MOUNTAIN. For location between Peaked and Round mountains.

MIDWAY SIDING. For location midway between Ashland and Mapleton.

MILE BROOK. For location approximately one mile from the Aroostook River.

MILL: BROOK (3), LITTLE-BROOK. For mills. Brook in Hersey Township, for a mill located on it in 1877. Brook and Little-Brook in Smyrna Township area, for a mill built in 1826 by Bradford Cummings. Brook in Moro Township, for a mill built there in 1867 by David B. Bates and Smith Gilman.

MILLER BROOK. For Sam Miller, old guide and trapper.

MILLS BROOK. For Mills, soldier who settled after Aroostook War.

MINK MARSH POND. For mink.

MINNOW BROOK. For minnows.

MITCHELL MOUNTAIN. Possibly for Albert Mitchell, settler, th 1870's.

MOCCASIN POND. Unknown.

MOLUNKUS: EAST BRANCH-STREAM, LAKE, LITTLE STREAM, settlement, STREAM, TOWNSHIP, UPPER-TOWN SHIP, WEST BRANCH LITTLE-STREAM. Abnaki: "a ravine high banks on each side."

MONARDA. Unknown.

MONSON LAKE. For the Monson family.

MONSON: MILL, MILL BROOK. For the Monson family o Houlton, who owned many area mills.

MONTICELLO: settlement, STATION, TOWNSHIP. For Mont cello, the home of Thomas Jefferson.

MONUMENT BROOK. (2). In Amity Township, for the monumen located in the northeast corner of town on the U.S.-Canadia border. In T4R3, for the surveying line, called the "Monumen Line," which runs nearby.

MOORE BROOK. For J. Moore, farmer, 1877.

MOORES BROOK. For the local Moore family.

MOOSE: BROOK (4), HILL, MOUNTAIN, POND (2), PONI STREAM, RIDGE. For moose.

MOOSEHORN STREAM. For a pair of moosehorns hung in a tre near the stream. Area people gave directions by the horns.

MOREHOUSE BROOK. Unknown.

MOREY BROW. Unknown.

MORGRIDGE POND. For George Morgridge, who farmed nearby i 1877.

MORIN MOUNTAIN. For Joseph Marin, early settler.

MORO TOWNSHIP. Unknown.

MORRIS CORNER. For L.G. Morris, resident, 1857.

MORRISON BROOK. (2). In Oakfield Township, probably for Samuel Morrison, early settler and farmer. In T18R13, unknown.

MORROW ROAD. (crossing). For J. Morrow, who had a large farm there.

MOSQUITO: BROOK, BROOK POND, POINT. For mosquitos.

MUD: BROOK (4), LAKE (8), LITTLE-POND, POND (11), POND STREAM. Descriptive.

MURPHEY ROAD. (crossing). For the name of the road which crosses the Bangor & Aroostook Railroad. The road was named for E. Murphy, resident, 1877.

MUSKET BROOK. Unknown.

MUSQUACOOK: DEADWATER, FIRST-LAKE, LITTLE-STREAM, MOUNTAIN, SECOND-LAKE, STREAM, THIRD-LAKE. Abnaki: "muskrat place" or "birch bark place."

NADEAU POND. (2). In Fort Fairfield Township, for E. Nedo, who farmed there in 1877. In T14R7, for Sefroi Nadeau.

NADEAU THOROUGHFARE. For Sefroi Nadeau, settler, 1840.

NASHVILLE TOWNSHIP. Unknown.

NEGRO: BROOK, BROOK LAKES, FIFTH-LAKE, SIXTH-LAKE. For a Negro working a log drive who was drowned in the brook.

NEW CANADA TOWNSHIP. For the many French-Canadians living there.

NEW LIMERICK: settlement, TOWNSHIP. For Limerick Township in York County, Maine, where many settlers came from.

NEW SWEDEN: settlement, TOWNSHIP. By the Swedish immigrants, for Sweden.

NICHOLS BROOK. For Howard Nichols, whose farm it traverses.

NICHOLS RAPIDS. For Nichols, lumberman and settler.

NICKERSON BROOK. Unknown.

NICKERSON LAKE. For Eugene F. Nickerson, area landholder, 1877.

NIGGER BROOK. For Negroes who logged there.

NIGHTHAWK MOUNTAIN. For nighthawks.

NINEMILE BROOK. For location about nine miles from Seven Islands on the St. John River.

NINEMILE DEADWATER. For its location on the Big Black River nine miles from where the Big Black River flows into the St. John River.

NINETEEN MOUNTAIN. Unknown.

NIXON. Unknown.

NORTH: BROOK, BROOK RIDGE, LAKE, POND (2), POND BROOK, RIDGE. Descriptive.

NORTH YARMOUTH ACADEMY GRANT TOWNSHIP. For the North Yarmouth Academy.

NORWAY: ISLAND, POINT. For Norway pines.

NOTCH, THE. Descriptive.

NOTRE DAME. For the Notre Dame parish.

NOWLAND: BROOK, HILL, SIDING. For J. Nowland, who had land in the area.

NOYES BROOK. Possibly for Josiah M. Noyes, resident, 1857.

NUMBER NINE: MOUNTAIN, STREAM. For the designation of the Number Nine Townships.

NUMBER ONE BROOK. For being the first brook to meet Rocky Brook after Little Rocky Brook.

NUMBER SEVEN RIDGE. For its location in Township 7, Range 3.

OAKFIELD: HILLS, settlement, TOWNSHIP. Named by the oldest resident in 1866, James Timoney, for the oaks and fields.

OAK: HILL, POINT (2), RIDGE. For oak trees.

OGREN. For C.J. Ogreen, whose land the Bangor & Aroostook Railroad crossed.

OLD MAID ROCK. Fancifully named.

ORCHARD BOG. Descriptive.

ORCUTT: BROOK, MOUNTAIN. Unknown.

ORIENT: settlement, TOWNSHIP. For its meaning of "east." It is located on the east boundary of Maine.

ORR: BROOK, RIDGE. Unknown.

OSGOOD DEADWATER. For William Osgood, who had a camp there.

OTTER: BROOK (4), BROOK BOG, LAKE, POND. For otters.

OUELLETTE. For the local Ouelette family.

OUELLETTE BROOK. (3). In St. Agatha Township, for Josephell Ouellette, Acadian. The others, unknown.

OUTLET MOUNTAIN. For its location next to the outlet of Pleasant Lake.

OWL POND BROOK. Unknown.

OWLS ROOST, THE. Unknown.

OXBOW. (bend). For a bend on Birch River.

OXBOW BROOK. For an oxbow, or bend, on it.

OXBOW: settlement, TOWNSHIP. Descriptive of an oxbow, or bend, on the Aroostook River.

PACKARD: HILL, LAKE. For David Packard, settler, 1857.

PAGE POND. For E. Page, who had a farm there in 1877.

PALMER BROOK. For Jim Palmer, who cleared the land in the area.

PALMER DEADWATER. Unknown.

PARADIS BROOK. For the logging Paradis family.

PARENT. For location near the Parent family home.

PARKHURST. For E.E. Parkhurst, prominent farmer, 1860.

PARKS BROOK. Unknown.

PARK SIDING. Unknown.

PATTEE BROOK. Probably for the family of S.B. Pattee.

PATTEN JUNCTION. For Patten Township in Penobscot County.

PAULETTE BROOK. For Hypholitic Paulette, who owned a farm here.

PAULS. For George Paul.

PEA COVE. Unknown.

PEAKABOO MOUNTAIN. Fancifully named.

PEAKED MOUNTAIN. Descriptive.

PEARCE BROOK. Probably for Varney Pearce, early settler.

PELLETIER: BROOK, SIDING. Unknown.

PENNINGTON: BROOK (2), MOUNTAIN, POND. For Pennington, an old logger.

PERCH POND. For perch fish.

PERHAM: settlement, TOWNSHIP. For Sidney Perham, Governor of Maine.

PERLEY: BROOK, NORTH BRANCH-BROOK, SOUTH BRANCH-BROOK. For the nickname — "Perley" — of an Englishman named Pearl.

PETERS COVE. For Marcus or Jacob Peters, settlers, mid 1800's.

PETES POND. Unknown.

PETITE BROOK. Cartographer's error for "Pitook Brook," for "Pitook" Cyr, who owned a grist mill there.

PETTINGILL BROOK. For Joshua Pettingill, who cleared the area land.

PETTINGILL RIDGE. For C. L. Pettingill, who logged here in the 1890's.

PEVERE RIDGE. Unknown.

PHAIR. Probably for Thomas H. Phair, owner of starch factories, 1880's.

PICARD: BROOK, HILL. Unknown.

PIERCE LAKE. For Henry Peers.

PIERRE. For Peter Daigle, who owned land where the siding is located.

PINE: BIG-BEND, ISLAND. For pine trees.

PINETTE BROOK. (2). In Fort Kent Township, for the Pinette family, whose farm it crossed. In Eagle Lake Township, for Old Man Pinette, one of the first area settlers.

PINNACLE, THE. (4). Descriptive.

PINNETTE HILL. For Charles and Phydime Pinette, residents.

PLAISTED. For Governor Plaisted.

PLEASANT LAKE. Descriptive.

PLISSEY LAKE. For its location near the farm of W. Plissey, farmer, 1877.

PLOURDE MILL. For Plourde, who constructed the mill.

PLUNKETT: BROOK, POND. For the ancestors of P. Plunkett, who lived nearby in 1877.

POCKET, THE. Descriptive of a cove.

POCWOCK: EAST BRANCH-STREAM, STREAM, WEST BRANCH-STREAM. Possibly Abnaki: "shallow water."

POLE HILL. For a pole left standing here by the first surveyors.

POLLARD MOUNTAIN. For the Pollard family, who ran a mill on the St. Croix.

POND BROOK. Descriptive.

POPLAR: ISLAND BROOK, ISLAND RAPIDS. For poplar trees.

PORTAGE: LAKE, LAKE TOWNSHIP, settlement. For the portage from the lake to Machias Lake.

PORTER SETTLEMENT. For the Porter family, who settled here before the Civil War.

PORTLAND LAKE. For location in an area granted to Portland Academy.

POWERS CORNER. For R. Powers, resident, 1877.

POWERS GORE. Unknown.

PRATT COVE. For Joshua Pratt, who settled there in 1870's.

PRATT: LAKE (2), LAKE STREAM. Lake in Washburn Township, for David Pratt, who owned much land in the area. The others, unknown.

PRESLEY: LAKE, LITTLE-LAKE. Unknown.

PRESQUE ISLE: EAST BRANCH-STREAM, JUNCTION, LAKE, NORTH BRANCH-STREAM, settlement, STREAM, TOWNSHIP, WEST BRANCH-STREAM. French: "almost an island," for a peninsula on the Presque Isle Stream.

PRESQUILE RIVER. For Presque Isle.

PRESTILE: BROOK, HILL. For Presque Isle.

PRETTY BROOK. Descriptive.

PRIDE. Unknown.

PRIESTLY: BROOK (2), RAPIDS. For the Priestly family, loggers.

PROUTY BROOK. For Levi Prouty, farmer and millwright, about 1833.

PUDDING ROCK. Descriptive of shape.

PUNCHARD BROOK. Unknown.

PUSHINEER POND. Unknown.

PYLE MOUNTAIN. For S. Pyle, who owned land here, 1877.

QUAGGY JOE. For a misspelling of "quaquajo": "boundary mountain." When the Micmacs were defeated by the Malecites, they set up this mountain as a boundary.

QUIGGLY BROOK. Unknown.

QUIMBY. Unknown.

RAMSAY BROOK. For the Ramsay family, residents.

RAND LANDING. For Rand, woodsland proprietor.

RAND POND. For N.N. Rand, on whose farm the pond was located.

RANDS. For J. Rand, who farmed nearby, 1877.

RANKIN: BROOK, RAPIDS. Unknown.

READ LAKE. For A. Reed, who lived near its shore, 1877.

RED: BROOK, BRIDGE (settlement), LEDGE, RIVER, RIVER FALLS. Descriptive of color.

REED: DEADWATER, POND, settlement, TOWNSHIP. Unknown.

REGIEST DAIGLE BROOK. For Regiest Daigle, who had a farm on the brook.

RESERVOIR HILL. (2). In Houlton Township, for the location of a reservoir there. In Van Buren Township, for the location of a reservoir used by the Van Buren fire department as an emergency water supply.

RICHARDSON BROOK. Unknown.

RIDEOUT BROOK. (2). In Weston Township, for Rideout, lumberman, who camped there. In TER2, probably for William Rideout, who lived in the area in 1847.

RIDEOUT: LAKE, POND. For a Rideout who drowned there.

RIDER BROOK. Unknown.

RISTA SIDING. Named by Swedish immigrants for a locality in the province of Jamtland, Sweden,—"Rista fallett"—"Rista Falls."

RIVIERE DES CHUTES. French: "river of falls," although the name hardly applies, for it is actually a fall-less brook. The name applies primarily to where the brook enters the St. John River, and possibly the turbulence of its emptying during high water gave the name.

ROACH POND. For roach, or sunfish.

ROBBINS: BROOK, BROOK POND. Unknown.

ROBERTS. For the Reverend J. Roberts, on whose land the flagstation was located.

ROBINSONS. Probably for William Robinson, mill builder, 1864.

ROCKABEMA LAKE. Possibly Abnaki: "woodpecker."

ROCK POND. Descriptive.

ROCKY: BROOK (5), BROOK MOUNTAINS, LITTLE-BROOK, MOUNTAIN, NORTH BRANCH-BROOK, POINT, RIDGE. Descriptive.

ROLL DAM BROOK. Descriptive of a dam where the logs rolled down to the brook below after being floated up a kind of inclined plane.

ROSINGNAL BROOK. For Honore, Fortunat, and Denis Rossignol, Acadian settlers.

ROSS LAKE. For the Ross family, residents, 1877.

ROUND: ISLAND (2), MOUNTAIN, MOUNTAIN POND, POND (2). Descriptive of shape.

ROWE: BROOK, LAKE. Unknown.

ROYS POINT. Unknown.

RUSSELL: BROOK, CROSSING. For a Russell who owned land in the area.

SADDLEBACK MOUNTAIN. Descriptive of shape.

SAFFORD POND. Probably for the earlier family of George Safford.

SAG POND. Descriptive of location in a sag, or low area.

ST. AGATHA: settlement, TOWNSHIP. For the St. Agatha parish church.

ST. ALMOND: BROOK, POND. Unknown.

ST. AMANTIS BROOK. Unknown.

ST. CLAIR ISLAND. Unknown.

ST. CROIX: LAKE, settlement, STREAM, TOWNSHIP, Unknown.

ST. DAVID. For the St. David parish church.

ST. FRANCIS: RIVER, settlement, TOWNSHIP. Unknown.

ST. FROID. For Sefroi Nadeau, early area settler. The spelling discrepancy is a surveyor's misunderstanding of "Sefroi."

ST. JOHN BROOK. For the local St. John family, who pronounced their name "Sin Jin."

ST. JOHN: RIVER, settlement, TOWNSHIP. By Samuel de Champlain, who discovered it on St. John the Baptist's Day in 1604.

ST. LUCE STATION. For the St. Luce parish church.

SALMON: BROOK LAKE, POINT, POOL, WEST BRANCH-BROOK. For salmon fish.

SAM DREW MOUNTAIN. For Samuel Drew, who lived nearby and was the descendant of an early settler.

SAND: COVE, ISLAND. Descriptive.

SANFORD STREAM. Unknown.

SAULS BROOK. Unknown.

SAVAGE BROOK. For Savage, a soldier who remained in the area after the Aroostook War.

SAVAGE ISLAND. For Daniel Savage, initiator of lumber operations in St. John Township.

SAWYER CORNER. For E. Sawyer, who lived at the corner, 1877.

SAWYER POND. For the Isaac Sawyer family, settlers, the 1850's.

SAWYERS BOG. For Daniel Sawyer, a farmer.

SCHEDULE BROOK. For a rapids that could be counted on to disrupt the schedule of any log drive because of the jams it precipitated.

SCHOOL BROOK. For the East End School located nearby.

SCHOOLHOUSE: BROOK, RAPIDS. For a schoolhouse located there.

SCOTT POND. Unknown.

SCUDDER BROOK. For Joseph Scudder, farmer, 1845.

SEALANDER BROOK. For the Sealander family, Swedish immigrants.

SEAMS BROOK. Unknown.

SEARWAY BROOK. For Searway, local lumberman.

SECOND: BROOK, LAKE (3). Descriptive.

SECRET POND. Descriptive of isolation.

SEMINARY BROOK. Unknown.

SEVEN ISLANDS. (2). Descriptive.

SEYMOURS POINT. For Dedime Seymore, who owned the point.

SHARP. For Henry Sharp. who had a mill nearby.

SHEEAN BROOK. For the local Sheean family.

SHELDON RIDGE. Unknown.

SHEPERD RIPS. Possibly for Shepard Boody, who owned a mill at Oxbow.

SHEPHERD: BROOK, BROOK MOUNTAIN, POND. Unknown.

SHERIDEN. Named by an old man who delivered mail in the area, for General Sheriden, whom he had served under during the Civil War.

SHERMAN: MILLS, settlement, TOWNSHIP. For Senator John Sherman of Ohio, statesman, financier, and abolitionist.

SHERWOOD MOUNTAIN. For Steve Sherwood, who settled at its foot.

SHIELDS: BRANCH, BROOK (2). For the logging Shield family.

SHINGLE BROOK. Possibly for a shingle mill.

SHOALER MOUNTAIN. Unknown.

SHOREY. Unknown.

SHOREY: BROOK, HILL. For Joseph E. Shorey, prominent settler, 1835.

SILVER: LAKE, SPRING BROOK. Descriptive.

SILVER RIDGE: settlement, TOWNSHIP. For a heavy growth of silver birch trees.

SINCLAIR. Unknown.

SINCLAIR BROOK. (2). In St. John Township, for the D. Sinclair family. In T14R12, for Sinclair, a soldier who remained after the Aroostook War.

SIXMILE BROOK. (2). In Garfield Township, for its meeting the Machias River six miles from where the Machias River meets the Aroostook River. In T12R15, for its location about six miles from Seven Islands in the St. John River.

SIX MILE ISLAND: For its location six miles from Van Buren.

SKAGROCK BROOK. Unknown.

SKERRY. Unknown.

SKEW FALLS. Descriptive of the varied angles the water takes as it runs down the falls.

SKITACOOK: LAKE, STREAM. Abnaki: "dead water."

SLY: BROOK, BROOK LAKES, LITTLE-BROOK. Descriptive of their winding courses.

SMITH: BROOK (5), BROOK DEADWATER, BROOK POND, BROOK RIDGE, LITTLE-BROOK (2), POND. Brook in Houlton Township, for the family of Henry J. Smith, settler, before 1829. Brook, Brook Deadwater, Little-Brook, and Brook Ridge in Oxbow Township, probably for the James Smith family, settlers, the 1880's. The others, unknown.

SMYRNA: CENTER, MILLS, TOWNSHIP. For the ancient city of Smyrna, Turkey.

SNAKE BROOK. (2). For snakes.

SNARE BROOK. For moose snares.

SNOW SETTLEMENT. For Thomas and Edward Snow, settlers, 1857.

SOLDIER POND. For soldiers who built a temporary quarters there on the bank of the Fish River during the Aroostook War. On December 24, 1839, the quarters caught fire and 2 guards were killed.

SOMES CORNER. For the P. Somers family, farmers in 1877.

SOUCIER BOG. For Fred Soucier, who had a logging operation in the area.

SOULE BROOK. Unknown.

SOUTH: BRANCH, BROOK (2). Descriptive.

SOWISH LAKE: Abnaki: "sluggish."

SPAULDING. For Charles I. Spaulding, who lived there about 1910.

SPAULDING: BROOK (2), PONDS. Brook in Silver Ridge Township, for the Spaulding family. Brook and Ponds in Wallagrass Township, unknown.

SPECTACLE: BROOK, MOUNTAIN, POND. Descriptive of shape like spectacles, or eyeglasses.

SPINNEY BROOK. Unknown.

SPLIT BROOK. Descriptive of its rising in 2 branches.

SPOFFORD RIDGE. Unknown.

SPOON MOUNTAIN. Unknown.

SPRAGUEVILLE. For a large number of Spragues living there in the last part of the 19th century.

SPRING: BROOK (2), HILL. For springs.

SQUAPAN. For Squa Pan Lake.

SQUA PAN: INLET STREAM, LAKE, MOUNTAIN, STREAM. Abnaki: "bear's den."

SQUARE: LAKE, LAKE RIDGE. For a mistranslation of an Indian word meaning "round."

SQUIRREL: BROOK (4), MOUNTAIN, POCKET, POND. For squirrels.

STAIR FALLS. Descriptive of shape.

STARKEY CORNERS. For Charles V. Starkey, who ran a general store here in the 1890's and reportedly bought for slaughtering cattle smuggled across the border from Canada.

STATE ROAD. (settlement). For the State Road cut from Presque Isle to Ashland in 1842.

STERLING: BROOK, POND. Unknown.

STERLING RIDGE. For the Sterling family, who lived there in the last half of the 19th century.

STETSON RIDGE. Unknown.

STEVENS HILL. For S. Walter Stevens, who owned a nearby gristmill.

STEVENSVILLE. For the numerous Stevens living here.

STEWART BROOK. For J. Stewart, who lived on its banks in 1877.

STEWART HILL. For the early Stewart family.

STINK POND. Descriptive.

STOCKHOLM: MOUNTAIN, settlement, TOWNSHIP. By Swedish immigrants, for Stockholm, Sweden.

STONE BROOK. For Lewis or William Stone, early settlers.

STONY BROOK. Descriptive.

STOREY HILL. Unknown.

STRATTON ISLAND. For Wilder Stratton, who lived there before 1837.

SUCKER BROOK. For sucker fish.

SUGAR BERTH RIDGE. For maple sugar operations there.

SUGAR HILL. Ezra McGary was driving a wagon with a barrel of sugar in it up the hill to the store of J.H. Haley. At the top of the hill, the barrel slipped out of the wagon, stove in the head, and spilled sugar out as it rolled down the hill.

SUGAR LOAF. Descriptive of shape.

SUGARLOAF MOUNTAIN. Descriptive of shape.

SUGAR RIDGE. For sugar maples there.

SUNSET PARK. Descriptive.

SWANBACK CLEARING. For Jonathon Swanback, who cleared the area.

SWEDE POINT. Unknown.

SWEENEY: BROOK (2), POND. Unknown.

SYLVESTER POINT. Unknown.

TAPLEY RIDGE. Unknown.

TENMILE: BROOK (2), LAKE. Brook in T11R7, for its meeting the Machias River about 10 miles from where the Machias meets the Aroostook River. Lake and Brook in T3R2 area, for the lake's location about 10 miles from Mattawamkeag Lake.

THIBADEAU BROOK. For a number of Thibedeaus living there, 1877.

THIBIDEAU BROOK. For the Thibideau family, Acadian settlers.

THIBODEAU BROOK. For Baptiste Thibodeau, Acadian settler, 1785.

THIBODEAU ISLAND. For 2 Thibodeau families who cultivated the island.

THIRD: LAKE (3), LAKE BROOK. Descriptive.

THOMAS BROOK. Unknown.

THOMPSON DEADWATER. Unknown.

THOROUGHFARE: BROOK, THE-. Descriptive.

THOUSAND ACRE: BOG, SWAMP. Descriptive of a very large bog and swamp.

THREE BROOKS: brooks, COVE, NORTH BRANCH-, SOUTH BRANCH-. Descriptive.

THREE BURNT MOUNTAIN. Descriptive.

THREEMILE BROOK. (2). In Moro Township, for location 3 miles from Molunkus. In T14R8, for location about 1 mile from Fourmile Brook.

THREEMILE ISLAND. For its location in the Allagash River about 3 miles from where the Allagash meets the St. John River.

THREEMILE POND. For its location 3 miles from the Allagash River.

TIE CAMP BROOK. Descriptive of where railroad ties were cut.

TIMONEY: LAKE, MOUNTAIN, settlement. For James Timoney, landowner, 1877.

TINHORN, THE. Unknown.

TOGUE: POINT, POND, STREAM. For togue fish.

TOTE ROAD POND. For a tote road that runs by.

TOWNLINE BROOK. Near the town line of Moro and T7R5.

TRACY BROOK. (5). In Hodgdon Township, possibly for Jonathon Tracy, settler, 1828. In Amity Township, for Asa Tracy, settler, 1827. The others, unknown.

TRAFTON: BROOK, POND. For Trafton, a logger.

TRAFTON SIDING. For E. Trafton, who lived nearby.

TROUT: BROOK (3), BROOK RIDGE, POND. For trout fish.

TRUEWORTHY BROOK. Unknown.

TURTLE BROOK. For turtles.

TUTTLE POND. For the early Tuttle family.

TWENTYFIVEMILE BROOK. For its meeting the Machias River about 25 miles from where the Machias meets the Aroostook River.

TWENTYMILE: BROOK, RIGHT FORK-BROOK. For its meeting the Machias River about 20 miles from where the Machias meets the Aroostook River.

TWIN: BROOK, BROOK ISLAND, BROOK RAPIDS, NORTH BRANCH-BROOK, POND, SOUTH BRANCH WEST-BROOK, WEST-BROOK. Descriptive.

TWOMILE BROOK, NORTH BRANCH-BROOK, SOUTH BRANCH-BROOK. For the brook meeting the Big Black River 2 miles from where the Big Black meets the St. John River.

UGH LAKE. Unknown.

UMCULCUS STREAM. Abnaki: "a whistling duck."

UMSASKIS LAKE. Malecite: "linked together like sausages."

UNION CORNERS. For the union, or junction, of 4 roads.

UPPER: DEADWATER, DEADWATER POND, FALLS, POND. Descriptive.

UPPER HUDSON POND. Unknown.

VALENTINE RIDGE. Unknown.

VAN BUREN: settlement, TOWNSHIP. For Martin Van Buren, the President of the U.S. during the Aroostook War.

VIOLETTE BROOK. Unknown.

VIOLETTE: POND (2), STREAM. In Caribou Township, possibly for Lewis Violette, or his earlier family. In T17R3, unknown.

VIOLETTE SETTLEMENT. For several resident Violette families.

VIOLETTE STREAM. For Augustin Violette, early settler.

WADE: NORTH-, TOWNSHIP. For Wade, early proprietor.

WADLEIGH: BROOK (2), MOUNTAIN, NORTH BRANCH-BROOK, SOUTH BRANCH-BROOK. Unknown.

WALKER BROOK. For the Walker family, who left New Brunswick during the War of 1812 to escape persecution.

WALKERS. Unknown.

WALKER SETTLEMENT. For Benjamin and Joseph Walker, who lived there in 1877.

WALLAGRASS: LAKES, settlement, STATION, STREAM, TOWNSHIP. If Indian, Micmac: "good river." Or Abnaki: "shallow, full of holes."

WARREN FALLS. Unknown.

WASHBURN: JUNCTION, settlement, TOWNSHIP. For Israel Washburn, a governor of Maine.

WATSON BROOK. For a Watson family who lived there in 1877.

WEBSTER BROOK. (3). In Limestone Township, for Hosea Webster, settler about 1857.

WEEKSBORO: RIDGE, settlement. Unknown.

WEEKS: BROOK, POND. Unknown.

WELLINGTON RIDGE. For General Joel Wellington, who bought much area land in 1828.

WELTS BROOK. For the John Wells family, who lived there in 1877. The spelling discrepancy is a cartographical error.

WESLEY BROOK. For the local Wesley family.

WEST: COVE, BRANCH, BROOK, INLET, LAKE, MOUNTAIN. Descriptive.

WESTFIELD: LAKE, settlement, TOWNSHIP. For Westfield, Massachusetts.

WESTFORD HILL. One source says for Westford, Massachusetts. Another says for the Westford family, who settled there in the 1820's.

WESTMANLAND TOWNSHIP. Named by Swedish settlers for the Westmanland area of Sweden.

WESTON: settlement, TOWNSHIP. For Weston, the surveyor of the 1835 town lines.

WHEELOCK: BROOK, ISLAND, LAKE, settlement, SIDING, WEST BRANCH-BROOK. For Walter Wheelock, early lumberman.

WHEELOCK MILL. For the Wheelock family, owners.

WHIRLY BROOK. Possibly descriptive.

WHITE BROOK. (2). In Allagash Township, for the local White family, loggers. In T13R5, unknown.

WHITEHEAD LAKE. Probably for Fred Whited, local farmer, 1854, whose ancestral name was "Whitehead."

WHITEHORSE REEF. Fancifully named.

WHITE: LAKE, POINT, POND. Unknown.

WHITMAN MOUNTAIN. Unknown.

WHITNEY: BROOK (3), NORTH BRANCH-BROOK, SOUTH BRANCH-BROOK. Brook, North Branch-Brook, and South Branch-Brook in Bridgewater Township, for Sumner Whitney, settler, 1840, who built the town's first hotel near the brook. The others, unknown.

WHITNEY POINT. For the Whitney family, owners, 1877.

WHITTAKER BROOK. Unknown.

WIGGINS BROOK. Unknown.

WILCOX SETTLEMENT. For Benjamin Wilcox and his 5 sons, who lived with their families there.

WILDCAT BROOK. For wildcats..

WILLARD BROOK. For N.D. Willard, who owned a sawmill there, and his son Howard, who later had a limemill on the same site.

WILLIAMS BROOK. For the William Williams family, settlers after 1828.

WINSHIP BROOK. For Benjamin Winship, settler about 1828.

WINSLOW LAKE . For S.P. Winslow, who farmed nearby, 1877.

WINTERVILLE: settlement, STATION, TOWNSHIP. Unknown.

WOLF ISLAND. For wolves.

WOLVERTON BROOK. Unknown.

WOODBRIDGE CORNER. For Harrison B. Woodbridge, who lived there, 1877.

WOODLAND: CENTER, settlement, TOWNSHIP. For the good area woods.

WORK: COVE, POINT, For the Work family.

WYLES BROOK. For the local Wyles family.

WYMAN BROOK. Unknown.

WYTOPITLOCK: LAKE, settlement, STREAM. Abnaki: "at the place where there are alders."

YANKEETULADI: BROOK, POND. Blend of English "Yankee"

and Malecite "tuladi": "togue" or "place where they make canoes."

YELLOW BROOK. Descriptive of color of water.

YERXA RIDGE. Unknown.

YORK RIDGE. For the York family who farmed there.

YOUNG BROOK. For the local Young family.

YOUNG HILL. For Jonathon and J.C. Young, who lived there.

YOUNGS: BROOK, LAKE. For John Young, settler, 1846.

ZELLA ISLAND. Unknown.

CUMBERLAND COUNTY

ABNER POINT. For Abner Johnson, born in Durham in 1824, who bought the area from a Sinnett.

ADAMS HEAD. Possibly for the family of Jacob Adam, early settler.

ADAMS HILL. For the Adams family, who lived there, 1871.

ADAMS POND. (2). In Bridgton Township, for the numerous Adams family. In Standish Township, for Fred Adams, owner of Wild Acres Turkey Farm.

AI BROOK. For Ai Plummer, through whose land it ran.

ALDEN ROCK. Unknown.

ALEWIFE BROOK. For alewives.

ALLEN BOG. For the Allen family, who lived nearby, 1871.

ALLEN RANGE BROOK. For Arnold Allen, settler, 1643.

ANDERSON: BROOK, HILL. For J.F. Anderson, resident, 1871.

ANDREWS: BEACH, NUBBLE. For John Andrews.

ARTIST POINT. For the artists who used to frequent it.

ASH: POINT, POINT COVE. For ash trees.

ATHERTON HILL. For the Atherton family.

BABB CORNER. For the Babb family, who lived there, 1871.

BACHELDER BROOK. For Loring and Hannible Bachelder, early settlers.

BACK: COVE, SHORE. Descriptive.

BAILEY: ISLAND, ISLAND (settlement). For Deacon Timothy Bailey, settler, the mid 1700's.

BAKER: BROOK, CORNER, MOUNTAIN. For W. Baker and his family, early settlers.

BALD: HILL, MOUNTAIN, PATE MOUNTAIN, ROCK. Descriptive.

BALDWIN: EAST-, NORTH-, TOWNSHIP, WEST-. For Loammi Baldwin, early proprietor.

BALLASTONE LEDGES. For stones that were used as ship's ballast.

BANGS ISLAND. Probably for Colonel Joshua Bangs, former owner of Cushing Island.

BAR ISLAND. Descriptive.

BARKER POND. Unknown.

BARNES: ISLAND (2), POINT. For the numerous Barnes family, 1871.

BARREN HILL. Descriptive.

BARTLETT POINT. Probably for the Nicholas Bartlett family, early settlers and area landholders.

BARTOL ISLAND. For the Bartol family of the late 18th century.

BASIN: COVE, POINT. Descriptive.

BASKET: ISLAND, LOWER-LEDGE, UPPER-LEDGE. Descriptive.

BATES ISLAND. For the Bates family, who lived on Great Chebeague Island.

BEACH COVE. Descriptive.

BEALS COVE. For the Beal family, who lived there before 1850.

BEAN ISLAND. For the early Bean family.

BEAR: BROOK, RIVER. For bears.

BEARCE BOG. For the Bearce family, who owned the bog in 1871.

BEAVER: BROOK, POND (2). For beavers.

BEECH: RIDGE (2), RIDGE BROOK. For beech trees.

BELL HILL. For a bell in the meetinghouse that was located there.

BEN ISLAND. Unknown.

BENNETT COVE. For D. Bennett, who lived there in 1871.

BETHEL: ISLAND, POINT. Unknown.

BETTYS NECK. For Aunt Betty Welch, the first woman born in Raymond Township, in 1775.

BIBBER HILL. For the local Bibber family.

BIG: BEACH, HILL. Descriptive.

BIGLOW SWAMP. Unknown.

BIRCH: ISLAND (2), ISLAND (settlement), ISLAND LEDGE, LITTLE-ISLAND (2), POINT (2). For birch trees.

BLACK: BROOK, ROCK (2). Descriptive.

BLACK POINT. For the heavy, dark growth of evergreen trees.

BLACKSNAKE LEDGE. Descriptive of shape.

BLACKSTRAP: HILL, settlement. For William Blackstrap.

BLANCHARD POND. For the O.D. Blanchard family.

BLANEY POINT. For Benjamin Blaney, who owned about an eighth of Cousins Island in 1730.

BLUEBERRY HILL. For blueberries.

BLUE: POINT, POINT HILL. To distinguish it from nearby Black Point.

BLUFF POINT. Descriptive.

BOG POND. Descriptive.

BOLD DICK . A frequent fanciful name for an island that sits off to itself.

BOLSTERS MILLS . For Isaac Bolster, who built a dam and sawmill here in 1819.

BOMBAZINE ISLAND. For Bombazeen, an Indian Chief killed in a battle. He probably never visited the island.

BOND BROOK. Unknown.

BONNY EAGLE POND. Tradition says that a Scotchman was crossing a bridge when he met another man. As an eagle flew over them, the Scotchman said, "See the bonnie eagle."

BOWMAN ISLAND. For the Bowman family, early settlers.

BRACKETT POINT. For Anthony Brackett, early settler.

BRADBURY MOUNTAIN. For the early Bradbury family.

BRADLEYS CORNER. Unknown.

BRAGDON ISLAND. For the Bragdon family.

BRANCH BROOK. Descriptive.

BRANDY BROOK. (2). In Gorham Township, for a bottle of brandy that was drunk by the chairman of the road committee at the brook when the road was being surveyed. In New Gloucester Township, for the color of the water.

BRANNING LEDGES. Unknown.

BRANT LEDGES. For brants (a variety of geese).

BREAKHEART HILL. Unknown.

BREAKNECK BROOK. One source says for the speed of the flowing water. Another says that a prize bull once fell into the brook and broke its neck.

BRICKYARD COVE. For a brickyard operated there by a Collins.

BRIDGTON: NORTH-, settlement, SOUTH-, TOWNSHIP, WEST-. For Moody Bridges of Andover, Massachusetts, proprietor.

BRIGHAM HILL. For W. Brigham, resident, 1871.

BRIGHTON CORNER. For its location on Brighton Avenue.

BRIMSTONE HILL. For a black type of rock called "brimstone" by the natives.

BROAD: COVE (3), COVE ROCK. Descriptive.

BROKEN COVE. Descriptive of the broken rock on its shore.

BROTHERS, THE. Fanciful name for two rocks.

BROWN COVE. Unknown.

BROWN COW: EAST-, WEST-. Fanciful name for two rocks.

BROWN HILL: For B. Brown, resident, 1871.

BROWNS POINT. For the Moses Brown family, seafarers.

BROWNS POND. For John B. Brown, early settler.

BRUCE HILL. For the Frederick Bruce family.

BRUNSWICK: settlement, TOWNSHIP. For Brunswick, Germany,

or the House of Brunswick, to which the King of England belonged.

BUNGANUC: BROOK, LANDING, POINT, ROCK. Abnaki: "at the boundary place."

BURGESS BROOK. For F. Burgess, resident, 1857.

BUSH ISLAND. Descriptive.

BUSTINS: ISLAND, LITTLE-ISLAND. For John Bustin, settler, late 17th century.

BUTTERMILK: COVE, MOUNTAIN, POINT. Unknown.

CALLEN POINT: For the calling for ammunition by men who were attacked by Indians while building a stockade there to men at the garrison on the other side of Royal River.

CAMP COVE. For the summer camps there.

CANADA HILL (2). In Windham Township, named during a drunken party at a barn raising when one of the men climbed a tree and said he could see "all over the world and a part of Canada." In Otisfield Township, because it was so high one might see Canada.

CAPE, THE. Descriptive.

CAPE COTTAGE. For cottages located there.

CAPE ELIZABETH TOWNSHIP. Named for Princess Elizabeth, eldest daughter of James I, by her brother, Prince Charles.

CAPE MONDAY. Named by Captain A.W. Libby, a canal captain, as a reference. Below it was another point he called "Cape Tuesday" for the same reason.

CAPISIC POND. Abnaki: "dammed up branch."

CARD COVE. For the early Card family.

CARSLEY BROOK. For John and Nathan Carsley, settlers, 1792.

CARTER: BROOK, HILL. For D., G.W., and B.F. Carter, who lived on the hill in 1871.

CASCO: BAY, settlement, SOUTH-, TOWNSHIP. Abnaki: "great blue heron," or Micmac: "muddy." Some say Spanish: "helmet," by a Spanish explorer, but doubtful.

CASH CORNER. For the many Cash families there in the latter part of the 1800's.

CATFISH ROCK. For catfish.

CEDAR: LEDGE (2), LEDGES. For cedar trees.

CENTER ISLAND. For location in the center of Quahog Bay.

CENTRAL LANDING. Descriptive of location.

CHAFFIN POND. For the Chaffin family.

CHAMBERS CORNERS. For Thomas Chambers, who built a store there about 1820.

CHANDLER COVE. For Jonathon and Zachariah Chandler, who owned the cove about the time of the Revolution.

CHANDLER RIVER. For the Chandler family, who lived up river in New Gloucester.

CHAPLIN HILL. For the Chaplin family who lived nearby in 1871.

CHARITY LEDGE. Humorous, for if one grounds out on it, he will have to accept charity to keep alive.

CHEBEAGUE: GREAT-ISLAND, LITTLE-ISLAND, POINT. Abnaki: "almost separated."

CHECKLY POINT. For Samuel Checkly, early settler.

CHENERY BROOK. For the Chenery family who lived on its banks, 1870.

CHIMNEY ROCK. Descriptive of shape.

CHIVERICKS COVE. Unknown.

CHIVER LEDGE. Unknown.

CHOATE HILL. For the Choate family who lived there.

CITY POINT. For a point on Peaks Island facing Portland.

CLAM COVE. For clams.

CLAPBOARD: ISLAND, LOWER-ISLAND LEDGE, UPPER-ISLAND LEDGE. Descriptive of shape.

CLARK BROOK. For the Clark family who settled in the early 1800's.

CLARK COVE. Probably for the family of Samuel Clark, settler, 1739.

CLARK POND. For D.W. Clark, resident nearby, 1871.

CLEAVES LANDING. Probably for George Cleaves, early settler.

CLIFF: ISLAND, ISLAND LANDING.. Descriptive of its granite cliffs.

COBB COVE. For Daniel Cobb, who lived nearby about 1810.

COBBS BRIDGE. (settlement). For the many area Cobbs.

COD: EAST-LEDGE, THE-ROCKS, WEST-LEDGE, WEST-LEDGE ROCK. For codfish.

COFFEE POND. For a supply of goods, primarily coffee, lost through the ice here.

COLD: BROOK, RAIN POND, SPRING, SPRING BROOK. Descriptive.

COLE BROOK. For the Cole family who inhabited its banks.

COLEMAN COVE. For the Coleman family who settled in the 1820's.

COLLEGE ISLAND. Unknown.

COLLEGE: SWAMP, SWAMP BROOK. For one of the town lots, where the swamp is located, being given to Harvard College.

COLLEY WRIGHT BROOK. For Colley Wright, who felt cheated in drawing a lot for his property and sold his interest in Windham Township for 1 pound.

COLLINS BROOK. Probably for J. Collins, who lived there about 1850.

COLLINS POND. For the Collins family.

COLLYER BRANCH. For Peter Collyer, who built a log cabin there during the Revolution to escape service in the British army.

CONVENE. The first name of the community was New Limington, but when a post office was being established, it was realized that there was already a New Limington Post Office in existence. The ladies discussing it said that they hoped a name could be found, for it would be very convenient to have a post office here. Another lady said, "Let's name it 'Convene' then."

COOK MILLS. For the Cook brothers who established the mills.

COOKS CORNER. For Stephen Cook, settler, 1764.

COOL ROCK. Descriptive.

COOMBS ISLAND: LOWER-, UPPER-. For the Coombs family who settled in the 1700's.

COON ROAD SWAMP. For nearby Coon Road, for raccoons.

CORNFIELD POINT. For a cornfield that used to be there.

CORNISH STATION. For Cornish Township in York County.

CORWIN ROCK. Unknown.

COUSINS: ISLAND, ISLAND (settlement), RIVER. For the John Cousins family, settlers, 1645.

COW: ISLAND, ISLAND LEDGE. For its use as a cow pen.

COX LEDGE. Unknown.

COX PINNACLE. For its location on the Cox farm.

CRAB: ISLAND, LEDGE. For crabs.

CRANBERRYHORN HILL. Possibly for cranberries being there and its shape.

CRESCENT BEACH. Descriptive.

CRESSEY HILL. For the Daniel Cressey family, who built a store in Gorham in 1795.

CROCKETT CORNER. For the Crockett family living there in 1871.

CROCKETTS CORNER. For W. Crockett, who lived there in 1871.

CROOKED RIVER. Descriptive.

CROWELL ROCK. Unknown.

CROW ISLAND. (4). For crows.

CRYSTAL LAKE. Descriptive.

CUMBERLAND: CENTER, CENTER STATION, COUNTY, FORE-SIDE, MILLS, TOWNSHIP, WEST-. For William, Duke of Cumberland, son of King George II.

CUNDY: EAST-POINT, HARBOR, HARBOR (settlement), WEST-POINT. For William Cundy, settler, 1733.

CURTIS COVE. For David Curtis, settler, 1744.

CUSHING BRIGGS. For the Briggs and Cushing Shipyard located there.

CUSHING: ISLAND, ISLAND (settlement). For Colonel Ezekiel Cushing, settler by 1762.

CUSHING POINT. (2). For the early Cushing family.

DANFORD CREEK. For A. Danford, who lived along the creek, mid-1800's.

DAVID CASTLE. Unknown.

DAY BROOK. For Charles and Martin Day.

DEAD HOLE BROOK. Descriptive of the flow of the water.

DEARBORN HILL. For the local Dearborn family.

DEEP CUT. Descriptive of a cut through a hill for the Maine Central Railroad.

DEER: BROOK, HILL, POINT. For deer.

DEERING: EAST-, JUNCTION, NORTH-, settlement. For the Nathaniel and John Deering families.

DELANO PARK. For J. Delano, resident, 1871.

DESERT OF MAINE. Descriptive.

DIAMOND: COVE, GREAT-ISLAND, ISLAND LANDING, ISLAND LEDGE, ISLAND ROADS, LITTLE-ISLAND, LITTLE-ISLAND LANDING. Some say for quartz crystals found there; however, it is likely it was chosen just to have a more elegant name than its previous one — Hog Island.

DICK SHOAL. Unknown.

DINGLEY: COVE, ISLAND (2). Island in Casco Township, for Captain Joseph Dingley, local landholder and settler. Cove and Island in Harpswell Township, for the Dingley family, who sailed in the area.

DIPPER: COVE, COVE LEDGES. Unknown.

DITCH BROOK. Descriptive.

DIVISION POINT. For the boundary line dividing Captain Waldo and Colonel Waite's land on Great Chebeague Island.

DOCK, THE. Descriptive.

DOG CORNER. For the many dogs that were there.

DOGS HEAD. For a fancied resemblance.

DOLLEY CORNER. For E.C. Dolley.

DOLLY BROOK. For Thomas Dolly, who lived there in the early 1800's.

DOLLYS ISLAND. For the father of Mira Dolley.

DORSEYS COVE. Unknown.

DOUGHTY: COVE, LANDING, POINT. For the Doughty family, numerous in the area.

DOUGLAS BROOK. Probably for Seth Douglas, early settler.

DOUGLAS: HILL, MOUNTAIN. For John and Andrew Douglas, settlers between 1825-30.

DOW CORNER. For Jabez Dow, early settler.

DOYLE POINT. For John Doyle, shipbuilder, 1780.

DRINKWATER POINT. For the Drinkwater family, noted mariners.

DRISCOLL ISLAND. For the local Driscoll family.

DRUNKERS LEDGE. Unknown.

DRY: MILLS, POND. Descriptive.

DUCK: LITTLE-POND, POND, ROCK. For ducks. Little-Pond in Windham Township was named for Duck Pond, the former name of Highland Lake.

DUG HILL BROOK. For a misspelling of "Doug Hill," for Douglas Hill.

DUMPLING POND. Descriptive of shape.

DUNDEE: FALLS, HILL, POND. For Dundee Bill Mason, early settler.

DUNKERTOWN. To get out of paying for a road through that part of the town, some of the people engaged in a lawsuit. Squire Keith, one of the counsels in the case, remarked, "Think of the poor donkeys toiling up those long hills." In derision the area was called "Donkeytown," later, through usage, shortened to "Dunkertown."

DUNNS. For numerous Dunn families there in 1871.

DUNSTAN: RIVER, settlement. For Dunster, England, former home of some of the settlers.

DUTTON HILL. For the Dutton family who first inhabited it.

DYER CORNER. For the numerous area Dyer family.

DYER: COVE (2), POINT. Cove and Point in Cape Elizabeth Township, for Ed and Enoch Dyer, who lived there in the early 1800's. Cove in Harpswell Township, for the E. Dyer family, who lived there in 1871.

DYER ICE POND. For the Dyer family who cut ice here.

DYKES MOUNTAIN. For the Dike family who lived there in 1871.

EAGLE: ISLAND, ISLAND LEDGE. For eagles.

EAST: END, END BEACH. Descriptive of location in Portland Township.

EASTMAN BROOK. For Dr. John Eastman, settler from Conway, New Hampshire.

EAST: POINT (2), BRANCH. Descriptive.

ECHO POND. Descriptive.

EDDY BROOK. Unknown.

EDES FALLS. For Thomas Edes, who operated a sawmill there.

EDWARDS BROOK. For H. and J. Edwards, residents, 1871.

EDWARDS COVE. For the William Edwards family, settlers, 1802.

EEL WEIR CANAL. Descriptive.

EIGHT CORNERS. Descriptive of the crossing of roads creating eight corners.

ELIZABETH PARK. For location in Cape Elizabeth Township.

ELM: ISLAND, TREE COVE, -WOOD. For elm trees.

ERWIN NARROWS. For the Ewing family, settlers from England in the Robert Tempo colony.

EVERGREEN LANDING. For evergreen trees.

FALES HILL. Unknown.

FALL BROOK. Descriptive.

FALMOUTH: FORESIDE, NORTH-, settlement, TOWNSHIP, WEST-CORNER. Probably by Sir Ferdinando Gorges, for Falmouth, England.

FARM BROOK. Descriptive.

FARNSWORTH BROOK. For George Farnsworth, who lived there.

FARWELL: BOG BROOK. For the Farwell family who owned the bog in 1870.

FILES BROOK. For the Files family, settlers, early 1800's.

FINNERD BROOK. For the Finnerd family farm, where it rose.

FISH POINT. For fish.

FITCH HILL. For the numerous Fitch family.

FLAG: ISLAND, UPPER-ISLAND. For flags, a local name for a flower growing there.

FLASH ISLAND. Descriptive of the sun reflecting on the grass and rocks in the summer.

FLINTS MOUNTAIN. For Eleazer Flint, settler in the 1800's.

FLYING: LITTLE-POINT, POINT, POINT NECK. For duck and geese that flew over to get from one bay to another.

FOGG: BROOK, HILL. For the numerous Fogg family.

FOGG MOUNTAIN. For D. Fogg, resident, 1871.

FOGG POINT. For A. Fogg, who lived at the point, late 1800's.

FOGGS CORNER. Probably for the Enoch Fogg family, settlers by 1774.

FORE RIVER. Descriptive.

FOREST LAKE. Descriptive.

FORT ALLEN. Probably for Ethan Allen, who had just taken Fort Ticonderoga in the Revolutionary War when the fort was built.

FORT GORGES. For Sir Ferdinando Gorges, first proprietor of the area.

FORT: HILL (2), HILL BROOK, POINT (2). Hill and Hill Brook in Gorham Township, for a fort located there in the 1740's. Hill and Point in Cape Elizabeth Township, for a small fort built there in 1744 in anticipation of a French invasion. Point in Harpswell Township, for a breastworks built there in 1812.

FORT LEVETT. Probably for Captain Levett, early settler on Cushings Island.

FORT LYON. Unknown.

FORT PREBLE. For Commodore Preble, prominent Revolutionary War naval veteran.

FORT SCAMMEL: fort, POINT. For Colonel Alexander Scammel, friend of General Henry Dearborn of Maine, U.S. Secretary of War.

FORT WILLIAMS. For Major General Seth Williams of Augusta, Civil War veteran.

FOSTER BROOK. For D.K. Foster, early settler.

FOSTERS CORNERS. For the Foster family who resided there.

FREEMAN HILL. For S. Freeman, who lived there.

FREEPORT: settlement, SOUTH-, TOWNSHIP. Possibly because it was a free, accessible port. Possibly for Sir Anthony Freeport, a character in one of Joseph Addison's plays (highly doubtful, although traditional).

FRENCH: ISLAND, LITTLE-ISLAND. Possibly for the early French family, but unknown for certain.

FROST GULLY BROOK. For Ichabod and Phineas Frost, settlers by 1782.

FRYE ISLAND. For Frye, who lived on it for many years.

FRYES LEAP. For the Frye of Fryes Island who jumped off the cliff here to escape pursuing Indians.

GAG CORNER. Unknown.

GALLOWS ISLAND. Unknown.

GAY BROOK. For Lewis Gay, settler, 1784.

GEORGE ISLAND. Unknown.

GLANTZ CORNER. For the Glantz family who lived there in the 1770's.

GLOUCESTER: HILL, NEW- (settlement). NEW-STATION, NEW-TOWNSHIP, UPPER-. For Gloucester, Cape Ann, Massachusetts, former home of some of the settlers.

GLOVERS WIG. For Glauber, a white man scalped by the Indians there in the early days.

GOAT ISLAND. For its use as a goat pen.

GOOGINS: ISLAND, LEDGE. For the Googins family, settlers in 1763.

GOOSE: COVE, LEDGE, LOWER-ISLAND, NEST LEDGE, POINT, UPPER-ISLAND. For geese.

GORHAM: NORTH-, settlement, SOUTH-, TOWNSHIP, WEST-. For Captain John Gorham, who served in King Phillip's War.

GOSLINGS, THE. Fanciful name for a number of small rocks near Upper and Lower Goose Islands.

GOTHAM HILL. Possibly a misunderstanding of Cotton Hill, for a Cotton living there in 1857.

GOUDY LEDGE. Unknown.

GOULD CORNER. Possibly for Elijah Gould, early settler.

GRAND: BEACH, -VIEW HILL. Descriptive.

GRASSY LEDGE. Descriptive.

GRAVES HILL. Probably for the John Graves family, early settlers.

GRAY: EAST-, MEADOWS, NORTH-, settlement, SOUTH-, STATION, TOWNSHIP, WEST-. For Thomas Gray, one of the Massachusetts proprietors.

GREAT: FALLS, HARBOR COVE, LEDGE COVE, POND. Descriptive.

GREELEY: BROOK, HILL. For John Greeley, who lived on its banks.

GREEN: HILL, INNER-ISLAND, ISLAND LEDGE, ISLAND PASSAGE, ISLAND REEF, LEDGES, OUTER-ISLAND, UPPER-ISLANDS. Descriptive.

GROWSTOWN. For the many Grows living there in the 19th century.

GULF OF MAINE. For the State of Maine.

GULLY BROOK. Descriptive.

GUN: POINT, POINT COVE. Descriptive of being a long, slender neck of land.

GURNET STRAIT. For any number of places named "Gurnet" in England, by early English settlers.

HADDOCK: COVE, ROCK. For haddock fish.

HALLICOM COVE. Unknown.

HALL POINT. For the Hall family who lived there by the time of the Revolution.

HAMBLEN BROOK. For Timothy Hamblen, who had a mill there about 1780.

HANCOCK POND. For John Hancock, local hunter and trapper.

HARBOR GRACE. Likely French: "haven harbor."

HARDING. For the Harding family who owned the Harding Fabricating Plant of the Bath shipyards.

HARDING HILL. For several Harding families who lived on it.

HARLAN SWAMP. For Harlan Lovewell.

HARMON BEACH. For Daniel Harmon, farmer and settler.

HARPSWELL: CENTER, COVE, EAST-, NECK, NORTH-, SOUND, SOUTH-, TOWNSHIP, WEST- Tradition says named by the Denning family, for Harpswell, England.

HARRASEEKET RIVER. If Indian, Abnaki: "full of obstacles." One source says possibly for an Indian of that name.

HARRISON: settlement, SOUTH-, TOWNSHIP. For Harrison Gray Otis, one of the chief proprietors.

HARVEY BROOK. For the Harvey family.

HASKELL ISLAND. For Captain Haskell, master of a coasting vessel.

HASKELL POND. For Ebenezer Haskell, settler, early 1800's.

HATCHERY BROOK. For a fish hatchery there.

HAYDEN BAY. For the Elias W. Hayden family.

HAYDEN BROOK. For J. Hayden, resident nearby, 1871.

HAYWARD POINT. Unknown.

HEATH BROOK. Descriptive.

HEDGEHOG MOUNTAIN. For hedgehogs (porcupines).

HEN: BIG-ISLAND, ISLAND, COVE. Fanciful.

HIGGENS: BEACH, CREEK. For the area Higgins family.

HIGGINS CORNER. For the Higgins family who lived there in 1871.

HIGH HEAD. (2). Descriptive.

HIGHLAND: LAKE (2), LAKE (settlement). Lake and settlement in Westbrook Township, descriptive, but primarily because the present name was more elegant than the former Duck Pond. Lake in Bridgton Township, although it is 160 feet higher than Long Lake, and highlands surround it, the inhabitants wanted something more impressive than Crotched Pond, its former name.

HIGHLANDS. Descriptive.

HILL BROOK. For Deacon Daniel Hill, settler, 1799.

HILLSIDE. (2) In Sebago Township, for the Hill family who lived there in 1871. In Brunswick Township, descriptive.

HOBBS BROOK. Unknown.

HOBBS HILL. For R. Hobbs, resident, 1871.

HOGFAT HILL. For the hogs pastured here on this oak-covered hill to fatten on the acorns.

HOLBROOK LEDGE. For the Jonathon Holbrook family.

HOLT POND. For Holt, area surveyor.

HOPE ISLAND. Possibly for a Hope family who were in the area early.

HOPKINS ISLAND. For Simeon and Elisha Hopkins.

HORSE ISLAND. (2). For use as pastures for horses.

HOUSE ISLAND. For a stone house built there in 1623 by Christopher Leavitt.

HOWARD POINT. For the local Howard family.

HUE AND CRY: EAST-, WEST-. Descriptive of the sailors on the lookout for these ledges and rocks as their ship entered these waters.

HUNGER: BAY, HILL, MOUNT-. For early settlers in these areas having a difficult time making a living.

HUNT HILL. For Daniel Hunt, settler, 1770's.

HUNTS POINT. For the Hunt family.

HUSSEY: SOUND, THE-. Although the Hussey family can be found in the Portland area early, it is possible that this shallow, dangerous area could be named for being a "hussy," difficult to contend with.

INDIAN: CAMP BROOK, COVE, ISLAND (2), POINT (2), ROCK. For Indians.

INGALLS: HILL, POND (2), settlement. Hill, Pond, and settlement in Brunswick Township, for Isaiah, Phineas, Nathan, Francis, Asa, and Reuben Ingalls, who all settled near one another before 1800. Pond in Baldwin Township, for Lieutenant Benjamin Ingalls, a Louisburg veteran.

INKHORN BROOK. For Rowland Houghton, surveyor, who lost his cow horn full of ink in the brook as he attempted to cross it when it was high.

INTERVALE. Descriptive.

IRELAND CORNER. Unknown.

IRON: ISLAND, LITTLE-ISLAND. Descriptive of a rock-bound island.

IRONY ISLAND. Descriptive of a rock-bound island.

ISLAND POND. Descriptive of a pond with an island on it.

JACK BROOK. For A. Jack or his ancestors.

JACKSON BROOK. For Captain Simon Jackson, early settler.

JAQUISH: GUT, ISLAND. For Lieutenant Richard Jaques, Indian fighter and settler, 1727.

JENKS LANDING. For Joshua E. Jenks, hotel proprietor.

JENNY: ISLAND, LEDGE. Unknown.

JERRY BROOK. For Jerry Edwards, resident about 1850.

JERRY POINT. Unknown.

JEWELL ISLAND. For George Jewell, who purchased it from the Indians in 1637. There is a local tradition that it is named for the glistening iron pyrites there.

JOHN COVE. Unknown.

JOHNS: LEDGE, POINT. Unknown.

JOHNSON BROOK. For the Johnson family.

JOHNSON COVE. For the James Johnson family, who lived there about 1800.

JONES CREEK. For the area Jones family.

JONES HILL. For D. Jones, resident, 1871.

JONES LEDGE. Unknown.

JONES WHARF. For William Jones, hotel owner.

JORDAN BAY. For Dominicus Jordan, settler, 1794.

JORDAN: POINT (2), REEF. Point and Reef in Cape Elizabeth Township, for the Jordan family, who has been there since the 17th century. Point in Harpswell Township, for John Jordan, settler, 1739.

JOSIAHS COVE. Unknown.

JOSIES BROOK. For John Jose, Revolutionary War veteran.

JUGTOWN PLAINS. For a former community that was named for the following incident. Once in Jonathon Smith's mill yard, the men engaged in a shooting match, using a drink of whiskey now and then to sharpen up their shooting. As the match progressed, one man set the jug of whiskey on a stump, and before long, it was shot by mistake.

JUNK OF PORK. (island). Descriptive of shape.

KEAZER POND. Unknown.

KELSEY BROOK. For Joel Kelsey, who operated a store nearby.

KENNY BROOK. Unknown.

KETTLE COVE. Descriptive of shape.

KNIGHT HILL. For several Knight families living there.

KNIGHTS BROOK. For John Knight, settler, about 1805.

KNIGHTVILLE. For numerous Knight families.

KRAMS POINT. For the local Kram family.

LAMBERT POINT. For Captain Lambert, who ran a nearby store.

LAMSON COVE. Unknown.

LAND OF NOD. Unknown.

LANES ISLAND. For Samuel and Henry Lane, who settled here in 1688.

LEACH HILL. For Mark Leach, early settler.

LEAVITT BROOK. For Dr. Joshua Leavitt, early settler.

LEAVITT ISLAND. For Christopher Leavitt, early settler.

LEDGE HILL. Descriptive.

LEDGES, THE. Descriptive.

LEIGHTON HILL. For numerous area Leightons in 1871.

LEWIS HILL. For Major L. and Deacon George Lewis.

LIBBY BROOK. For the numerous Libby family in the area since at least the 18th century.

LIBBY HILL. For A., I., and G.L. Libby, who lived there in 1857.

LIBBY RIVER. Probably for the James Libby family, settlers by 1747.

LIBBYTOWN. For the many Libbys who lived there.

LIGONIA. For the grant of land which included much of Maine, named "Ligonia" in 1643 by Alexander Rigby.

LILY POND. For lilies.

LINCOLN WEEKS BROOK. Unknown.

LINDSAY ISLAND. Possibly for the J. Lindsley family, who lived nearby in 1871.

LITTLE: BEACH, COVE, FALLS, HILL, ISLAND, MOUNTAIN, NORTH BRANCH-RIVER, POND (2), RIVER (2). Descriptive.

LITTLE BULL LEDGE. For White Bull.

LITTLEJOHN: ISLAND, ISLAND (settlement). Possibly for John Cousins, namesake of Cousins Island, who owned both and needed to distinguish between them. Also, there have been a number of Littlejohn families in the Yarmouth area.

LOMBARD HILL. For the Lombard family who lived there and owned much area land.

LOMBOS HOLE. Unknown.

LONG: BEACH, COVE (2), CREEK, ISLAND (2), ISLAND (settlement), LAKE (2), LEDGE, MEADOWS, POINT (2), REACH, REACH MOUNTAIN. Descriptive.

LOOKOUT POINT. During the Indian Wars a sentinel was stationed here to watch for Indians attacking by canoe.

LOON ISLAND. For loons.

LORENZEN HILL. Unknown.

LOVELLS HILL. For Dennis Lovell, who settled here before 1790.

LOWELL COVE. For 3 Lowell brothers who settled in the area.

LOWER: BAY, NARROWS. Descriptive.

LUCKSE SOUND. Unknown.

LUMBO LEDGE. Unknown.

LUNTS CORNER. Unknown.

LYON POINT. For the local Lyon family.

MACKWORTH: ISLAND, POINT. For Arthur Mackworth, who was given the island by his friend Sir Ferdinando Gorges about 1631.

MADELON POINT. For the steamer "Madelon" which loaded there in the 1890's.

MAIDEN COVE. Unknown.

MAPLE RIDGE. For maple trees.

MAQUOIT BAY. Abnaki: "a wet place."

MARE BROOK. Probably for John Mare, early settler.

MARINER. For James Mariner, early settler.

MARK: GREAT-ISLAND, ISLAND, ISLAND LEDGE, LITTLE-ISLAND. Great-Island and Little-Island mark the entrance to Merriconeag Bay. Island and Island Ledge, for use as position marks for fishermen hunting their fishing grounds.

MARSTON HILL. For the Marston family who lived there.

MARTIN BROOK. For the local Martin family.

MARTIN ISLAND. Unknown.

MARTIN POINT. For Richard Martin, settler, 1658.

MASSACRE POND. For the massacre of 19 whites by Indians in 1702.

MAST COVE. For masts rafted there.

MAST LANDING. For being the receiving point for masts for the Royal Navy.

MAXWELL: COVE, POINT. For J. Maxwell, who lived there in 1871.

MAYBERRY HILL. For Richard, Edward, and William Mayberry, brothers.

McINTOSH BROOK. For Duncan McIntosh, emigrant from Scotland.

McKENNY POINT. For the McKenny family.

MEADER BROOK. For J.A. Meader, who lived here in the 1850's.

MEADOW BROOK. (4). Descriptive.

MEETING HOUSE HILL. For a meeting house located there.

MERE: POINT, -POINT (settlement), -POINT BAY, -POINT NECK. Possibly for John Mare, early settler. Others say French: "sea."

MERRICONEAG SOUND. Malecite: "lazy portage."

MERRILL BROOK. (2). For many area Merrills.

MERRIMAN COVE. For Walter Merriman, early settler.

MERROW LANDING. For Merrow, who lived there in 1857.

MIDDLE: BAY COVE, BROOK, BROOK BOG, GROUND ROCK, ROCK. Descriptive.

MILE BROOK. Descriptive of its length.

MILL: BROOK (5), COVE, CREEK, POND, STREAM. For mills.

MILLER: CREEK, POINT. For the local Miller family.

MILLIKEN: BROOK, HILL. Unknown.

MINISTERIAL ISLAND. For being set aside for use by the ministry of Cumberland Township.

MINK ROCKS. For mink.

MINNOW BROOK. For minnows.

MISERY HILL. Unknown.

MITCHELL HILL. For A. Mitchell, who lived there in 1871.

MITCHELL LEDGE. For Captain Josiah A. Mitchell.

MITCHELL ROCK. Unknown.

MOLLY GUT. Possibly Abnaki: "steep."

MOORE POINT. Unknown.

MOOSE: MEADOW, POND (2). For moose.

MORGAN MEADOW; For the Morgan family, owners.

MORRILLS CORNER. Possibly for the Peter Morrill family.

MOSHER: BROOK, CORNER. For M. Mosher, among others who have lived there.

MOSHIER: ISLAND, LEDGE, LITTLE-ISLAND. For John Moshier, early settler.

MOSQUITO BROOK. For mosquitos.

MOUNTAINVIEW PARK. Descriptive and promotional name.

MOUNT HENRY. Tradition says for Henry Plummer, son of Aaron Plummer, but the name seems to predate this family's settlement.

MUDDY RIVER. Descriptive.

MUD PONDS. Descriptive.

MUNJOY HILL. For George Munjoy, resident, 1652.

MUSSEL COVE. (2). For mussels.

NAPLES: BAY OF-, settlement, SOUTH-, TOWNSHIP. For Naples, Italy.

NASON BROOK. (2). In Gorham Township, for Uriah Nason, who built a mill here about 1804. In Sebago Township, for the early Nason family.

NASONS CORNER. Unknown.

NEWHALL. For the Newhall family, who ran a gunpowder factory there.

NONESUCH: COVE, POINT, RIVER. Some say for its erratic course. Others, for Nonsuch, the summer home of Queen Elizabeth. Still others, for the goodness of the land on its west side — "no such land."

NORTH: BRANCH, LEDGES, -WEST RIVER. Descriptive.

NORTON BROOK. For the numerous Norton family.

NOTCH, THE. Descriptive.

NOTCHED POND. Descriptive.

NUBBIN, THE. Descriptive.

NUBBLE: HILL, POND, ROCK. Descriptive.

NUTTING LEDGE. For Peter Nutting, who lived here about 1820.

OAK: -DALE, HILL (4), ISLAND, LEDGES. For oak trees.

OBEDS ROCK. Unknown.

OLD ANTHONY ROCK. Unknown.

OLD PROPRIETOR. Unknown.

OLD TOM ROCK. Unknown.

ORRS: COVE, HILL, ISLAND, ISLAND (settlement). For the families of Joseph and Clement Orr, settlers, 1742. Island specifically for Joseph Orr.

TISFIELD: EAST-, COVE, GORE, settlement, SOUTH-, TOWN-SHIP. For Harrison Grey Otis, Mayor of Boston, Senator from Massachusetts, and a nephew of James Otis, one of the proprietors. Others say for James and Samuel Otis, two of the proprietors.

TTER: BROOK, POND, PONDS. For otters.

UTLET BROOK. Descriptive.

VERSET ISLAND. Descriptive of appearance.

WL POND. For owls.

ANTHER: POND, RUN. For panthers.

APOOSE ISLAND. For nearby Squaw Island.

ARKER POINT. Probably for James Parker, innkeeper.

ARKER POND. For the former name of Casco Township—Parkerville, probably for Captain Nathaniel Parker, a proprietor.

ARROT POINT. Unknown.

EABLES POINT. For J., M., and A.W. Peables, residents, 1871.

EABODY POND. For Richard Peabody, early settler.

EACOCK HILL. For peacocks kept there by Simon Greenleaf.

EAKED MOUNTAIN. Descriptive.

EAKS: ISLAND, ISLAND (settlement). Possibly for Joseph Peaks, a soldier in the company of Captain Dominicus Jordan in 1744. It is known that he lived a while in Cape Elizabeth, but what connection, if any, he had with Peaks Island is unknown.

ENNELLVILLE. For the Thomas Pennell family, settlers of the 1700's.

ERLEY MOUNTAIN. For Enoch Perley, settler, 1775.

ERLEY POND. For the local Perley family.

ETER COVE. Unknown.

ETTINGILL ISLAND. For the pioneer Pettingill family who lived at Flying Point.

PETTINGILL POND. For J. Pettengill, resident, 1857.

PHILLIPS BROOK. Unknown.

PIGEON BROOK. For pigeons.

PIG KNOLL. For pigs kept there not long ago.

PIKE CORNER. For Pike, who lived there.

PINE HILL. For pine trees.

PINE POINT. For Charles Pines, who lived near.

PINETREE LEDGE. Possibly for pine trees.

PINKHAM: ISLAND, POINT. For the area Pinkham families in 1871.

PINNACLE, THE. Descriptive.

PISMIRE MOUNTAIN. For either its approximate shape like an anthill or the ants that infest it.

PISCATAQUA: EAST BRANCH-RIVER, RIVER. Abnaki: "the place where the river divides."

PISGAH HILL. A frequent Maine place-name for the biblical Mount Pisgah; however, if Indian, Abnaki: "dark," or Mahican: "muddy."

PLEASANT: -DALE, HILL (2), HILL (settlement), POND RIDGE, RIVER. Descriptive.

PLUMMER ISLAND. For the local Plummer family.

PLUMMER LANDING. For Aaron Plummer, early settler.

POLE ISLAND. For poles cut there for fish weirs.

POLLACK CREEK. For pollock fish.

POMROY ROCK. Unknown.

PONCE LANDING. Unknown.

POND: COVE, COVE (settlement), ISLAND, ISLAND LEDGE. Descriptive.

POORS HILL. For W.C. Poor, resident, 1871.

POPEVILLE. For Nathan Pope, who owned a sawmill here.

POPLAR RIDGE. (2). For poplar trees.

PORCUPINE MOUNTAIN. For porcupines.

PORTERS LANDING. For Seward Porter and his 11 sons, who ran a salt works about 1782.

PORTLAND: HARBOR, HEAD, settlement, SOUTH-, SOUTH-GARDENS, SOUTH-TOWNSHIP, TOWNSHIP. For Portland, Dorsetshire, England.

POTTS HARBOR. For Richard Potts, settler by 1672.

POUND OF TEA. (island). A pound of tea was one of the articles in a trade made for the island by a fisherman.

POWELL POINT. For John Powell, settler in the 1700's.

POWNAL: CENTER, NORTH-, TOWNSHIP, WEST-. For Governor Thomas Pownal of Massachusetts.

PRATTS BROOK. For the seafaring Pratt family.

PRESUMPSCOT: FALLS, RIVER. Abnaki: "ledges in channel."

PRIDES CORNER. For Peter Pride.

PRINCE: POINT (3), LEDGE. Point and Ledge in Falmouth Township, for the Prince family who settled in the 1850's. Point in Brunswick Township, for the H. Prince family. Point in Yarmouth Township, probably for Otis Prince, early settler.

PROSPECT HILL. Descriptive.

PROUTS: NECK, NECK (settlement). For Timothy Prout, who purchased part of the area in 1728.

PULPIT ROCK. Descriptive.

PUMPKIN HILL. The story is told that a man living at the foot of the hill raised a good crop of pumpkins that disappeared one night. He found them in a neighbor's barn at the top of the hill. When asked how they got there, the neighbor said they must have rolled up the hill.

PUMPKIN KNOB. (2). Descriptive of shape.

PUMPKIN VALLEY. Some say for pumpkins growing there. Othe for pumpkin pines growing there.

PUNCHBOWL. Descriptive of shape of a small cove.

QUAHOG BAY. For quahogs. Natick: "round clam."

QUAKER: BROOK, HILL. For the area Quakers.

RAGGED ISLAND. Descriptive.

RAM: ISLAND (3), ISLAND LEDGE. For their use as sheep pe

RANDALL HILL. For John Howard Randall, who lived there aft 1907.

RATTLESNAKE: LITTLE-POND, MOUNTAIN, POND. For t many rattlesnakes early settlers found there.

RAYMOND: CAPE, EAST-, HILL, NECK, NORTH-, settleme TOWNSHIP. For Captain William Raymond, who served in t Canadian Expedition of 1690.

RAYVILLE. For David Ray, who built a mill here in 1785.

RED BROOK. Descriptive of the color of the water.

REED COVE. Owned by Joseph Orr, who had no children of own. He married Letitia Reed, a widow with several children. son of hers inherited the cove and the Reed name derived fro him.

RICHARDS POND. Unknown.

RICH: HILL, MILL POND, -VILLE. For C.S. and G.M. Ric sawmill owners, 1871.

RICHMOND: ISLAND, ISLAND HARBOR. For George Richmon who had a business enterprise on it early.

RICKER HEAD. For the Ricker family, shipbuilders.

RIDGE: THE-, UPPER-. Descriptive.

RIDLEY COVE. For James Ridley, a pre-Revolutionary War settle

RIVERTON. For its location on the Presumpscot River.

ROBINSON HILL. For A.J. Robinson.

OCK: LEDGE, POINT. Descriptive.

OCKY HILL. (3) Descriptive.

ODGERS BROOK. For George Rogers, who lived nearby in 1850.

OGUE ISLAND. Probably because it was a menace to navigation.

OGUES ISLAND. Probably because it was a menace to navigation.

OHRS HILL. Unknown.

OLFE BROOK. For the Rolfe family living there in the 1870's.

OSEMONT. Promotional name.

OUND ROCK. Descriptive.

OYAL: JUNCTION, RIVER. For William Royal, who lived on its banks about 1640.

UNAROUND BROOK. Descriptive.

USSELL BROOK. For John Russell, farm owner in 1835, who sold to Calvin Russell in 1840.

YE POND. Unknown.

ABBATHDAY POND. For a number of beaver trappers who agreed to meet here to keep the Sabbath, before the area was settled.

ACO RIVER. Abnaki: "flowing out."

ADDLEBACK: HILLS, LEDGE. Descriptive.

AGAMORE VILLAGE. Promotional name.

AMBORN BROOK. For Josedick Samborn, settler, late 1700's.

AND: BROOK, ISLAND (2), POND. Descriptive.

ANDY: COVE, CREEK, HILL, POINT, POINT LEDGES. Descriptive.

ARGENT BROOK. For Daniel Sargent, early settler.

ATURDAY POND. Unknown.

AWYER BROOK. For the local Sawyer family.

CARBOROUGH: BEACH, BEACH STATION, NORTH-, RIVER, TOWNSHIP, WEST-. For Scarborough, Yorkshire, England.

COTLAND. For its location on "Highland" Lake and "McIntosh" Brook.

SCOTTOW: BOG, HILL. For Captain Scottow and his family, very early settlers.

SCRAG ISLAND. Descriptive of a worthless, ragged island.

SCRIBNER HILL. For Samuel Scribner, settler, 1784.

SCRIBNERS MILL. For Elijah Scribner, the mill owner.

SEAL: COVE (2), LEDGE, ROCK. For seals.

SEBAGO: EAST-, LAKE, LAKE BASIN, LAKE (settlement), LITTLE-LAKE, NORTH-, settlement, TOWNSHIP, WEST-. Abnaki: "big lake."

SEBASCODEGAN ISLAND. Abnaki: "carry or passage almost completed."

SHAD GULLY. For shad fish.

SHAKER VILLAGE. For the Shaker colony, which was established in 1791.

SHARK COVE. For sharks.

SHAW MILLS. For T.M. Shaw, who had a sawmill there.

SHEEP: ISLAND, ISLAND LEDGE, ISLAND NORTH LEDGES. For its being used as a sheep pen.

SHELLDRAKE: COVE, POINT. For sheldrakes.

SHELTER ISLAND. For its use by early settlers as a refuge from Indians. A blockhouse was located there.

SHIP COVE. Where ships could weather storms.

SHOOTING ROCK. Descriptive of where hunters shot ducks.

SHORE ACRES HILL. Promotional name.

SILVER BROOK. Descriptive.

SIMPSON: BROOK, POINT. For William Simpson, settler, 1759.

SINKHOLE, THE. Descriptive.

SISTER: ISLAND, ISLAND LEDGE. For its appearance, much like a neighboring island.

SISTERS: GROUND, rocks. Fanciful name for a number of rocks.

SISTERS, THE. Fanciful name for 3 rocks.

SKUNK: KNOLL, KNOLL BROOK. For skunks.

SMALL: BROOK, HILL. Possibly descriptive of size, but more likely for the Small family.

SMALLS HILL. Probably for John Small, surveyor of Gorham.

SMITH BROOK. (2). In Brunswick Township, for the area Smith family in 1871. In Otisfield Township, for Jonathon Smith, mill owner there after 1828.

SMUGGLERS COVE. Descriptive.

SMUTTYNOSE ISLAND. A frequent name descriptive of black rocks among lighter colored ones.

SNOW ISLAND. For the area Snow family.

SNOWS HILL. For J. Snow, resident, 1871.

SODOM. For a group of Italian or Irish workers hired by the Maine Central Railroad who lived in railway cars there and were much given to drinking and wild parties. Because they were thought to be wicked by the local people, the area was called "Sodom" for the biblical evil city.

SOLDIER LEDGE. Unknown.

SONGO: LOCK, RIVER. Abnaki: "the outlet."

SOW AND PIGS. Fanciful name for a large rock and a bunch of smaller ones.

SPAR COVE. (2). In Falmouth Township, for trees that were felled and then floated to Mast Landing. In Portland Township, possibly for the same reason.

SPEARS HILL. For David Spears, merchant and owner of Spears' Wharf about 1800.

SPICERS COVE. Unknown.

SPIDER ISLAND. (2). For spiders.

SPRING: COVE, POINT, POINT LEDGE. Descriptive.

SPRUCE POINT. For spruce trees.

SPURWINK: HILL, RIVER. Although it is unknown why the nam is applied, "Spurwink" is an English surname and the are probably was named for or by an early settler. It is not Indian f almost certain.

SQUAW ISLAND. Only because Indians formerly occupied it.

SQUIDERE GUSSET. For Squidere Gusset, Indian sachem who ga his lands to England. The name translates possibly as Abnaki-En lish: "flows rapidly."

SQUIRREL ISLAND. For squirrels.

STANDISH: settlement, SOUTH-, TOWNSHIP. For Miles Standis military leader of Plymouth Colony.

STAPLES BROOK. For the Staples family, first family in the are who were still there in 1871.

STAPLES: COVE (2), POINT (2). Point and Cove in Cape Elizabe Township, for the Staples family who lived there in 1857. Poi and Cove in Falmouth Township, for Joseph Staples, settler the 1700's.

STAVE ISLAND. For lumber for barrel staves being obtained ther

STEEP FALLS. Descriptive.

STEPPING STONES. Descriptive.

STEVENS BROOK. (2). In Brunswick Township, for Jacob Steven who had a saw and cornmill here. In New Gloucester Townshi for William Stevens, early settler.

STEVENS ROCK. Unknown.

STICKEY RIVER. For many small, sunken logs, referred to a sticks, which protrude above the water.

STOCKBRIDGE POINT. For Josiah Stockbridge, early settler.

STOCKMAN ISLAND. For C. Stockman, who owned it.

STOVER: COVE, POINT. For John Stover, early settler.

STRAWBERRY CREEK. For wild strawberries.

STROUDWATER: RIVER, settlement, SOUTH BRANCH-RIVER. For Stroudwater, England.

STROUT BROOK. (2). In Standish Township, for E. Strout, who lived there in 1871. In Gorham Township, for many Strouts living in the area in 1871.

STUART BROOK. For its rising on the Stuart family farm.

STURDIVANT: ISLAND, LANDING LEDGES. For numerous Sturdivant families.

SUCKER: BROOK (2), -VILLE. For sucker fish.

SUMMIT SPRING HILL. Descriptive.

SUNSET: LANDING, PARK, POINT, ROCK. Descriptive.

SYLVESTER RIDGE. For Ezekiel Sylvester, early settler.

TANNERY BROOK. For a number of tanneries located there in the early days.

TARKILL POND. A cartographical error for "Tarkiln Pond," for a tar kiln there.

TARKILN HILL. For a tarkiln located there.

TAYLOR REEF. Unknown.

TEA SWAMP. For quantities of Labrador tea growing there.

TENNEY RIVER. For a large number of Tenney families that lived along it in the late 1800's.

TENNY HILL. (2). In Raymond Township, for H. Tenney, who lived on it in 1871. In Casco Township, for W. Tenny, who lived there.

THAYER BROOK. For the Thayer family who lived along it in the late 1800's.

THOITS BROOK. For J. Thoits, who lived there in 1871.

THOMAS BAY. Possibly for J.K. Thomas, who lived there in 1852.

THOMAS POND. (2). For the early Thomas families.

THOMES BROOK. For M. and S. Thomes, who lived there.

THOMPSON HILL. For numerous area Thompsons.

THOMPSON POINT. For Roland Thompson, who operated a summer hotel and camp there.

THORNTON HEIGHTS. Unknown.

THREE ISLANDS. Descriptive.

THRUMCAP. Descriptive of shape like a thrumcap, a sailor's rope cap.

TIGER HILL. Unknown.

TINGLEY BROOK. For the early Tingley family.

TODDY BROOK. For the water from the brook being used to make moonshine liquor.

TONDREAUS POINT. Unknown.

TORREY HILL. For the Torrey family that settled about the time of the Revolution.

TORRINGTON POINT. Unknown.

TORY ROCK. For a Tory who was shot by a local seaman as he escaped from the mainland to this rock.

TOWN FARM HILL. For the town farm located there.

TOWN LANDING. (2). Descriptive.

TREASURE ISLAND. Fancifully named.

TREFETHEN. For the Trefethen family.

TRICKEY POND. Tradition says named by the Indians, for the bottom being very irregular and the ice freezing in varying thicknesses, thus making it dangerous and tricky to cross; however, there were Trickey families located in the area.

TROUT BROOK. For trout fish.

TRUNDY: POINT, REEF. For J. Trundy, point resident, 1871.

TRYON MOUNTAIN. For the Tryon family who inhabited the mountain in the 19th century.

TUCKER BROOK. For the William and G.M. Tucker families.

TURNER ISLAND. For George W. Turner, who owned part of it.

TURNIP: ISLAND, ISLAND LEDGE. Descriptive of shape.

TWO BUSH ISLAND. Descriptive of a very small island.

TWO TRAILS. Descriptive of where 2 roads branch.

UPPER: BAY, NARROWS. Descriptive.

VAILL ISLAND. Unknown.

VALLEY BROOK. Descriptive.

VARNEY HILL. For the Varney family who lived there.

VERRILLS LEDGES. For the Verrill family who lived there.

WAITES LANDING. For the Waite family who had a shipping wharf.

WALDO POINT. For Captain Waldo, who was part owner of Chebeague Island.

WALNUT: HILL, HILL (settlement). For walnut trees.

WARD BROOK. For John Ward, settler, 1779.

WARDS COVE. For a number of Wards who lived at the cove.

WARDTOWN. For the Ward brothers who raised large families there.

WATCHIC: BROOK, LITTLE-POND, POND. Of relatively recent origin. Possibly a synthesized word to sound as if it were Indian. But possibly Abnaki: "muddy place."

WATTS: LEDGE, POINT. Possibly for the Henry Watts family, settlers after 1640.

WEBB MILLS. For Richard Webb, owner about 1850.

WEBB ROWE MOUNTAIN. For Lazarus Rowe and his wife, Molly Webber, who owned much area land.

WESCOTT BROOK. (2). In Gorham Township, for Reuben Wescott, settler about 1783. In New Gloucester Township, for the early Wescott family.

WESTBROOK: settlement, TOWNSHIP. For Colonel Thomas Westbrook.

WESTCUTOGO HILL. Abnaki: "gullied river banks," for an area of Royal River.

WEST END. Descriptive of a section of Portland.

WESTERN: BEACH, COVE, HEAD, LANDING. Descriptive.

WEST: LEDGE, POINT, SHORE SANDY BEACH. Descriptive.

WHALEBACK. (2). Descriptive of a ledge.

WHALEBOAT: ISLAND, LITTLE-ISLAND, LITTLE-LEDGE. Descriptive of shape like a whaleboat.

WHALE ROCK. Descriptive of shape.

WHARF COVE. For an old wharf located there.

WHARTON POINT. For Thomas Wharton, settler, 1717.

WHITE BULL. Fanciful name for a white rock.

WHITE COVE. For the White family who lived there about 1900.

WHITEHEAD: PASSAGE, rock. For an outcropping of white rock that resembles a man's head.

WHITE: ISLAND, POINT (2). Island and Point in Harpswell Township, for Nicholas White, settler, 1675. Island in Standish Township, for E. White, who lived there in 1871.

WHITE MOUNTAIN: For J. White, who lived there in 1871.

WHITE ROCK. For a large, white boulder that used to stand on the hill in front of the church until the rock was destroyed with dynamite.

WHITES CORNER. For Albion P. White, who set up a shoe factory there in 1844. His family had lived there since the 1700's.

WHITNEY HILL. For the Whitney family who lived there in the latter half of the 19th century.

WIDGEON COVE. For widgeons (a variety of duck).

WIGGINS BROOK. For the local Wiggins family.

WILDWOOD PARK. Descriptive.

WILLARD: BEACH, ROCK. For Captain C.J. Willard.

ILLETT BROOK. For the Willett family.

ILLIAMS ISLAND. Unknown.

ILLOW BROOK. For willow trees.

ILSON: COVE, LEDGES. For Alexander Wilson, settler, 18th century.

INDHAM: CENTER, HILL, HILL (settlement), NORTH-PLAINS, SOUTH-, TOWNSHIP. For Windham or Wymonham (pronounced "Windom"), England.

IND MOUNTAIN. For the Winn family who lived there.

INNOCKS NECK. For Joseph Whinick, settler about 1667.

INSTON HILL. For the local Winston family.

ITCH ROCK. Unknown.

OLF NECK. For Henry Wolf, settler about 1675.

OODFORDS CORNER. Unknown.

OODSUM BROOK. For John Woodsum, settler, 1798.

OODWARD: COVE, POINT. For Samuel and Peter Woodward, settlers, 1750's.

RECK COVE. For an early shipwreck there.

RIGHT CORNER. For the Wight family who lived there.

YER ISLAND. For Robert Wyer, settler, 1762.

ARMOUTH: ISLAND, JUNCTION, LEDGES, NORTH-TOWN-SHIP, RESERVOIR, settlement, TOWNSHIP. North Yarmouth was named first and given the "North" to distinguish it from Yarmouth, Massachusetts. It was named for Yarmouth, England.

ELLOW ROCK. Descriptive.

ORK HILL. Probably for the John York family, settlers, 1684.

ORK LANDING. For the York family living there by 1759.

EB COVE. Unknown.

FRANKLIN COUNTY

BRAHAM: MOUNT-, MOUNT-TOWNSHIP. Unknown.

DAMS BROOK. For the Adams family.

DAMS HiLL. For A. Adams, resident, 1864.

DLEY POND. For the Adley family, one of the earliest groups of settlers.

LDER: BROOK (2), LITTLE-STREAM, SOUTH BRANCH-STREAM, STREAM (3), STREAM TOWNSHIP. For alder trees.

LLEN BROOK. For the William Allen family.

LLEN PINNACLE. For B.B. Allen, resident, 1864.

LLENS MILLS. For Benjamin and Newman Allen, who purchased Gowers Mills and changed the name in 1823.

NDERSON BROOK. Unknown.

NDROSCOGGIN RIVER. Abnaki: "the place where fish are cured."

NTLER HILL. For a large set of antlers found there many years ago.

RNOLD POND. For Benedict Arnold's expedition to Quebec, which passed near here.

VON: CORNER, settlement, TOWNSHIP. Said to be for the English Avon River.

ACHELOR BROOK. For the Batchelder family. "Bachelor" is a cartographical error.

AG POND MOUNTAIN. For its nearness to a small pond shaped like a bag.

AKER STREAM. Probably for Barnabas Baker, settler by 1778.

ALD: MOUNTAIN (2), MOUNTAIN (settlement), PATE. Descriptive.

BALLARD POND. For Jonathon Ballard, who first settled in Temple Township in 1799.

BANNOCK MOUNTAIN. For a survey party that camped on the north side in 1780 and baked a bannock (a type of bread) there. Others say it resembles a bannock.

BARKER BROOK. For Dyer Barker, resident, 1864.

BARKER STREAM. For T. Barker, landholder, 1864.

BARNARD: BROOK, LITTLE-POND, MOUNTAINS, POND. For Barnard, early settler.

BARNJUM. Unknown.

BASIN BROOK. Descriptive.

BAUDS POND. Unknown.

BEAL POND. For Fred N. Beal, who built Twin Camps here.

BEALS BROOK. For Daniel Beale, settler and businessman, 1797.

BEAN: BROOK, MOUNTAIN. For Jeremiah Bean.

BEANS CORNER. Some say for the Israel Bean family. Others, for James Bean, settler about 1800. Still others, for Dearborn Bean.

BEAR: BROOK (2), HILL. For bears.

BEATTIE: POND, TOWNSHIP. Unknown.

BEAVER: (2), BOG BROOK, MOUNTAIN, POND (4). For beavers.

BEECH HILL. For beech trees.

BEMIS: MOUNTAIN, settlement, STREAM. For Bemis, who built a camp in the area.

BERDEEN STREAM. Unknown.

BERLIN TOWNSHIP. For Berlin Mills of New Hampshire, which owned much area land.

BERRY MILLS. For Jacob Berry, early settler.

BIGELOW: MOUNTAIN, settlement. For Major Timothy Bigelow, one of Benedict Arnold's officers on his march to Quebec, who climbed the mountain hoping to sight Quebec.

BIG: ISLAND (settlement), ISLAND POND. Descriptive of an island in the pond.

BIG SAG. For its being a deep depression with hills all around.

BLABON HILL. For the early Blabon family.

BLACK: BROOK, MOUNTAIN, NUBBLE (2), SPUR. Descriptive.

BLACKCAT MOUNTAIN. For the woodsmen's name for the fisher.

BLANCHARD POND. For the local Blanchard family.

BLANCHARD PONDS. Although there is no record of their being here, the Blanchard family was in the area early.

BLUEBERRY MOUNTAIN. For blueberries.

BLUE: LITTLE-, MOUNT-, MOUNT-POND, MOUNT-STREAM, OLD-MOUNTAIN. Descriptive of color in the afterglow of the sunset.

BOARDMAN MOUNTAIN. For Esquire Herbert Boardman, who settled at its base in 1795.

BOG: BROOK, POND. Descriptive.

BOIL MOUNTAIN. Some say it is descriptive of its shape.

BONNEY POINT. For the early Bonney family.

BOUNDARY: BROOK, POND, SOUTH-POND, For the location near the U.S. -Canadian boundary.

BOWLEY BROOK. For William Bowley, settler, 1803.

BOWLEY ROCK. For a man named Bowley who was marooned on the rock all night.

BRADBURY BROOK. For the local Bradbury family.

BRAGDON BROOK. For Timothy Bragdon, resident, 1864.

BRAY HILL. For the early Bray families.

BRIMSTONE MOUNTAIN. For a kind of black granite called "brimstone" by the local inhabitants.

BROWNS PEAK. For the Frank Brown family, who lived nearby.

BUGLE COVE. Descriptive of the shape of the shoreline.

BULLEN MILLS. For the early Bullen family who owned the mill.

BURNHAM HILL. For Squire Burnham, who bought the land from Squire Rangeley.

BURNT HILL. Descriptive.

BUTTERFIELD HILL. For Samuel Butterfield.

BYRON NOTCH. For its being an entrance to Byron Township.

CALDWIN HILL. For the local Caldwin family.

CAPE COD HILL. For Prince, Baker, and other families, who came from Cape Cod, Massachusetts.

CARIBOU: FLOW, MOUNTAIN, POND, VALLEY. For caribou.

CARRABASSETT: RIVER, settlement, SOUTH BRANCH-RIVER, WEST BRANCH-RIVER. Abnaki: "small moose place[?] sturgeon place[?]"

CARTHAGE: settlement, TOWNSHIP. For the classical city of Carthage, North Africa.

CASCADE: BROOK, STREAM. Descriptive.

CASWELL MOUNTAIN. For Caswell, foreman at Skinner's sawmill.

CENTER HILL. (2). Descriptive of location.

CHAIN: LAKES, OF PONDS TOWNSHIP. Descriptive of lakes connected like links of a chain.

CHANDLER: HILL, MILL STREAM. For the respective Chandler families.

CHASE CORNER. For Charles Chase, farm owner. Others say for Nathan Chase.

CHASE POND. For the local Chase family.

CHERRY: HILL, RUN BROOK. For cherry trees.

CHESTERVILLE: NORTH-, settlement, TOWNSHIP. For Chester, New Hampshire, named by Samuel Linscott and Dummer Sewall. Others say for the hymn "Chester," a favorite of the settlers.

CHICK HILL. For the early Chick family.

CHISHOLM. For Hugh J. Chisholm, mill builder.

CHITTENDEN POND. Unknown.

CITY COVE. For Rangeley settlement.

CITY POND. For being the reservoir for Sand River.

CLAY: BROOK (2), BROOK MOUNTAIN. For clay.

CLEAR: POND, POND MOUNTAIN, -WATER POND. Descriptive.

CLOUTMAN: POND, RIDGE. For Cloutman, a man from Massachusetts who shot a twelve point buck on the ridge.

COBBLE HILL. Descriptive.

COBURN GORE. The inhabitants say it was named for the Coburn family who got the grant.

COLD STREAM. Descriptive.

CONANT: BROOK, STREAM. For the respective Conant families.

COPLIN TOWNSHIP. Unknown.

COTTLE BROOK. For the early settling Cottle family.

COUBERS BROOK. For the early Colburn family; cartographical error.

COVE BROOK. Descriptive of where the brook empties.

COWEN HILL. For David B. Cowan, settler, 1787. Others say for Ephraim Cowen of Dunstable, Massachusetts.

COW: HILL, POND, RIDGE. Unknown.

CRANBERRY: PEAK, POND. For cranberries.

CROCKER: MOUNTAIN, -TOWN TOWNSHIP. For the local Crocker family, the only family there for some time.

CROCKETT MOUNTAIN. For the early Crockett family.

CROSBY POND. Unknown.

CROSSMAN STREAM. For C.H. Crossman, resident, 1864.

CROWELL POND. For Nathan Crowell, resident, 1864.

CROWLEY BROOK. Unknown.

DAKAIN BROOK. For the early settling Dakin family.

DALLAS: settlement, TOWNSHIP. One source says probably for George M. Dallas, a vice-president of the United States.

DAVIS: settlement, TOWNSHIP. Unknown.

DAY: MOUNTAIN, MOUNTAIN POND. For the early Day family.

DAY POND: For William Day, resident, 1864.

DEAD: BROOK, NORTH BRANCH-RIVER, RIVER (settlement), SOUTH BRANCH-RIVER, STREAM. Descriptive of flow.

DEAN MOUNTAIN. For the local Dean family.

DELAWARE GAP. Possibly for the Delaware Indians, but unlikely.

DERBY MOUNTAIN. For the Derby family.

DICKEY BROOK. For Ed Dickey, who had a mill there.

DILL POND. For Henry Dill, Rangeley guide.

DOCTOR BROOK. Unknown.

DOCTORS ISLAND. For a doctor who bought it.

DODGE POND. For the early Dodge family.

DOME MOUNTAIN. Descriptive.

DOUGLAS POND. For A. S. Douglas, Maine guide.

DRAKES BROOK. Unknown.

DRURY POND. For the Drury family.

DRYDEN. For John Dryden, Farmington insurance company director, the 1850's.

DUNNING BROOK. For Robert Dunning.

DURGIN BROOK. Unknown.

DYER HILL. Unknown.

EAGLE POINT. For eagles.

EAST BROOK. Descriptive.

EAST DIXFIELD. For Dr. Elijah Dix of Boston.

ECHO COVE. Descriptive

EDDY POND. Unknown.

EDES BROOK. For the Edes family.

ELEPHANTS HEAD. Descriptive.

ELLIS POND. For Joe Ellis, landowner.

EPHRAIM RIDGE. For an early settler.

ETHEL POND. For the daughter of a man named LaSalle, owner of the pond.

EUSTIS: settlement, RIDGE, TOWNSHIP. For Charles L. Eustis of Lewiston, who owned part interest in the township.

FAIRBANKS. For Colonel Joseph Fairbanks, millowner, 1792.

FALLS BROOK. Descriptive

FARMER MOUNTAIN. For a farm located at its foot.

FARM HILL. For a farm located on it in the 1800's.

FARMINGTON: FALLS, settlement, TOWNSHIP, WEST-. For being a good farming region.

FELLOWS POND. For the early Fellows family.

FILLIBROWN BROOK. For the local Fillibrown family.

FISH BROOK. For Elisha Fish, settler, 1853.

FLATIRON POND. Descriptive of shape.

FOSTER HILL. For Benjamin Foster, one of the first settlers.

FOUR: PONDS BROOK, PONDS MOUNTAIN. For Moxie, Sabbath Day, Round, and Long Ponds.

FRAN BROOK. Unknown.

FRANKLIN COUNTY. For Benjamin Franklin.

FREEMAN: RIDGE, TOWNSHIP. For Samuel Freeman of Portland, one of the proprietors.

GAMMON POND. For the A. Gammon family, residents, 1864.

GAMMON RIDGE. For Simon Gammon, one of the early settlers.

GENEVA BOG BROOK. For Geneva, a girl who grew up nearby.

GILKEY BROOK. Unknown.

GLEASON MOUNTAIN. For the local Gleason family.

GOLD BROOK. For gold once found there.

GOODRICH: BROOK, CORNER. For Jonathon Goodrich (Goodridge), who was a blacksmith and the first postmaster i 1804, and his brother John.

GORDON HILL. For the local Gordon family.

GORHAM GORE. For being part of land granted to Gorha Academy.

GRANTS. For Ed Grant, who started a sportsman's camp there.

GRANTS POND. (2). For the Grant families.

GRAYS MOUNTAIN. For John Gray, who lived there.

GREELY POND. For the local Greely family.

GREEN BROOK. For the local Green family.

GREENBUSH: LITTLE-POND, MOUNTAIN, POND. Possibly de criptive.

GREEN HILL: Descriptive.

GREENVALE COVE. For the Greenvale House, run by a ma named Kimball.

GREENWOOD STREAM. For Thaddeus Greenwood of Farmingtor settler, 1844.

GRIFFIN MOUNTAIN. Unknown.

GRINDSTONE POND. For Joseph Tufts, who quarried rocks on th shore of the pond and made them into grindstones.

GULF: LITTLE-STREAM, WEST BRANCH-STREAM. For Gul Stream in Somerset County, for a "gulf" or depression.

GULL POND. For seagulls.

HACK INLET. Unknown.

HAINES POINT. For the Haines family, farmers.

HALEY BROOK. (2). In Dallas Township, for Charles Haley, Main guide. In Sandy River Township, for Clarence Haley, who owne property beside it as early as 1914. He burned to death in 1947

HALEY POND. For John Haley, who had a split-shingle mill there

HALFMILE BROOK. Because it runs into Horseshoe Stream, half a mile from the Chain Lakes.

HALFMOON POND. Descriptive.

HAMMOND: FIELD BROOK, POND. For Will Hammond, who lived there.

HAMPSHIRE HILL. For New Hampshire, former home of many of the settlers.

HANSCOM BROOK. For the Hanscom family who owned area land.

HARDY STREAM. For Hiram G. Hardy, who settled in the 1800's.

HARTWELL: INTERVALE, MOUNTAIN. For the Hartwell family.

HARVEY POND. For the local Harvey family.

HATCHERY BROOK. For a fish hatchery attempted on the outlet of Ross Pond.

HATHAN: LOWER-BOG, UPPER-BOG, Unknown.

HAY BOG BROOK. For hay meadows.

HAYNO BOG. For William Hayno, landowner.

HEDGEHOG HILL. (2). For headgehogs (porcupines).

HID POND. For its isolation.

HILDRETHS MILL. Unknown.

HILLS POND. Unknown.

HOGANS BROOK. For Hogan, who built a camp nearby.

HOLMAN POND. For Elisha Holman, who had a mill there.

HOLT HILL. For Caleb Holt, second settler there, from Wilton, New Hampshire, 1802.

HOOPER BROOK. Unknown.

HORN, THE. For being a peak on Saddleback Mountain, like a saddlehorn.

HORN HILL. Descriptive.

HORNS, THE: POND, PEAKS. Descriptive.

HORSESHOE: POND (2), STREAM. Descriptive.

HOUGHTON: BROOK, LEDGES. For James Houghton, settler, early 1800's.

HUNTER BROOK. For William Hunter, who built a camp there.

HUNTER MOUNTAIN. For Henry Hunter, resident, 1864.

HURRICANE: BROOK, MOUNTAIN, POND. For a hurricane that struck from the coast in the late 1800's and blew down much timber.

HUSTON BROOK. Unknown.

HUTCHINSON BROOK. For Ebenezer Hutchinson, settler, early 1800's.

ICK NORTON MOUNTAIN. For Icabod Norton, who settled between 1788-96.

INDIAN: LITTLE-POND, POND, ROCK, STREAM (2), STREAM MOUNTAIN. For Indians.

INDUSTRY TOWNSHIP. Named by the wife of Reverend J. Thompson, for the character of the people. Others say for a Mr. Allen, who gave the name to the first militia formed in the late 1700's, and the Township took its name from it.

IRA MOUNTAIN. For Ira S. French, early settler.

JACKSON: LITTLE-MOUNTAIN, MOUNTAIN, POND. For the early Jackson family.

JAY: NORTH-, settlement, TOWNSHIP. For John Jay, first Chief Justice of the Supreme Court.

JERUSALEM TOWNSHIP. Unknown.

JESSIE POND. For the first name of an early owner.

JIM: POND, POND BROOK, POND TOWNSHIP. For an old hunter, Jim, who ranged the area.

JOHNS: POND, POND (flagstation). Unknown.

JOLLY BROOK. Unknown.

JONES POND. Unknown.

JONT STREAM. For the first name of one of the first settlers there.

KAMANKEAG: BROOK, flagstation, POND. Abnaki: "near the weir."

KENNEBAGO: DIVIDE, EAST-MOUNTAIN, LAKE, LITTLE-LAKE, RIVER, settlement. Abnaki: "long pond" or "large lake."

KENNEDYS CORNERS. For the local Kennedy family.

KEOUGH. Unknown.

KEYES BROOK. For Simon Keyes, who had a sawmill there.

KIBBY: BROOK, EAST BRANCH-STREAM, MIDDLE BRANCH-STREAM, MOUNTAIN, STREAM, TOWNSHIP. Unknown.

KINGFIELD: settlement, TOWNSHIP. For William King of Bath, first governor of Maine and developer of the township, named by his wife.

KING MOUNTAIN. For William King, first governor of Maine.

KINNEYS HEAD. For John Kinney, early settler.

KITTRIDGE BROOK. For the Kittridge family.

KNOWLES HILL. For the Knowle family who owned a large farm there.

KNOWLTONS CORNER. For Samuel Knowlton and his son John, settlers, 1786.

LAKE MOUNTAIN. For nearby Halfmoon Pond.

LAKIN HILL. For the ancestors of William Larkin, Maine guide.

LANDING, THE. Descriptive of a log driving landing.

LANG: -TOWN MILL, TOWNSHIP. For the local Lang family.

LAPHAM BROOK. For James Lapham.

LAW MOUNTAIN. For Reuben Law, resident.

LEAVITT HILL. Unknown.

LEDGE: BROOK, POND. Descriptive.

LEMON STREAM. Unknown.

LILY POND. For lilies.

LITTLE ISLAND POND. For a pond with a small island in it.

LITTLE: MOUNTAIN, POND. Descriptive.

LITTLE NORRIDGEWOCK STREAM. Possibly Abnaki: "where swift river descends," or Malecite: "two torrents at this place."

LOCKE POND. For a Minister Locke, reported to have been "an unscrupulous promoter who changed denominations with the season."

LONE MOUNTAIN. Descriptive.

LONG: POND (3), POND STREAM. Descriptive.

LOOKOUT HILLS. For being a high stretch of hills where one can see for miles.

LOON: LAKE, LAKE (settlement). For loons.

LOST LOGAN. Descriptive of its isolation.

LOUISE MOUNTAIN. Unknown.

LOWELLTOWN: settlement, TOWNSHIP. For many area Lowells.

LOWER HATHAN BOG. Unknown.

L POND. Descriptive of shape.

LUFKIN POND. For the early Lufkin family.

LUTTON BROOK. For Lutton, an old hunter.

MACOMBER HILL. For the Reverend Joseph Macomber of Bridgewater, Massachusetts, in 1795.

MACQUILLIS CORNER. For a McCrillis who built a cotton mill there. The spelling discrepancy is a cartographer's error.

MACY. For Macy, who built a camp there.

MADRID: EAST-, JUNCTION, settlement, TOWNSHIP. For Madrid, Spain. Tradition says that when the town was being organized, a Spaniard was there and asked that it be named for Spain's capital to honor Spain's struggle for independence.

MAPLE HILL. For maple trees.

MARTIN BROOK. For a lumberman named Martin.

MASSACHUSETTS: BOG, BOG STREAM, GORE. For Massachusetts retaining the timber rights after Maine became a state.

McGURDEY STREAM. For the early McGurdey family.

McINTIRE POND. For H. McIntire, farm owner there in 1861.

McLEARY BROOK. For G.H. and J.E. McLeary, residents, 1864.

MEADOW BROOK. Descriptive.

MECHAM HILL. For the early Mecham family.

MERRILL MOUNTAIN. Unknown.

MIDWAY POND. Descriptive of location between Sandy River Ponds and Saddleback Lake.

MILL: BROOK (2), POND. For mills.

MINGO SPRINGS. Delaware: "treacherous, stealthy, sneaky," a term applied to the Mohawks.

MITCHELL BROOK. (3). In Carthage Township, for Franklin Mitchell, settler, 1823. In Industry Township, for the Mitchell family. In Temple Township, for Asa M. Mitchell.

MOOSE AND DEER POND. For moose and deer, frequently seen.

MOOSE: HILL, LITTLE-HILL, MOUNTAIN, RIVER, SOUTH BRANCH-RIVER, WEST BRANCH-RIVER. For moose.

MOOSEHORN. Unknown.

MOOSELOOKMEGUNTIC: LAKE, settlement. Abnaki: "portage to the moose-feeding place," or "moose feeding among trees."

MOSHER: HILL, POND. For John Mosher, settler, 1855.

MOTT STREAM. Unknown.

MOUNTAIN: BROOK, POND, POND STREAM, -VIEW. Descriptive.

MOUNT PISGAH. For the biblical Mount Pisgah, where Moses saw the promised land.

MOXIE POND. Said to mean "dark water."

MUD: BROOK, POND (4), POND RIDGE. Descriptive.

MUDDY BROOK. Descriptive.

NASH: POND, STREAM, WEST BRANCH-STREAM. For the early settling Nash family.

NEBO MOUNTAIN. Some say an Indian named Nebo lived there. Others say it is descriptive of a bended knee, "knee-bow."

NEW SHARON: settlement, TOWNSHIP. For Sharon, Massachusetts.

NEW VINEYARD: BASIN, MOUNTAINS, settlement, TOWNSHIP. For Martha's Vinyard, Massachusetts, by settlers in 1791.

NILE BROOK. For Luke Nile.

NO. 1 BROOK. For being the 1st brook on Moose River in Beattie Township.

NO. 6 BROOK. For being the 6th brook after No. 1 Brook on the South Branch Moose River.

NOON MOUNTAIN. Unknown.

NORCROSS POND. For Seth Norcross.

NORTH: LITTLE-WEST POND, POND, -WEST INLET, -WEST POND. Descriptive.

NORTON: BROOK (2), BROOK POND. For the respective Norton families.

NORTON MOUNTAIN. For Cornelius and Samuel Norton, purchasers of much of New Vinyard Township.

NUTTING POND. For John Nutting, nearby farm owner.

OAKES NUBBLE. For the early Oakes family.

OLD: BLUFF, BLUFF HILL. Descriptive.

ONION HILL. Descriptive of shape.

OQUOSSOC. Abnaki: "a slender blue trout."

ORBETON STREAM. For the Orbeton family.

OTTER: BROOK, POND. For otters.

OVERLAKE. Descriptive of location.

OWLS HEAD. Descriptive of shape.

PAINE HILL. For Thatcher Paine, settler, 1802.

PARKER POND. For Scarborough Parker, settler, 1798.

PARLIN POND. For Vincent Parlin.

PEAKED MOUNTAIN. Descriptive.

PEARL POND. Descriptive.

PEASE POND. For the Pease family.

PERHAM HILL. For Lemuel and Silas Perham, settlers by 1788.

PERHAM: JUNCTION, STREAM. For the early Perham family.

PERKINS TOWNSHIP. For Dr. Perkins, who owned much area land.

PERK POND. For "Old Man" Perk, who lived there.

PERRY: MOUNTAIN, POND. For the Perry family who farmed nearby.

PHILBRICK HILL. For the Philbrick family who owned it.

PHILLIPS: MOUNTAIN, settlement, TOWNSHIP. For Jonathon Phillips of Boston, early settler.

PINE BROOK. For pine trees.

PINNACLE POND. Descriptive.

PODUNK POND. Natick: "place where the foot sinks."

POPE MOUNTAIN. Unknown.

POPLAR: BROOK, LITTLE-MOUNTAIN, MOUNTAIN, RIDGE, STREAM. For poplar trees.

PORTER HILL. For Ezekiel Porter, farmer and settler, 1790.

PORTER LAKE. For Alexander Porter, mill owner.

POTATO: HILL (2), NUBBLE. Descriptive of shape.

POTTER HILL. (2). In Carthage Township, for the Potter family who settled there. In Wilton Township, for Robert Potter, resident, 1814.

POWDERHOUSE HILL. For a powder magazine built there for the militia, 1817.

PRATT MOUNTAIN. For Paul and Joel Pratt, pioneer settlers.

QUICK STREAM. Descriptive.

QUILL: HILL, POND, POND BROOK. For porcupines.

QUIMBY: BROOK, POND. For the early Quimby family.

RAND: BROOK, RIDGE. For Moses Rand, early settler.

RANGELEY: RIVER, settlement, TOWNSHIP, TOWNSHIP T3R1 For Squire Rangeley of Yorkshire, England, who bought the area in 1825 and wanted to establish a semi-feudal system in the wilderness.

RAPID: STREAM, STREAM VALLEY. Descriptive.

RECORDS. For Will Record's Sporting Camp established there.

REDINGTON: POND (2), POND RANGE, settlement, STREAM TOWNSHIP. For the local Redington families.

REED: BROOK, HILL, POND. For Abraham Reed of Kingfield settler after 1871.

REEDS. For the early Reed family.

RIDLEY BROOK. For Jonathon Ridley, early settler.

RILEY. For Edwin Riley of New York, who was brought in to manage mills built by Hugh Chisholm.

ROBINSON BROOK. Unknown.

ROCK: POND (2), STREAM. Descriptive.

ROSS POND. For the early Ross family.

ROUND: MOUNTAIN (2), MOUNTAIN POND, POND (3). Descriptive.

ROWE HILL. For the early Rowe family.

SABBATH DAY POND. Unknown.

SABLE: MILL BROOK, RIDGE. For sables.

SADDLEBACK: JUNIOR, LAKE, LITTLE-POND, MOUNTAIN (2) STREAM. Descriptive.

SALEM: settlement, TOWNSHIP. For Salem, Massachusetts.

SAMPSON HILL. For the Sampson family who lived there.

SANBORN HILL. For the early Sanborn family.

SAND POND. Descriptive.

SANDY: RIVER, RIVER PONDS, RIVER TOWNSHIP, SOUTH BRANCH-RIVER. Descriptive.

SAWYER: BROOK, HILL RIDGE. For the local Sawyer family.

SECRET: BOG, POND. Descriptive of its isolation.

SEVENMILE STREAM. Runs into the Androscoggin River approximately 7 miles from Livermore Falls.

SEVEN PONDS TOWNSHIP. For Little Island, Secret, Long, Beaver, Big Island, White Cap, and L Ponds located within its boundaries.

SHADAGEE BROOK. Pennacook: "the principal stream," but likely for Shadogee Stream in Carroll County, New Hampshire.

SHALLOW POND. Descriptive.

SHILOH POND. The previous name was changed by a resident who named it for the biblical Shiloh.

SIBERIA MEADOWS. For its isolated location and its temperature in the winter.

SISK MOUNTAIN. Unknown.

SKEDADDLE COVE. In local 19th century slang, "to hide, to get out of sight"; applied to men who hid out in this area to avoid the Civil War draft.

SKINNER. For Skinner, who ran a sawmill.

SKUNK BROOK. For skunks.

SMALLS FALLS. For the Small family that owned much of the surrounding land.

SMART: BROOK, MOUNTAIN. For a man named Smart who worked at Skinner's sawmill.

SMITH BROOK. For Smith, who worked at Skinner's sawmill.

SMITH COVE. For H.P. Smith.

SNOWMAN BROOK. For either James or John Snowman, early settlers.

SNOW: MOUNTAIN, MOUNTAIN POND. Because it had snow on it longer than any other mountain in the area except Sugarloaf.

SOL: BROOK, RIDGE. Unknown.

SOULE MILL. For Soule, the man who operated the mill.

SOUTH: BOG, BOG BROOK, BOG ISLANDS, BROOK, COVE, POND, -WEST POND. Descriptive.

SPAULDING MOUNTAIN. Unknown.

SPENCER: BALE MOUNTAIN, BOG, POND, WEST BRANCH-STREAM. Unknown.

SPOTS POINT. For R.L. Spot's camp.

SPOTTED MOUNTAIN. Descriptive.

SPRUCE MOUNTAIN. (4). For spruce trees.

SQUAW MOUNTAIN. Undoubtedly named for an Indian woman, but for no known reason.

STANLEY STREAM. For Solomon Stanley of Winthrop Township, early settler who was an ancestor of Frank E. and Freeland O. Stanley, inventors of the Stanley Steamer.

STAPLES POND. For Gideon and George S. Staples, early settlers.

STETSON POND. For the early Stetson family.

STOCKBRIDGE BROOK. For John Stockbridge, settler before 1833.

STONES CORNER. For the family of Major Moses Stone.

STONEY BROOK. Descriptive.

STORER HILL. For John Storer, settler, early 1800's.

STRATTON: BROOK, BROOK POND, settlement. For the early Stratton family.

STRONG: settlement, SOUTH-, TOWNSHIP. For Caleb Strong, the governor of Massachusetts who signed the incorporation papers.

STUBBS MOUNTAIN. For the local Stubbs family.

SUGAR BROOK. Probably for the maple sugar trees there.

SUGARLOAF MOUNTAIN. Descriptive of shape.

SUMMIT. For the surrounding mountains.

SWETT BROOK. For Benjamin Benson Swett.

SWIFT: EAST BRANCH-RIVER, LITTLE-RIVER POND, RIVER, RIVER POND, WEST BRANCH-RIVER. Descriptive.

SYLVESTER HILL. For the early Sylvester family.

TAINTER: BROOK, CORNER. For the Tainter family who settled here before 1816.

TANTRATTLE MOUNTAIN. Unknown.

TAYLOR: HILL, HILL POND. For the local Taylor family who lived there.

TEA: LITTLE-POND, MOUNTAIN, POND. Descriptive of the coloration of the water.

TEMPLE: BROOK, settlement, STREAM, TOWNSHIP. For Temple, New Hampshire, former home of many of the settlers.

TEN DEGREE. For a railroad in the area that held a grade which did not exceed 10 degrees for a considerable distance.

TIM: BROOK, MOUNTAIN, POND. For Tim, an old hunter.

TITCOMB HILL. For Stephen Titcomb, settler, 1776.

TOENAIL RIDGE. Reputedly so steep one had to hang on by his toenails.

TOOTHAKER: BROOK, ISLAND. For John R. Toothaker, lumberman.

TOOTHAKER POND. For Squire Toothaker.

TORRY: HILL, HILL POND. For a number of Tories who settled on this hill and remained for the duration of the Revolutionary War.

TOWNSEND BROOK. For the early Townsend family.

TOWNSEND RIDGE. For "Old Man" Townsend, who owned it.

TRASK BROOK. For the Trask family.

TREAT HILL. For Captain Ezekiel Treat, who owned much area land.

TROUT: BROOK, POND. For trout fish.

TRUE HILL. For George True.

TRUE MOUNTAIN. For J. or Moses True.

TUFTS: POND, POND BROOK. For Joseph Tufts, settler, 1810.

TUMBLEDOWN: BROOK, MOUNTAIN, POND. Descriptive of condition of the mountain.

TWIN ISLAND POND. Descriptive of two islands in a pond.

UNKNOWN POND. Because it has no other name.

VALLEY BROOK. Descriptive of location.

VAN DYKE MOUNTAIN. Unknown.

VARNUM MOUNTAIN. For Varnum, a man who owned much of it.

VARNUM: POND, STREAM. For Varnum, resident of Temple Township.

VILES: LITTLE-POND, POND. For the local Viles family.

VOSE MOUNTAIN. For Eben Vose, who moved here in 1816.

WALKER HILL. For William Walker, early settler.

WARREN HILL. For the early Warren family who lived here.

WASHINGTON TOWNSHIP. For George Washington.

WEBB: LAKE-, RIVER. Dummer and Henry Sewall of Bath, Reuben Colburn and John Beeman of Pittston, Samuel Butterfield and William Tufts of Sandy River, and Samuel Dutton of Hallowell set out to explore the country from the Kennebec River to Connecticut. They found here a rusty gun, several old traps, and the name "Thomas Webb" carved on a tree.

WEEKS MILLS. For Weeks, owner of the mill.

WELCH BROOK. For the early Welch family.

WELCOME HILL. For Timothy Welcome, early settler.

WELD: CORNER, settlement, TOWNSHIP. For Benjamin Weld of Boston, one of the early proprietors.

WELHERN POND. For Welhern, who lived near.

WEST: BROOK, -BROOK. Descriptive.

WEST MILLS. For Captain Peter West, who built the mill in 1803.

WHETSTONE BROOK. For the rocks found here which could be made into whetstones.

WHISKEY BROOK. Probably for the color of the water.

WHITE CAP: MOUNTAIN, POND. Descriptive.

WIGGLE BROOK. Descriptive of its irregular course.

WILBUR BROOK. Unknown.

WILDER HILL. For the Wilder family.

WILSON: POND, STREAM. For Thomas Wilson, hunter and explorer, who served as a guide for early settlers.

WILTON: EAST-, settlement, TOWNSHIP. For Abraham Butterfield of Wilton, New Hampshire, who agreed to pay the expenses of incorporation for the privilege of naming it for his former home.

WINSHIP STREAM. For the Winship family.

WINSLOW POND. For the Winslow family who lived nearby.

WINTER BROOK. Unknown.

WITHAM BOG. For Peter Witham, early settler.

WYMAN TOWNSHIP. For the ancestors of Miles Wyman, early Maine guide.

YEATON BROOK. Unknown.

YORK HILL. For the Rufus and Samuel York families.

ZION HILL. Named for the biblical Zion by Minister Sewall.

HANCOCK COUNTY

ABBOTT BROOK. Unknown.

ABRAMS POND. Unknown.

ACADIA MOUNTAIN. Named by Giovanni Verrazan, who explored for Frances I of France, probably for a mispronunciation of the Malecite: "Passamaquoddy" - "Passam - acadie": "place of abundance of pollack."

ALAMOOSOOK LAKE. Garbled Malecite: "at the fish spawning place."

ALDEN RIDGE. Unknown.

ALDER BROOK. (2). For alder trees.

ALLAGASH BROOK: Abnaki: "birch bark shelter."

ALLEN: BROOK, LOWER-POND, MIDDLE-POND, POND, UPPER-POND. Unknown.

ALLEN COVE. For Nehemiah Allen, settler by 1780, and later Allens, such as Captains D.M. and J. Allen, residents, 1881.

ALLEY ISLAND. For E.C. Alley, resident, 1881.

ALLEYS POINT. For a Captain Alley who retired there. It is rumored that he was an ex-pirate and was buried in the uniform of a British naval officer whom he had forced to walk the plank.

ALLIGATOR: LAKE, STREAM. Descriptive of the shape of the lake.

AMES POND. For the many area Ames in 1881.

AMHERST: settlement, TOWNSHIP. For Amherst, New Hampshire.

AMPHITHEATER, THE. Descriptive of shape of a valley.

ANDERSON POND. Unknown.

ANDREW ISLAND. For the Andrew family who owned and occupied it.

ANEMONE CAVE. For sea anemones.

ANNS POINT. Unknown.

ANVIL, THE. One source says that the island is locally called the "Devil's Anvil" because of its shape and what appears to be a giant footprint nearby. The devil was supposed to come here to sharpen his spear. Another source says that the name "Devil's Anvil" came from its shape and because a cave there was inhabited by a lynx called the "Devil Cat" by an old farmer fisherman who kept a small flock of sheep that it occasionally raided.

ARCHER BROOK. For Robert G. and Ansalem Archer, among the first settlers, early 1800's.

ARCHERS CORNERS. For G.F. Archer, who lived here in 1881.

AREY COVE. For Thomas ("Honest Tom") Arey, who lived there.

ASH: BOG STREAM, ISLAND, MOUNTAIN, POINT. For ash trees.

ASHVILLE. For the Benjamin Ash family, early settlers.

ASTICOU. For Asticou, an Indian sagamore about 1613, when the whites arrived. The name translates as Old Abnaki: "deep river."

ATKINS HILL. For the Atkins family who inhabited the hill.

ATKINSON BROOK. Unknown.

ATLANTIC. For its location on the Atlantic Ocean.

AUNT BETSYS BROOK. Unknown.

AUNT BETTY POND. Unknown.

AURORA: settlement, TOWNSHIP. Named by the Reverend Sylvester Clapp Williams for the goddess of dawn.

BABSON: ISLAND, LITTLE-ISLAND. For Joseph and Abraham Babson.

BACK: COVE (2), MEADOW. Descriptive.

BACKWOOD MOUNTAIN. Descriptive of its inaccessibility, in the "back woods."

BACON ISLAND. Unknown.

BAGADUCE RIVER. Micmac: "large tidewater stream."

BAKER HILL. (2). In Sullivan Township, for M. Baker, who lived there in 1881. In T29M9, unknown.

BAKER: ISLAND, ISLAND BAR. For the Baker family who settled before 1774.

BAKER ISLANDS. Unknown.

BAKER RIDGE. For John Baker, old lumberman.

BALD: BLUFF, ISLAND, MOUNTAIN (3), PEAK, PORCUPINE ISLAND, ROCK (2), ROCK LEDGE. Descriptive.

BALDWIN CORNERS. For J. Baldwin, resident, 1881.

BARBLESS POND. Because it did not resemble Tunk Lake nearby, which has a barb-like projection.

BARE ISLAND. Descriptive.

BARGE: EAST-, WEST-. Two islands that from a distance appear to be two barges rowing a ship (Ship Island).

BAR HARBOR: harbor, settlement, TOWNSHIP. For Bar Island, which is located in its main harbor.

BAR: ISLAND (5), OUTER-ISLAND, POINT. Descriptive.

BARRED ISLAND. Descriptive of its being attached to the mainland by sandbars.

BARREL BROOK. Unknown.

BARR HILL. For S.F. Barr, early summer resident.

BARTLETT: ISLAND, NARROWS. For Christopher Bartlett, settler by 1762.

BASIN: POND, THE-. Descriptive of shape.

BASKING RIDGE. Unknown.

BASS: HARBOR, HARBOR HEAD, HARBOR MARSH. One source says for sea bass. Another, for an early family.

BATTLE ISLAND. In the early 1800's, two men became embroiled in an argument over the ownership of this small island. They agreed to fight it out there, the winner to receive it. Although they came armed with a scythe and pitchfork, they both returned home unhurt, and the neighbors said that they did not guess the battle amounted to much.

BAY: LOWER WEST-POND, SOUTH-, WEST-, WEST-POND. Descriptive.

BAYSIDE. Descriptive.

BEACH ISLAND. Descriptive.

BEAN ISLAND. Unknown.

BEAR: BROOK, DEN HILL, HEAD, ISLAND (3), POINT, POND. For bears.

BEAVER BROOK. For beavers.

BECKWITH HILL. For Samuel M. Beckwith, from Cornwallis Township in Nova Scotia, who owned timberland in the 1800's.

BEECH: CLIFF, HILL, HILL POND, ISLAND POND, MOUNTAIN, RIDGE. For beech trees.

BEEHIVE, THE. Descriptive of the shape of the mountain.

BENJAMIN RIVER. For Benjamin Friend.

BENNET COVE. For the Bennet family, stone quarriers.

BERNARD: MOUNTAIN, settlement. For Sir Francis Bernard.

BERRY COVE. For Edward Berry, son-in-law of the first settler.

BIG: HILL, MOUNTAIN, ROCKS. Descriptive.

BIG CHIEF SPRING. Fancifully named.

BILL EMERSONS NECK. For H. William Emerson, summer resident and master teacher.

BILLINGS BROOK. For B.F. and J.H. Billings, residents, 1881.

BILLINGS COVE. For the Abel Billings family, settlers, 1780.

BILLINGS HILL. For Captain S. and J. Billings, residents, 1881.

BIRCH: HARBOR, HARBOR (settlement), HARBOR POND, HILL (2), ISLAND, SPRING, STREAM. For birch trees.

BIRD ROCK. For sea birds.

BLACK: -CAP MOUNTAIN, CAP MOUNTAIN, CORNER, ISLAND (4), LEDGE, LITTLE-CAP MOUNTAIN, LITTLE-ISLAND, MOUNTAIN, ROCK BROOK, THE-WOODS. Island in Ellsworth Township, probably for John Black, a land agent. Island in Bar Harbor Township, for Black, a hermit who lived there in the early 1800's. The others, descriptive.

BLACK POND. For Andrew Black, first permanent settler, 1759.

BLACKWOOD MOUNTAIN. Unknown.

BLAISDELL HILL. For the Blaisdell family who lived here.

BLAKE POINT. For D., C., W., and M. Blake, residents, 1881.

BLASTOW COVE. Probably for Samuel Blaster, early settler.

BLOCKHOUSE POINT. For a small fortification located there.

BLOOD MOUNTAIN. For Reverend Mighill Blood, the first minister in 1797.

BLOXTON HEATH. For Bloxton, the man who cleared the area but never lived there. He was from Ellsworth or Number Eight Township.

BLUE: EAST-HILL, HILL, HILL (settlement), HILL TOWNSHIP, HILL FALLS, HILL HARBOR, HILL NECK, NORTH-HILL, SOUTH-HILL. For its blue look from a distance due to the spruce and pine trees there.

BLUFF: HEAD, POINT. Descriptive.

BLUFFS, THE. Descriptive.

BLUNTS POINT. For the early Blunt family.

BLUNTS POND. For Colonel John Blunt and his brother, who bought the surrounding land.

BOG: BROOK (2), LITTLE-RIVER, MOUNTAIN, POND, RIVER. Descriptive.

BOGGY RIVER. Descriptive.

BOGUS MEADOW. Unknown.

BOLD ISLAND. A frequently used descriptive name for an island that stands somewhat by itself.

BOWDEN ISLAND. For its long ownership by the Bowden family—Arthur Bowden before 1923 and at present by Ford Bowden.

BOWL, THE. Descriptive of shape.

BOXAM COVE. Unknown.

BRACEY POND. Unknown.

BRACY COVE. For John Bracey, settler, early 1800's.

BRADBURY ISLAND. Unknown.

BRANCH: LAKE, LAKE STREAM, MIDDLE-RIDGE. Descriptive.

BRANDY: POND, STREAM. Descriptive of the color of the water.

BREAKNECK BROOK. Descriptive of a fast flowing brook.

BREWER MOUNTAIN. For Edward Brewer, known as "Master Brewer," shipbuilder.

BRIDGES POINT. For Job Bridges, settler, 1780.

BRIMSTONE ISLAND. Descriptive of a black type of rock called "brimstone" by the settlers.

BROAD COVE. Descriptive.

BROOKLIN: NORTH-, settlement, TOWNSHIP, WEST-. Brooklin and Sedgwick Townships are divided by Salt Pond and Benjamin River, which are connected by a brook: the town line is a "brook line."

BROOKSVILE: NORTH-, settlement, SOUTH-, TOWNSHIP, WEST-. For John Brooks, Governor of Massachusetts between 1816-20.

BROWNS BROOK. Probably for James H. Brown, settler between 1820-23.

BUBBLE POND. For The Bubbles.

BUBBLES, THE. These are two hemispheric shaped hills which

resemble human breasts. The settlers referred to them in their dialect as "the Bubbies," but the cartographers changed the name so that it would not be so suggestive.

BUCK: HARBOR, ISLAND, For Jonathon Buck, area surveyor, founder of Bucksport.

BUCKLE: HARBOR, ISLAND (2). Descriptive of shape.

BUCKMASTER NECK. For E. and W. Buckminster, residents, 1881.

BUCKS MILLS. For Colonel Jonathon Buck, who owned the mill about 1764.

BUCKSPORT: EAST-, NORTH-, settlement, TOWNSHIP. For Colonel Jonathon Buck, leading citizen and founder of Bucksport.

BUFFALO: HILL, LITTLE-STREAM, STREAM. Unknown.

BUGGY POND. For bugs.

BULGER HILL. For M. Bulger, resident, 1881.

BULL: HILL, LITTLE-HILL. Unknown.

BUNKER COVE. For the numerous Bunkers living there in 1881.

BUNKER: HEAD, NECK. For the Bunker family who settled in the area by the late 1700's.

BUNKERS HARBOR. For the Captain George Bunker family, residents in the 1800's.

BURNTCOAT HARBOR. For the former name of Swans Island, "Brule Cote." The name was given by the French meaning "burned coast." The English, through folk etymology, changed the name to something that they could understand.

BURNT: COVE, HILL, -LAND COVE, LAND LAKE, POND (2), PORCUPINE ISLAND. Descriptive.

BURNT COVE. For a fire set by Joseph Colley, early settler.

BURNT HUB HILL. Descriptive of its condition and location, near a road intersection (a hub).

BURYING ISLAND. One source said that it is believed to be an old Indian burial ground. Another says that the present is a misspelling of "Berrying Island," as it used to be a popular berrying and picnic spot.

BUTLER POINT. For Moses Butler, the first settler in 1764.

BUTTERFIELD ISLAND. Unknown.

BUTTER ISLAND. Descriptive of its color when it is heavily covered with goldenrods in the summer.

BUTTERMILK BROOK. Descriptive of the color of the water.

BUTTON HILL. Probably descriptive of its shape.

BYARD. For W. Byard, resident, 1881.

CADILLAC: CLIFFS, MOUNTAIN. For Antoine de Lamothe Cadillac, the grantee of the area by the King of France.

CALF: ISLAND, LITTLE-ISLAND. For cattle kept there.

CAMPBELL ISLAND. For John Campbell, early settler.

CAMPBELL LAKE. Unknown.

CAMP: BROOK, FIELD STREAM, ISLAND, LITTLE-ISLAND, STREAM, STREAM BOG. For people who have camped on them.

CANADA CLIFF. So high that one can "see to Canada."

CANCER HILL. Unknown.

CANOE POINT. Possibly named for the Canoe Clubs that abounded during tourist season in the early 20th century.

CANON BROOK. Unknown.

CAPE CARTER. For James Carter, resident, 1780.

CAPE LEVI. For Levi Higgins, early settler of Hulls Cove.

CAPE ROSIER. For James Rosier, who accompanied Captain George Weymouth on a voyage here and wrote an account of it in 1605.

CARD BROOK. For Joseph Card, settler, 1780, who had a mill there.

CARD MILL STREAM. For S. Card, resident, 1881.

CARIBOU MOUNTAIN. For caribou.

CARLETON: ISLAND, STREAM. For the Carleton family who settled in Blue Hill before the Revolution.

CARNEY ISLAND. For Michael Carney, settler, 1762.

CARRYING PLACE. Descriptive of where boats were carried across Newbury Neck.

CARRYING PLACE INLET. Descriptive of the carry between Skillings River and Taunton Bay.

CARTER BLUFF. Probably for Daniel Carter, settler between 1820-33.

CARTER NUBBLE. For John and Mary Carter, owners.

CARTER POINT (2). In Blue Hill Township, for the many area Carters in 1881. In Sedgwick Township, for the Allen Carter family, settlers by 1780.

CARTER SPRING. For its location on land owned by the Carter family.

CASCO PASSAGE. Micmac: "muddy" Probably named, however, for its use by ships heading to Portland and the Casco Bay area.

CASEBOTTLE HEATH. Unknown.

CASTINE: HARBOR, NORTH-, settlement, TOWNSHIP. For Baron Vincent de St. Castine, who lived here from 1667-97.

CAT COVE. Unknown.

CATERPILLAR MOUNTAIN. Descriptive of shape.

CATHERINE MOUNTAIN. Unknown.

CAVE HILL. (2). For caves there.

CEDAR SWAMP MOUNTAIN. For cedar trees.

CENTER HARBOR. For its location near the center of Eggemoggin Reach in Brooklin Township.

CHAIN: MIDDLE-LAKE, UPPER-LAKE. Descriptive of lakes in a chain pattern.

CHAMPLAIN MOUNTAIN. For Samuel de Champlain, explorer of the 1600's.

CHANDLER PARKER MOUNTAIN. For Chandler Parker, grandson of the early settling Parker family.

CHANNEL ROCK. (3). Descriptive.

CHASE BROOK. A cartographical error for Chasm Brook, named for its depth.

CHASE MOUNTAIN. For Z.B. Chase, resident, 1881.

CHATTO ISLAND. For G. Chatto, resident, 1881.

CHICK BROOK. For the Elisha Chick family, settlers before 1808.

CHICKEN MILL: POND, STREAM. Named by men working at a sawmill who lived in a nearby boarding house. The lady of the house seldom went to the store for groceries, but simply used whatever was at hand, which was mostly chickens. The men were served chicken almost every day. They and the neighbors soon started calling it the "Chicken Mill."

CHINA HILL. For Daniel Cough, a Chinaman, who owned it, but would not live there because he thought it was haunted.

CLAM ISLANDS. For clams.

CLARK: COVE, MEADOW BROOK. Unknown.

CLARK POINT. (2). In Gouldsboro Township, for the early Clark family. In Southwest Harbor Township, for Nathan Clark, who ran an early store there.

CLARK POND. For L. and B. Clark, residents, 1881.

CLARK RIDGE. Probably for the Nathan Clark of Clark Point or his family.

CLEFT, THE. Descriptive.

CLEMENTS BROOK. For F., G., and J. Clements, residents, 1881.

CLOSSON COVE. (2). For E. and D. Closson, residents, 1881, and the Closson family.

CLOSSON POINT. For Z. Closson, resident, 1881.

COD LEDGES. For codfish.

COLBY BROOK. For S. A. Colby, resident, 1881.

COLLAR BROOK. For N. Collar, who lived on its banks in 1881.

COLLINS COVE. For the Collins family who owned property there early.

COLSON BRANCH. For the Colson family who settled along the coast in the early 1800's.

COLT HEAD ISLAND. To make a fanciful pair with nearby Horse Head Island.

COMPASS: HARBOR, ISLAND. Unknown.

CONARY: COVE, HEAD, ISLAND. For Thomas Conary, early settler.

CONARY: NUB, POINT. For the many area Conarys in 1881.

CONDON HILL. For the Condon family who lived there.

CONDON POINT. For John Condon, settler before 1780.

CONE HILL. Descriptive of shape.

CONNERS NUBBLE. Unknown.

CONNOR POINT. For a Connor family who lived there in 1881.

CONTENTION COVE. For a disagreement over the place of settlement by some pioneers in 1763. The settlers put in at the cove to argue the issue and reach an agreement. When they finished, in agreement, they sailed up the Union River, which they named for their "union" of opinion.

COOK BROOK. For G.W. Cook, resident, 1881.

COOMBS: BROOK, ISLAND. For the early Coombs family.

COON BOG. For raccoons.

COOT ISLANDS. For coots.

COPELAND BROOK. For the Copeland family who settled on an adjacent hill.

COREA: HARBOR, settlement. Named for the nation of Korea, for no reason, by Eva Talbut, daughter of the first postmaster.

COW ISLAND. For cows kept there.

CRABTREE: LEDGE, NECK. For Agreen Crabtree, who lived there early.

CRAIG POND BROOK. For Samuel Craig, who helped lay out the first road in 1771.

CRANBERRY: GREAT-ISLAND, HARBOR, ISLAND, ISLES TOWNSHIP, LITTLE-ISLAND, POINT. For cranberries.

CRANES CORNERS. For G. Crane, who lived there in 1881.

CRIPPENS BROOK. For J. Crippens, who lived there by 1860.

CROCKER POND. For Crocker, who ran a lumber camp there.

CROCKETT COVE. For Josiah Crockett, one of the original settlers of Deer Isle Township.

CROMWELL: BROOK, COVE. For Oliver Cromwell, military dictator of England after the English Civil War.

CROTCH: HILL, ISLAND. Descriptive.

CROW ISLAND. (5). For crows.

CROWNINSHEILD POINT. Unknown.

CRYSTAL: COVE, POND. Descriptive.

CURTIS COVE. For A.S., F.A., and Calvin Curtis, residents, 1881.

DANE BROOK. For F. Dana, who lived nearby in 1881.

DARK BROOK. Descriptive of the color of the water.

DARLING ISLAND. For the early Darling family.

DAY MOUNTAIN. For morning, or "day," first breaking there from over the ocean.

DAYTON ISLAND. Unknown.

DEADMAN BROOK. For a peddler who was murdered and his body hidden under the bridge crossing the brook.

DEADMAN COVE. For a ship that was wrecked outside the cove, and one of the drowned sailors who washed ashore here.

DEADMAN POINT. For a corpse washed up here 100 years ago.

DEAD: RIVER, STREAM. Descriptive of their flow.

DEAN BROOK. Unknown.

DEBEC POND. For Whittaker Debec.

DEDHAM: settlement, TOWNSHIP. Named by Reuben Gregg, for his former home of Dedham, Massachusetts.

DEEP: COVE (6). HOLE. Descriptive.

DEER: HILL (2), ISLAND THOROUGHFARE, ISLE, ISLE (settlement), ISLE TOWNSHIP, LAKE, LITTLE-ISLE, LITTLE-ISLE (settlement), NORTH-ISLE, SOUTH-ISLE. For deer.

DENNING BROOK. For the previous name of Echo Lake, "Denning Pond." Denning operated a sawmill here.

DEVILS HEAD. (2). For a fancied resemblance.

DEVILS ISLAND. For the prison island in French Guiana. The Maine island was the site of a granite quarry where men sentenced to hard labor by the courts had to work.

DICE HEAD. For John Jacob Dyce, settler before 1784.

DINGLE MEADOW HEATH. Unknown.

DIX POINT. For the numerous Dix families in the area in 1881.

DODGE HILL. For the early Dodge family.

DODGE POINT. For Ezra Dodge.

DOG: BROOK, CORNERS. For the many area dogs.

DOGFISH: COVE, POINT. For dogfish.

DOLLARD HILL. For B. Dollard, who lived there in 1881.

DOLLAR: ISLAND, POINT. Descriptive of shape (round).

DOLLY HILL. Unknown.

DONNELL POND. Unknown.

DORR: MOUNTAIN, POINT. For George Buckman Dorr, who turned the mountain over to the Federal Government.

DOW LEDGE. For the Nathan Dow family.

DOWNING: BOG STREAM, POND. Unknown.

DRAG BROOK. Descriptive of logs being dragged to its banks by teams.

DRAM ISLAND. Descriptive of its size.

DRESSERS MOUNTAIN. For the Dresser family who bought the mountain from the Blood family.

DRUM ISLAND. Descriptive of shape.

DRY: ISLAND, MONEY LEDGE. Unknown.

DUCK: BROOK, COVE (2), COVE BROOK, GREAT-ISLAND, ISLAND, LAKE LAKE BROOK, LAKE COVE, LITTLE-IS-LAND, LITTLE-POND, MOUNTAIN, POND (3), POND BROOK, POND HILL. For ducks.

DUCKTAIL POND. Descriptive of shape.

DUDS POND. For Dud Sumner, a lumberman.

DUFFY: COVE, POINT. For A. Duffy, resident, 1881.

DUMB: BROOK, LITTLE-BROOK. Possibly a nautical term meaning "not self propelling," therefore slow flowing; or for its running quietly.

DUNHAM POINT. For Elijah Dunham, early settler.

DUNHAMS COVE. For S. Dunham, resident, 1860.

DUNKER HILL. Unknown.

DUTTON: LITTLE-POND. Unknown.

EAGLE: BROOK, ISLAND (2), LAKE (2), MOUNTAIN. For eagles. Lake in Bar Harbor Township; specifically for an eagle seen there by Frederick Edwin Church.

EAGLES CRAG. For eagles' nests.

EASTBROOK: settlement, TOWNSHIP. Because drainage of the southern half of the town flows into the East Branch Union River.

EAST BUNKER LEDGE. Known locally as Bunkers Whore. Captain

Bunker of the Cranberry Isles sailed to Bar Harbor one night to take the town prostitute for a boat ride. Not giving his sailing his undivided attention, he grounded his boat on this ledge. Another version of the story says that the prostitute was rowing out to meet him when her boat capsized, and her body washed up on the ledge.

EAST: COVE, POINT (3), POND. Descriptive.

EASTERN: BAY, CHANNEL, POINT (2), POINT HARBOR. Descriptive of location.

EATON: ISLAND, LITTLE-ISLAND. For the large area Eaton family, possibly Theophilus Eaton, early settler.

ECHO: LAKE, LITTLE-LAKE. Descriptive. The later inhabitants felt the old name, Denning Pond, too inelegant.

EDDIE BROOK. Unknown.

EDEN. For the earlier name of Bar Harbor, for the English statesman Richard Eden, or because the beauty of the town reminded one of the Garden of Eden.

EGGEMOGGIN: REACH, settlement. Malecite: "fish weir place."

EGG ROCK. (2). For eggs there.

EGYPT: BAY, settlement, STREAM, WEST BRANCH-STREAM. Some say because the shoreline resembles that of Egypt. Another says that there was a gristmill on the stream, and many people had to go a long distance to it, so far, in fact, that it was like having to go to Egypt.

ELIOT MOUNTAIN. For Charles William Eliot, the president of Harvard, considered the "father of Acadia National Park.."

ELLSWORTH: FALLS (settlement), NORTH-, settlement, TOWN-SHIP, WEST-. For Oliver Ellsworth, a delegate from Massachusetts to the Constitutional Convention.

ELM BROOK. For elm trees.

EMERY COVE. For the numerous Emery families there in 1881.

ENCHANTED ISLAND. For the sound of footsteps that follows one about the island. The local people say that this is not an echo, but the sound of continued walking, after one stops.

ENOCH MOUNTAIN. For Enoch Leland, who lived near.

FALLS POINT. For nearby Sullivan Falls.

FARREL ISLAND. For the Farrell family.

FAWN POND. For fawns.

FERNALD COVE. For Tobias Fernald, an early settler.

FERN SPRING. For fern plants.

FERRY SPRING. For a ferry that operated there.

FIDDLEHEAD. Descriptive of shape. Also some people say it was so named because fiddleheads (edible ferns) grow there.

FIERY MOUNTAIN. When the sun breaks over it in the morning, it is a splash of fire.

FIFIELD POINT. For T.S., J.T., and S.W. Fifield, residents, 1881.

FIFTH LAKE: MOUNTAIN, STREAM. Descriptive.

FIR POINT. For fir trees.

FIRST POND. Descriptive.

FISH: CREEK, ISLAND, POINT (2). For fish.

FITZ MOUNTAIN. For the Fitz Mills on Fitz Pond (now Phillips Lake), for the Fitz family who settled in the early 1800's.

FIVE MILE CORNERS. For its location 5 miles from Bucksport.

FLAG HILL. For flag flowers.

FLANDERS: BAY, POND, STREAM. Some say named by the former French settlers, for the Flanders area of Belgium. Others say for Steven Flanders, of Flemish origin, who was shipwrecked here.

FLAT ISLAND. Descriptive.

FLEA ISLAND. For its small, one-half acre size. It has remained in the same family for 100 years and is always deeded to a seven-year-old child of the family when it changes hands. Annie Thurlow, when seven, wanted her own island, and her grandfather gave her this one. She later gave it to a much younger brother who in turn gave it to a nephew. At the time of this writing, another seven-year-old is about to receive it.

FLETCHER BLUFF. For the Fletcher family who lived there.

FLETCHERS LANDING. Unknown.

FLING ISLAND. For an early Eagle Island resident who reportedly killed a bear on Bear Island and flung the carcass to this island, about a mile away. Rather obviously folklore.

FLOODS POND. For the early Flood family.

FLOOD STREAM. For Andrew Flood, settler before 1800.

FLYE: ISLAND, POINT. For James Flye, who settled before 1780.

FLYING MOOSE MOUNTAIN. Unknown.

FLYING MOUNTAIN. For an Indian legend that tells of a piece of another mountain flying off and making a new mountain.

FOGG COVE. For A. Fogg, resident, 1881.

FOLLY ISLAND. Over a century ago, two men got into a lawsuit over the ownership of the island. The judge said that it was folly to argue over such a small, worthless island.

FORBES POND. For Eli Forbes, selectman, 1789.

FORT, THE. Descriptive of shape.

FORT GEORGE. For George III of England in 1779.

FOSTERS BROOK. Probably for Jacob Foster, early settler.

FOURTH POND. Descriptive of its location near 3 others.

FOX POND. For foxes.

FRANKLIN: EAST-, ROAD (settlement), settlement, TOWNSHIP, WEST-. For Benjamin Franklin.

FRAZER PASSAGE. Unknown.

FRAZER POINT. For Frazier, runaway slave aided by the Underground Railroad, who settled in Maine and started a plant making salt from sea water on the site.

FREEMAN BROOK. For Freeman Archer, landowner.

FREEMAN RIDGE. Probably for the James Freeman family.

FREESE ISLAND. For George Freeze, early settler.

FREMONT PEAK. Unknown.

FRENCHBORO. Unknown.

FRENCH ISLAND. For the local French family.

FRENCHMAN BAY. For its being the staging area for French warships which were fighting the English. Another source says for Sieur D'Iberville's frigate "Poly," which was seen here so often.

FRESH MEADOW. Descriptive.

FROST POND. (2). In Mariaville Township, for the many area Frost families. In Sedgwick Township, unknown.

GALLEY POINT. For J. Gally, who lived there in 1860.

GANDER ISLAND. To make a fanciful pair with Goose Island.

GARDEN: ISLAND, POINT. For gardens planted there.

GARLAND BROOK. For the farm of J. Garland, which was there in 1881.

GASSABIAS: LAKE, STREAM. Abnaki: "small clearwater lake."

GEORGE: HEAD ISLAND, HEAD LEDGE, LITTLE-HEAD ISLAND. For the local George family.

GEORGES: BROOK, HEATH, POND (2). In Stonington Township, for George Butler, who owned the pond by 1795. The others, unknown.

GERRISHVILLE. For Andrew Gerrish, early settler, and his later family.

GILES: POND, POND BROOK. For Daniel and Joseph Giles, who settled nearby, early 1800's.

GILL POND. Unknown.

GILLY LEDGE. For the William Gilly family, settlers about 1800.

GILMORE: MEADOW, PEAK. For the Gilmore family who owned the area.

GILPATRICK BROOK. For Captain Isaac Gilpatrick, settler, 1774, from Biddeford.

GOLD STREAM. For traces of gold discovered there.

GOODWIN. Unknown.

GOOGINS LEDGES. For location off the Googin family property.

GOOSEBERRY: ISLAND (2), POINT. For gooseberries.

GOOSE: COVE (3), FALLS, ISLAND, MARSH POND, MARSH POINT, POND (3), POND HEATH, POND MOUNTAIN, ROCK, ROCK COVE. For geese.

GORHAM MOUNTAIN. Unknown.

GOTT BROOK. For T.A. and L. Gott, residents, 1881.

GOTT: GREAT-ISLAND, LITTLE-ISLAND. For Daniel Gott, owner of the 2 islands by 1789.

GOULD: BROOK, RIDGE. For Zebediah Gould, who built a house there and cleared the land in 1822.

GOULDSBORO: settlement, SOUTH-, TOWNSHIP, WEST-. For Robert Gould, one of the grantees.

GRAHAM LAKE. For Edward M. Graham, Sr., of the Bangor Hydro-Electric Company.

GRAND MARSH BAY. Descriptive.

GRANT COVE. For N. and Captain W. Grant, residents, 1881.

GRASS: ISLAND, LEDGE (2). Descriptive.

GRASSY POND. Descriptive.

GRAVEL ISLAND. Descriptive.

GRAY: CORNER, RIDGE. For the Reuben Gray family, who lived there before the Revolution.

GRAY COVE. For Josiah and Jeremiah Gray, early settlers.

GRAYS POINT. For W.P. and R.L. Gray, residents, 1881.

GREAT: BROOK, BROOK HILL, COVE, HEAD (2), HEATH, HILL, LEDGE, MEADOW (2), POND (2), POND (settlement), POND MOUNTAIN. Descriptive.

GREAT WORKS: EAST-POND, STREAM. When lumbering first started in the area, there were great stacks of logs along the stream, waiting for the spring thaw so that they could be driven to the mills. These stacks constituted "great works."

GREEN: COVE, ISLAND (6), LAKE (2), LEDGE. Descriptive of color.

GREEN HEAD. For the former name of Stonington, Greens Landing.

GREENING ISLAND. For Greening, who lived in an old house on its southwest point in 1860.

GREENLAW: COVE, NECK. For William Greenlaw, who settled nearby in 1762.

GREEN NUBBLE. Possibly for the Michael Green family of the mid 1800's.

GREYS BROOK. For I.P. Grey, settler, 1881.

GRINDLE POINT. For John Grindle, settler, 1761.

GRINDSTONE: NECK, POINT. For a vessel from Nova Scotia, loaded with grindstones, which wrecked here. The stones were salvaged by local people.

GROG: ISLAND, LEDGE. One of the points where rum ("grog") was smuggled into Maine.

GROTTO HILL. Descriptive.

GUAGUS: LITTLE-STREAM, STREAM. Micmac: "low flooded ground," or "rough stream."

GULCH BROOK. Descriptive.

GULL: LEDGE, LEDGES. For seagulls.

GUNNING ROCK. For the old days when hunters went here to shoot coots.

GUPTIL POINT. For John Gubtail, early settler.

GUT, THE. Descriptive.

HADLEY POINT. For Simeon Hadley, early settler.

HADLOCK: BROOK, COVE, LOWER-POND, POINT, UPPER-POND. For Samuel Hadlock, who first settled near the brook in Mount Desert Township but later moved to the point in Cranberry Isles.

HALFMILE POND. (2). For being approximately a half mile long.

HALFTIDE LEDGE. For being uncovered at half tide.

HALFWAY BROOK. For location halfway between Bernard and West Tremont.

HALFWAY MOUNTAIN. For location halfway between 2 old roads.

HALIBUT: HOLE, ROCKS. For halibut fish.

HALL POINT. For W. Hall, resident, 1860.

HALL QUARRY. For Cyrus Hall, who had a quarry there about 1870.

HAMILTON STATION. For William Pierson Hamilton, wealthy New Yorker, who operated the farm as a horse-breeding enterprise, mid 1930's.

HANCOCK: COUNTY, POINT, POINT (settlement), POND, settlement, SOUTH-, TOWNSHIP. For John Hancock, Governor of Massachusetts, 1780-85 and 1787-93.

HANSON POND. For the Hanson family who lived nearby in 1860.

HAPWORTH BROOK. Unknown.

HARBOR: ISLAND (4), INNER-(2), LITTLE-BROOK, -SIDE, SOUTHWEST-, SOUTHWEST-(settlement), SOUTHWEST-TOWNSHIP. Descriptive.

HARDHEAD ISLAND. For being composed of barren rock.

HARDWOOD: HILL (3), ISLAND, LITTLE-HILL, RIDGE. For hardwood trees.

HARPER MEADOW BROOK. For the Harper family who owned the meadow.

HARRIMAN COVE. For Asabel Harriman, settler, 1766-67.

HARRIMAN POND. For L. Harriman, settler, 1881.

HARVEY BROOK. Unknown.

HASKELL POINT. For A.J.T., T., and numerous other Haskells who were living there in 1881.

HATCASE: LITTLE-POND, POND. Fancifully named. It would serve as the hatcase for nearby Black Cap, a hill now named Eagle Mountain.

HATCH COVE. For Fredric Hatch, settler, 1773.

HATCH POINT. For the Hatch family who owned it.

HAT ISLAND. Descriptive of shape.

HAULOVER, THE. For a neck of Deer Isle where boats could be hauled over rather than sailed around.

HAVEN. A descriptive name for a summer colony.

HAWES POINT. For David Hawes, Revolutionary War veteran, one of the first settlers.

HAYCOCK POND. Unknown.

HAYNES POINT. (2). For Perley Haynes, settler by 1797, and the later Haynes family.

HEAD: HIGH-(4), LITTLE-, LOWER-, WESTERN-. Descriptive.

HEART: ISLAND, POND. Descriptive of shape.

HEATH: BIG-(2), THE-(2), BROOK (2). Descriptive.

HEDGEHOG HILL. For hedgehogs (porcupines).

HEIFER HILL. To make a pair with Bull Hill.

HELL BOTTOM SWAMP. For its having a deep, oozy bottom that seems to have no end and seldom freezes.

HELLS HALF ACRE. For being a dangerous area to sail in because of the many rocks, and for nearby Devil Island.

HEMLOCK POINT. For hemlock trees.

HEN ISLAND. (2). Fancifully named.

HENRY COVE. For Henry Sargent, who had his house there.

HENRY: ISLAND, POINT. For numerous Henrys in the area, 1881.

HERRICK BAY. For John Herrick, one of the proprietors in 1780, and many later Herricks.

HERRICKS. For numerous Herricks, descendants of the early family.

HERRIMAN POINT. For Peter Harriman, proprietor, 1780.

HERON ISLAND. (2). For herons.

HIGH SHERIFF. Unknown.

HILLER RIDGE. For Asa Hiller, early settler.

HILLS COVE. Unknown.

HINCKLEY BROOK. For Hinckley, lumberman.

HIO HILL. For Ohio Gros, whose nickname was "Hio."

HODGDON; BROOK, POND. Probably for the Joseph Hodgdon family, who lived in the area by 1789.

HODGDON COVE. For W. and J. Hodgdon, residents, 1881.

HOG BAY. Where hogs were driven across the ice in winter.

HOG ISLAND. For hogs kept there.

HOLBROOK ISLAND. For Jonathon Holbrook, resident by 1786.

HOOPER HEATH. For D. Hooper, resident, 1881.

HOP, THE. Only a short distance (a "hop") from Long Porcupine Island.

HOPKINS HILL. For S. Hopkins, resident, 1881.

HOPKINS POINT. For E. and R. Hopkins, residents, 1881.

HOPPER BROOK. Unknown.

HORSEBACK, THE. (2). Descriptive of a ridge.

HORSE HEAD ISLAND. Descriptive of shape.

HORSESHOE: COVE, LAKE, MOUNTAIN. Descriptive of shape.

HOSPITAL ISLAND. For buildings located there during War of 1812 to treat the wounded.

HOTHOLE: BROOK, MOUNTAIN, POND, STREAM. Because the stream seldom freezes.

HOUSE POINT. For a house located there.

HAZLAM POND. Unknown.

HUB, THE. Descriptive of shape.

HUGUENOT HEAD. Fancifully named by George B. Dorr.

HULLS: COVE, COVE (settlement). For Captain Samuel Hull, settler before 1796.

HUMPBACK: BOG, BROOK. For the shape of a nearby mountain.

HUMPKINS ISLAND. Unknown.

HUNTERS: BEACH, BROOK. Probably for duck hunters.

HURD POND. For P.S. Hurd, resident, in 1881.

HURDS CORNER. For early settlers.

HUTCHINS COVE. For Charles Hutchings, settler, 1765.

INDIAN: BROOK (2), CAMP BROOK, CAMP PONDS, POINT, POINT (settlement). For Indians.

INGALLS ISLAND. For Samuel and William Ingalls, early settlers.

INGRAHAM POINT. Unknown.

INNER DAWES LEDGE. Unknown.

IRESON HILL. For Ireson, who owned the hill.

IRISH POINT. For a group of Irishmen who cut all the timber off the point.

IRONBOUND ISLAND. For its being rocky.

ISLESFORD. For its location on Little Cranberry Isle.

ISRAEL POINT. For Israel Higgins, one of the first 2 settlers of Bar Harbor.

JACOB BUCK: MOUNTAIN, POND. For Jacob Buck, later member of the early Buck family in Bucksport Township.

JED ISLAND. Unknown.

JELLISON BROOK. Probably for William Jellison, early settler.

JELLISON COVE. For J., E., and I. Jellison, residents, 1881.

JELLISON: HILL, HILL POND, LITTLE-HILL POND, MEADOW BROOK, POND BROOK. For R. Jellison, resident, 1881, and his early family.

JERICHO BAY. Unknown.

JERRYS BROOK. Unknown.

JESSE BOG. Unknown.

JETTEAU POINT. Unknown.

JIMMIES MOUNTAIN. Unknown.

JIM POINT. Unknown.

JIMS HILL. For Old Jim, who lived there.

JOE MOORE BROOK. Unknown.

JOHN B. MOUNTAIN. For John B. Gray.

JOHN BROWN BROOK. Unknown.

JOHN ISLAND. For the John family.

JOHN GRAY POND. For John Gray, who was in the area by 1787.

JOHNS: BROOK, ISLAND (4), ISLAND DRY LEDGE. Island in Tremont Township, for John Galley. The others, unknown.

JOHN SMALL COVE. For John Small of Ashville.

JOHNSON BROOK. For Johnson, who owned timberland here.

JOHNSON POINT. For Giles Johnson, early settler.

JONES: COVE, POND. For Nathan Jones, first settler, 1762.

JORDAN BROOK. For the many area Jordans in 1881.

JORDAN: HARBOR, ISLAND. For H.W. Jordan, resident, 1881, and his earlier family.

JORDAN LEDGE. For B. and I. Jordan, residents, 1881.

JORDAN: POND, RIDGE. For George N. and J.S. Jordan, brothers who had a permanent lumber camp at the pond.

JORDAN RIVER. For the numerous area Jordan families.

JOYCE BEACH. For the James Joyce family, settlers, 1806.

JOYCE POINT. For the early Joyce family.

JOYVILLE. For Benjamin Joy, settler, 1763, and his descendants, such as L.P., H.N., and B. Joy, residents, 1881.

JUNK OF PORK: (island). Descriptive of shape.

KEBO: BROOK, MOUNTAIN. If Indian, Abnaki: "I fall."

KENCH MOUNTAIN: For Thomas Kench, early settler.

KILKENNY: BROOK, COVE, Unknown.

KILLMAN POND. Unknown.

KIMBALL POINT. Unknown.

KINGMAN BROOK. Unknown.

KING POND. For King Jackson, old lumberman.

KINGS POINT. For Captain David King, resident.

KITTERIDGE BROOK. For the descendants of Dr. Kendall Kitteridge, first English settler of Mount Desert Island.

KNIGHT NUBBLE. Unknown.

LAKE: WEST-, WEST-RIDGE. Descriptive.

LAKEWOOD. For location near Green Lake and surrounding woods.

LAKE WOOD. Probably for the area woods, but possibly for the Wood family.

LAMOINE: BEACH, EAST-, NORTH-, settlement, TOWNSHIP. For DeLamoine, an early French landholder.

LAMP ISLAND. Descriptive of shape.

LATTY COVE. For J.G. and other area Lattys, residents, 1881.

LAWRENCE COVE. For E. Lawrence, resident, 1881.

LAZYGUT ISLAND. Because the island and its ledges were irregular in shape and resembled excrement.

LEACHES POINT. For F.W. and D. Leach, residents, 1881.
LEAD: LOWER-MOUNTAIN, MIDDLE-MOUNTAIN POND, MOUNTAIN, UPPER-MOUNTAIN POND. For an old man who discovered lead there.
LEDGE FALLS RIDGE. Descriptive.
LEDGES, THE. Descriptive.
LEIGHTON BROOK. For the Leighton family.
LELAND POINT. For Amariah Leland, settler before 1800.
LILLY POND. Possibly a cartographical mistake for "Lily Pond."
LILY POND. (4). For lilies.
LITTLEFIELD COVE. For Averill and Solomon Littlefield, settlers.
LITTLE POND. Descriptive.
LOIDS BROOK. A cartographical error for Lords Brook, for James, Isaac and George Lord, settlers by 1790.
LONG: COVE (3), HEATH, ISLAND (2), ISLAND HEAD, ISLAND HUB, ISLAND TOWNSHIP, LEDGE (3), LITTLE-POND, MILL COVE, MOUNTAIN, POINT (3), POND (6), POND HILL, PORCUPINE ISLAND. Descriptive.
LOOKOUT LEDGE. For being the highest point on Bartlett Island.
LOOKOUT POINT. Because it served as a lookout for British ships during the War of 1812.
LOON POND. For loons.
LOPAUS POINT. For the Lopaus family, settlers, early 1800's.
LORDS COVE. For numerous area Lords in 1881.
LOVEJOY POND. Unknown.
LUCE COVE. For A. Luce, resident, 1881.
LUCERNE-IN-MAINE. Promotional name given by its developer Harold M. Saddlemire, for its resemblance to Lucerne, Switzerland.
LUNT HARBOR. For Joseph Lunt, settler, early 1800's.

LURVEY: BROOK, SPRING. For Jacob Lurvey, Revolutionary War veteran.
MACE BROOK. Unknown.
MACKEREL COVE. For mackerel fish.
MAHANON BROOK. Unknown.
MAHONEY ISLAND. Unknown.
MAIN STREAM. Descriptive.
MANCHESTER POINT. For John or Thomas Manchester, settler by 1789.
MANN: BOG, BROOK. For M. Mann, resident by 1860.
MANN MEADOW. For the Mann family.
MAN OF WAR BROOK. For being the place where the English war-ships filled their watercasks, where the stream runs over a granite ledge into Somes Sound.
MANSELL MOUNTAIN. For Sir Robert Mansell, early grantee of the island.
MANSET. For Sir Robert Mansell, early grantee of the island. When the postal department was petitioned for a post office, a clerk accidentaly crossed the "l's" and made them look like "t's." The final "t" was later dropped.
MARIAVILLE: NORTH-, settlement, TOWNSHIP. For Maria Matilda, daughter of William Bingham, owner of much Maine land.
MARK: EASTERN-ISLAND, ISLAND (2). Island and Eastern-Island in Stonington Township, marks the end of the Thoroughfare Island in Winter Harbor Township, marks entrance to Winter Harbor.
MARKS CORNER. For S. Marks, resident, 1881.
MARLBORO: BEACH, settlement. For Marlboro, England.
MARSHALL BROOK. For J.L. Marshall, resident, 1881.
MARSH: HEAD, POINT. Descriptive.

MARTIN: RIDGE, RIDGE BROOK, RIDGE COVE. For the early Martin family.

MASON LEDGE. Unknown.

MASON MOUNTAIN. For T., A., and G.W. Mason, residents, 1881.

MASON POINT. For Timothy Mason, early settler and shipbuilder.

MAYPOLE, THE. For a maypole erected here by Marguerite, a French indentured servant girl of the Joel Sargent family, to divert the Indians.

McCABE MOUNTAIN. Unknown.

McCASLIN STREAM. For the descendants of Alexander McCaslin, who settled in the area shortly after the Revolution.

McCLOUD MOUNTAIN. For J. McCloud, resident, 1881.

McFARLAND MOUNTAIN. Possibly for John McFarland, early shipbuilder.

McGANN BOG. For the McGann family who owned extensive land.

McGLATHERY: ISLAND, LITTLE-ISLAND. For the McGlathery family who owned them.

McHEARD: BROOK, COVE. For McHeard, first settler of Blue Hill Township.

McKINLEY. For President McKinley.

McNEIL POINT. Unknown.

MEAD MOUNTAIN. Unknown.

MEADOW: BROOK (4), OLD-BROOK, POINT, STREAM. Descriptive.

MIDDLE: LOWER-BRANCH POND, UPPER-BRANCH POND. Descriptive.

MILL: BROOK (2), COVE (3), POND (2), OLD-BROOK, STREAM (4). For mills.

MILLET ISLAND. For Millet, an Irishman who set up a plant here extracting salt from sea water.

MILLS POINT. For G.V. Mills, resident, 1881.

MILLS RIDGE. For the early Mills family.

MILLVALE. For a mill there owned by a Small family.

MINTURN. Unknown.

MITCHELL: COVE, MARSH. For C.B. and J. Mitchell, residents, 1881.

MITCHELL HILL. For the early Mitchell family.

MITCHELL POND. For S. Mitchell, resident, 1881.

MOLASSES POND. For an Indian woman, Molasses, who claimed to have been born in a canoe, as her mother was crossing the pond. It could quite possibly mean "deep" in Old Abnaki.

MONTGOMERY MOUNTAIN. For J. and H. Montgomery, residents, 1881.

MOORE BROOK. (3). For numerous Moores living in the area in 1881.

MOOSE: BIG-ISLAND, COVE, HILL, ISLAND (2), LITTLE-ISLAND. For moose.

MOOSEHORN STREAM. Unknown.

MORANCY: POND, STREAM. For John Morancy.

MORGAN BAY. For a number of Morgans there in the late 19th century.

MORRISON HEATH. For Morrison, a man who owned it for a short period.

MORRISON KNOLL. For A. and E.E. Morrison, residents, 1881.

MORRISON POND. For the Morrison family.

MORRISON: POND MOUNTAIN, PONDS, RIDGE. For James Morrison, old lumberman.

MORSE COVE. Unknown.

MOSELY POINT. For D. Mosely, resident, 1881.

MOSQUITO BROOK. (2). For mosquitoes.

MOTHER BUSH POND. For an old woman named Bush who lived there, whom many considered a witch. Instead of calling her "Witch Bush," they called her "Mother."

MOULTON POND. For M.P. Moulton, resident, 1860.

MOUNTAIN: BROOK, -VILLE. Descriptive.

MOUNTAINY POND. Descriptive.

MOUNT CROMER. For Old Cromer, a hermit who lived on the mountain.

MOUNT DESERT: ISLAND, NARROWS, TOWNSHIP. By the French, meaning "bare mountain," for many of the peaks were bare of trees.

MOUNT GILBOA. Unknown.

MOUNT OLIVE.Local legend says that while Fort Knox was being built across the Penobscot River in 1843-45, a young lady named Olive lived on the hill. Since there was little entertainment for the workers it became customary for them to go across the river on Saturday night to "mount Olive."

MOUSE ISLAND. Descriptive of size.

MUCKLEBERRY POND. For a small berry so named by natives.

MUD: BROOK, POND (3). Descriptive.

MUDDY POND. Descriptive.

MURPHY: HILL, SWAMP. For the numerous area Murphys in 1881.

MYRA. By Luther Jackson, for his wife Elmyra. He formerly lived in Greenfield Township before it was incorporated. After it was incorporated and he received his tax bill, he objected and moved to an area where there were no taxes.

MYRICK COVE. For J. and M.V. Myrick, residents, 1881.

MYRICK RIDGE. For the Myrick family.

NARRAGUAGUS: LAKE, LITTLE-RIVER, WEST BRANCH-RIVER. Abnaki: "above the boggy place."

NARRAMISSIC RIVER. Undoubtedly Indian, but meaning unknown.

NARROWS, THE. (4) Descriptive.

NASKEAG: HARBOR, POINT, settlement. Abnaki: "place at the end."

NATS RIDGE. Unknown.

NED ISLAND. For Ned Rodick, owner.

NEGO ISLAND. For the "Negew," ship commanded by Edward Naylor, 1662.

NEGRO POINT. For a number of Negro families who settled here after the Civil War.

NEWBURY NECK. For Newbury, Massachusetts, former home of many of the settlers.

NEWMAN COVE. For Tom Newman.

NEWPORT COVE. For settlers from Newport, Massachusetts.

NICATOUS STREAM. Abnaki: "the little fork."

NICK RIDGE. Unknown.

NICOLIN. It is said this is an Indian word meaning "wolves run in packs."

NO MANS ISLAND. For being unclaimed.

NO. 33 PLANTATION. Descriptive of plantation designation.

NOOK, THE. Descriptive.

NORRIS ISLAND. For the Norris family who lived on it.

NORTH: -EAST CREEK, -EAST HARBOR, -EAST HARBOR (settlement), -EAST POINT, POINT (3), -WEST COVE (3), -WEST HARBOR. Descriptive.

NORTHERN: BAY, NECK. Descriptive.

NORUMBEGA: MOUNTAIN, settlement. Some say that this is an European transplant. Others, that it might be Abnaki: "still water between falls."

NORWAY POINT. For Norway pine trees.

NORWOOD COVE. Probably for members of the Joshua Norwood family.

NORWOOD RIDGE. For Joshua and William Norwood.

NOYES POND. Unknown.

NUB, THE. Descriptive.

NUTTER POINT. For William Nutter, settler before 1808.

OAK: HILL (6), HILL CLIFF, MOUNTAIN, POINT (2), RIDGE. For oak trees.

OCEANVILLE. For the Atlantic Ocean.

OGDEN POINT. For David B. Ogden, summer resident from New York.

OLD FIELD HILL. For an abandoned field.

OLDHOUSE COVE. For an old house located there.

OLD: POND, POINT (2). Because settlers have been here a long time.

OLD SOAKER. Fanciful name for a ledge that is covered and uncovered by the tides.

OLD WHALE LEDGE. Descriptive of shape.

OLIVERS POND. For its location on the Oliver family homestead.

OPECHEE ISLAND. Chippawa: "a robin," probably an imported name.

ORAN POND. Unknown.

ORCUTT HARBOR. For Malichi and Jacob Orcutt, early settlers.

ORCUTT MOUNTAIN. For its location on the Orcutt family land.

ORLAND: EAST-, NORTH-RIVER, settlement, SOUTH-, TOWNSHIP. Tradition says that it was named by its first settler Joseph Gross in 1764, when he found an oar on the shore of the river.

ORONO ISLAND. For Chief Joseph Orono of the Abnakis or Orono Township, as Chief Orono was probably never here.

ORR COVE. For the local Orr family.

OSBORN TOWNSHIP. Unknown.

OTIS, settlement, TOWNSHIP. For Joseph Otis, original proprietor.

OTTER: BOG, BOG MOUNTAIN, CLIFFS OF-, COVE, CREEK, CREEK (settlement), POINT, POND, PONDS. For otters.

OVENS, THE. Descriptive of shape.

OXBOW: MOUNTAIN, THE-. Descriptive of a curve in the Narraguagus River.

OXHEAD: LOWER-POND, MIDDLE-POND, STREAM, UPPER-POND. Unknown.

OX HILL. One source says because it is so steep only an ox can climb it.

PARKER POINT. (2). In Blue Hill Township, for Colonel Parker, who fought at the Siege of Louisburg. In Bar Harbor Township, for Silas Parker, settler by 1776.

PARKER POND. For Oliver Parker, early settler.

PARKMAN MOUNTAIN. For Francis Parkman, historian.

PARTRIDGE: BROOK, COVE, ISLAND, POND. Probably for partridges.

PATTEN: BAY, LOWER-POND, UPPER-POND, STREAM. For the John Patten family, early settlers.

PATTON HILL. For S. and M. Patton, residents, 1881.

PATTY LOT HILL. Unknown.

PEAKED MOUNTAIN. (3). Descriptive.

PEAT BOG. For peat.

PEMETIC MOUNTAIN. Abnaki: "range of mountains."

PENOBSCOT: BAY, EAST-BAY, MOUNTAIN, NORTH-, RIVER, settlement, SOUTH-, TOWNSHIP, WEST-. Malecite? Abnaki? "at the descending rocks or at the extended ledges." Probably specifically for the river, and the river for the Penobscot Indians.

PERCH ISLAND. For perch fish.

PERKINS MOUNTAIN. For N. Perkins, resident, 1881.

PERKINS POINT. For John and Joseph Perkins, settlers between 1762-84, and their descendants.

PETERS: BROOK, POINT. For the Peter family who settled here before the Revolution.

PETTEES POINT. For William Pette, first settler on the point.

PHILLIPS LAKE. For Nathan Phillips, settler about 1810.

PHINNEY ISLAND. Unknown.

PHOEBE ISLAND. One source said for a Phoebe family, but this is rather doubtful. Probably for phoebes, birds.

PICKEREL: LITTLE-POND, POND. For pickerel fish.

PICKERING: COVE, ISLAND, LITTLE-ISLAND. For Samuel Pickering, early settler.

PIERCE HEAD. For E. Pierce, resident, 1881.

PIERCE POND. For the Pierce family who lived here in the 1800's.

PINE: HILL (2), KNOLL. For pine trees.

PINKHAM BROOK. For W. Pinkham, resident, 1881.

PINNACLE. Descriptive.

PISTOL: GREEN, LOWER-LAKE, MIDDLE-LAKE, SIDE-LAKE, STREAM, UPPER-LAKE, STREAM. Unknown.

PLACENTIA ISLAND. Probably settled by a Frenchman who called it "Plaisance" — "beautiful island."

POINT FRANCIS. For Francis, the first settler.

POND: ISLAND (3), LOWER-, UPPER-. Descriptive.

POOL, THE. Descriptive.

POPLAR POINT. For poplar trees.

POPPLESTONE LEDGE. For popplestones.

PORCUPINE: ISLAND, LEDGE. For porcupines.

PORCUPINES, THE. Descriptive of shape.

PORK BROOK. Unknown.

PORTER: BROOK, COVE, POND. Unknown.

POTATO ISLAND. (2). Descriptive of shape.

PRAYS BROOK. For Ephraim Pray, early settler.

PREBLE COVE. (2). In Cranberry Isles Township, for the ancestor of William H. Preble. In Sullivan Township, for John Preble, settler about 1762.

PREBLE ISLAND. For John, Nathaniel, and Samuel Preble, early settlers.

PRESSEY COVE. For John Pressey, who lived nearby.

PRETTY: MARSH, MARSH HARBOR. Descriptive.

PROSPECT: HARBOR (settlement), HARBOR POINT, POINT. For the view from the hills surrounding the harbor.

PUG: HOLE, -HOLE POND, POND. Descriptive of a small shallow pond or stream.

PUMPKIN ISLAND. Descriptive of shape.

PUNCHBOWL. Descriptive of shape.

PUZZLE BROOK. Because it appears that it should flow toward the sea, but it flows toward Toddy Pond.

QUILLPIG MOUNTAIN. For quillpigs (porcupines).

RACOON COVE. For raccoons.

RAINBOW POND. Unknown.

RAM ISLAND. (3). For sheep kept on them.

RAVENS NEST. For ravens that built nests there.

REACH. For Eggemoggin Reach.

REDFIELD HILL. For Redfield, resident of Seal Harbor before 1900.

RED: POINT, ROCK CORNER. Descriptive.

REED POINT. For the numerous area Reeds in 1881.

REMICK POINT. For E. Remick, resident, 1881.

RESOLUTION ISLAND. Unknown.

RICE POINT. For the Rice family living on the southwest tip of Sutton Island.

RICHARDSON BROOK. Probably for Stephen Richardson, settler before 1776.

RIFT POND. Probably for being located in a geological fault or "rift."

RILE POND. Unknown.

RIPPLE POND. Descriptive.

ROARING BROOK. (2). Descriptive.

ROBBINS HILL. For the numerous area Robbins in 1881.

ROBERTS BLUFF. For the John Roberts family, settlers between 1820-33.

ROBERTS BROOK. For D. Roberts, resident, 1881.

ROCK: DAM HEATH, ISLAND, POINT. Descriptive.

ROCKY: BROOK, LITTLE-POND, POND (3). Descriptive.

RODERICK HEAD. Unknown.

ROLLING ISLAND. Unknown.

ROUND: ISLAND, LITTLE-POND (2), MOUNTAIN, POND (3), POND NUBBLE. Descriptive.

RUM: COVE, KEY. For rum being smuggled into Maine here.

RUMELL ISLAND. For the many Rumells in 1881.

RUM ISLAND. For an early settler who built his cabin here. Being an alcoholic, he drank everything, but "Rum" was as good a name for his home as any. Another source says that liquor was smuggled into Maine here during Prohibition.

RUNT BROOK. Descriptive.

RUSS ISLAND. For the Russ family.

SABAO: LOWER-LAKE, MOUNTAIN, UPPER-LAKE. Malecite: "almost through."

SADDLEBACK: ISLAND, MOUNTAIN, ridge. Descriptive.

ST. HELENA ISLAND. For the island where Napoleon was held prisoner. This Maine island was the site of a granite quarry where prisoners were used for labor.

ST. SAUVEUR MOUNTAIN. For the nearby St. Sauveur French colony.

SALISBURY: COVE, COVE (settlement). For Ebenezer Salisbury, settler about 1770.

SALISBURY POINT. For N. Salisbury, resident, 1881.

SALLY ISLAND. For the Scilly Islands off the coast of Cornwall, England; named by early English settlers.

SALMON ISLAND BROOK. Named by Freeman Archer for a friend, Sam Nye, and himself — "Sam and I land brook."

SALMON POND. For salmon fish.

SALT CAMP COVE. For a salt camp located there which made salt by boiling seawater.

SALT POND. Because it was a saltwater pond.

SAMPSON POINT. Unknown.

SAND: COVE (4), ISLAND (3), POINT (4), THE -BAR. Descriptive.

SARGENT: BROOK, HEAD, MOUNTAIN, POINT. For the Sargent family who owned much land north of the mountain.

SARGENTS: ISLAND, POINT. For Abijah Sargent, early settler.

SARGENTVILLE. For the many area Sargents in 1881.

SAULTER POND. For J. Salter, resident, 1881.

SAWPIT BROOK. For an old abandoned sawpit located there. A sawpit is a hole in the ground with a platform over it. One man in the hole and another on the platform saw with a crosscut saw.

SAWYERS COVE. For many Sawyers living there, 1881.

SAWYERS ISLAND. For the Sawyer family, early settlers.

SCAMMON POND. For the Scammon family.

SCHIEFFELIN POINT. For the Schieffelin family, who owned a wholesale drug firm in New York.

SCHOODIC: BAY, BOG, HARBOR, HEAD, ISLAND, MOUNTAIN, NUBBLE, PENINSULA, POINT, settlement. Abnaki or Malecite: "point of land" or "trout place."

SCHOOLHOUSE; BROOK, COVE. For a schoolhouse located there by 1860.

SCHOOLHOUSE LEDGE. For a schoolhouse located there.

SCHOONER HEAD. For a British warship which fired at the head because it appeared in the fog to be the sails of a schooner.

SCHOPPE RIDGE. Unknown.

SCOTCH BROOK. Unknown.

SCOTT ISLAND. (2). In Deer Isle Township, for Nathaniel Scott, settler before 1800. In Stonington Township, for the early Scott family.

SCRAG ISLAND. (2). Descriptive.

SCRAGGY ISLAND. Descriptive.

SCULPIN POINT. For sculpin fish.

SEAL: COVE (4), COVE (settlement), COVE HEAD, COVE POND, HARBOR, HARBOR (settlement), ISLAND, POINT. For seals.

SEAWALL: POINT, POND, settlement. For the boulders which line the shore of Somes Sound like a seawall.

SECOND POND. (2). Descriptive.

SEDGWICK: NORTH-, RIDGE, settlement, TOWNSHIP. For Major Robert Sedgwick of Charleston, Massachusetts, Indian and French fighter.

SENECA BROOK. Natick: "place of stones."

SEVENMILE; BROOK, BROOK BLUFF, MIDDLE BRANCH-BROOK. Because it is approximately 7 miles in length from Lower Lead Mountain Lake to the Middle Branch Union River.

SEVEN STAR HILL. For the 7 stars of the Pleiades, which can be seen over the hill at certain times of the year.

SHARK COVE. For sharks.

SHACKFORD BROOK. For Increase Shackford, who owned the land the brook traverses.

SHAG LEDGE. For shags (cormorants).

SHEEPHEAD ISLAND. For a fancied resemblance.

SHEEP: ISLAND (5), ISLAND LEDGE, LITTLE-ISLAND. For use as sheep pens.

SHEEP PORCUPINE ISLAND. For a group of islands that look like a large porcupine and several small ones. The large one was originally called the "She Porcupine" but this was changed by folk etymology to "Sheep."

SHELDRAKE: ISLAND, LEDGE. For sheldrakes.

SHEPARDSON BROOK. For O.L. Shepardson.

SHILLALAH POND. Unknown.

SHINGLE ISLAND. Descriptive of shape.

SHIP ISLAND. When this island had a few trees and was viewed from the right angle, it resembled an ancient high pooped ship being rowed by two barges — East Barge and West Barge (islands).

SHIVERS, THE. A number of rocks and very small islands that were difficult and dangerous to navigate. They gave a sailor "the shivers."

SHORT POINT. Descriptive.

SIBLEY POND. For the Lincoln Sibley family.

SIEUR de MONTS SPRING. For Pierre du Guast, Sieur de Mont who sent Champlain to explore the Maine coast.

SIGHTLY HILL. Unknown.

SILSBY: HILL, PLAIN. For Samuel Benjamin, David, and Roswell Silsby, the first settlers about 1805.

SILVER LAKE. Descriptive.

SIMMONS POND. Unknown.

SISTER: EAST-ISLAND, WEST-ISLAND. Two islands fancifully named.

SKILLINGS RIVER. Tradition says that the river was named for a small Swiss river by early French settlers.

SLOOP: ISLAND, ISLAND LEDGE. With its one tree, it resembles a sloop.

SMALLIDGE POINT. For John Smallidge.

SMALLS COVE. For Thomas and Job Small, brothers who lived there.

SMELT BROOK. (2). For smelt fish.

SMITH COVE. For the Joseph Smith family, who owned the cove and operated a tidewater mill.

SMITH RIDGE. Unknown.

SMUTTYNOSE ISLAND. Descriptive of a dark rock on a lighter background.

SNAIL POND. For snails.

SNAKE POND. For snakes.

SNOW COVE. For Joshua Snow, resident, 1780.

SNOWSHOE POND. Descriptive of shape.

SOLS CLIFF. For Solomon Higgins, son of an early settler.

SOMES: COVE, HARBOR, POND, SOUND, -VILLE. For Abraham Somes, early settler.

SORRENTO: HARBOR, settlement, TOWNSHIP. One source states that it was named by Frank Jones, brewer of Portsmouth, for Sorrento, Italy, which the area supposedly resembles. Another source says that this is only tradition, and it was named for a Mr. Soren who was one of a company that founded a summer resort.

SOUND, THE. Descriptive.

SOUTH: -EAST HARBOR, -WEST COVE, -WEST POINT (2), -WEST VALLEY. Descriptive.

SOUTHERN: COVE, NECK. Descriptive.

SPARKS ISLAND. For Isaac and Jacob Sparks, settlers, 1765.

SPARROW HILL. For sparrows.

SPAULDING RIDGE. For Spaulding, early lumberman.

SPECTACLE: ISLAND (2), POND, POND RIDGE. For shape like spectacles (eyeglasses).

SPENCER: BROOK, POND. For Spencer, lumberman.

SPERRY POND. For the Sperry family who lived on the shore in 1881.

SPIRIT LEDGE. For the spirits of drowned sailors who are supposed to congregate here.

SPRING: BROOK, BROOK POND, LAKE, RIVER, RIVER LAKE, RIVER MOUNTAIN. Descriptive of being fed by springs.

SPRINGY: BROOK, MOUNTAIN, LOWER-POND. Descriptive.

SPRUCE: GREAT-HEAD, HEAD, ISLAND, LITTLE-HEAD ISLAND, MOUNTAIN, POINT. For spruce trees.

SPURLING POINT. For Benjamin Spurling and family, settlers, 1768.

SQUANTUM POINT. Natick: "a door or gate." Narragansett: "angry god."

SQUID: BAY, ISLAND. For squid.

STANLEY BROOK. Probably for John Stanley, early settler.

STANLEY POINT. For William Stanley, settler and farmer, 1814.

STARVATION BRANCH. Unknown.

STAVE: ISLAND (2), ISLAND BAR, ISLAND HARBOR. For barrel staves made there.

STEEP LANDING. Descriptive.

STEVE ISLAND. Unknown.

STEVENS POINT. For the Stevens family of the early 1800's.

STEVES HILL. Unknown.

STEWARD BROOK. Unknown.

STILES LAKE. Unknown.

STINSON: NECK, POINT. For Thomas and Samuel Stinson, who settled here before the Revolution.

STOCKBRIDGE: HILL, POND. For John Stockbridge, settler, 1816.

STONINGTON: settlement, TOWNSHIP, WEST-. For the good granite quarries.

STONY BROOK. Descriptive.

STOVER: CORNER, COVE. For numerous area Stovers in 1881.

STOVER HILL. For Jonathon Stover, mine owner in 1881.

STRICKLEN RIDGE. For the Stricklen family who settled it.

STUBBS BROOK. For S.E. Stubbs, resident, 1881.

SUCKER BROOK. For sucker fish.

SUGAR HILL. For maple sugar operations.

SULLIVAN: EAST-, FALLS, HARBOR, NORTH-, settlement, TOWNSHIP. For Daniel Sullivan, early settler, about 1762.

SUMMER: HARBOR, HARBOR (settlement). Descriptive.

SUNKEN HEATH. Descriptive.

SUNKHAZE STREAM. Abnaki: "concealed outlet."

SUNSET. Descriptive.

SUNSHINE. Descriptive.

SURRY: EAST-, settlement, SOUTH-, TOWNSHIP. For Surry, England, because John Ross wrote General David Cobb, president of the Massachusetts Senate, that he wanted it named anything that was short.

SUTTON ISLAND. For Eben Sutton, who bought it from the Indians for 2 quarts of rum.

SWAINS COVE. For Captain William Swain, early settler.

SWAN BROOK. For D.T. Swan, resident, 1881.

SWANS: ISLAND, ISLAND TOWNSHIP. For James Swan, 18th century land speculator.

SWAZEY LEDGE. For the area Swazey family, residents in 1881.

SYLVESTER COVE. Probably for Captain Benjamin Sylvester, early settler.

TAFT POINT. For G.F. Taft, resident, 1881.

TANNERY; BROOK (2), HILL. For tanneries. Brook in Ellsworth specifically for a tannery there before 1859.

TAPLEY COVE. For J.P. Tapley, resident, 1881.

TARN, THE. Descriptive.

TAUNTON BAY. Probably for Taunton, Massachusetts, home of General David Cobb, who was a manager of the Bingham Purchase in 1795.

TAYLOR: LOWER-BROOK, UPPER-BROOK. Unknown.

TEN HILL. By early teamsters for being the 10th hill away from Milford.

THIRD: LAKE, POND. Descriptive.

THIRTY-FIVE BROOK. For its location in Township 35 Middle Division.

THIRTY-NINE TANNERY. For its location in Township 39 Middle Division.

THOMAS: BAY, ISLAND. For the John Thomas family, one of the first 2 settlers of Bar Harbor.

THOMPSON BROOK. Unknown.

THOMPSON COVE. For Thomas Thompson, owner of the adjoining land.

THOMPSON ISLAND. For Colonel Cornelius Thompson, Resolutionary War veteran and captain of the privateer brig "Chase."

THOMPSON LEDGES. Unknown.

THREE BUSH ISLAND. Descriptive of a small island.

THRUMCAP: ISLAND, island (2), THE-. Descriptive of shape like a thrumcap, a skull cap made of rope yarn by early sailors.

THUNDER HOLE. For the sound the water makes rushing in at high tide.

THURLOW: HEAD, KNOB. For David Thurlow, early settler who lived there.

THURSTON POND. For the Thurston family who lived on the Orrington end of the pond.

TILDEN POND. For Tilden, owner of much land in 1881.

TILLS: COVE, POINT. For Tillden Wardwell.

TIMBER: BROOK, COVE, POINT. Descriptive.

TINKER: BROOK, HILL (2), ISLAND. Hill in Mariaville Township, unknown. The others, for a Tinker family who bought the island for a keg of rum from a Robertson or Robinson.

TITCOMB: BROOK, POND. For Titcomb, lumberman.

TODDY POND. (2). In Blue Hill Township, for a British soldier who dropped his liquor, or toddy, into the pond as he crossed it on a pontoon bridge. In Orland Township, for a man who used the water to make liquor.

TOOTHACHER COVE. For Joseph Toothacker, settler by 1792.

TOOTHACHER LEDGE. For Elijah Toothacker, farmer in 1798.

TORREY: CASTLE, ISLAND, POND. For Jonathon Torrey, settler by 1763.

TOURTELOTTE RIDGE. Unknown.

TOWN HILL. Because the town owned 450 acres on this hill.

TRAP ROCK. For lobster traps.

TREASURE ISLAND. Named by a Mr. Glover who owned it and wanted a more elegant name than the former "Sowards Island."

TREMONT: TOWNSHIP, WEST-. For the tree-covered mountains.

TRENTON: settlement, TOWNSHIP, WEST-. For the battle of Trenton, New Jersey, in the Revolution.

TRIAD: PASS, THE-. For three peaks.

TRIANGLES, THE. For three islands forming a triangle.

TROUT: BROOK, BROOK RIDGE, POND (2), POND MOUNTAIN. For trout fish.

TRUEWORTHY POND. Unknown.

TRUMPET ISLAND. Descriptive of shape.

TUCKER: BROOK, CREEK, MOUNTAIN. Unknown.

TUNK: LAKE, LAKE (settlement), LITTLE-POND. Abnaki: "principal or large swift stream." There is disagreement that this is an Indian word. One source says that a family invited a number of men to a supper of stew filled with "doeboys" (a soft bread dumpling). There were also plates of doeboys on the table for a sidedish. After the meal was finished, one of the guests asked the host what they were going to do with all the extra doeboys. "This," the host said as he hurled one at him. The battle was on, and the doeboys flew fast and thick. When one missed its target, it hit the wall with a "tunk." The men, noticing this sound, shouted, "Tunk him!" when they wanted a certain person hit. The scene of the battle was henceforward called "Tunk" in honor of the battle and was soon transferred to the surrounding landmarks.

TURNER: LITTLE-MOUNTAIN, MOUNTAIN. For Turner, early lumberman.

TURNER POINT. For J. and O. Turner, residents, 1881.

TURTLE: ISLAND, ISLAND LEDGE. Descriptive of shape.

TURTLE POND. For turtles.

TWINNIES, THE. Descriptive of 2 small islands.

TWO BUSH: ISLAND, island. Descriptive of a small island.

ULMER BROOK. For P. and L. Elmer, residents, 1881.

UNCLE DICK HILL. For Richard ("Uncle Dick") Heath, original owner.

UNION: BAY, EAST BRANCH-RIVER, RIVER, WEST BRANCH--RIVER. In 1763 a disagreement erupted among a shipload of settlers as to where they should settle. To settle the dispute, they sailed into Contention Cove and argued. When a unanimity of opinion was reached, they sailed up the Union River, so-named for their "union" of opinion.

UNKNOWN: LOWER-, MIDDLE-LAKE, POND, STREAM, UPPER--LAKE. Because the pond had no name.

VALLEY: COVE, PEAK. Descriptive.

VERONA: ISLAND, PARK, settlement, TOWNSHIP. For Verona, Italy.

WADSWORTH COVE. For General Peleg Wadsworth, who waded across the cove and was wounded in 1780 in his escape from Fort George.

WALKER POND. For John Walker, Revolutionary War veteran.

WALLAMATOGAS MOUNTAIN. Abnaki: "coves in little river," or "the clear, cold water where we stop to get a fresh drink."

WALLS POINT. For D. Walls, resident, 1860.

WALTHAM: RIDGE, settlement, TOWNSHIP. For Waltham, Massachusetts.

WARM BROOK. Descriptive, as it seldom freezes.

WARREN POINT. Possibly for Richard Warren, 19th century settler.

WASHINGTON JUNCTION. A railroad junction for lines leading to Washington County.

WATTS HILL. For the Watts family.

WAUKEAG: NECK, settlement. Abnaki: "a great knoll."

WEAVER RIDGE. Unknown.

WEBB: BROOK, LITTLE-POND, POND. Unknown.

WEBB COVE. For Seth Webb, early settler.

WEBSTER BROOK. For Captain H. and F. Webster, residents, 1881.

WEEDS POINT. Probably for Benjamin Weed, among the first settlers.

WEIR COVE. For fish weirs.

WEST BROOK. For the West family, residents, 1881.

WEST: COVE, POINT (2), POND. Descriptive.

WESTERN: BAY, BROOK, COVE, ISLAND (2), MOUNTAIN, PASSAGE, POINT (2). Descriptive.

WEYMOUTH POINT. For one of the first English settlers of that name who settled there before 1800.

WHALEBACK: ridge (2), THE-. Descriptive of ridges.

WHITECAP, THE. Descriptive.

WHITES BROOK. For Charles and Clarence White, residents, 1881.

WHITES MOUNTAIN. For W. White, resident, 1881.

WHITMORE NECK. For Joseph Whitmore, early settler.

WHITTEN PARRITT STREAM. Unknown.

WIGHT HEATH. For T., O.S., and D. White, residents in 1860. The spelling discrepancy is due to the Maine pronunciation of "white" as "wight."

WIGHT POND. For a Wight who lived there in 1881.

WILEY BROOK. For Wiley, lumberman.

WILLIAMS POINT. Unknown.

WILLIAMS POND. (2). In Bucksport Township, for J. Williams, resident, 1860. In T28MD, unknown.

WILSON CORNER. For N. Wilson, resident, 1881.

WILSON POINT. For C. Wilson, resident, 1881.

WINCHE MOUNTAIN. For quarry men who set up winches here.

WINKUMPAUGH: BROOK, CORNERS. Abnaki: "a good enclosed pond."

WINSLOW: ISLAND, STREAM. For Elijah Winslow, settler, 1765.

WINTER: HARBOR, HARBOR (settlement), HARBOR TOWN-SHIP. For the harbor, which does not freeze.

WITCH HOLE BOG. Before the 1947 fire, Witch Hole Bog was rimmed by tall evergreens. The stillness of the water and surroundings prompted the eerie name.

WIZARD POND. Unknown.

WONDERLAND. A promotional name given by Ike Stanley, who had an eating place here.

WONSQUEAK HARBOR. Possibly Abnaki: "shallow bay."

WOODCHOPPING RIDGE. Descriptive.

WOODS POINT. For Joseph Wood, one of the first settlers in 1762.

WORMWOOD POND. For Eli Wormwood, settler, 1765.

WRECK ISLAND. For a number of ships wrecked there.

YELLOW: ISLAND, LEDGES. Descriptive.

YOUNGS: BAY, POINT. For W. and R.H. Young, residents, 1881.

YOUNGS ISLANDS. For the early Young family.

YOUNGS MOUNTAIN. Probably for Ezra Young, who was elected captain of the militia during the Revolution.

YOUNGS POND. For the Young family, settlers, early 1800's.

YOUNGS POINT. For any number of area Youngs in 1881. One source says that the point so designated is really Long Point and not Young's Point.

KENNEBEC COUNTY

ADKINS POINT. For the early Adkins family.

ALBION: settlement, SOUTH-, TOWNSHIP. For Albion, ancient name of England.

ALLEN HILL. For the Thomas Allen family, settlers before 1800.

ANDERSON POND. Unknown.

ANDROSCOGGIN: ISLAND, LAKE, RIVER. Abnaki: "the place where fish are cured."

ANNABESSACOOK: flagstation, LAKE. Abnaki: "at that particular lake where small fish are caught," or "at the beautiful body of stillwater."

ASHFORD BROOK. For Robert Ashford, settler, 1812.

AUGUSTA: NORTH-, settlement, TOWNSHIP. For Pamela Augusta Dearborn, daughter of General Harry Dearborn, Revolutionary War figure.

AUSTIN BOG. Possibly for the Charles Austin family, early settlers.

BAILEY CORNER. For Hannah or Nathaniel Bailey, settlers, 1803.

BAKER BOGS. For the Baker family who owned the land.

BAKER HILL. For Ralph Baker, who ran an inn and store in 1824 and helped select the name of Albion Township.

BALLARD BAY. For Jabez S. Ballard, who kept summer boarders in the 1890's.

BANGS BEACH. For Captain Dean Bangs, early settler.

BASIN POND. Descriptive.

BATCHELDERS CROSSING. For Asa Batchelder, settler from New Hampshire who ran Batchelder's Tavern.

BATTLE RIDGE. Tradition says that the ridge was named for the 18th century settlers who feuded so much.

BEAVER: BROOK (2), POND. For beavers.

BEECH HILL. For beech trees.

BELGRADE: LAKES, NORTH-, NORTH-STATION, settlement, STREAM, TOWNSHIP. Tradition says named for Belgrade, Yugoslavia (then Serbia), by John V. Davis, who had traveled in Europe. (Some contend that Mr. Davis had never been to Europe.)

BELLE ISLAND. French: "pretty."

BELLOWS STREAM. For F. Bellows, resident, 1879.

BENTON: EAST-, FALLS, settlement, STATION, TOWNSHIP. For Thomas Hart Benton, a prominent Democrat and congressman from Missouri.

BERRY HILL. For the Berry family.

BERRY POND. For Rufus Berry, settler by the early 1800's.

BICKFORD HILL. For Asa Bickford.

BIG ISLAND. (2). Descriptive.

BIRCH: ISLAND (3), POINT. For birch trees.

BLACK ASH SWAMP. For black ash trees.

BLACK: ISLAND, POND. Descriptive.

BLODGETT ISLAND. Unknown.

BOG: BROOK (3), POND (2), STREAM. Descriptive.

BOLTON HILL. For Savage Bolton, early settler.

BOND BROOK. For Thomas Bond, who received a nearby lot in 1762.

BONNY POND. For Bonney, a deserter from the Continental forces in the American Revolution, who hid here.

BOODY POND. Unknown.

BOWEN HILL. For a man named Bowen from Lewiston, who was on a timber hunting expedition there.

BRAINARD POND. For Asahel and Benjamin Brainard, settlers by 1828.

BRANCH, THE. Descriptive.

BRANN BROOK. For Frank Brann, resident by the 1840's.

BRICKETT POINT. For Asa Brickett, who ran a chowder house here about 1870.

BROWNS CORNER. Probably for the Alexander Brown family, the first settlers about 1670.

BROWNS ISLAND. For J. and G. Brown, residents nearby in 1856.

BUKER POND. For Daniel Buker, settler, 1812.

BULL BROOK. While there is no confirmation of this, it is likely that it was named for its swift flowage.

BURGESS POND. For the Burgess family who owned it.

BURNT HILL. Descriptive.

CAMP ABENA POINT. For Camp Abena, a summer camp located there.

CARLTON POND. For Carlton, a man who built a mill there.

CASTLE ISLAND. For Leighton Castle, who built summer cottages there.

CAUSEWAY ISLAND. Because it serves as a causeway to Spruce Island.

CHAFFEE BROOK. For James H. Chaffee, farmer, mid-1800's.

CHELSEA: settlement, TOWNSHIP. For Chelsea, Massachusetts.

CHINA: LAKE, settlement, SOUTH-, TOWNSHIP. For "China," an old, sad hymn that the settlers liked.

CHOATS BROOK. For Aaron Choate, settler by 1800.

CHUTE ISLAND. For the Moses Chute family.

CLINTON: settlement, TOWNSHIP. For Dewitt Clinton, builder of the Erie Canal, U.S. Senator, and Governor of New York.

COBBOSSEECONTEE: LAKE, LITTLE-LAKE, STREAM. Abnaki: "plenty of sturgeon."

COCHNEWAGEN LAKE. Abnaki: "closed-up route."

COE POINT. Unknown.

COLD STREAM. Descriptive.

COOK HILL. For the Elijah Cook family, settlers, early 1800's.

CRAMS POINT. Probably for John H. Cram, settler by 1851.

CRANBERRY POND. For cranberries.

CROOKED ISLAND. Descriptive.

CROSS HILL. Because the settlers had to cross this hill to get from South Vassalboro to the Kennebec River. Others say for Zebediah and William Cross.

CROTCHED POND. Descriptive.

CUBA ISLAND. Descriptive of its shape.

DAVID POND. For David Ingham, one of the early settlers.

DAVIS POND. Possibly for Captain Samuel Davis, early settler.

DAM POND. Descriptive.

DANFORTH HILL. For Samuel, Enoch, and Isaac Danforth, early settlers.

DEARBORN BROOK. For J.F. Dearborn, settler, early 1800's.

DECKER CORNER. For the Stephen Decker family, who ran a store in the 1820's.

DEER HILL. For deer.

DENNIS HILL. For the early settling Dennis family.

DESERT POND. For its location in a desolate, deserted area.

DEXTER POND. For Isaac Dexter, settler, 1799.

DILNOW BROOK. For Ebenezer Delano, who settled here early.

DIRIGO CORNER. For the name of a post office established there in 1860 with Horatio Nelson as postmaster. The post office was named for the state motto, "Dirigo."

DISMAL SWAMP. Descriptive.

DIXON CORNER. For the local Dixon family.

DOCTOR POND. Unknown.

DOLOFF POND. For the Doloff family, settlers, late 1700's.

DUNN POINT. For the Dunn family.

DUNNS CORNER. For Peter Dunn, tavernkeeper before 1800.

DUTTON POND. For Coffram Dutton ad his son Charles E., who had settled by 1851.

EAST LIVERMORE FALLS. For Livermore Falls in Androscoggin County.

EATON MOUNTAIN. For the ancestors of Fritz Eaton.

EGYPT POND. For area called Egypt for an unknown reason.

ELLIS POND. For William Ellis, settler by 1802.

EMERY SWAMP. For the Emory family who owned it.

EVANS POND. For Joseph Evans, settler before 1776.

FAIRBANKS POND. For the prominent Fairbanks family, settlers, early 1800's.

FARMINGDALE: settlement, TOWNSHIP. For the many area farms.

FAYETTE: CORNER, HILL, NORTH-, TOWNSHIP. For La-Fayette, who aided the colonies in their war for independence against England.

FELLOWS BROOK. For Nathaniel Fellows, a settler of 1794.

FIELDS BROOK. For Nathan Field, who built a saw and gristmill in 1845 with Nathan Blackman.

FIFTEENMILE STREAM. Because it empties 15 miles up the Sebasticook River from where the Sebasticook flows into the Kennebec River.

FLYING POND. The Indians discovered the pond, and when they attempted to lead some of their friends back to it and could not locate it, they said that it must have flown off.

FOSS HILL. (2). In Benton Township, for the Foss family who lived there. In Rome Township, for J. Foss, resident, 1856.

FOSTER POINT. For Edgar and Dexter Foster, who built the first camp on the point.

FOWLER BROOK. For Fowler Bog in Waldo County.

FOX POND. For foxes.

FRENCHS CORNER. Probably for Charles G. and Enoch French, residents by 1851.

FRENCH MOUNTAIN. For the Moses French family who lived here in 1865.

FRINK: HILL, ISLAND. Unknown.

FROG ISLAND. For frogs.

GARDINER BROOK. For Captain Benjamin Gardiner, shipmaster, who settled about 1832.

GARDINER: settlement, SOUTH-, TOWNSHIP, WEST-TOWNSHIP. For Dr. Sylvester Gardiner, proprietor.

GETCHELL CORNER. For John Getchell, settler, 1775.

GIVENS HILL. For the Givens family, early settlers.

GOFF BROOK. For L.S. Goff, resident, 1879.

GOODWIN CORNER. For Simon Goodwin, mill operator before 1793.

GOODWIN POINT. (2). In Litchfield Township, for Simon Goodwin, mill operator before 1793. In Pittston Township, for either Jordan or Abiel Goodwin, settlers of 1850.

GOOSENECK ISLAND. Descriptive.

GOULD POND. For Mosiah Gould, better known as St. Gould for his reputed piousness, who came from Boston in the 1770's. It is reported that he usually slept near the water's edge with a fish line tied to his wrist so that he would always have fresh fish.

GRANITE HILL. Descriptive.

GRAPE ISLAND. For wild grapes.

GREAT: MEADOW STREAM, POND. Descriptive.

GREELEY ISLAND. For Joseph Greeley, settler, 1780's.

GREELEY POND. For Moses and Seth Greeley, settlers, 1765.

GREEN ISLAND. (2). Descriptive.

GROVER BROOK. For the Benjamin Grover family, settlers, 1803.

HALES BROOK. Probably for Jonathon Hale, Revolutionary War veteran.

HALL CORNER. For Albert Hall, who lived there about 1950, and his earlier family.

HALLOWELL: settlement, TOWNSHIP. For Benjamin Hallowell, substantial proprietor in the Kennebec Patent.

HAMILTON POND. For the J. Nudd Hamilton family, in the area by the 1790's.

HAMMOND BROOK. For Paul and Elijah Hammond, early settlers.

HATCH COVE. For Dr. Theron Hatch, who built a summer cottage there.

HATHORNE HILL. For Captain James A. Hathorne.

HAYDEN CORNER. For Colonel Joseph Hayden, early settler.

HEMLOCK POINT. For hemlocks.

HERSEY ISLAND. For L.P. Hersey, owner, late 1800's.

HEWITT BROOK. For the Hewitt family.

HODGDON ISLAND. For the Hodgdon family of East Winthrop.

HOPKINS: POND, STREAM. For Joseph Hopkins, millowner, early 1800's.

HORNBEAM MOUNTAIN. For hornbeam trees.

HORSE POINT. For the first horse brought to Belgrade Township, from Sidney Township, by Simeon Wyman. It is reported that the horse grew homesick, waded out from this point, and swam back to Sidney.

HORSESHOE: ISLAND, POND. Descriptive of shape.

HOWARD HILL. For James Howard, the only commander of Fort Western, built in 1754. He lived there after the Indian wars and made the fort his place of business.

HOWLAND HILL. For John Howland, original Pilgrim Father of Plymouth Colony and commander of a trading post in the Upper Kennebec River region. Another source claims that this is a misspelling of Howling Hill, a place where wolves used to congregate and howl at the sheep located on Mutton Hill. This explanation, while possibly true, is likely folk etymology.

HOYT BROOK. (2). In Belgrade Township, for the Hoyt family, early settlers. In Winthrop Township, for the Francis Hoyt family, early settlers.

HOYT HILL. For G. and N.H. Hoyt, residents by 1879.

HOYT ISLAND. For the early Hoyt family.

HUNTER BROOK. Unknown.

HUSSEY HILL. For the Robert Hussey family, settlers by 1815.

HUTCHINSON POND. For Israel and Andrew Hutchinson, early settlers and farmers.

ICEBORO. For the men who worked in the icehouses and built their homes here.

INDIAN ISLAND. (2). For Indians.

INGHAM: POND, STREAM. For David Ingham, the man who gave his first name to David Pond.

IRON MINE HILL. For the large amount of iron ore there.

ISLAND PARK. Because the park, used for dances and picnics, was located on an island in Cobbosseecontee Lake.

JAMAICA POINT. Possibly for ice cut here and sent to Jamaica. If Indian, Natick: "beaver."

JIMMIE POND. Unknown.

JIMMY POND. Unknown.

JOCK STREAM. For John (Jock) Munyaw, who lived on its banks.

The name is an actual shortening of the original Jockomunyaw Stream.

JOE POND. Unknown.

JOHN BROWN MOUNTAIN. For John Brown, who lived on its crest, mid 1800's.

JONES BROOK. (2). In Sidney Township, for Atwood F. Jones, settler, 1849. In Waterville Township, for the Jones family who lived there prior to 1900.

JOYCE ISLAND. Unknown.

JOYS POND. Unknown.

JUG STREAM. Tradition says for a number of drunks who christened the area Juggernaut after one said, when he had finished all the whiskey in the jug, "Jug or not?" When no one answered him, he broke the jug. This is likely folk etymology and folklore.

KENNEBEC: COUNTY, RIVER. Abnaki: "long, quiet water."

KENTS: HILL, HILL (settlement). For Captain Warren and Charles Kent, settlers before 1793.

KEZAR POND. For the John Kezar family, settlers, 1790.

KIDDER POND. For the Kidder ancestors of Hazel Eaton.

KILDEER POINT. Colorful name given in the 1830's by a developer of a resort area; there are no kildeer in the area.

KIMBALL BROOK. Possibly for George Kimball, resident by 1850.

KIMBALL POND. For S. Kimball, resident, 1856.

LAMBS CORNER. For Luther Lamb, early settler.

LeCLAIR ISLAND. For Edmund LeClair, who built a small summer hotel on it. When the hotel was later being moved over the ice to the mainland, it burned.

LIBBY HILL. For the early Libby family.

LILY POND. (4). For lilies.

LITCHFIELD: CORNERS, PLAINS, settlement, TOWNSHIP. For Litchfield, England.

LITHGOW HILL. For Captain William Lithgow, who served at Fort Richmond and helped establish Fort Halifax. The Lithgow Hill site of Fort Richmond was Captain Lithgow's home, 1748-54.

LITTLE POND. Descriptive.

LITTLE PURGATORY POND. For a pond formerly called Purgatory Pond by William Gardiner in 1776. When asked where he had spent the night, he replied, "In Purgatory. The black flies and mosquitoes were so thick we couldn't sleep."

LOCKS CORNER. For the father of Samuel Locke, 1824 tannery operator.

LONE TREE ISLAND. Descriptive.

LONG: ISLAND, POINT (2). POND. Descriptive.

LOON: ISLAND, POND. For loons.

LORD HILL. For the Simon and William Lord families, who settled before 1800.

LOVEJOY POND. For Daniel Lovejoy, among the first settlers, 1790.

LOVERS ISLAND. For a couple caught in "flagrante delicto."

LUNTS HILL. For Johnson Lunt, settler, 1790.

MAGGOTTY MEADOW BROOK. Unknown.

MANCHESTER: settlement, TOWNSHIP. For Manchester, Massachusetts, former home of some of the settlers.

MANTER HILL. Probably for David Manter, settler by 1790.

MAPLE RIDGE ISLAND. For maple trees.

MARANACOOK: LAKE, settlement. Abnaki: "plugged-up lake, deep lake," or "black bass here."

MARTIN HILL. For L. Martin, resident, 1879.

MAYFLOWER HILL. For mayflowers.

McCOY CROSSING. For the McCoy family.

McGAFFEY MOUNTAIN. For Charles McGaffey.

McGRATH POND. For Thomas McGrath, settler by 1815.

MEADOW: BROOK (3), HILL. Descriptive.

MEARS BROOK. For Mary Mears.

MERRILL ISLAND. For the Joseph Merrill family, early settlers.

MESSALONSKEE: LAKE, STREAM. Abnaki: "white clay here."

MIDWAY ISLAND. Descriptive of being halfway out in Messalonskee Lake.

MILL: POND, STREAM (2). For mills built there.

MINNEHONK LAKE. Abnaki: "many geese."

MOLAZIGAN ISLAND. One source says that it is an Indian word meaning "black bass." Another says it is for the Molazigan Club of Boston, the name of which was made from a combination of the names of the members.

MONKS HILL. For Benjamin Monk, one of the first area homesteaders.

MONMOUTH: EAST-, NORTH-, RIDGE, settlement, SOUTH-, TOWNSHIP. Named by General Henry Dearborn for the Battle of Monmouth in the American Revolution.

MOODY POND. For the early Moody family.

MOOSE: POND, POND STREAM. For moose.

MORRILL HILL. For J.H. Morrill, resident, 1879.

MORRISON HEIGHTS. For the John Morrison family, settlers of about 1800.

MORRISON CORNER. For James Morrison, who ran a store there about 1830. Another source states for Dependence Morrison, early settler.

MORTON BROOK. For the Morton family.

MOSHER HILL. For Trip Mosher, early settler.

MOSHER POND. For David or Baxter Mosher, early settlers.

MOUNTAIN, THE. Descriptive.

MOUNT PHILIP. For Philip Snow, first settler of the area, 1774, and a hunter.

MOUNT PISGAH. For the biblical Mount Pisgah, where Moses saw the Promised Land.

MOUNT VERNON: settlement, TOWNSHIP, WEST-. For Mount Vernon, home of George Washington.

MUD POND. (3). Descriptive.

MUTTON HILL. For sheep kept there.

NARROWS: LOWER-POND, THE-, UPPER-POND. Descriptive.

NEHUMKEAG POND. Abnaki: "eels run out."

NORRIS HILL. For James Norris, early settler.

NORRIS: ISLAND (2), POINT. Island and Point in Litchfield Township area, for the Nathanial Norris family, millowners in the 1790's. Island in Wayne Township, for the Norris family, settlers before 1800.

NORTH BAY. Descriptive.

OAK: HILL (2), ISLAND, -LAND (settlement), -LAND TOWNSHIP. For oak trees.

OTTER ISLAND. For otters.

OUTLET STREAM. Descriptive.

PACKARD LEDGE. For 4 Packard brothers who settled here about 1800.

PAINES CORNER. For Lemuel Paine, settler, 1805.

PALMER BROOK. Probably for Edward or Samuel Palmer, settlers, 1803.

PARKER POND. For any of several Parker families who settled, late 1700's

PATTEE: POND, POND BROOK. For Ezekiel Pattee, early settler.

PELTON HILL. Unknown.

PENNY POND. For the George Penney family, settlers before 1800.

PICKEREL POND. For pickerel fish.

PINE: HILL, ISLAND (2). For pine trees.

PINKHAM: ISLAND, SOUND. Probably for the Noah Pinkham family, early settlers.

PISHON FERRY. For Charles Pishon, ferry operator before 1800.

PITTSTON: EAST-, NORTH-, TOWNSHIP. For the family of John Pitt, people who had been instrumental in procuring settlers.

PLEASANT HILL. Descriptive.

POCASSET LAKE. Natick: "the stream widens."

PORCUPINE HILL. For porcupines..

POTTERS BROOK. For Jeremy and Amos Potter, millowners.

PRATT STREAM. For Vincent Pratt, millowner, 1827.

PRESCOTT HILL. For Captain James Prescott, settler, 1792.

PRIEST HILL. For Jonas Priest, settler, 1792.

QUAKER HILL. For a Quaker cemetery there.

RANDOLPH: settlement, TOWNSHIP. For Randolph, Massachusetts.

READFIELD: DEPOT, settlement, TOWNSHIP. Tradition says for Peter Norton and his mother, who were avid readers.

RICHARDS ISLAND. Unknown..

RICHMOND MILL. For the Richmond family, who operated the mill.

RICKER HILL. Unknown.

RIGGS BROOK. Unknown.

RING HILL. For Amasa Ring, early farmer.

RIVERSIDE. For its proximity to the Kennebec River.

ROBBINS MILL STREAM. For Luke Robbins, millowner, 1830.

ROBBINS POINT. For Daniel Robbins, settler by 1782.

ROBERTS HILL. For the Frank Roberts family.

ROCKWOOD BROOK. For G. Rockwood, resident, 1856.

ROLLING DAM BROOK. For a "rolling dam" built there, a dam where the logs float up a kind of inclined plane and roll over to the water below.

ROME: CORNER, settlement, TOWNSHIP, TROUT BROOK. For Rome, Italy.

ROUND: POND, TOP. Descriptive.

SANDERS HILL. Unknown.

SANDERSON CORNER. For John Sanderson, settler before 1850.

SAND POND. Descriptive.

SANDS, THE. (island). Descriptive.

SANFORD BROOK. For the Sanford family.

SAVADE POND. For a misunderstanding by the surveyors when they asked the name of the pond. Obviously not being familiar with the Maine dialect, they wrote more or less phonetically the Maine pronunciation of "surveyed."

SAWYER HILL. For the Harlow Sawyer family, early settlers.

SCHOOLHOUSE POND. For a schoolhouse built there in the 1820's.

SCOTT ISLAND. Unknown.

SEAVEYS CORNER For H.B. and E. Seavey, residents, 1856.

SEAWARD MILLS. For Giles Seaward, millowner.

SEBASTICOOK RIVER. Penobscot-Abnaki: "almost-through place."

SENNETTS CORNER. For the many Sennetts living there.

SEVENMILE: BROOK, ISLAND. For where it empties, 7 miles north of Augusta on the Kennebec River.

SHED POND. Unknown.

SHEEP ISLAND. For sheep kept there.

SHORE HILL. Probably for the Shorey family who settled in 1790.

SIDNEY: BOG BROOK, CENTER-, GREAT-BOG, NORTH-, settlement, TOWNSHIP, WEST-. For the Englishman, Sir Philip Sidney.

SILVER LAKE. Descriptive.

SISTER: LOWER-ISLAND, UPPER-ISLAND. Fanciful names for a pair of islands.

SNAKE POINT. For snakes.

SPEARS CORNER. For many Spears who lived there.

SPECTACLE POND. For its eyeglass shape.

SPIDERS ISLAND. Unknown.

SPRING BROOK. For being spring fed.

SPRINGER HILL. For David and Thomas Springer, settlers about 1785.

SPRUCE ISLAND. For spruce trees.

STICKNEY BOG. For Benjamin Stickney, one of the first area settlers.

STONE BROOK. For the Reverend Daniel Stone, one of the first ministers to settle permanently in Old Hallowell.

STONEY: BROOK, MEADOW BROOK, POINT. Descriptive.

STUART POND. For Samuel, Wentworth, and Calvin, sons of Duncan Stuart, settlers before 1800.

STURTEVANT HILL. For Albert and Leonard Sturtevant, sons of an early settler.

SUMMERHAVEN. Descriptive of a summer settlement.

TABER HILL. For Paul Taber, settler before 1800.

TACOMA: LAKES, settlement. Nisqually: "great white breast." The Nisqually Indians are indigenous to Washington State and not to Maine. The name was probably given by some traveler.

TALLWOOD. Descriptive.

TANNERY BROOK. For Joseph Ham's tannery, built in the 1800's.

TAYLOR POND. For O.E. Taylor, resident, 1856.

TELEGRAPH HILL. This hill was used as a landmark by boats navigating the Kennebec River, but it is not known whether this is in any way connected with the name.

THAYER CORNER. For Barnabas, Jeremiah, and Timothy Thayer, early settlers.

THOMPSON HILL. Probably for Jonathon Thompson, settler, 1777.

THREECORNERED POND. Descriptive of shape.

THREEMILE POND. Descriptive of length.

TILTON POND. For Tilton Richards, early settler. Sometimes his name is given as Richards Tilton.

TINGLEY BROOK. This brook is mislocated on the Geological Survey map, as it should be farther to the north; however, it was named for the Tingley family who lived on its banks.

TINKHAM POND. One source says for a family who lived there. Another says it is a misspelling of "tinkers," as the pond is no longer than a "tinker mackerel."

TOGUS: LITTLE-POND, LOWER-POND, POND, settlement, STREAM. One source says it was named by a Mr. Beals for another stream formerly called the "Worromontogus." The word is Abnaki, however: "brook entering cove."

TOLMAN POND. For Samuel Tolman, who received an early lot.

TORSEY LAKE. For Dr. Henry P. Torsey, former president of Kent's Hill School, who fished there frequently.

TOWN FARM BROOK. For the town farm.

TOWN HOUSE HILL. The town meeting house was located there in 1833.

TRUE COVE. For John and David True, early settlers.

TWELVE CORNERS. Where roads meet, creating 12 corners.

TWELVEMILE BROOK. For where it empties into the Sebasticook River, 12 miles from where the Sebasticook flows into the Kennebec River.

TWO TREES ISLAND. Descriptive.

TYLER CORNER. For a Tyler who ran a store there.

TYLER POND. For the Tyler family, settlers as early as 1808.

UNDINE BAY. For a classical female water spirit.

UNITY: (unorganized area). For Unity Township in Waldo County.

VASSALBORO: CENTER-, EAST-, NORTH-, settlement, SOUTH-, TOWNSHIP. Some say for Florentine Vassal of London, one of the proprietors of the Plymouth Colony, who owned some land in the area. Others say for the Honorable William Vassal, prominent citizen of Massachusetts.

VAUGHN BROOK. For Dr. Benjamin Vaughn, who, before coming to Hallowell in 1796, was a member of the English Parliament. The story is told that the famous French statesman Talleyrand, while visiting Dr. Vaughn on his estate in the late 1790's, fell into this brook and narrowly escaped drowning.

VIENNA: MOUNTAIN, settlement, TOWNSHIP. For Vienna, Austria.

WARD BROOK. For B.S. and S.H. Ward, residents, 1879.

WATERVILLE: settlement, TOWNSHIP. For its location on water, the Kennebec River.

WATSON POND. For John Watson, who owned a farm on the east side in 1882.

WAYNE: NORTH-, settlement, TOWNSHIP. For General "Mad" Anthony Wayne, of George Washington's staff.

WEBBER POND. For Charles Webber, settler by 1790.

WEEKS MILLS. For Major Abner Weeks and his father, who had a mill and tannery there.

WELCH POINT. For the Welch family.

WELLMAN POND. For Joseph Wellman, resident, 1820's-40's.

WENTWORTH POINT. For George Wentworth, the owner when it was developed as a resort area.

WESTON MEADOWS. For Joseph Weston, who cleared this area in 1771. This and more land was bestowed on Weston's son William for Joseph's service as a guide to Benedict Arnold on the Quebec expedition.

WEST POINT. Descriptive.

WHITTIER: BROOK, POND (2). Brook and Pond in Vienna Township, for Lyman Whittier and his son Perley, millowners, mid-1800's. Pond in Rome Township, for Thomas Whittier, millowner, 1840.

WILLIAMS HILL. For the Williams family.

WILSON BROOK. For Ephraim Wilson, millowner and settler by 1791.

WILSON: POND, STREAM. For Wilson, white hunter drowned in the stream by Indians.

WINDSOR: NECK HILL, NORTH-, STATION, settlement, SOUTH-, TOWNSHIP, -VILLE, WEST-. For the Windsors, the royal house of England.

WINGS MILLS. For Silas B. Wing, millowner before 1840.

WINSLOW; EAST-, settlement, TOWNSHIP. For General John Winslow, who helped construct Fort Halifax.

WINTER HILL. For Samuel Winter, who bought the hill in 1820.

WINTHROP: CENTER, EAST-, settlement, TOWNSHIP. For Governor John W. Winthrop, first colonial governor of Massachusetts Bay Colony.

WOODBURY: HILLS, POND. For True and Hugh Woodbury, settlers, 1806.

YALLALY HILL. Unknown.
YORK HILL. For the York family.

KNOX COUNTY

ALDEN ROCK. Possibly for Alden Shea, early settler.

ALFORD LAKE. For the Nathan Alford family, settlers, early 1800's.

ALLEN BROOK. Unknown.

ALLEN: ISLAND, LEDGE. For Alexander Allen, owner in 1774.

AMESBURY POINT. For Edwin T. Amesbury, sea captain.

AMES COVE. For Am Simmons, who lived there.

AMES POINT. For the Ames family who settled about 1765.

ANDREWS ISLAND. For Captain Stephen Andrews and his brothers, who lived near Waldoboro and traded along the coast.

APPLETON: NORTH-, RIDGE, settlement, TOWNSHIP, WEST-. For Samuel Appleton of Ipswich, New Hampshire, among the first settlers.

AREY: COVE LEDGES, NECK. For Isaac Arey, settler, 1770.

ASH: ISLAND, ISLAND LEDGE, POINT, POINT (settlement). For ash trees.

ATHEARNS CORNER. For the George L. Athearn family, about 1888.

ATLANTIC POINT. For the Atlantic Ocean.

BABBIDGE ISLAND. Some say for William Babbidge, early settler. Others, for E.G. Babbidge, sea captain.

BABCOCK POINT. For William Babcock from Massachusetts, who had a summer home here, late 1800's.

BACK: COVE, RIVER (2). Descriptive of location.

BAILEY: LEDGE, POINT. For the early Bailey family.

BALD MOUNTAIN. (2). Descriptive.

BALLYHAC COVE. For the early Ballyhac family, Irishmen.

BANKS COVE. For the Banks family who settled about 1765.

BAR ISLAND. (2). Descriptive.

BARLEY HILL. For barley grown there by the Burgess or Calderwood families.

BARREL, THE. Descriptive of shape.

BARRETT HILL. For the Charles Barrett family, settlers by 1793.

BARTER SHOAL. For James Barter, who wrecked a ship there.

BARTLETT HARBOR. For the early Bartlett family.

BARTON ISLAND. For the Barton family, settlers about 1800 who mended herring weirs.

BASIN, THE. Descriptive.

BATTERY: area, POINT. For being the location of naval gun batteries.

BAY LEDGE. Descriptive.

BEACH HILL. For beech trees, cartographical error.

BEAR HILL. For bears.

BEAUCHAMP POINT. Probably for the John Beauchamp family, one of the 1629 proprietors.

BEAVERDAM BROOK. For beaverdams.

BENNER: HILL, ISLAND. For the John Benner family.

BEYER SHIP LEDGE. There was a Captain John Geyer in the area, but a connection is not certain.

BILLS ISLAND. For Bill Folsom, who ran his boat aground on nearby rocks.

BIRCH: ISLAND (2), POINT (3). For birch trees.

BIRD POINT. One source says for birds. Another, for a local family.

BLACK DINA. Fanciful name for a black rock face.

BLACK: EAST-LEDGE, ISLAND, ISLAND LEDGE, LEDGES ROCK (2), ROCKS, WEST-LEDGE. Descriptive.

BLACKHORSE ISLAND. Fanciful name for a black granite island.

BLACKINTON CORNERS. For the local Blackinton family.

BLANK POINT. Likely a misspelling of "Black Point."

BLUBBER ISLAND. Tradition says a place where blubber was rendered.

BLUFF HEAD. Descriptive.

BRADFORD POINT. For the Bradford family.

BRANCH BROOK. Descriptive.

BREWSTER: POINT, POINT LEDGE. For the early Brewster family.

BRIG LEDGE. For a brig wrecked there in 1835, drowning 5 sailors.

BRIMSTONE: ISLAND, LITTLE-ISLAND. For a black granite rock.

BROAD COVE. (2). Descriptive.

BROOM ISLAND. Descriptive of shape.

BROTHERS, THE. Fanciful name for 3 rocks.

BROWNS COVE. For the Brown family, settlers about 1765.

BROWNS HEAD. For Cyril Brown, who lived nearby.

BROWNS ISLAND. For the Brown family who were in the area by 1785.

BOG, THE. Descriptive.

BOOT NECK. When viewed from the Waldoboro bridge, it resembles the neck of a boot.

BULL BROOK. Tradition says for a bull that broke its leg there.

BULL COVE. For a bull pushed overboard from a boat, which swam to the island and came ashore at this cove.

BURGESS COVE. For Ezekiel Burgess, settler, between 1820-30.

BURKETTVILLE. For Andrew K. Burkett, who built 2 mills there.

BURNT: ISLAND (6), ISLAND THOROUGHFARE, LITTLE-IS-LAND. Descriptive.

BURTON POINT. For Major Burton, who commanded a fort in the area.

CALDERWOOD: ISLAND, NECK, POINT. For the John Calderwood family, settlers, 1769.

CALDWELL: ISLAND, LITTLE-ISLAND. There was a Caldwell family in the area early, but on a 1758 map the island is called "Colvel," which might be a family name itself, or a corruption of "Caldwell."

CALF ISLAND. Although there is no record of it here, islands were frequently so named for being used as pens for cattle.

CAMDEN: settlement, TOWNSHIP. For Charles Pratt, Earl of Camden.

CAMP: COVE, COVE LEDGE, ISLAND. Used as campsites.

CAREY ROCK. For Mother Carey's chickens (gulls and small sea birds), which swarm it.

CARVER: COVE, HARBOR, ISLAND, POND. For Thaddeus Carver and his sons John and Reuben, who settled about 1766.

CAT LEDGE. Unknown.

CATO: COVE, LEDGE. Unknown.

CEDAR: ISLAND (2), POND, SWAMP. For cedar trees.

CHANNEL ROCK. (3). Descriptive.

CHICKAWAUKIE POND. Although this is not a legitimate Indian term, it is a composite attempt at "good, sweet, fresh, drinkable water."

CLAM: COVE, HIGH-LEDGES, LEDGES. For clams.

CLAREY HILL. For Edward Clarey, settler by 1850.

CLARK: COVE, ISLAND, ISLAND (settlement), ISLAND LEDGE, POINT. Probably for the Benjamin Clark family, early settlers.

COGGANS HILL. For the William Coggans family, early settlers.

CONDON POINT. For Benjamin Condon, settler between 1810-20.

CONWAY POINT. Probably for the Conway family from Northern Ireland.

COOMBS: HILL, NECK. For Anthony Coombs, settler by 1775.

COOMBS ISLAND. For Joseph Coombs, settler about 1773.

GINN POINT. For Jeremiah Ginn, who had a fishery here in the 1800's.

GLEN COVE. For its location on Clam Cove. The "Glen" is descriptive.

GLENMERE. Suggested by the U.S. Postal Service for no reason.

GLOBE. The name of a post office set up by Robert Sukeforth. People said that the mail had to go "around the globe" to get there.

GOOSE: EAST-ROCK, ISLAND, RIVER (2), ROCK (2), ROCKS. For geese. In Rockport Township, specifically for a goose nest found there by Nathaniel Hosmer.

GRACE ROCK. Unknown.

GRAFFAM ISLAND. For the Grafton family, early settlers.

GRANTS TURN. For Grant, summer resident who had his home there in 1902.

GRASSY POND. Descriptive.

GRAVES, THE. Before the installation of navigational aids, they were the graveyard of many ships and sailors.

GREEN: ISLAND (3), ISLAND SEAL LEDGES, LARGE-ISLAND, LEDGE (5), LITTLE-ISLAND (2), POINT SHOALS. Island in Vinalhaven Township, for Joseph Green, who escaped from the Indians when they massacred his family about 1757, when he was twelve years old. The others, descriptive.

GREER ISLAND. Possibly a cartographical mistake from "Green."

GRINDSTONE: INNER-LEDGE, LEDGE. Because they could grind the bottom out of a boat.

GULL ROCK. For gulls.

GUNDELL ISLAND. Unknown.

GUNNING ROCKS. For hunters who hunted ducks and geese there.

GURNEY HILL. For Elisha Gurney, settler by 1811.

GUSHEES CORNER. For the many Gushees living here in the 1880's.

HALIBUT: ROCK, WEST-LEDGES. For halibut fish.

HALL ISLAND. (2). For the early Hall families.

HALLS COVE. For Ebeneezer Hall, settler, 1750.

HARBOR: HEAD-, ISLAND (2), LEDGES, POINT. Descriptive.

HARDWOOD ISLAND. For hardwood trees.

HARPOON LEDGE. For a drunk whaler who mistook the ledge for a whale and threw his harpoon at it.

HARRIET BROOK. Unknown.

HARRINGTON COVE. For John Harrington, who lived there in 1803.

HART: ISLAND, ISLAND LEDGES, LEDGES, NECK. For John Hart, settler, 1700's.

HARTNEY HILL. Possibly for Harkness, a man who laid out roads in the 1800's.

HATCHET: COVE, MOUNTAIN. Tradition says they were named for the Indians burying a hatchet as a symbol of peace.

HATHORNE POINT. Probably for the Samuel Hathorn family who settled not far away in 1750.

HAWTHORN POINT. For the Samuel Hathorn family, settlers in 1750.

HAYDEN POINT. For Luther Hayden, early settler.

HAY: ISLAND (2), LEDGE. Because of the hay growing there.

HEAD: EASTERN-, WESTERN-(2). Descriptive.

HEN ISLAND. (2). First called "Heron Island" for herons; corrupted to "Hern," then to "Hen."

HENDRICKSON POINT. For Hendrickson, an eighteen-year-old boy who lived with the Maddox family. He married a Waterville girl, came back, and settled on this point.

HERON: NECK, NECK LEDGE. Descriptive of shape.

HERRING LEDGE. For herring fish.

HEWETT: ISLAND, ISLAND ROCKS. For Captain Solomon Hewet, who lived there and traded along the coast.

HIBBERTS CORNER. For T. Hibbert.

HIGH: HEAD, ISLAND (2), LEDGE. Descriptive.

HOBBS POND. For James P. Hobbs, resident, 1888.

HOG: COVE, COVE LEDGE. The location of Jere McIntire's pig sty.

HOG ISLAND. (2). For hogs kept there.

HOGSHEAD, THE. To make a fanciful pair with The Barrel. It is larger.

HOLDEN LEDGE. Unknown.

HOLIDAY BEACH. Descriptive of a summer colony.

HOME HARBOR. Descriptive.

HOOPER: ISLAND, ISLAND SHOAL, POINT. For Thomas Hooper.

HOPE BROOK. For Edgar Hoak, who lived nearby.

HOPE: NORTH-, settlement, SOUTH-, TOWNSHIP. Some say it was "a land of hope." Others say that James Malcolm, surveyor, marked the 4 corner posts of the township with the letters "EHPO." When a name was desired for the township, they simply rearranged the letters to "Hope."

HOPKINS POINT. For Dr. Theophilus Hopkins, first doctor in the area, about 1805.

HORNBARN COVE. For a barn located on the Horn farm, used by fishermen as a navigational aid.

HOSMER POND. For Nathaniel Hosmer, settler, 1785.

HOSPITAL POINT. For a military hospital located there.

HOUGH LEDGE. Unknown.

HOUSE LEDGE. Unknown.

HOWARD: POND, POINT. For Daniel Howard, landowner, 1784.

HOWIE ROCK. Possibly for Simeon Howe, settler before 1849.

HURRICANE: ISLAND (2), LEDGE, LITTLE-ISLAND, SOUND. For hurricanes that struck along the coast. In Vinalhaven Township, some say that a hurricane struck on the same day that William Vinal bought the island.

HYLER COVE. For Charles Hyler, or his earlier family.

INDIAN: CREEK, LEDGE. For Indians.

INDIAN ISLAND. For the many Indians seen there by Captain Blaisdell in the French and Indian War. It was long an Indian camping place.

INGRAHAM HILL. For the early Ingraham family.

INNER BREAKERS. Descriptive.

IRON POINT. A term meaning "rocky."

ISLE AU HAUT: BAY, ISLAND, MOUNTAIN, settlement, THOROUGHFARE, TOWNSHIP. French: "high island," given by Samuel de Champlain. The Mountain in Vinalhaven Township was so named because from it one could see Isle au Haut.

JAMESON POINT. (2). In Friendship Township, for Samuel, Alexander, and Paul Jameson, settlers about 1754. In Rockland Township, for Robert Jameson, settler before 1800.

JERUSALEM MOUNTAIN. Unknown.

JOHNSON: HILL, POND. For Levi Johnson, who settled in 1844.

JONES BROOK. For Henry Jones, resident, 1859.

JONES HILL. For a number of Jones families in the area by 1888.

KENT COVE. For Benjamin Kent, settler about 1765.

KIMBALL: HEAD, ISLAND. For Solomon Kimball, settler, 1775.

KNOX COUNTY. For General Henry Knox, U.S. Secretary of War.

LAIREYS: ISLAND, LEDGE, NARROWS. For the numerous Lairey family, sometimes spelled "Larry."

LAKE CITY. Descriptive of location.

LANE ISLAND. For Benjamin Lane, settler, 1762.

LARK LEDGES. For larks.

LASELL ISLAND. For Ellison Laselle, first settler there.

LAWREY. Although the Lawrey name goes back to 1754, named only a few years ago for the Lawrey families in the area, descendants of the first.

LEADBETTER: ISLAND, NARROWS. For Increase and John Leadbetter, settlers about 1767.

LERMOND COVE. For John Lermond and his 2 brothers, who came in 1767 and built a camp there.

LERMOND POND. For the early Lermond family.

LILLY POND. (2). For water lilies.

LITTLE FRANKLIN LEDGE. For its location near an island formerly called Franklin Island, for its first owner.

LITTLE: ISLAND (2), THOROUGHFARE. Descriptive.

LOBSTER GUT. For lobsters.

LOBSTER POND. (2). For lobsters kept there.

LONG: COVE (3), COVE (settlement), ISLAND, LEDGE, POND (2). Descriptive.

LOOKOUT. A point that forms a "lookout."

LOWELL LEDGE. For its location off the Lowell family's property.

LOWELL ROCK. For the Lowell family.

LUCIA BEACH. For Lucia Burpee.

MACES POND. For Thomas Mace, settler by 1791.

MACKEREL LEDGE. For mackerel.

MADDOCKS CORNER. For Ambrose Maddocks, early settler.

MAIDEN CLIFF. For Elenora, daughter of Zadock French, who accidentally fell to her death here on a Maying party, 1864.

MALCOLM LEDGES. Unknown.

MANSFIELD POND. For Daniel H. Mansfield, resident by 1888.

MAPLE JUICE COVE. Descriptive of the color of the water that is emptied here by Alder Stream.

MARBLEHEAD ISLAND. Some say for Sebastian Marble, who was from the Broad Bay area and a governor of Maine. Others, for Marblehead, Massachusetts.

MARKEY BEACH. Unknown.

MARK ISLAND. Marks the entrance to the Fox Island Thoroughfare.

MARSHALL POINT. For Samuel Marshall, who lived there in 1802.

MARSH: BROOK, COVE (3), COVE HEAD, THE-. Descriptive.

MARTIN: POINT, settlement. For the Martin or Morton family who lived there.

MARTINS CORNER. For the family of Ruth Martin, who lived there about 1870.

MARTINSVILLE. For the later family of Thomas Martin early settler.

MATINICUS: HARBOR, ISLAND, ISLE TOWNSHIP, ROCK, settlement. Abnaki: "far out island."

McCARTHY POINT. For John McCarter, settler, 1750, and his later family.

MEADOW: BROOK, MOUNTAIN. Descriptive.

MEDOMAK: LITTLE-RIVER, RIVER. Abnaki: "place of many alewives."

MEDRIC ROCK. For medrics, ocean birds, that frequent it.

MEDUNCOOK RIVER. Abnaki: "blocked by sandbars."

MEGUNTICOOK: LAKE, MOUNTAIN, RIVER. Malecite or Micmac: "big mountain harbor."

MELVIN HEIGHTS. For Isaac B. Melvin, long-time resident.

MERCHANT: BROOK, ISLAND, ROW. For Anthony Merchant, settler, 1772.

METINIC: GREEN ISLAND, ISLAND, ISLAND LEDGE. Abnaki: "far out island."

MIDDLE MOUNTAIN. Descriptive.

MILL: COVE, POND, -POND, RIVER (2), STREAM. For mills located on them.

MILLERITE LEDGES. For the mineral millerite (nickel oxide).

MINISTER GUT. Unknown.

MINK ISLAND. For minks.

MIRROR LAKE. Descriptive.

MITTEN LEDGE. Tradition says that a lobsterman lost his mittens there while hauling up his traps.

MONROE ISLAND. For Hugh Monroe, owner.

MONTGOMERY POINT. For N. Montgomery, resident, 1859.

MOORE: HARBOR, HEAD. For Captain John Moore, who anchored his ship there.

MORANG CORNER. For the Morang family who came here about 1910.

MORSE: ISLAND, LEDGE. For the early Morse family.

MOSQUITO: HARBOR, HEAD, ISLAND. For mosquitoes.

MOUNT BATTIE. Tradition says that it was named for Elizabeth Richards before the 1800's. She supposedly loved the mountains and called the one nearest her home "my mountain." It was called "Bettys Mountain" for her, then "Mount Battie." Another reliable source said that it was called "Betty" 10 years before Miss Richards settlement and is probably an Abnaki word with a meaning having to do with alewives.

MOUSE ISLAND. (2). Descriptive of size.

MOUSE RIDGE. Unknown.

MOXY REEF. Possibly for Captain Mouncey, commander of the frigate "Furieuse," which harried these waters in 1814. Possibly for the Indian Chief Moxus.

MUDDY PONDS. (2). Descriptive.

MUD POND. Descriptive.

MULLEN COVE. For the early Mullen family.

MUSCLE RIDGE: CHANNEL, ISLANDS. For mussels.

MUSCONGUS BAY. Abnaki: "many rock ledges."

NABBY COVE. Unknown.

NARROWS ISLAND. For a small channel between it and Vinalhaven Island.

NASH POINT. For the Nash family who settled in 1814.

NATHAN ISLAND. For Nathan Merchant.

NECK, THE. Descriptive.

NEDS POINT. For Edward Thomas, who lived there.

NETTLE ISLAND. For nettles.

NEWBERT POND. For Albert H. Newbert, who settled here about 1880 and was once a postmaster in Appleton.

NO MANS LAND. A worthless island that no one claimed.

NORTH: -EAST COVE, -EAST LEDGE, -EAST PASSAGE, -EAST POINT (2), -EAST POINT REEF, -EAST POND LEDGE, HAVEN (settlement), HAVEN ISLAND, HAVEN TOWNSHIP, POND, -WEST LEDGE. Descriptive.

NORTHERN ISLAND. Descriptive.

NORTON: ISLAND, ISLAND LEDGES. For Jonathon, Ezra, and Samuel Norton, early settlers.

NORTON POINT. For Uriah Norton, early settler.

NUBBINS. Descriptive.

NUBBLE, THE. Descriptive.

OAK: HILL, ISLAND (2), -LAND PARK. For oak trees.

OAKS CORNER. For Francis J. Oakes, wealthy New York dye manufacturer who built a mansion here in 1856.

OGIER POINT. For Abraham Ogier, settler about 1771.

OHIO ISLAND. Abnaki: "big or beautiful river." It does not seem to apply here; therefore, probably so named for another reason.

OLD: COVE, HARBOR, HARBOR POND. Descriptive.

OLD HORSE LEDGE. Fanciful.

OLD HUMP: CHANNEL, LEDGE. In this very deep channel there are some very shallow ledges or "humps."

OLD: MAN LEDGE, WOMAN LEDGE. Fanciful names to make a pair.

OTIS: COVE, POINT. For Samuel Otis, settler, 1797.

OTTER: ISLAND (3), ISLAND PASSAGE, LEDGE, POINT, POND. For otters.

OUTER SCRAG LEDGE. For Scraggy Island in Hancock County.

OWLS: HEAD, HEAD BAY, HEAD HARBOR, HEAD (settlement), HEAD TOWNSHIP. Descriptive of shape; named by Governor Thomas Pownal in 1759.

OYSTER: EAST BRANCH-RIVER, RIVER, WEST BRANCH-RIVER. For oysters.

PASTURE COVE. For a nearby pasture.

PATRICK MOUNTAIN. Probably for Charles Patrick of Washington Township.

PATS BROOK. For its location on Patrick Conley's property.

PATTEN POINT. Unknown.

PAYSON CORNER. For John Payson, early settler.

PEASE: BROOK, CORNER. For Nathan Pease, who settled at the corner in 1828.

PELL ISLAND. For Pelitiah Barter, settler before 1792.

PERRY CREEK. For John Perry, settler by 1779.

PETTENGILL STREAM. For the early Pettengill family.

PHILBRICK MOUNTAIN. For the early philbrick family.

PITCHER BROOK. For Josiah O. Pitcher, who lived there in 1860.

PITMANS CORNER. For Hermon Pitman, resident, 1888.

PLEASANT: BEACH, ISLAND, MOUNTAIN, POINT, POINT GUT. Descriptive.

POND: COVE, GREAT-ISLAND, LITTLE-ISLAND, POINT, SUNKEN-LEDGE. Descriptive.

POOL, THE. Descriptive

POPPLESTONE: NORTH-LEDGE, POINT, SOUTH-LEDGE. Descriptive.

PORT: CLYDE, CLYDE HARBOR. Suggested by the U.S. Postal Department, for no reason.

PORTERFIELD LEDGE. For William Porterfield, settler before 1776.

POTATO ISLAND. For its use as a potato patch by an early settler.

POVERTY HUMP. For a rough, rocky area where many lobster traps have been lost.

PROCTORS CORNER. For John Proctor, settler, 1835.

PUDDING ISLAND. Descriptive of shape.

PULPIT: HARBOR, HARBOR (settlement), ROCK. For the shape of the rock.

QUIGGLE BROOK. Unknown.

RABBITS EAR. Descriptive of shape.

RACKLIFF: BAY, ISLAND. For William Rackliff, settler before 1802.

RAGGED ISLAND. Originally Abnaki: "Raggertask" — "island rocks." By folk etymology it changed to "Ragged Ass" and "Ragged Arse." The cartographers "cleaned" it up to the present "Ragged."

RAGGED MOUNTAIN. Descriptive.

RAM ISLAND. (5). Used as a pen for sheep.

RAZORVILLE. For George Razor, son of John Martin Reiser, 1754 settler of Waldoboro Township.

REACH, THE. Descriptive.

RICE HEATH. For Nathan D. Rice, who owned it in the 1880's.

RICHS: COVE, POINT. For John Rich, early settler.

ROBERTS: HARBOR, ISLANDS. For Elisha Roberts, settler, 1800's.

ROBINSON POINT. For Spencer Robinson, who homestead was nearby.

ROBINSON ROCK. For the Robinson family.

ROCKLAND: settlement, TOWNSHIP. For the limestone quarries.

ROCKPORT: HARBOR, settlement, TOWNSHIP, WEST-. For being a port located in a rocky area.

ROCKVILLE. For the area rock.

ROCKY: MOUNTAIN, POND. Descriptive.

ROSEBUD ISLAND. Descriptive.

ROUND: POND (2), ROCK. Descriptive.

SADDLE: ISLAND, -BACK LEDGE. Descriptive.

ST. GEORGE: RIVER, RIVER NARROWS, settlement, TOWNSHIP. For St. George, patron saint of England; named by Captain George Weymouth in 1605, when he claimed the area for England.

SAND: COVE, ISLAND. Descriptive.

SANDY BEACH. Descriptive.

SAWPIT CORNER. For the location of a sawpit, a pit where a man stands in a depression and another stands on a platform to saw wood with a two-man, straight saw.

SAWYER MOUNTAIN. For Ebenezer Sawyer, settler about 1800.

SEAL: BAY, COVE, HARBOR, ISLAND, LEDGE (3), LEDGES. For seals.

SEAL ISLAND. In Matinicus Isle Township, for shape.

SEAL TRAP, THE. For being a narrow, long cove where seals could be trapped and slaughtered. Others say folk etymology of French "Ciel Trappe" "sky trapped." Descriptive.

SEAVEY: COVE, ISLAND, LEDGES. For Stephen Seavey, early settler.

SENNEBEC POND. Abnaki: "rocks in the pond."

SEVEN TREE POND. Descriptive.

SHAG: INNER-LEDGE, LEDGE, LEDGES, ROCK, ROOST, OUTER-LEDGE. For shags, a variety of bird.

SHARKEYVILLE CREEK. For a Sharkey who ran a quarry nearby.

SHARK ISLAND. For sharks.

SHEEP: ISLAND (3), ISLAND SHOALS. For sheep.

SHEPARDS HILL. For Daniel Shepard, settler, 1795.

SHERMAN COVE. For Ignatius Sherman, resident about 1800.

SHERMANS MILL. For Willard Sherman. millowner until 1886.

SIMMONS HILL. For Jethro Simmons, resident, 1888.

SIMONTON CORNERS. For James Simonton, Jr., settler about 1813.

SLINS ISLAND. For Leonard Fales, the owner in 1810. Probably the name came about in a manner like this: someone asked whose island that was, and the reply was "That's Len's island." The "s" of "that's" combined with the short form of "Leonard" "Len" to give the "Slins."

SMITH: COVE, ISLAND. For Peter Smith and family, early settlers.

SOUTH: BREAKER (2), POINT, POND, -WEST COVE, -WEST LEDGES. Descriptive.

SOUTHERN: ISLAND, POINT. Descriptive.

SOUTHERN MARK ISLAND. Marks the entrance to Merchant Row.

SPARROW ISLAND. For sparrows.

SPAULDING ISLAND. For Captain H. Spaulding, owner.

SPEARS ROCK. For the Jonathon Spear family, settlers about 1762.

SPECTACLE. ISLAND. (2). Descriptive of eye-glass shape.

SPECTACLES. Descriptive of eye-glass shape.

SPOON: GREAT-ISLAND, LEDGE, LITTLE-ISLAND. Descriptive of shape.

SPRING BROOK. For springs.

SPRUCE: HEAD ISLAND, HEAD (settlement), MOUNTAIN. For spruce trees.

SQUEAKER GUZZLE. For a variety of duck called a "squeaker" and a fault in a rock that extends for some distance, where the sea rushes in, called a "guzzle."

STAHLS HILL. Probably for the Henry Stahl family, early settlers.

STALLION LEDGE. For a stallion on Green Island who swam from there to the mainland and stopped on this ledge to rest.

STAND IN POINT. Used as a navigation guide to turn in or "stand in" from Penobscot Bay to the Fox Island Thoroughfare.

STARBOARD ROCK. Descriptive..

STEPHENS HEAD. Unknown.

STICKNEY CORNER. For the Stickney family.

STIMPSONS ISLAND. For a local family.

STODDART ISLAND. For the Stoddart family.

STONE: ISLAND, POINT. Descriptive.

STOVERS CORNER. For Jacob Stover, settler there about 1840.

SUGAR LOAVES. Descriptive.

SUNKEN LEDGE. Descriptive.

SUNSET POINT. Descriptive.

TEEL: COVE, ISLAND. For Adam Teel, early settler.

TENANTS: HARBOR, HARBOR (settlement). Tradition says for Joshua Tenant or Joshua Tenant Maker, his grandson; however, the name antedates these men according to one authority.

TENPOUND ISLAND. (2). In Matinicus Isle Township, for a ten-pound cannonball found there. In St. George Township, because it is very small, "only about ten pounds."

THOMAS MOUNTAIN: For the early Thomas family.

THOMASTON: SOUTH-(settlement), SOUTH-TOWNSHIP, settlement, TOWNSHIP. For Major General John Thomas, a general in the Revolution.

THOMPSON ISLAND. For James Thompson.

THORNDIKE POINT. For Ebenezer Thorndike from Cape Elizabeth, for whom Eben Island was also named.

TIPTOE MOUNTAIN. Tradition says that during the Indian troubles, the Indians would tiptoe up to the top of the mountain and swoop down on the settlers.

TOMMY ISLAND. Unknown.

TRIAL POINT. For being a trial for sailors to navigate.

TRIANGLE: NORTHERN-, SOUTHERN-. For groups of 3 rocks.

TUCKANUCK LEDGE. Wampanoag: "a round loaf of bread."

TURKEY: COVE, POINT. Unknown.

TURNIP ISLAND. In 1845 a ship wrecked nearby and much turnip seed washed up on the shore and was picked up by a man named Glidden. Each year the seed from the turnips was saved, and "Glidden Turnips" are still grown in the area.

TURNIP YARD. For the rocks protruding from the water like the tops of turnips.

TWO BUSH: CHANNEL, ISLAND (2), LEDGE, LITTLE-ISLAND, REEF. Descriptive of a small island.

UNION: EAST-, NORTH-, settlement, SOUTH-, TOWNSHIP . For the people's forming a union to incorporate.

VARMAH CREEK. For H. Vannah, who lived near. The spelling is a cartographical error.

VAUGHN NECK. Probably for Joseph Vaughn, settler before 1800.

VINAL: COVE, -HAVEN ISLAND, -HAVEN (settlement), -HAVEN TOWNSHIP. For John Vinal, Boston merchant who helped many of the settlers get clear titles to their land.

WARREN: EAST-, settlement, SOUTH-STATION, TOWNSHIP. For General Joseph Warren, who fell at Bunker Hill.

WASHINGTON: BROOK, POND, settlement, TOWNSHIP, WEST-. For General George Washington.

WASH LEDGE. Because the sea washes over it.

WATERMAN: BEACH, POINT. For Winslow Waterman, owner in 1861.

WATERMAN COVE. For the Waterman family who settled about 1765.

WATTONS MILL. For Charles F. Watton, millowner after 1862.

WATTS: COVE, POINT. For Captain Samuel and John Watts, early settlers.

WESBSTER HEAD. For the Webster family that settled about 1765.

WENTWORTH CORNERS. For Benjamin Wentworth, Sr., who settled here with his family.

WENTWORTH MOUNTAIN. For Betty Wentworth, daughter of an early settler.

WESKEAG RIVER. A shorter form of a longer Abnaki word: "tidal creek at the peninsula."

WESTERN BIGHT. Descriptive. A "bight" is a bend or curve in a shoreline.

WESTERN LEDGE. Descriptive.

WEST: PENOBSCOT BAY, POINT. Descriptive.

WHALEBACK. Descriptive of shape.

WHARTON ISLAND. For the Watton family who once lived there. When the surveyor heard it pronounced, he probably thought it to be the local pronunciation of "Wharton."

WHEAT ISLAND. Cartographical mistake for Weed Island.

WHEATON ISLAND. Unknown.

WHEELER: BAY, BIG ROCK. For William Wheeler, early landowner.

WHITE: ISLANDS, LEDGE, -HEAD ISLAND, -HORSE ISLAND. Descriptive of limestone formations.

WHITEOAK: CORNER, POND. For whiteoak trees.

WHITNEY CORNER. For John Whitney, settler, 1819.

WIDOW ISLAND. For the widow of Thomas Winslow, who lived there.

WIGGINS ROCK. For the early Wiggins family.

WILDRAKE BEACH. For wildrakes.

WILEY CORNER. For the local Wiley family.

WILEY HILL. For Joseph Wiley, who lived here about 1880.

WILSON: COVE, HEAD. For Robert Wilson, settler by 1850.

WINTER HARBOR. For being a harbor that seldom froze.

WOLSGRAVE ISLAND. For Charles Wolfgrover, who lived there.

WOOD COVE. For its location on Wooden Ball Island.

WOODEN BALL ISLAND. For the highest point on the island that is shaped like a knob, or ball, and was covered with trees at one time.

WOOSTER COVE. For the Wooster family who settled about 1765.

YELLOW: LEDGE (2), RIDGE ISLAND, ROCK. Descriptive of color.

YORK ISLAND. For Benjamin York, first settler and owner.

YOUNG POINT. (2). In Matinicus Isle Township, for the early Young family. In Vinalhaven Township, for Samuel Young, early settler.

ZEKE POINT. For Ezekiel Calderwood.

ZEKES LOOKOUT. Unknown.

ZEPHER LEDGES. For the winds or "zephers" that blow there.

LINCOLN COUNTY

ADAMS POND. For Samuel Adams, settler and millowner, 1768.

ALBEE HIGH HEAD. For the early settling Albee family.

ALFORD BROOK Unknown.

ALNA: CENTER, settlement, TOWNSHIP. For its earlier name Alno, from the Latin *alnus*, "alder trees."

APPLACHIE POND. Probably Old Abnaki: "bare place, devoid of trees."

ARK, THE. A rock shaped somewhat like the biblical ark.

BACK: BROOK, COVE, MEADOW BROOK, NARROWS (settlement), RIVER, RIVER COVE. Descriptive.

BAILEY POINT. For 6 generations of the Bailey family who have lived there.

BAR ISLAND. Descriptive.

BARTERS ISLAND. For the Samuel Barter family, who settled there about 1755-56.

BARTLETT POINT. For Joel Bartlett, settler, 1857.

BAYVILLE. Descriptive.

BEAVER: -DAM BROOK, ISLAND. For beavers.

BEECH HILL. For beech trees.

BEN BROOK. Unknown.

BENNER: BROOK, CORNER, HILL. For John Henry Benner, a German immigrant in 1753.

BENNETT NECK. Unknown.

BERRY ISLAND. For blueberries.

BIRCH: ISLAND, POINT. For birch trees.

BISCAY POND. Unknown.

BLACK: BROOK, HEAD. Descriptive.

BLINN HILL. For David Blenn, early settler who bought the hill in 1794.

BODGE HILL. For the Bodge family, early settlers.

BOGUES CORNER. For the Bogue family.

BOOTHBAY: CENTER, EAST-, HARBOR, HARBOR (settlement), HARBOR TOWNSHIP, TOWNSHIP, WEST-HARBOR. In 1764 the local settlers petitioned to be incorporated as Townsend Township, but one already existed in Massachusetts. The story is told that the agent sent with the petition was asked by the legislative committee, when attempting to decide upon a new name, about the geography of the place. He said they had a harbor that was "snug as a booth." On his replying "Yes" to the question, "Do you have a bay?" the committee named it "Boothbay." The explanation smacks of folklore.

BOOT NECK. Descriptive of shape.

BOSTON ISLAND. Because it was owned by summer residents from Boston.

BOYD POND. For James Boyd, settler before 1766.

BRADSTREET COVE. Unknown.

BRANCH, THE. Descriptive.

BRANN BROOK. For the Brann family, settlers, early 1800's.

BREMEN: LONG ISLAND, TOWNSHIP. For Bremen, Germany.

BRIAR COVE. For a man named Briar.

BRISTOL: MILLS, SOUTH-, TOWNSHIP, WEST-. For Bristol, England.

BROAD: COVE, COVE (settlement). Descriptive.

BROOKS: COVE, POINT (settlement). For Charles Stockbridge Brooks, early settler.

BROOKS TURNER HILL. Unknown.

BROWNS: COVE, HEAD COVE. For John Brown, who bought much of the area in 1639 from the Indians.

BRYANT ISLAND. For the Bryant family, settlers about 1776.

BULLDOG, THE. Fancifully named.

BUNKER HILL. Unknown.

BURNHAM COVE. For the Solomon Burnham family, settlers before 1800.

BURNT: HEAD, ISLAND. Descriptive.

BUTTER POINT. Unknown.

CABBAGE ISLAND. For a man named Holbrook who grew cabbages there for the Boston market.

CALL HILL. For Philip and Obadiah Call, the first settlers.

CAMERON POINT. For the Daniel Cameron family, settlers, 1758.

CAMPBELL CREEK. Not for the Campbell family of about 1791, for the creek is mentioned by name before that.

CAPE: HARBOR, ISLAND. Descriptive of location.

CAPE NEWAGEN. Abnaki: part of a long word meaning "route across the land." The "cape" is not English but folk etymology of the Abnaki "kep."

CAPITOL ISLAND. Selected only for its better sound than the former Pig Cove, by summer residents.

CARD: COVE, LEDGE. For the Card family.

CARLISLE: ISLAND, POINT. For Josephus Carlisle, settler, between 1767-70.

CARLTON BROOK. For S.C. and William Carlton, residents, 1857.

CAT LEDGE. Fancifully named. Nearby are some small rocks, not listed on the map, but called by the natives "The Kittens."

CAVIS POINT. Unknown.

CEDAR: -BUSH ISLAND, GROVE. For cedar trees.

CHAMBERLAIN. Possibly for the William Chamberlain family, settlers about 1800.

CHEWONKI: COVE, NECK. Abnaki: "a great bend."

CHRISTMAS: COVE (3), COVE (settlement). On Monhegan Island, legend says for Captain John Smith, who supposedly spent Christmas day, 1614, here. In South Bristol Township, one source states for Norsemen spending the Christmas of 1014 here. In Southport Township, one source says called Little Christmas Cove locally to distinguish it from Christmas Cove, South Bristol Township. (It is likely all of these are confused and to some extent erroneous. There are other sources which contradict them.)

CLAM ISLAND. For clams.

CLARK COVE. For Clark, the earliest settler in the area.

CLARY LAKE. For the Robert Cleary family, among the 12 first settlers.

CLOUGH POINT. For Captain Samuel Clough, master of the merchantman "The Sally," who was supposed to rescue Marie Antoinnette from France, but she was beheaded first.

COD COVE. For cod fish.

COLBY COVE. For Captain William Colby, settler in the 1800's.

COLLECTOR LEDGE. For being a dangerous ledge which "collected" fishermen's traps and boats.

COOKS POND. For the Cook family who lived there after the Revolution.

COOMBS: COVE, LEDGE. Probably for the Joshua Coombs family, settlers before 1790.

COOPERS MILLS. For Leonard Cooper, settler, about 1833.

CORDWOOD HILL. For cordwood cut there.

CORK COVE. For the name of the first verified attempted settlement in Dresden Township, 1718, named for County Cork, Ireland, the home of some of the settlers.

COTTAGE POINT. For cottages.

COURTHOUSE POINT. For the old courthouse built there in the 1760's.

COW: ISLAND, ISLAND DRY LEDGE, ISLAND LEDGES. For cows kept there.

COWSEAGAN NARROWS. Malecite: "rough rocks."

CRANBERRY LEDGE. For cranberries.

CROCKER HILL. Unknown.

CROSS: POINT, RIVER. Because it forms a cross where it crosses the north end of Barters Island between the Sheepscot and Back rivers. Others say for being a cross-over from the Sheepscot River to Back River.

CROTCH ISLAND. Descriptive.

CROW ISLAND. (2). For crows.

CRUMMETT: BROOK, MOUNTAIN. For the ancestors of Orrin Crummett.

CUCKOLDS, THE. For being rocks which have deluded sailors into hitting them.

CUNNINGHAM ISLAND. For the John Cunningham family, settlers, 1733.

CUSHMAN: COVE, HILL. For Kenelm Cushman, settler by 1813.

DAMARISCOTTA: LAKE, MILLS, RIVER, settlement, TOWN-SHIP. Abnaki: "plenty of alewives."

DAMARISCOVE ISLAND. A shortened form of Damarills Cove, named for Humphrey Damarill, seaman resident about 1614.

DAVID ISLAND. For David Pierce, settler in West Southport between 1764-69. This island and another, Pratts, guard the entrance to Hendricks Harbor. Pratts was formerly called Joe Island for Joseph Pierce, brother of David.

DAVIS CORNER. For the local Davis family.

DAVIS ISLAND. For George Davis, settler, the 1600's.

DAVIS POINT. For S. Davis, resident by 1857.

DAVIS STREAM. For the Davis family.

DAYS COVE. For the Day Ship Yard located there.

DEADMAN COVE. For two bodies found in the water there in the 19th century.

DEEP COVE. Descriptive.

DEER: MEADOW BROOK, MEADOW POND. For deer.

DEMUTH: BROOK, HILL. For the Johannes Heinrich Demuth family, settlers about 1754.

DODGE: LOWER COVE, POINT, UPPER COVE. For the Colonel Paul D. Dodge Family, settlers, 1733, and the later Dodge Brickyard.

DODGE POND. For Arthur Dodge, who had a shingle mill there.

DOGFISH HEAD. For dogfish.

DOVER. For Dover, New Hampshire, former home of many of the settlers.

DRESDEN: MILLS, SOUTH-, TOWNSHIP, WEST-. For Dresden, Germany, because, some say, an honored ex-Hessian doctor, Dr. Theobald, was from there.

DRY POINT. Descriptive.

DUCK: INNER-ROCK, ROCKS, -SPUDDLE POND. For ducks.

DUTCH NECK. For an English mispronunciation of what the early German settlers called themselves, "Deutsch."

DYER: HILL, LITTLE-POND, RIVER. For the Christopher Dyer family, among the earliest settlers.

EASTERN: BRANCH, BROOK, DUCK ROCK, RIVER. Descriptive.

EAST NECK. Descriptive.

EBENECOOK HARBOR. Abnaki: "opens out behind the entrance place."

EDDY, THE. Descriptive.

EDGECOMB: EAST-, FORT-, NORTH-, settlement, TOWNSHIP. For Lord Edgecomb, a friend of the American colonies.

EUGLEY CORNER. For Hudson Eugley, who ran a general store.

EUGLEY HILL. For the Bernhardt Eugley family, settlers in 1752.

FARMERS ISLAND. For farming operations carried on there.

FARNHAM POINT. For Jonathon Farnham, settler before the Revolution.

FARNSWORTH: BROOK, POINT. For William Farnsworth, settler, 1760's.

FEYLERS CORNER. For the Gottfried Feyler family, settlers, 1742.

FINN BROOK. For Edward or James Finn, early settlers.

FISHERMAN: ISLAND, ISLAND PASSAGE. For fishermen.

FISH HAWK ISLAND. For fishhawks.

FISH POINT. For fish dried there by the early settlers before shipping them to Europe.

FITCH: COVE, POINT. For Jonas Fitch, settler, 1753.

FLANDERS CORNER. For the Flanders family who settled about 1781.

FLOOD POND. For M. Flood, resident, 1857.

FLYING PASSAGE. For a place where geese flew from one body of water to another.

FORT: ISLAND, POINT. For an old blockhouse and other earth and stone fortifications constructed during the War of 1812.

FOSSETTS COVE. For Alexander Fossett, settler, 1700's.

FOSTER ISLAND. For the Foster family who were in the area early.

FOSTER POINT. For Thomas Foster.

FOWLE: COVE, POINT. For Joshua Fowles, settler by 1765.

FOXBIRD ISLAND. Unknown.

FRENCH POND. For John Henry French, who had a lumber mill.

GALL ROCK. A cartographer's mistake for "Gull Rock," for sea gulls.

GARDINER POND. Probably for John Gardiner, settler about 1760.

GEM ISLAND. Descriptive.

GIVENS POND. For the early Givens family.

GLENDON: settlement, STATION. Unknown.

GOOSEBERRY ISLAND. For gooseberries.

GOOSE: ROCK, ROCK PASSAGE. For geese.

GREAT BAY. Descriptive.

GREEN ISLAND. For a rich cornfield fertilized by gull droppings.

GREEN: ISLANDS, POINT (2). Descriptive.

GREENLAND COVE. One source says it is descriptive.

GREENLEAF COVE. For Stephen Greenleaf, settler, 1743.

GROSS: NECK, POND. For the John Martin Gross family, settlers in 1753.

GUT, THE. A term descriptive of a narrow passage.

HADDOCK ISLAND. For haddock fish.

HAGGETT HILL. For the early Haggett family.

HALFTIDE LEDGE. Descriptive.

HALL POINT. For Hall, early resident shoemaker.

HARDY ISLAND. Unknown.

HARPERS ISLAND. Unknown.

HARRINGTON CORNER. For the Harrington family who settled about the time of the Revolution.

HASKELL HILL. For the Haskell family who settled about 1800.

HASTINGS POND. For William Hastings, resident, 1857.

HATCHS CORNER. For the many descendants of David, Reuben, and Eben Hatch, settlers before 1800.

HAVENER: COVE, LEDGE, POINT. For Charles Heavner, settler 1752.

HAY ISLAND. For hay.

HEAD TIDE. Descriptive of location.

HEAL: COVE, POND. For David Heal, early settler.

HEATH POINT. Descriptive.

HENDRICKS: HARBOR, HARBOR (settlement), HEAD. Possibly for Hendricks, prominent Mohawk chief who was a delegate to a conference in Portland.

HERON: INNER-ISLAND, ISLAND, OUTER-ISLAND, OUTER-IS-LAND LEDGE. For herons.

HIBBERTS GORE. For the T. Hibbert family, residents, 1857.

HIGH: HEAD, ISLAND. Descriptive.

HILLTON POINT. For the early Hilton family.

HILTON COVE. For William Hilton, who had a tide mill there after 1754.

HOCKOMOCK: CHANNEL, POINT. Abnaki: possibly "place of palisades made of sharp logs driven in ground."

HODGDON: COVE, ISLAND. For the Thomas and William Hodgdon families, settlers, early 1800's.

HODGSONS ISLAND. For Hodson, the man who ran Hodson Mills in East Boothbay.

HOE ISLAND. For an early German settler named "Hoch," whose name would be pronounced like "hoe." Another says that it is descriptive of its shape. Another says that an Indian gave a settler the island for repairing his hoe.

HOFFSE POINT. For the Matthias Hoffse family, settlers 1751-52.

HOG: ISLAND (2), ISLAND BAR, ISLAND LEDGE. For being used as hog pens.

HOLLIS POINT. For the local Hollis family.

HOPKINS HILL. For the Hopkins family who ran a stable there.

HORN POND. Descriptive of shape.

HOWARD HILL. For Joshua Howard, settler 1769, Revolutionary War veteran.

HUBBARD POINT. Probably for the family of Daniel Hubbard, early settler.

HUNGRY ISLAND. Because the settlers found it poor farmland.

HUNT HILL. Unknown.

HUNTING ISLAND. For duck hunting.

HUSTONS BAY. For the James Huston family, settlers, 1730.

HYPOCRITES, THE. For a mispronunciation of the former name of Fishermans Island, "Hippocras," which was folk etymology for its former name of "Epituse": Abnaki, "it lies in the water." The name was transferred from the island to the rocks.

INDIAN: ISLAND, -TOWN ISLAND. For the Indians who formerly inhabited them.

ISLE OF SPRINGS. Descriptive, named in 1887 for promotional purposes.

JACKS POINT. Unknown.

JAMES POND. For a man named James who drowned there.

JEFFERSON: NORTH-, settlement, SOUTH-, TOWNSHIP. For Thomas Jefferson, third President of the U.S.

JEWETT: COVE, POINT. For the James Jewett family, settlers by 1767.

JIMS: ISLAND, ISLAND LEDGE. Unknown.

JOHNS: BAY, ISLAND, RIVER. Some say because on a map of 1614 the name of Sir John Towne is placed near here. Another says for John Smith, first accurate mapper of the area.

JOHNSON: HILL, ISLAND. For the ancestors of W. Johnson, resident, 1857.

JONES CORNER. For Tom Jones, who ran a grocery store there.

JONES: COVE, POINT. For A. Jones, resident, 1857.

JONES GARDEN ISLAND. Possibly for William Jones, settler, 1700's.

JONES HILL. Possibly for Jonathon Jones, early area settler.

JONES: NECK, POINT. For the Jones family, one of the earliest, about 1680.

JUNIPER POINT. For juniper trees.

KALERS: CORNER, POND. For the Johannes Koehler family, settlers, 1753.

KEENE: NARROWS, NECK. For the early Keene family.

KEHAIL POINT. For Henry Kehail, early settler.

KELSEY POINT. For the Kelsey family who lived there.

KENNEDY CORNER. For Nathaniel Kennedy, son of an early settler.

KENNISTON HILL. For David Kenniston, settler about 1785.

KERR POND. Unknown.

KEYES CORNER. Unknown.

KILLICK STONE ISLAND. Because stones could be obtained here for anchors. A "killickstone" is an anchor stone.

KNICKERBOCKER LAKES. Owned by the Knickerbocker Ice Company for ice-cutting purposes.

KNOWLES ROCKS. Unknown.

KNOWLTON CORNER. For the Knowlton family who lived in a corner of Back Meadows.

KNUBBLE BAY. Descriptive.

LABRADOR MEADOW. An area of bog land that has a rich growth of moss. The local fishermen who went to the Grand Banks off Labrador in the 1800's saw tundra of the same type moss and named it, when they returned, for its resemblance.

LEHMAN ISLAND. For the Captain John Lermond family.

LEVENSALER BROOK. For the John Adam Levensaler family, settlers before 1753.

LEWIS COVE. For Allen Lewis, farmer before 1850.

LINCOLN COUNTY. For Governor Thomas Pownal, colonial governor of Massachusetts, whose home was Lincoln, England.

LINEKIN: BAY, NECK, settlement. For Benjamin Linekin, settler 1743.

LITTLE: FALLS BROOK, ISLAND, POINT, POND (2), RIVER. Descriptive.

LOBSTER: COVE, POINT. For lobsters.

LOCUST ISLAND. Some say for locust trees. Others for grasshoppers.

LONG: COVE (4), COVE POINT, ISLAND LEDGES, LEDGE POND. Descriptive.

LOOKOUT HILL. Descriptive of a tall hill that served as a lookout.

LOUDS ISLAND. For the many Louds being there.

LOUDVILLE. For the many Louds living there.

LOVE COVE. For George Love, early settler.

LOVEJOY NARROWS. For Captain Abiel Lovejoy, settler before 1800.

LOVEJOY STREAM. For Elijah Lovejoy, celebrated Abolitionist.

LOWER HELL GATE. For fast, dangerous water.

LOWER MARK ISLAND. Marks Sheepscot Bay.

LOWER POND. Descriptive.

LOWES COVE. For S.P. Low, resident, 1857.

MADDOCK COVE. For Palgrave Maddock, settler before 1800.

MANANA ISLAND. Abnaki: originally "Monanis," "the small island," and corrupted.

MANKS CORNER. For the George Mink family, German settlers in 1753.

MARRS HILL. For William Marr, resident, 1857.

MARSH: HARBOR, ISLAND, RIVER. For marshes.

McCARTY COVE. For James McCarty, early settler.

McCOBB HILL. For Samuel McCobb, settler about 1730.

McCURDY POND. Unknown.

McFARLANDS: COVE, POINT. For Solomon McFarland, early settler.

McFARLANDS ISLAND. For John M. McFarland, who had a fishery and store there, early 1800's.

McGUIRE POINT. For the early McGuire family.

McKOWN POINT. For William McKown, who lived here about 1800.

MEADOW: BROOK (2), COVE. For meadows.

MEARS COVE. For the Mears family.

MEDOMAK: LITTLE-POND, POND, RIVER, settlement. Abnaki: "place of many alewives."

MEETINGHOUSE COVE. For the Lutheran Church built there, 1762.

MERRILL COVE. For the Merrill family.

MERROW ISLAND. Possibly for Willard Merry, settler before 1850.

MERRY ISLAND. For Admiral John Merry, early settler.

MIDDLE: GROUND, LEDGES. Descriptive.

MILES ISLAND. For the Miles family.

MILL COVE. For a mill located there.

MILLER ISLAND. For the early Miller family.

MOLLYS HEAD. For Molly Casey, who ran an unlicensed tavern frequented by fishermen, early 1800's.

MONHEGAN: ISLAND, HARBOR, settlement, TOWNSHIP. Malecite, Micmac: "out to sea island."

MONTGOMERY POINT. For Robert Montgomery, settler by 1758.

MONTSWEAG: BAY, BROOK. Abnaki: "narrow, dugout channel."

MORANG COVE. For the Morang family, settlers about 1776.

MOSER LEDGE. Unknown.

MOTIONS, THE. Sunken ledges that can be detected by the motion of the sea.

MOUNT PISGAH. Named by the Reverend John Murray, whose parsonage was there, for the biblical Mount Pisgah.

MOUSE ISLAND. Descriptive of size.

MOXIE COVE. One source says for the Indian Chief Moxus.

MUDDY POND. Descriptive.

MUSCONGUS: BAY, HARBOR, settlement, SOUND. Abnaki: "many rock ledges."

MUSQUASH POND. Abnaki: "reddish-brown animal (muskrat)."

NARROWS, THE. (2). Descriptive.

NEGRO ISLAND. One source says for a Negro who once lived there. Another says because it is heavily wooded with spruce, which look black from a distance.

NEQUASSETT BROOK. Abnaki: "at the pond."

NEWAGEN. For Cape Newagen.

NEWCASTLE: NORTH-, settlement, SOUTH-, SQUTH-STATION, TOWNSHIP. For the Duke of Newcastle, principal secretary to the King and a friend of the colonists.

NEW: HARBOR, HARBOR (settlement), HARBOR DRY LEDGES. Descriptive.

NOBLEBORO: settlement, STATION, TOWNSHIP. For James Noble, landholder. Others say for Colonel Arthur Noble, leader of the English forces killed attempting to drive the French from Nova Scotia in 1747.

NORRIS POINT. For Charles Norris, shipbuilder of Medcafe and Norris Shipyard.

NORTH BRANCH. Descriptive.

NORTON LEDGE. For Captain Ackley Norton, formerly of Addison Township, who left Maine for Palestine to teach the people better methods of farming.

OAK: HILL, ISLAND, LITTLE-ISLAND. For oak trees.

OCEAN: HARBOR, POINT. Descriptive.

ORFFS CORNER. For the Nicholas Orff family, settlers, 1752.

OVEN MOUTH. The Abnakis borrowed the word "oven" from the English and gave it a new pronunciation "abann" and the additional meaning of "bread." They applied the word to this passage as a descriptive term, and the whites adopted the name, re-anglicizing it to "oven."

OYSTER CREEK. For oysters.

PALMER HILL. For the local Palmer family.

PALMER ISLAND. For John Palmer, one of the survivors of an attack by the Canada, Norridgewock, and Penobscot Indians in October 1689.

PARADISE ISLAND. Descriptive name given by summer residents.

PARSONS CREEK. For Stephen Parson, who had a mill there prior to 1800.

PEABOW ISLAND. Unknown.

PEMAQUID: BEACH, HARBOR, LEDGE, NECK, POINT, POINT (settlement), POND, RIVER, settlement. Micmac: "extended land."

PERCH ISLAND. For perch fish.

PERKINS POINT. For D.D., J., B., and R.D. Perkins, residents, 1857.

PETER MOUNTAIN. Unknown.

PETERS ISLAND. Unknown.

PIERCE COVE. For the Samuel Pierce family, settlers before the Revolution.

PIG COVE. Although it is not recorded, this cove was probably named for pigs raised there, as many other coves and islands so named were.

PINE CLIFF. For pine trees.

PINKHAM POND. For the Pinkham family, owners.

PITCHERS: COVE, POINT. For Nathaniel Pitcher, settler, 1760's.

PLEASANT COVE. Descriptive.

PLUMMER POINT. For the early Plummer family.

POLINS LEDGE. Unknown.

POOLS LANDING. For Isaac Poole, early settler.

POORHOUSE COVE. Unknown.

POTTLE COVE. For Azariah Pottle, early settler.

POWDERHORN ISLAND. Descriptive of shape when its ledges are included.

PRATTS ISLAND. For Ezra Pratt and his son Earl, who bought it in 1922 and built summer cottages on it.

PRENTISS ISLAND. For Captain Prentiss.

PROCKS LEDGE. For Peter Prock, German settler, 1751.

PUMPKIN: COVE, ISLAND, ISLAND NORTHEAST LEDGE, LEDGES. Descriptive of shape.

QUARRY POINT. For a granite quarry located nearby.

RAM: ISLAND (3), LEDGES. For sheep kept on them.

REEDS ISLAND. For Benjamin Reed, former owner.

ROBINSON RIDGE. For the early settling Robinson family.

ROSS: ISLAND, POND. Unknown.

ROUND: POND, POND (settlement). Descriptive.

RUM COVE. While there is no record of it, this cove was probably used to smuggle rum into the U.S.

RUTHERFORD ISLAND. For the Reverend Robert Rutherford, resident, 1729, and chaplain to Governor Dunbar.

SALT BAY. For being the first bay of salt water after the fresh water of Damariscotta Lake. It was named to show the contrast of fresh and saltwater fish that could be taken in the respective areas.

SALT MARSH COVE. Descriptive.

SAMPSON COVE. For Captain Charles Samson, settler, 1769.

SANDHILL CORNER. Descriptive.

SASANOA RIVER. For Chief Sasano, Abnaki sachem in 1607, who met Samuel de Champlain.

SAWYER ISLAND. For Ebenezer Sawyer, settler about 1776.

SEAL: COVE, LEDGES, ROCK. For seals.

SHEEPSCOT: RIVER, settlement. Abnaki: "many rocky channels."

SHERMAN LAKE. For Fred L. Sherman, first selectman of Newcastle Township. When Route One was built in 1930 a marsh was flooded to form the lake.

SIDENSPARKER POND. For Mathias Seidensberger, settler, 1742.

SLAIGO BROOK. Unknown.

SMITH HILL. For the Seba Smith family, settlers before 1776.

SMUTTY NOSE ISLAND. Descriptive of a black point in surrounding lighter colored rock.

SOMERVILLE: settlement, TOWNSHIP. Unknown.

SOUTHPORT: ISLAND, settlement, TOWNSHIP, WEST-. For its southerly location in the county.

SPECTACLE ISLAND. (2). Descriptive of eyeglass shape.

SPRAGUES CORNER. For Nathan Sprague, settler just before the Revolution.

SPROUL POINT. For the early Sproul family.

SPRUCE: POINT, POINT LEDGES, SHORE. For spruce trees.

SQUAM CREEK. Westport Island was formerly known as "Jeremy Squam." "Squam" is Abnaki for "salmon."

SQUIRREL: COVE, ISLAND, ISLAND (settlement). For squirrels.

STEARNS POINT. For Amos Stearns, shoemaker and early settler.

TARBOX COVE. For Samuel and Ezekiel Tarbox, early settlers.

THIEF ISLAND. Unknown.

THOMAS HILL. For Anthony Thomas and his son Waterman, settlers, 1770.

THOMAS POINT. For J. Thomas, resident, 1857.

THREAD OF LIFE LEDGES. There is a very narrow ship's channel, "the thread of life," running between the ledges.

THREE CORNER POND. For its location near a 3-corner crossroads.

THRUMCAP: ISLAND (2), LEDGE. Descriptive of shape. A thrumcap is a sailor's homemade rope cap.

THURSTON POINT. For G. and W. Thurston, residents, 1857.

TIBBET ISLAND. For Nathaniel Tibbetts, settler about 1759.

TOBIAS POND. For the early Tobias family.

TOWNSEND GUT. For the former name of Boothbay Township, which was named for Lord Charles Townshend of England.

TRAINOR CORNER. Unknown.

TRAVEL: BROOK, POND. Unknown.

TREVETT. For Captain Joshua R. Trevett, born in Wiscassett Township.

TROUT BROOK. For trout fish.

TUMBLER ISLAND. Unknown.

TURNER POND. For Benjamin Turner, resident.

TURNERS CORNER. For Caleb Turner, resident, 1700's.

TURNIP ISLAND. Descriptive of shape.

TYLER: HILL, ISLANDS. For Samuel Tyler, settler before 1800.

UPPER MARK COVE. Because it marked a clear channel for about 4 miles up the Sheepscot River.

UPPER POND. Descriptive.

WADSWORTH COVE. For Deacon Wadsworth, who resided there.

WALDOBORO: NORTH-, settlement, SOUTH-, TOWNSHIP,

WEST-. For General Waldo, who served at the siege of Louisburg and helped the early settlers.

WALPOLE. One of three townships laid out and named for prominent Englishmen — Townsend, Harrington, and Walpole. Some say for Walpole, England.

WALTZ POINT. For Jacob Waltz, settler, mid-1700's.

WARD BROOK. For Nehemiah Ward, early 18th century settler.

WATERMAN BROOK. For the Abijah Waterman family, settlers, 1760's.

WEARY POND. A source states that this is a family name.

WEBBER: DRY LEDGE, SUNKEN LEDGE. For the Webber family, numerous in the area.

WEBBER POND. For the many Webbers in the area in 1857.

WEEKS HILL. For James Weeks, one of the first 12 settlers.

WENTWORTH POINT. Unknown.

WEST: BROOK (2), HARBOR POND, NECK. Descriptive.

WESTERN: BROOK, EGG ROCK. Descriptive.

WESTPORT: ISLAND, settlement, TOWNSHIP. Descriptive.

WHITEFIELD: NORTH-, settlement, TOWNSHIP. For George Whitefield, minister from England.

WHITE: HEAD, ISLANDS, POINT. Descriptive.

WHITTUM ISLAND. For Joseph Whittam, settler by 1765.

WILEY: BROOK, COVE, POINT. Probably for the Isaac Wiley family, settlers before 1790.

WILLETT HILL. For Thomas Willett, settler, 1797.

WINSLOW: HILL, MILLS. For the John Winslow family.

WISCASSETT: settlement, TOWNSHIP. Abnaki: "at the hidden outlet."

WITCH ISLAND. For Grace Courtland Chittenden. Purchased early 1900's by Daniel Chittenden and his wife as a summer home. They lived in New York where Mrs. Chittenden published a stock exchange paper. Her judgment and foresight on the stock market was so uncanny she was known as the "Witch of Wall Street."

WOODBRIDGE ISLAND. For Christopher Woodbridge, settler early 1800's.

WRECK: ISLAND, ISLAND LEDGES. For a ship wrecked here in the 1800's.

YOUNG POINT. Probably for John Young, settler about 1734.

OXFORD COUNTY

ABBIE POND. Unknown.

ABBOTT: BROOK (2), LITTLE-BROOK. In Lincoln Township, unknown. In Andover Township, for Jonathon and John Abbott, settlers before 1800.

ABBOTTS MILLS. For the many Abbotts in the area.

ABBOTTS POND. For James Abbott, early settler.

ACADEMY HILL. Because on a tract granted for the purpose of building an academy.

ADAMS MOUNTAIN. For the Adams family who cleared the area and operated a farm.

ADAMSTOWN TOWNSHIP. Unknown.

ALBANY: BASIN, BROOK, MOUNTAIN, NORTH, settlement, TOWNSHIP. For James Stuart, Duke of Albany and York, later King James II of England, who was granted this area in 1664.

ALDER: BROOK, RIVER. For alder trees.

ALDRICH LAKE. For Aldrich, a logger.

ALLEN BROOK. For the early Allen family who owned the land where the brook rises.

ALLEN HILL. (2). In Oxford Township, for Christopher and Samuel Allen, sons of an early settler. In Peru Township, for the early Allen family.

ALLEN MOUNTAIN. (2). In Denmark Township, for the early Allen family. In Peru Township, for Benjamin Allen, settler, 1847.

AMOS MOUNTAIN. For Amos Andrews, early settler.

ANDERSON BROOK. For the early Anderson family.

ANDOVER: EAST-, NORTH SURPLUS TOWNSHIP, settlement, SOUTH-, TOWNSHIP, WEST SURPLUS TOWNSHIP. For Old Andover, Massachusetts.

ANDREWS BROOK. For Ziba Andrews, millowner and early settler.

ANN BROOK. Unknown.

ASH BROOK. For ash trees.

AUNT HANNAH BROOK. For Aunt Hannah Mitchell, who owned a farm there with her husband.

AZISCOHOS: LAKE, LOW-MOUNTAIN, MOUNTAIN, POND. Abnaki: "small pine trees."

BACON HILL. For E.H. Bacon, resident, 1858.

BAD MOUNTAIN. One source says for a family named Bad who lived there. Another says for being a difficult mountain to climb.

BAILEY: BROOK, POINT. Unknown.

BAKER HILL. For Edward Baker, early settler.

BALD: BLUFF, LEDGE, LITTLE -PATE MOUNTAIN, MOUNTAIN (2), -PATE, -PATE MOUNTAIN, PEAK. Descriptive.

BAR, THE. Descriptive.

BARKER MOUNTAIN. For Benjamin Barker and his two brothers, who settled here first.

BARKER POND. (2). In Hiram Township, for Thomas Barker, who built a mill and dam there. In Bowman Township, unknown.

BARKERS BROOK. (2). In Bethel Township, for a group of Barker brothers who lived on the bank. In Albany Township, for the early settling Barker family.

BARKERS HIGH LEDGE. For Samuel Barker, early settler.

BARNES: BROOK. (2). In Hiram Township, for Henry W. Barnes, early settler. In Newry Township, unknown.

BARNETT POND. For the Barnett family who took up residence here after the Paine family departed.

BARNEY BROOK. Unknown.

124

BARRETT. For Simon Barrett, early settler.

BARTLETT BROOK. For Jonathon Bartlett.

BARTLETT HILL. For Malachi or John Bartlett, early settlers.

BASIN: FALLS, FALLS BROOK. Descriptive.

BATCHELDERS GRANT TOWNSHIP. For Richard Batchelder, the original grantee.

BAY: LOWER-, UPPER-. Descriptive.

B: BROOK, BROOK COVE, EAST-HILL, POND. For location in Upton Township, formerly known as B Plantation.

BEAN MOUNTAIN. (2). In Milton Township, for the area Bean family who settled about 1800. In Newry Township, unknown.

BEAR: LITTLE-MOUNTAIN (2), LITTLE-POND, MOUNTAIN (2), POND (2), RIVER. For bears. Bear Mountain in Waterford Township, specifically for a bear killed while trying to swim a nearby pond.

BEAVER: BIG-ISLAND, BROOK (7), ISLAND, LITTLE-POND, POND (3), POND BROOK, WEST-BROOK. For beavers.

BEECH HILL. For beech trees.

BELL MOUNTAIN. For the Bell family, settlers about 1815.

BEN BARROWS HILL. For Ben Barrows, son of an early settler.

BENNETT BROOK. For the Bennett family who settled before 1776.

BENSON HILL. For the early Benson family, farmers.

BEREAU BROOK. Unknown.

BERRY LEDGE. For William Berry, early settler.

BERRY POND. For the early Berry family.

BETHEL: EAST-, NORTH-, NORTHWEST-, settlement, TOWN-SHIP, WEST-. Named by the Reverend Chapman, for the frequent biblical name, "Bethel."

BICKFORD BROOK. For the early Bickford family.

BICKFORD POND. For Benjamin Bickford, settler, 1787.

BICKNELL BROOK. For the early Bicknell family.

BIG: BROOK, NORTH FORK-BROOK. Descriptive.

BIG BUCK MOUNTAIN. For a big buck deer killed there in the 19th century.

BIG: CANYON, FALLS. Descriptive.

BIGELOW POND. Unknown.

BILLINGS HILL. For John Billings, who lived here.

BILLINGS PONDS. For Billings, member of the Parmanchenee Club.

BILL MERRILL MOUNTAIN. For William Merrill, trapper and hunter, who froze to death there.

BILLY BROOK. For Uncle Billy, an old man who formerly lived there.

BIRCH: BROOK (2), HILL (2), ISLAND (2), POINT, POND. For brich trees.

BIRD: BROOK, POND. For the Bird family who lived there by 1797.

BISCO FALLS. For Josiah Bisco, surveyor, 1772.

BLACK: BROOK (4), BROOK COVE, BROOK NOTCH, LOWER-POINT, MOUNTAIN (5), POINT (2), POND (2), UPPER-POND. Descriptive.

BLACK: CAT BROOK, -CAT BROOK, CAT MOUNTAIN, NORTH BRANCH-CAT BROOK, SOUTH BRANCH-CAT BROOK. For the black cat, woodsmen's name for the fisher.

BLAKE ISLAND. For the early Blake family.

BLUEBERRY: ISLAND, MOUNTAIN. For blueberries.

BOBBY BROOK. For Bobby, son of an early settler.

BOB GOULD HILL. For Robert Gould, resident.

BOG: BROOK (6), POND. Descriptive.

BOGG BROOK. A cartographical error for "Bog Brook." Descriptive.

BOND ISLAND. For Jonas Bond, early owner.

BOSEBUCK MOUNTAIN. Abnaki: "at the outlet of the spread out stream."

BOSTON: HILLS, POND, For Daniel Boston, settler, 1775.

BOTTLE MOUNTAIN. Unknown.

BOULDER BROOK. For a large rock that marks the sight of John Lovewell's battle with the Indians.

BOWMAN: HILL, PONDS, TOWNSHIP. For the Bowman family who farmed there.

BRADLEY: BROOK (2), POND. Brook in Stow Township, for the Bradley family who lived nearby. Brook and Pond in Lovell Township, for the Bradley family who owned the surrounding timberland.

BRANCH BROOK. Descriptive.

BRANDY POINT. Unknown.

BRETT HILL. For the early Brett family.

BRIDGTON JUNCTION. For Bridgton, Cumberland County.

BRIGHAM LEDGE. For the Luther Brigham family, early settlers.

BRIGHTON HILL. When cattle were collected for market, this was the point of assembly. Their destination was the abattoir at Brighton, Massachusetts.

BRIMSTONE CORNER. The location of a church where "fire and brimstone" was preached.

BROADVIEW. Descriptive.

BROKEN BRIDGE POND. For an old, decrepit bridge which crossed the pond outlet.

BROWNFIELD: EAST-, settlement, STATION, TOWNSHIP, WEST-. For Captain Henry Y. Brown, grantee, for his service in the French and Indian War.

BROWN: HILL (2), LEDGE. Hill and Ledge in Albany Township, for Daniel Brown, an 1830 landowner. Hill in Norway Township, for the local Brown family.

BROWN MOUNTAIN. For Aunt Hepsey Brown, an early settler.

BROWNS ISLAND. Unknown.

BRUSH MOUNTAIN. Descriptive.

BRYANT HILL. For Christopher Bryant, settler, 1798.

BRYANT MOUNTAIN. For A. and M. Bryant, residents, 1858.

BRYANT: POND, POND (settlement). For Christopher and Soloman Bryant.

BUCKFIELD: EAST-, NORTH-, settlement, TOWNSHIP. For Abijah Buck, early settler.

BUCK: ISLAND, MEADOW BROOK. For buck deer.

BUCKS LEDGE. For John Buck, early settler from Buckfield Township.

BULL: BRANCH, MOUNTAIN. Unknown.

BULL BROOK. For a logging team of bullocks.

BULL ROCK. For a bull that fell off the rock into a deep crevice.

BUNGANOCK: BROOK, POND. Abnaki: "at the boundary place."

BUNKER: MOUNTAIN, POND. For John Bunker.

BURBANK POND. For John Burbank, Revolutionary War veteran, who settled in 1788.

BURGESS HILL. For Seth Burgess and his son Samuel, early settlers.

BURNELL HILL. For the Samuel Burnell family, settlers by 1819.

BURNT: HILL, MEADOW BROOK, MEADOW MOUNTAINS, MEADOW POND, MOUNTAIN. Descriptive.

BURROUGHS BROOK. For the local Burroughs family.

BUTTERS MOUNTAIN. For the Butters family who cleared the land for a farm.

BYRON: settlement, TOWNSHIP. For George Gordon, Lord Byron, who died nine years before the incorporation.

CABBAGE YARD POND. Unknown.

CALDWELL CORNER. Probably for the John Caldwell family, settlers, 1783.

CAMPBELL BROOK. For the early Campbell family.

CAMPBELL HILL. For the local Campbell family.

CAMPBELL MOUNTAIN. Unknown.

CANTON: MOUNTAIN, POINT, settlement, TOWNSHIP. For Canton, Massachusetts.

CARIBOU: MOUNTAIN, POND. For caribou.

CARR MOUNTAIN. For Elbridge Gary Carr, resident.

CARRY RIDGE. For a shortcut from Lower Richardson Lake to Umbagog Lake where one had to carry his canoe over this ridge.

CARTER HILL. (2). In Fryeburg Township, probably for Ezra Carter, early proprietor. In Norway Township, for James Carter, settler, 1839.

CARY HILL. For Dr. Bethel Cary, first settler.

CATARACTS, THE. Descriptive.

CAT POND. For blackcats (fishers).

C: BLUFF, BLUFF MOUNTAIN, POND, SURPLUS TOWNSHIP. For extra land from Township C.

CECIL MOUNTAIN. For Cecil, daughter of E. Lester Jones, director of the U.S. Coast and Geodetic Survey, who owned land nearby.

CEDAR BROOK. For cedar trees.

CHALK POND. (2). For chalk rock.

CHAMBERLAIN MOUNTAIN. Possibly a cartographical error, for a W. Chandler lived there in 1858.

CHANDLER BROOK. For Jeremiah Chandler, settler, 1782.

CHAPMAN BROOK. (2). In Newry Township, for the local Chapman family. In Riley Township, unknown.

CHAPMAN POND. For Abraham Chapman, one of the first settlers.

CHARLES: POND, RIVER. For the large Charles family who settled before 1800.

CHASE BROOK. For Skipper Chase, who had run away from some kind of unknown duty.

CHASE HILL BROOK. For the Chase family who owned the land it crossed.

CHILDS BROOK. For the Childs family who settled there in 1821.

CHILDS HILL. For William Child, early settler.

CHRISTIAN HILL. For the early residents here, who were very religious. People referred to them as "those Christians on the hill."

CLARK BROOK. For the Clark family, settlers by 1880.

CLAYS POND. For the Clay family, early settlers.

CLEARWATER BROOK. Descriptive.

CLEMONS: LITTLE-POND, POND. For John Clemons and family, settlers, 1779.

CLEVELAND POND. Unknown.

CLOUGH HILL. For the Clough family who settled here early.

COBB BROOK. For William Cobb, Revolutionary War veteran and early settler.

COBBLE HILL. Descriptive.

COBURN BROOK. For the early Coburn family.

COFFIN BROOK. For the Coffin family, large landholders.

COLCORD POND. For Davis, Phineas, and Jesse Colcord.

COLD: BROOK (5), LITTLE-RIVER, RIVER. Descriptive.

COLE BROOK. (2). In Brownfield Township, because it flowed through an area called Coleville for the many Cole families. In Paris Township, probably for Eleazer Cole, settler by 1798.

COLONEL HOLMAN MOUNTAIN. For Colonel Jonathon Holman, first proprietor.

COLTEN: BROOK, HILL. For the Colton family who first settled there.

CONCORD: LITTLE-POND, POND, RIVER, WEST BRANCH-RIVER. Unknown.

COON HOLLOW. For raccoons.

CRANBERRY: COVE, POND. For cranberries.

CREEPER HILL. For Greeber ("Creeper") Johnson.

CROCKER HILL. For Thomas Crocker, settler, 1808.

CROCKETT RIDGE. For Ephraim Crockett, who first settled there.

CROOKED RIVER. Descriptive.

CUMMINGS HILL. For Joseph Cummings, early settler.

CUMMINGS MOUNTAIN. For Deacon Asa Cummings, settler, 1798.

CUPSUPTIC: EAST BRANCH-RIVER, LAKE, LITTLE EAST BRANCH-RIVER, LOWER-TOWNSHIP, MOUNTAIN, POND, RIVER, UPPER-TOWNSHIP. Abnaki: "a closed up stream."

CURTIS HILL. Probably for the Noah Curtiss family, first settlers in Woodstock Township.

CUSHMAN BROOK. For Gideon Cushman, settler, 1781.

CUSHMAN: HILL, POND (2). In Lovell Township, for Dr. Joseph Cushman, first doctor in Lovell village. In Sumner Township, for Isaiah and Andrew Cushman, early settlers.

DAMON HILL. For the early Damon family.

DAN CHARLES POND. For Daniel Charles, resident, 1858.

DARNIT BROOK. For an old man who lived close by whose byword was "darn it."

DAVIS MOUNTAIN. Probably for Aron Davis, who settled from Salem, Massachusetts, in 1816.

DAVIS POND. For Robert Davis, who lived nearby.

DAYS RIDGE. For Hiram Day, owner.

DEACON PINNACLE. For Deacon Increase Robinson, the first settler there.

DEAD CAMBRIDGE RIVER. For its slow flowage and because it flowed through Cambridge, New Hampshire.

DEAD LAKE. Descriptive of flow.

DEAN BROOK. For Charles Dean.

DEAN HILL. For the Henry Chase Dean family.

DEER: BROOK, HILL (3), HILL SPRING, LITTLE-HILL, MOUNTAIN, MOUNTAIN STREAM, POND. For deer.

DENMARK: EAST-, settlement, TOWNSHIP, WEST-. One source says just prior to its naming, Danish seamen had fought Lord Nelson of England, and it was named in honor of their bravery, since there was no great love for the British. Another says that it was a promotional name, in hopes of attracting European settlement. Yet another says that an early settler named Mark lived there and called his home the "Den of Mark." All these derivations are questionable. Probably it was named for a foreign nation just because it was a custom of the time.

DENNISON BOG. Unknown.

DEVILS DEN. One source states that during storms people have heard strange noises coming from this cave and assumed it must be the devil making them. Another states that it was for the trick played on his guests by a proprietor of a local resort. When they started to enter the cave where he had hidden, he made a great noise with washboards, chains, and cowbells. They thought it was the devil and fled.

DICKVALE. For its proximity to Tumbledown Dick Mountain.

DIXFIELD: CENTER, settlement, TOWNSHIP. For Dr. Elijah Dix, who agreed to give the town a library if they would name it for him.

DOCK BROOK. For Doc, one of several men who went smelting there. He, being drunk on hard cider, fell into the creek, so they named it for him.

DOLLAR ISLAND. Descriptive of round shape.

DOLLY MOUNTAIN. Unknown.

DOTEN HILL. For Timothy Doten, early settler.

DOWNS HILL. For the early Downs family.

DRAGON MEADOW BROOK. For dragonflies.

DRESSER MOUNTAIN. For the early Dresser family.

DREW BROOK. For Stephen Drew, early settler.

DUCK: POND, POND BROOK. For ducks.

DUNHAM BROOK. For the Eleazer Dunham family, settlers, 1799.

DUNHAM HILL. Unknown.

DUNN LEDGE. For the early Dunn family.

DUNN NOTCH. For the Henry Dunn family, who lived here in the last half of the 19th century.

DURGIN BROOK. For J. and J., Jr., Durgin, residents, 1858.

DURGIN MOUNTAIN. For Levi Durgin, one of 6 very early settlers.

DURGINTOWN. For Samuel, Joseph, and David Durgin, holders of the Durgin Grant, who settled in 1809.

DURRELL HILL. One source says for Peter Durrell, one of the original grantees. Another says for David Durrell, earliest settler.

DYER POND. For the early Dyer family.

EAST: BRANCH, PEAK. Descriptive.

EASTMAN HILL. (2). In Lovell Township, for Noah Eastman, settler, 1789. In Paris Township, for Horatio Eastman, settler, mid-1800's.

EAST ROYCE MOUNTAIN. For West Royce Mountain in Beans Purchase Township, New Hampshire.

EDGECOMB HILL. For the Edgecomb family.

EDMUNDS BOG BROOK. For Benjamin Edmunds, early settler.

ELEPHANT MOUNTAIN. Descriptive of shape.

ELIZABETH MOUNTAIN. For Elizabeth, daughter of E. Lester Jones, director of the U.S. Coast and Geodetic Survey, who owned land in the area.

ELKINS BROOK. For the early Elkins family.

ELLINGWOOD MOUNTAIN. For Jacob Ellingwood, the first settler there.

ELLIS FALLS. Unknown.

ELLIS: LITTLE-POND, POND. For the early Ellis family.

ELLIS: RIVER, WEST BRANCH-RIVER. The outlet of Roxbury Pond, formerly called Ellis Pond.

ELM HILL. For elm trees.

ELWELL MOUNTAIN. For Sam Elwell, who operated a farm at its foot.

EMERY HILL. For A. and P. Emery, residents, 1858.

EMERYS MISERY. For a man named Emery, who attempted to log this very steep mountain. About everything that could happen to a logging operation happened to him that winter.

EVANS: BROOK, NOTCH. One source says for the Amos Evans family, settlers, 1832. Another says for an Evans who came down this brook to repel an Indian attack on Shelbourne, New Hampshire.

EVANS HILL. For the local Evans family.

EVANS LEDGE. Unknown.

FAIRVIEW HILL. Descriptive.

FALLS, THE. Descriptive.

FARMERS HILLS. For a Mr. Abbott, who cleared and farmed the area about 1800.

FARRINGDON MOUNTAIN. Unknown.

FARRINGTON HILL. Because it was cleared and farmed by the Farrington family.

FARRINGTON ISLAND. Unknown.

FARRINGTON POND. For John Farrington of North Cambridge, Massachusetts, who built a grist and sawmill here.

FARWELL MOUNTAIN. (2). Both of the mountains were named for Absalom Farwell, an early settler. He settled first near the mountain in Bethel Township and then moved to the mountain in Albany Township.

FESSENDEN HILL. For William Fessenden, first minister of the First Congregational Church of Fryeburg.

FIELDS HILL. For Joseph Fields, early settler.

FIGHT BROOK. The scene of Captain John Lovewell's fight with the Indians in May 1725, in which he and 9 of his men were killed while on a scalp-hunting expedition.

FIRST EAST BROOK. The first major brook running from the east on the Magalloway River.

FISH HILL. For the Fish family who lived there.

FISH POND BROOK. For fish.

FISH STREET. A section of road where the Old Channel of the Saco River looped around and made an eddy. The neighborhood supplied itself with fish from here.

FISK HILL. For the early Fisk family.

FLAT: -HEAD MOUNTAIN, HILL. Descriptive.

FLETCHER BROOK. For James Fletcher, early settler.

FLINTS: BROOK, MOUNTAIN. For James Flint, settler, 1803.

FOREST POND. Descriptive.

FORK HILL. Cartographical mistake for Fox Hill, for foxes.

FOSTER HILL. (2). In Lovell Township, for the Foster family, settlers, mid 1800's. In Stoneham Township, for the Fosters.

FOX POND. For foxes.

FRENCH BROOK. For the French family.

FRENCH HILL. For J. and W. French, residents, 1858.

FRENCH ISLAND. For the French family who settled about 1800.

FROG POND. For frogs.

FROST HILL. For the David Frost family, who settled here.

FROST MOUNTAIN. For George A. Frost, professional painter who went to Siberia with the George Kenner Expedition in 1885, to illustrate Kenner's forthcoming book.

FRY. For the Fry family, settlers about 1800.

FRYE BROOK. For the Frye family who settled here.

FRYEBURG: CENTER, EAST-, HARBOR, NORTH-, settlement, TOWNSHIP, WEST-. For Captain Joseph Frye, grantee.

FULLER BROOK. For a number of Fuller families who lived there.

FULLER HILL. For Consider Fuller, early settler.

FULLING MILL MOUNTAIN. Unknown.

FURLONG POND. For Thomas Furlong, early settler.

GAMMON HILL. For the early Gammon family.

GARDNER BROOK. For John Gardner, Revolutionary War veteran.

GARLAND BROOK. Unknown.

GILBERTVILLE. For the Gilbert family who had a saw and pulp mill there.

GILEAD: settlement, TOWNSHIP. For the many Balm of Gilead trees in the center of the town.

GLASSBY COVE. Unknown.

GLASS FACE MOUNTAIN. For its sheer face, which looks glassy when iced over in the winter.

GOLD BROOK. For bits of gold that can be found there.

GOODWIN POND. Unknown.

GOOSE EYE: BROOK, MOUNTAIN. Unknown.

GORDON BROOK. For Tom Gordon, early settler.

GOSS LEDGE. For Samuel Goss, early settler.

GOULD MOUNTAIN. For Moses and Aaron Gould, settlers before 1800.

GRAFTON: NOTCH, settlement, TOWNSHIP. Named by James Brown for Grafton, Massachusetts.

GRANGER POND. A corruption of Grandeur Pond, descriptive.

GREAT BROOK. (2). Descriptive.

GREELEY BROOK. For John Greeley, settler before 1800.

GREEN BROOK. For J.H. Green, resident, 1858.

GREEN: ISLAND, TOP. Descriptive.

GREEN POND. For Jeremiah Green, one of the earliest settlers.

GREENWOOD BROOK. Probably for Alexander Greenwood, early surveyor.

GREENWOOD HILL. For John Greenwood, one of the first settlers.

GREENWOOD: settlement, TOWNSHIP. Some say descriptive. Others, for Alexander Greenwood, area surveyor.

GREGG MOUNTAIN. For Gregg, a lumberman.

GRIFFIN ISLAND. Unknown.

HALE. For Hale, a man who ran a post office in Mexico Township.

HALEY POND. For William Haley, who lived nearby.

HALFMOON: COVE, POND. Descriptive.

HALL MOUNTAIN. For the Hall family.

HALL POND. Probably for Abijah Hall, farmer and settler, 1786.

HALLS: HILL, RIDGE. For the Hateevil Hall family, early settlers.

HAMBLEN HILL. For the Hamblen family who farmed here in the mid 1800's.

HAMLIN HILL. For the Hamlin family, owners.

HAMMEL BROOK. Unknown.

HAMMOND BROOK: NORTH-, SOUTH-. Unknown.

HAMMOND LEDGE. For Benjamin Hammond, early settler.

HANCOCK BROOK. For John Hancock, hunter and trapper, who was murdered in 1765 by John Brown. Sometimes his name is given as William Hancock, but the story is the same.

HANNAH BROOK. For the Hannah family who cleared and farmed the land.

HANOVER: settlement, TOWNSHIP. For the province in Germany and for King George III, whose family name was Hanover, by settlers from Germany.

HARDING HILL. For the early Harding family.

HARDSCRABBLE ISLAND. Because it was difficult to land and climb on.

HARLOW RIDGE. For the many Harlow families in the area.

HARTFORD: settlement, TOWNSHIP. For Hartford, Connecticut.

HARVEY BROOK. For Harrison Harvey, early settler.

HASTINGS. For Hastings, who had a lumber and wood alcohol mill there.

HASTINGS ISLAND. For Amos Hastings, early settler.

HATCH HILL. For the Hatch family, who farmed here, mid-1800's.

HATHAWAY HILL. For Lorenzo Hathaway, settler, 1838.

HAWK MOUNTAIN. For hawks sighted there by lumbermen.

HAYES POINT. For Dennis Hayes, settler, mid-1800's.

HAYFORD: BROOK, HILL. For William Hayford, early settler.

HAYSTACK: MOUNTAIN, NOTCH. Descriptive of shape.

HEADS CORNER. For the Head family.

HEALD POND. For Josiah Heald, one of the first settlers in 1800.

HEATH HILL. For Benjamin Heath, early settler.

HEBRON: settlement, STATION, TOWNSHIP. Some say it was just chosen from the Bible for no reason, other than it being a custom of the time. Others feel that the Baptist Society that gathered in

1791 bore the name of Hebron Baptist Society, and the name was taken from it.

HEDGEHOG: HILL (5), LEDGE. For hedgehogs (porcupines).

HEMENWAY RIDGE. For the early Hemenway family.

HEMINGWAY MOUNTAIN. For the early Hemingway family.

HEMLOCK KNOLL. For hemlocks.

HERRICK BROOK. For Benjamin Herrick.

HICKS POND. For John Hicks, early settler.

HIGHLAND PARK. Descriptive. The name of a sanitorium developed by Dr. John Buzzell of Portland, in the 1880's.

HIRAM: settlement, SOUTH-, TOWNSHIP. Named by General Peleg Wadsworth, Timothy Cutler, and Captain Charles L. Wadsworth, for the biblical King Hiram of Tyre.

HOBBS BROOK. For the Hobbs family, early settlers.

HOGAN POND. For Hogan, who fell through the ice on the pond and lost his horse and sled, but saved himself.

HOLMAN MOUNTAIN. For Colonel Jonathon Holman.

HOLMES HILL. Possibly for Zenas Holmes, early settler.

HOLT HILL. For the Holt family who lived there.

HORSE BEEF POINT. Unknown.

HORSE HILL. For a group of horses struck and killed by lightning there.

HORSESHOE POND. (5). Descriptive.

HOUGHTON. Unknown.

HOWARD: BROOK, MOUNTAIN. For the early Howard family.

HOWARD: POND, settlement. For Phineas Howard, early settler.

HOWE BROOK. For Silas Howe, who lived nearby.

HUBBARD POND. For Isaac Hubbard, early settler.

HUGH BROOK. Unknown.

HUNT POND. For the early Hunt family.

HUNTS CORNER. For Hunt, early tavern owner.

HURRICANE BROOK. For a hurricane, or storm, that blew down timber in the area.

HUTCHINSON HILL. For Daniel Hutchinson, early settler.

HUTCHINSON POND. For the R. Hutchinson Clover Seed Mill, which operated there in the 1800's.

ICE CAVE. Because it has ice in it for most of the summer.

ICICLE BROOK. Descriptive of its coldness.

INDIAN: COVE, POND. For Indians.

INGHAM HILL. For R. Ingham, resident, 1858.

INLET RIDGE. Descriptive.

IRISH HILL. (2). In Buckfield Township, probably for John Irish, settler, 1764. In Hartford Township, for Edmund Irish, early settler.

ISAIAH HILL. For Isaiah Hall, early settler, farmer, and millwright.

ISAIAH MOUNTAIN. For Isaiah, first settler in the area.

JACKSON POINT. Unknown.

JAKES NOTCH. Unknown.

JAM HILL. Possibly for a windmill, called a "windjammer," located there. Also, it could have been named for Jamb Bridge.

JAYBIRD POND. For jaybirds.

JERSEY BOG. For a jersey cow that became mired and died here.

JEWETT HILL. For the Jewett family who lived at its foot.

JIM HILL. For Jim Gill, who lived near.

JOCKEY CAP. For its resemblance to a skull or jockey cap. Possibly folk etymology of Abnaki "ajok" — "hill."

JOE McKEEN HILL. For Joe McKeen, who lived there.

JOHNSON MOUNTAIN. Unknown.

JORDAN: BROOK, MOUNTAIN. For Benjamin Jordan, settler by 1843.

KEDAR BROOK. Unknown.

KEEWAYDIN LAKE. For the wife of E. Lester Jones, director of the U.S. Coast and Geodetic Survey, Virginia Keewaydin. Her name translates in Chippawa: "people of the north wind" or "north wind."

KENDALL BROOK. (2). In Bethel Township, for Bezaleel Kimball, Jr., early settler. In Greenwood Township, for the Kendall family who had a dam and mill there.

KENNEBAGO: RIVER, MOUNTAIN. Abnaki: "long pond."

KENNISTON HILL. For the Kenniston family, farmers, mid-1800's.

KEOKA LAKE. Abnaki: "where they get red earth for pots[?]."

KETCHUM. Unknown.

KEYS: BROOK, POND. For Keys (or Kize) who was traveling near the pond when he was attacked by Indians. To escape, he swam across the pond.

KEZAR: FALLS, FALLS BROOK, FIVE-PONDS, HILL, LAKE, OUTLET, POND, RIVER. For George Kezar, famous hunter and trapper in the area in 1788.

KIDDER MOUNTAIN. For Jacob Kidder, early settler.

KIMBALL BROOK. Probably for Clarence Kimball, early settler.

KIMBALL HILL. (2). In Bethel Township, for Jacob Kimball, early farmer. In Waterford Township, for Isaac Kimball, early settler.

KINGMAN BROOK. For William Kingman, settler, 1831.

KNEELAND POND. For Cyrus Kneeland, millowner, 1835.

KNIGHTS HILL. For Merrill Knight, first settler and land grantee.

LABRADOR: LITTLE-POND, POND. Because the settlers said the pond was as cold as Labrador, since it took the ice so long to leave it in the spring.

LADIES DELIGHT HILL. In the early days, several homes were built here, and in the winter, the women were lonely and unhappy; hence, the ironical name.

LAKE ANASAGUNTICOOK. Abnaki: "at the river with the sandy bottom."

LANES BROOK. For Eliphalet Lane, early settler.

LANGDON BROOK. For Paul Langdon, who surveyed the area.

LARY: BROOK, BROOK MOUNTAIN, ISLAND, LITTLE-BROOK. For Joseph Lary, early settler.

LAWRENCE MOUNTAIN. For R.M. Lawrence, resident, 1858.

LEDGE RIDGE. Descriptive.

LIBBY HILL. For Meshack Libby, grantee.

LIBERTY CORNER. Unknown.

LIGHTNING LEDGE. Because it attracts lightning, probably because of an iron ore deposit.

LILY POND. (2). For lilies.

LINCOLN: BROOK, POND, TOWNSHIP. For Enoch Lincoln, governor of Massachusetts.

LITTLE ANDROSCOGGIN RIVER. For the Androscoggin River. Abnaki: "the place where fish are cured."

LITTLE BOY FALLS. For an Indian boy who went over the falls in a raft and was killed.

LITTLE: FALLS, MOUNTAIN, POND (3). Descriptive.

LOCKE HILL. For the early Locke family.

LOCKE: MILLS, MOUNTAIN. For Samuel Locke of Bethel Township, who built a mill there in 1830. He settled early near Locke Mountain in Bethel Township.

LOGAN BROOK. A corruption of Lagoon Brook. Descriptive.

LOMBARD BROOK. For the John Lombard family.

LOMBARD POND. A corruption of Lumbered Pond. Descriptive.

LONE: BROOK, MOUNTAIN. Descriptive.

LONG: MEADOW BROOK, MOUNTAIN (2), POND (3). Descriptive.

LOON ISLAND. (2). For loons.

LOST BROOK. (2). Descriptive of isolation.

LOU ANN BROOK. For Lou Ann Cooledge, an unmarried woman who lived nearby and killed a peddlar, who still haunts the place.

LOVEJOY HILL. For the nearby Lovejoy family.

LOVEJOY MOUNTAIN. (2). In Albany Township, for Joseph Lovejoy, early proprietor. In Mexico Township, for the Lovejoy family.

LOVELL: CENTER-, NORTH-, settlement, TOWNSHIP. For Captain Lovewell, Indian fighter, who led the white forces in 1724 and 1725, and was killed in Fryeburg Township.

LOVEWELL POND. For Captain John Lovewell, who was killed here with nine companions in May 1725, while on a scalp-hunting expedition.

LOWER KIMBALL LAKE. For Kimball Lake in New Hampshire.

LUDDEN BROOK. For Jacob Ludden, early settler.

LUNCH ISLAND. Unknown.

LUNT POINT. For Joshua Lunt, early settler.

LYNCHTOWN TOWNSHIP. Unknown.

LYNCHVILLE. Unknown.

LYNX BROOK. For lynxes.

MAD: MIDDLE BRANCH-RIVER, NORTH BRANCH-RIVER, RIVER, SOUTH BRANCH-RIVER. Descriptive of its flow. But possibly Abnaki: "bad, useless river."

MAGALLOWAY: LITTLE-RIVER, MIDDLE BRANCH LITTLE-RIVER, RIVER, SECOND EAST BRANCH-RIVER, THIRD EAST BRANCH-RIVER, TOWNSHIP, WEST BRANCH-RIVER. Malecite: "the shoveller [the caribou]."

MAHOOSUC: ARM, MOUNTAIN, NOTCH, RANGE. Abnaki: "home of hungry animals." Possibly Natick: "a pinnacle." The Abnaki word might refer to the Monhegan-Pequot refugees who fled from Connecticut to Maine following the Pequot War in 1637.

MARBLE MOUNTAIN. Descriptive.

MARR HILL. For the early Marr family.

MARSHALL POND. For David Marshall, who operated a sawmill there about 1781.

MARTINS BROOK. For the early Martin family.

MASON HILL. For the early settling Mason family.

MASON TOWNSHIP. For Mason, Massachusetts.

MASTERMAN HILL. For Cleveland Masterman, early settler.

MAYVILLE. Unknown.

McCOLLISTER HILL. For the McCollister family who lived there for generations.

McCRILLIAN BROOK. For the early McCrullian family.

McDANIELS HILL. (2). In Lovell Township, for the McDaniels family, farmers, mid-1800's. In Stoneham Township, for the early settling McDaniels family.

McINTIRE BROOK. For the McIntire family who settled by 1848.

McKie Fork. Unknown.

McWAIN: HILL, POND. For David McWayne, settler about 1775.

MEADOW: BROOK (9), -VIEW. Descriptive.

MERRILL: BROOK, HILL. For the Merrill family who lived there.

MERRILL CORNER. For Nathaniel Merrill, early miller.

METALLAK: BROOK, ISLAND, MOUNTAIN, POND, STREAM. Metallak was the last Coosuck Indian, who died at Stewartstown, New Hampshire, about 1850. He lived in Maine for quite some time. His name probably means in Pennacook, "the last man."

MEXICO: settlement, TOWNSHIP. Supposedly for Mexico, the nation, which was revolting against Spain when the township was named in 1818. Probably simply because the choice of foreign place-names was a custom of the time.

MIDDLE: BAY, BRANCH, INTERVALE. Descriptive.

MILES: BROOK, NOTCH (2), NOTCH BROOK. Notch and Notch Brook in Mason and Riley Townships, for the early Miles family. In Stoneham Township, unknown.

MILL BROOK. (6). For mills. Specifically in Bethel Township, for Joseph Twitchell, who built a grist and sawmill there in 1774.

MILLS BROOK. For mills located there.

MILTON TOWNSHIP. Unknown.

MINE NOTCH. For a mine nearby.

MINE POND. For a nearby lead mine.

MINISTER BROOK. Unknown.

MITCHELL BROOK. (3). In Hartford Township, for Jonas Mitchell, early settler. In Roxbury Township, for Franklin Mitchell, settler, 1832. In Mexico Township, for Zebediah Mitchell, early settler.

MOLLEDGEWOCK POND. Abnaki: possibly "at the deep place."

MOLL OCKETT MOUNTAIN. Abnaki: "at the sheer cliffs." But tradition says for Mary Agatha, last of the Pequakett Indians, who died in 1816. Another says for Moll Ockett, an Indian woman who roamed in the area for about seventy years.

MOODY: BROOK (2), MOUNTAIN (2). Brook and mountain in Andover North Surplus Township, for a man named Moody who fell from a cliff and was killed. Brook in Paris Township, for Benjamin Moody, early settler. Mountain in Woodstock Township, for Josiah Moody of Portland, one of the first settlers.

MOORE BROOK. For Aron Moore, early settler.

MOOSE: BOG, BROOK, LITTLE-POND, MOUNTAIN, POND (3), POND BROOK (2). For moose.

MORRILL LEDGES. For Peter Morrill, who lived nearby.

MORRISON BROOK. For the Morrison family.

MORSE BROOK. For the Morse family who lived near.

MOSQUITO BROOK. (2). For mosquitoes.

MOTHER WALKER FALLS. For Mother Walker, who owned the surrounding land.

MOULTON RIDGE. For David Moulton, Revolutionary War veteran who settled there, early 1800's.

MOUNT ABRAM. Probably for Abraham Wentworth, who lived at its foot in 1856.

MOUNTAIN BROOK. (2). Descriptive.

MOUNT CARLO. Unknown.

MOUNT CHRISTOPHER. For Christopher Bryant of Woodstock Township, who settled here early.

MOUNT CUTLER. For Timothy Cutler, landholder and tavern-keeper by 1778.

MOUNT DIMMOCK. Unknown.

MOUNT GLINES. For V. Glines, resident, 1880.

MOUNT HITTIE. For an old lady, Aunt Hittie, who was lost on the mountain.

MOUNT MARIE. For Marie, wife of a man named Willis who ran a mine there.

MOUNT MICA. For the mineral mica.

MOUNT MISERY. Unknown.

MOUNT OXFORD: MOUNT, SPRING. Originally called Hedgehog Hill until the Oxford Bottling Company began using a spring there for its water supply. The name was changed when the company called it "Mount Oxford" in an advertisement.

MOUNT TIRE'M. According to tradition, Indians who climbed this mountain always said that the climb would "tire'm Indians." Probably essentially true, except for the reference to Indians.

MOUNT TOM. (2). In Fryeburg Township, for a Massachusetts mountain of the same name that it resembles when viewed from a certain angle. In Sumner Township, for Tom, an old Indian.

MOUNT WILL. Unknown.

MUD: BROOK, POND (8). Descriptive.

MUSKRAT POND. For muskrats.

MUTINY BROOK. Unknown.

NARROWS, THE. (2). Descriptive.

NEW BOSTON. For Boston, Massachusetts.

NEWCOMB MOUNTAIN. For T.L. Newcomb, resident by 1880.

NEW ENGLAND BROOK. For New England.

NEWRY: NORTH-, NORTH-POST OFFICE, settlement, TOWN-SHIP. For settlers from Newry, County Down, Ireland.

NEWTON: BROOK, HILL. For Levi Newton, millowner.

NEZINSCOT: EAST BRANCH-RIVER, RIVER, WEST BRANCH-RIVER. Abnaki: "place of descent."

NILES BROOK. Unknown.

NOAH EASTMAN POND. For Noah Eastman, who settled in 1789.

NOBLE BROOK. For Charles Noble, who had a farm there.

NOBLES CORNER. For Nathan Noble, who built a store there in 1823.

NOISEY BROOK. Descriptive.

NORTH: -EAST POND, HILL, PEAK, POND (4), -WEST COVE. Descriptive.

NORWAY: CENTER, LAKE (settlement), NORTH-, settlement, TOWNSHIP. The citizens petitioned for the township to be named "Norage" for the Indian word for "falls." When the incorporation papers returned from the legislature, it had been given the name "Norway" by mistake. Probably some clerk "corrected" the poor spelling of the settlers.

NOTCH TWO. Counting Grafton Notch as number one, this is the second notch below it.

NOYES MOUNTAIN. Possibly for John Noyes, who lived nearby.

NUBBLE, THE. Descriptive.

NUMBER EIGHT POND. For its location on lot number 8 of the township.

NUMBER FOUR. For a former school district that included 4 square miles now in Sweden Township. "Four" was the number of the district.

NUMBER FOUR HILL. For a road called Number Four Road, for a plantation designation.

OAK HILL. (5). For oak trees.

OBSERVATORY MOUNTAIN. For its use as a lookout by the Indians.

OLD BLUE MOUNTAIN. Descriptive of color.

OLD SPECK MOUNTAIN. For several different varieties of trees there which give a speckled appearance, especially in the fall.

OLD TURK MOUNTAIN. One source says it resembles a Turk's turban.

OSSIPEE RIVER. Abnaki: "water on the other side."

OTTER: BROOK (2), POND. For otters.

OVERSET: MOUNTAIN, POND. Descriptive of how it overhangs the pond.

OWLS HEAD. Descriptive of shape.

OXBOW TOWNSHIP. For the province of Quebec, Canada, which makes a deep "oxbow" into Maine.

OXFORD: COUNTY, settlement, STATION, TOWNSHIP. Named for Oxford, Massachusetts, by David Leonard, one of the early settlers, who came from there.

PACKARD HILL. For the Packard family.

PADDY MEADOW BROOK. For the early settler Levi Masterman, whose nickname was "Paddy."

PAGE MOUNTAIN. For Samuel Page, early settler.

PAINE BROOK. (2). In Brownfield Township, for William Paine, early settler. In Grafton Township, for the Paine family who lived nearby.

PAINE CORNER. For Abijah M. Paine, Civil War veteran.

PALMER MOUNTAIN. For the early Palmer family.

PAPOOSE: LITTLE-POND, POND (2). In Albany Township, unknown. In Waterford Township, for a papoose drowned there before the whites settled.

PARADISE HILL. Descriptive.

PARIS: HILL, NORTH-, settlement, SOUTH-, TOWNSHIP, WEST-. Probably for Alfron Paris, leading Democrat who helped in Maine's separation from Massachusetts. Others say for Paris, France, because the French were admired for their help in the Revolution. If the name was for the French city, it was probably not for the above reason, but because the selection of foreign names was customary.

PARKER: HILL (2), -TOWN, TOWNSHIP. Unknown.

PARMACHENEE: LAKE, TOWNSHIP. For Parmanchenee, a daughter of an Indian chief. Her name means in Abnaki, "across the usual path."

PARSONAGE HILL. (2). For parsonages located there.

PARTRIDGE PEAK. One source says for partridges. Another says for the Partridge family.

PATCH MOUNTAIN. For Timothy Patch, who lived nearby.

PATTE: BROOK, HILL. For Moses Patte, an early millowner.

PATTERSON: BROOK, HILL. For the Patterson family, settlers by the mid-1800's.

PAULS BLUFF. For Will Paul, recent owner.

PAYNE LEDGE. For Isaac Payne, early settler.

PEABODY: BROOK, ISLAND. For Oliver and John Peabody, chief proprietors of Gilead Township.

PEABODY MOUNTAIN. (2). In Albany Township, for B. Peabody, resident, 1858. In Mason Township, for Oliver and John Peabody, who obtained the Peabody Grant, now Gilead Township.

PEAKED: HILL (2), MOUNTAIN (2). Descriptive.

PEARY MOUNTAIN. For Jacob Peary, soldier in the War of 1812.

PEAT POND. For peat.

PEBLEY MOUNTAIN. For Joseph Peverly, early settler.

PENNESSEEWASSEE: LAKE, LITTLE-LAKE. Natick: "a strange, shining, then fading, light."

PEPPERPOT POND. Descriptive of shape.

PERLEY POND. For John Perley, part owner in a sawmill there.

PERRY HILL. For the local Perry family.

PERU: EAST-, settlement, TOWNSHIP, WEST-. For the South American country of Peru which was liberated from Spanish rule in 1821, the same year the township was incorporated.

PETER GROVER HILL. For Peter Grover, original owner.

PETER MOUNTAIN. Unknown.

PHELPS BROOK. For S. Phelps, resident, 1858.

PHILBRICK BROOK. For Nathaniel Philbrick.

PHILBRICK ISLAND. For the early settling Philbrick family.

PICKETT HENRY MOUNTAIN. For Pickett Henry, early settler.

PICKETT HILL. A mispronunciation of Peaked Hill. Descriptive.

PIGEON POINT. For pigeons.

PIKE HILL. For Dudley Pike, who first settled there.

PINE: HILL (5), ISLAND (2), MOUNTAIN (2). For pine trees.

PINNACLE, THE. (4). Descriptive.

PLAIN POND. Descriptive of location.

PLAINS, THE. Descriptive.

PLEASANT: EAST BRANCH-RIVER, ISLAND, MOUNTAIN (2), POND (2), RIVER, WEST BRANCH-RIVER. Descriptive.

PLEASURE BROOK. Descriptive.

PLUMBAGO MOUNTAIN. For the mineral plumbago (graphite).

PLUMMER: BROOK, MOUNTAIN. For Plummer Enfield, who lived at the foot of the mountain.

POLAND MOUNTAIN. Possibly for John Poland.

POND: BROOK (2), IN THE RIVER. Descriptive.

POPPLE: Hill, HILL BROOK. The hill was formerly covered with poplar trees, called "popples" in the local dialect.

PORTAGE BROOK. Descriptive of the portage between Cupsuptic River and Aziscohos Lake.

PORTER BROOK. Unknown.

PORTER: -FIELD, settlement, TOWNSHIP. For Dr. Aaron Porter of Biddeford, who owned much of the township.

PORTLAND POINT. Unknown.

POWERS BROOK. For William Harmon Powers, settler about 1851.

PRATT CORNER. For H.K. Pratt, settler by 1880.

PRAYS BROOK. For the Pray family.

PROCTOR POND. Unknown.

PULPIT ROCK. Descriptive of shape.

PUZZLE: LITTLE-MOUNTAIN, MOUNTAIN. Unknown.

QUINT BROOK. For J. and C. Quint, residents, 1858.

RABBIT KNOLL. For rabbits.

RAGGED JACK MOUNTAIN. For shale rock which frequently slides off the mountain. The settlers said that it looked like a "ragged assed jackass" or a "ragged jackass" when it shed its winter coat. Another source says for a man named Jack who fell and tore his pants there. The mountain was formerly called "Ragged Ass Jack." The cartographers toned it down.

RAND BROOK. For Bert Rand, who had a camp there.

RANKINS MILL. For Joseph Rankin, millowner, 1813.

RATTLESNAKE: BROOK, ISLAND, MOUNTAIN (3), POND. For rattlesnakes that formerly inhabited the area. Pond in Brownfield Township, specifically for a man who raised snakes on the east shore of the pond and mistakenly got rattlesnakes mixed in with his crop. One night some boys dug a ditch to let water out of the pond for a July 4th joke. A heavy rain widened the ditch, and in a short time the pond lowered its level ten feet, washing the snake farm away.

REALTY. Unknown.

RECORD HILL. Unknown.

RED: BROOK, HILL, RIDGE, ROCK MOUNTAIN. Descriptive of color. Ridge in Grafton Township, specifically for a fire in 1908 which burned on the ridge for three months, until the first snow fell. The fire left the red soil exposed. Hill in Peru Township, for the oak trees whose leaves turn red in the fall.

REDDING. For the Redding brothers who built a mill there.

RICE HILL. For Eben Rice, the first justice of the peace in 1799.

RICHARDSON: EAST-PONDS, LOWER-LAKE, POND, .-TOWN TOWNSHIP, UPPER-LAKE. For the Richardson family, one of the first settlers in the township.

RIDLON BROOK. For Joshua Ridlon, settler, 1800's.

RIDLONVILLE. For Ridlon, who had a store there for years and ran the post office.

RIFLE POINT. Descriptive of shape.

RILEY: HILL, TOWNSHIP. For Luke Riley and family, early settlers of Newry Township.

ROBERTSON HILL. For Jonathon Robertson, early settler.

ROBBINS HILL. For Joshua Robbins, part Abnaki Indian, Revolutionary War veteran.

ROBINSON HILL. (2). In Hartford Township, for Increase Robinson, early settler. In Oxford Township, for Joseph Robinson, settler from England.

ROBINSON PEAK. Unknown.

ROCK DUNDEE. Unknown.

ROCK-O-DUNDEE HILL. Unknown.

ROUND: MOUNTAIN (2), POND (3). Descriptive.

ROWE HILL. For Steven Rowe, who lived on the crest.

ROXBURY: MOUNTAIN, NOTCH, settlement, TOWNSHIP. For Roxbury, Massachusetts.

RUMFORD; CENTER, CORNER, FALLS, POINT (settlement), settlement, TOWNSHIP. For Sir Benjamin Thompson, Count of Rumford, one of the proprietors.

RUMP: MOUNTAIN, POND. Descriptive of the shape of the mountain.

RUSSELL BROOK. (2). In Hartford Township, unknown. In Sumner Township, probably for Thomas Russell.

RUSSELL HILL. Possibly for Andrew Russell.

RYEMOOR HILL. For the Ryerson and Moore families who lived nearby. Finally a Ryerson married a Moore and the blend "Ryemoor" resulted.

RYERSON HILL. For Luke and George Ryerson, settlers, 1798.

SABATTUS. For the Abnaki Indian chief, Sabattus. The name is an Abnaki rendering of the French "St. Jean Baptiste."

SABLE: HILL, MOUNTAIN. The woodsmen's name for the martin.

SACO: LITTLE-RIVER, OLD COURSE-RIVER, RIVER. Abnaki: "the outlet."

SADDLE HILL. Descriptive of shape.

SANBORN RIVER. Possibly for Steven Sanborn.

SANDERSON BROOK. Unknown.

SAND POND. (2). Descriptive.

SANDY COVE. Descriptive.

SANTIAGO BOG. For its location in the Santiago tract of land. In 1898 or 1899 a group of men from Andover, Bethel, and Bridgton Townships purchased about 600 acres of land and built a bobbing mill. Because of the Spanish-American War, they named it in memory of the Battle of Santiago Bay.

SARGENT: BROOK, MOUNTAIN. For the Reuben Sargent family, settlers by 1842.

SATURDAY POND. For a group that camped on it on Saturday before they camped on Sunday Pond the next day.

SAWYER: BROOK, MOUNTAIN. For the local Sawyer family.

SCOGGINS BROOK. Because it crossed the old Scoggins Trail. "Scoggins" is possibly a corruption of an Indian word.

SCREW AUGER FALLS. For the small, round holes at the foot of the falls which appear to have been augered.

SEVERY HILL. For Aaron, Archibald, and Asa Severy, early settlers.

SHACK HILL. For Meshack Keene.

SHAGG POND. Possibly for shags (seabirds).

SHAKING BOG. Descriptive.

SHAVE HILL. Much horse trading was carried on here, and the hill was named for "close shaves" in the trading.

SHAW LEDGE. For Eaton Shaw, who owned much area land.

SHEEP ISLAND. For its use as a sheep pen.

SHELL: POND, POND BROOK. For shells.

SHELTER BROOK. For a woods shelter located there.

SHELTER ISLAND. Where people sheltered from rough water.

SHEPARDS RIVER. For a hunter named Shepard who liked it there.

SHIRLEY BROOK. For the early Shirley family.

SILVER: RIPPLE CASCADE, STREAM. Descriptive.

SIMONS BROOK. For the early Simons family.

SINGEPOLE: LITTLE-MOUNTAIN, MOUNTAIN. For the many forest fires that had left the trees "singed poles," limbs burned off and trunks blackened.

SKILLINGS HILL. For the Skillings family who settled here in the mid-1800's.

SKUNK POND. For skunks.

SLAB CITY. For a sawmill where there were stacks of slabs (outside cuts of lumber which contained bark).

SLIDE MOUNTAIN. Descriptive.

SMALLS MOUNTAIN. For Francis Small, who ran an Indian trading post in 1668.

SMITH CROSSING. For Smith, who ran a ferry there.

SNOW: MOUNTAIN, MOUNTAIN BROOK. Unknown.

SNOWS FALLS. For a trapper named Snow who was killed there before the settlement of the town.

SODOM. Named by the surrounding inhabitants because they felt the people living there to be immoral.

SONGO POND. Abnaki: "cold water."

SOUTH: ARM, ARM (settlement), BROOK, -EAST POND, HILL, MOUNTAIN, POND (2). Descriptive.

SPARROWHAWK MOUNTAIN. For sparrowhawks.

SPAULDING COVE. For Spaulding, who had a logging operation there years ago.

SPEARS STREAM. For Indians who speared fish there.

SPECKLED MOUNTAIN. (2). For their speckled appearance because of the different kinds of trees growing there.

SPECK POND. For Old Speck Mountain.

SPECK PONDS. Descriptive of size.

SPECTACLE PONDS. Descriptive of eyeglass shape.

SPILLMAN COVE. Unknown.

SPIRIT ISLAND. Unknown.

SPLIT BROOK. For its divided course.

SPRUCE: HILL, HILLS, MOUNTAIN (2). For spruce trees.

SQUARE DOCK MOUNTAIN. For the square-faced rocks at its summit. The "Dock" is probably a cartographical error for "Rock."

STACY HILL. For John Stacey, settler, 1804.

STANLEY HILL. For the Stanley family.

STANLEY POND. For William Stanley, millowner, 1822.

STAPLES HILL. For the Staples family who lived there for generations.

STARKS MOUNTAIN. For Captain William Starks, early settler.

STEARNS HILL. (2). In Paris Township, for Ebenezer Stearns, one of the original grantees, or possibly William Stearns. In Waterford Township, for the Stearns family who lived there in 1879.

STEARNS POND. For the local Stearns family.

STEVENS ISLAND. For John Stevens, early settler and large landholder.

STOCKBRIDGE BROOK. For John Stockbridge, settler before 1833.

STONEHAM: EAST, TOWNSHIP. For Stoneham, Massachusetts.

STONE HILL. (2). In Hebron Township, for Isaac Stone, early settler. In Waterford Township, for stone.

STONE MOUNTAIN. Descriptive.

STONY BATTER POINT. Descriptive of the appearance of the weathered rock.

STONY: BROOK (4), LOWER-BROOK, UPPER-BROOK. Descriptive.

STOWE MOUNTAIN. For the Stowe family who lived there.

STOW: settlement, TOWNSHIP. For Stow, Massachusetts.

STREAKED MOUNTAIN. Descriptive.

STUDENTS ISLAND. Unknown.

STURTEVANT: COVE, MOUNTAIN, POND, STREAM. For Joseph Sturtevant, who moved here in 1836.

SUCKER: BROOK (2), BROOK HILL. For sucker fish.

SUGARLOAF: mountain (2), MOUNTAIN (2). Descriptive of shape.

SUMNER: EAST-, HILL, settlement, TOWNSHIP, WEST- For Increase Sumner, governor of Massachusetts.

SUNDAY: COVE, POND (2). For groups that camped there on Sundays.

SUNDAY: RIVER, RIVER WHITECAP, SOUTH BRANCH-RIVER. The river was first discovered on a Sunday.

SURPLUS: MOUNTAIN, POND. For their location, in Andover North Surplus Township.

SWAINS: NOTCH, POND. For John Swain, early settler.

SWAN HILL. For James Swan, Jr., early settler.

SWAN: POND, POND BROOK. For the Swan family who lived near.

SWANS FALLS. For Caleb Swan, early settler.

SWEDEN: EAST-, settlement, TOWNSHIP. Probably just another foreign name to go with Norway, Denmark, Paris, Naples, and townships.

SWETT BROOK. Unknown.

SWIFT CAMBRIDGE RIVER. Descriptive, and runs into Cambridge, New Hampshire.

SWIFT RIVER. Descriptive.

SWIMMING BOG. Descriptive.

TABLE ROCK. Descriptive of shape.

TEAR CAP. For a fight witnessed by Dr. Joseph Benton on one of his calls. In the fight the two women tore up each other's lace caps.

TEMPLE HILL. For settlers from Temple, Massachusetts.

TENMILE: POND, RIVER, WEST BRANCH-RIVER. The river runs into the Saco River about 10 miles north of Hiram settlement.

THOMAS BROOK. For the local Thomas family.

THOMAS FARM POND. For the Thomas family who owned a farm here about 1800.

THOMAS HILL. For Elisha Thomas, settler before 1776.

THOMPSON: BROOK, HILL (2). Hill and brook in Hartford Township, for Ira, Cyrus, Oakes, and John Thompson, Township, unknown.

THOMPSON LAKE. For Thompson, who drowned while attempting to cross the lake.

THRASHER PEAKS. Unknown.

THURSTON BROOK. (2). In Rumford Township, for the early Thurston family. In Porter Township, unknown.

THURSTON: MOUNTAIN, POND. For the early Thurston family.

TIBBETTS MOUNTAIN. (2). In Brownfield Township, for Abraham Tibbetts, War of 1812 veteran. In Greenwood Township, for the Tibbetts family who owned the wood-turning mill at Locke Mills.

TIGER HILL. The original Tiger Hill was located between Whitney and Hogan ponds. Here the Keene brothers built two houses and a barn. The brothers fought constantly, and after a particularly big fight, the neighbors said they fought like tigers and named their home "Tiger Hill." Later the brothers moved to a new hill and the name moved with them.

TIMBER ISLAND. Descriptive.

TOOTHAKER BROOK. Unknown.

TOWN FARM BROOK. Location of the town farm.

TOWN HOUSE. This settlement was named for the town house that was there by 1858.

TOWNSHIP C. Township designation.

TRAFTON POND. Unknown.

TRAP CORNER. One source says that for a long time no store stood here. Ebenezer Drake finally built his store to "trap" the business that would go to other localities. Another says that there is a tradition that Indians put a trap in a tree to mark the place where some money was hidden.

TRASK LEDGE. For Amos Trask, early settler.

TRASK MOUNTAIN. For several Trask families who owned much area land.

TROUT: BROOK (2), LITTLE-BROOK. For trout fish.

TUCKER VALLEY BROOK. For Eliphalet Tucker, early settler.

TUMBLEDOWN DICK MOUNTAIN. (2). In Gilead Township, one source says for a horse named Dick that fell to his death there. Another says for a shepherd named Dick who fell off the mountain while trying to rescue a sheep. In Peru Township, for an Indian named Dick who fell to his death one foggy night. All of these derivations are probably folklore. It is quite possibly just a fanciful name for a mountain that sometimes had slides.

TURNER HILL. For Jesse Turner, settler about 1797.

TWIN: BROOK, MOUNTAIN, MOUNTAINS, NORTH-MOUNTAIN, PEAKS, SOUTH-MOUNTAIN. Descriptive.

TWITCHELL: BROOK (3), POND. Brook in Gilead Township, for Captain Eleazer Twitchell, early settler. Brook and Pond in Greenwood Township, for Joseph Twitchell of Bethel Township, early proprietor. Brook in Paris Township, for Jacob Twitchell, early farmer.

TYLER BROOK. For Gilbert Tyler, early settler.

TYLER: MOUNTAIN, NOTCH. For the Tyler family who lived in the area in 1880.

UMBAGOG LAKE: Abnaki: "clear lake."

UNCLE TOM MOUNTAIN. Unknown.

UPTON: settlement, TOWNSHIP. For Upton, Massachusetts.

VIRGINIA LAKE. For Virginia Keewaydin, wife of E. Lester Jones, director of the U.S. Coast and Geodetic Survey, who owned land in the area.

WADSWORTH BROOK. For General Peleg Wadsworth, owner of much area land.

WALKER BROOK. (2). In Albany Township, unknown. In Roxbury Township, for John Walker, who settled here in 1814.

WALKER ISLAND. For the Walker family, who farmed the island in the 1800's.

WALKER MOUNTAIN. Unknown.

WALKERS: MILL, MOUNTAIN. For Daniel Walker, early owner.

WARDS POND. For the Ward family who had a mill there.

WARREN BROOK. For William Warren.

WARREN HILL. Probably for John Warren, early settler.

WASHBURN POND. For Ebenezer Washburn, early settler.

WATERFORD: EAST-, NORTH-, settlement, SOUTH-, TOWNSHIP. For the many ponds and brooks.

WEBBER BROOK. For David Webber, settler, 1817.

WEBBER POND. For Benjamin Webber, settler about 1798.

WELCHVILLE. For John W. Welch, wealthy Boston merchant who owned much land.

WELLS POND. For Henry P. Wells, former president of the Parmanchenee Club.

WEST: ARM, BROOK, MOUNTAIN, PEAK. Descriptive.

WEYMOUTH: HILL, POND. Unknown.

WHALE BACK MOUNTAIN. Descriptive.

WHALES BACK. Descriptive.

WHEELER: BROOK, MOUNTAIN. Unknown.

WHITECAP: BROOK, MOUNTAIN. Descriptive of snow on the mountain.

WHITEHOUSE HILL. For the early Whitehouse family.

WHITES: BROOK, NOTCH. Unknown.

WHITING HILL. For John Whitney, settler about 1800.

WHITMAN: HILL, MOUNTAIN. Probably for Jacob Whitman, settler, 1781.

WHITNEY BROOK. For Whitney, a soldier sent here from Massachusetts in 1780 to help pacify the Indians. They killed him, and he is buried near the brook.

WHITNEY HILL. (2). In Canton Township, for a settler named Whitney. In Paris Township, for David Whitney, one of the original grantees.

WHITNEY POND. (2). In Oxford Township, for William Clark Whitney, agent for Andrew Carnegie. In Stoneham Township, for the early Whitney family.

WHITTEMORE BLUFF. For Edwin Whittemore, early settler, who lived there.

WIGHT BROOK. For the Wright family.

WILBUR MOUNTAIN. For James Wilbur, who made the first clearing there.

WILD: BROOK, RIVER, -WOOD COVE. Descriptive.

WILEY MOUNTAIN. For Joe Wiley, who settled here in 1883.

WILLARD BROOK. For Samuel S. Willard, early settler.

WILLIS MILLS. For Frank Willis, who built a mill there long ago.

WILLOW BROOK. For willow trees.

WILSONS MILLS. For Wilson, who owned a saw and gristmill there.

WINNS HILL. For the local Winn family.

WITT HILL. Unknown.

WITT SWAMP. For Benjamin Witt, settler, 1791.

WOODBURY HILL. For Andrew Woodbury, settler about 1792.

WOOD ISLAND. Descriptive.

WOODSTOCK: NORTH-, SOUTH-, TOWNSHIP. For the area woods.

WORTHLEY: BROOK, POND. For the Worthley family who owned much land.

WYMAN BROOK. For Henry M. Wyman, early settler.

WYMAN MOUNTAIN. The Wyman family cleared the area about 1900.

YAGGER. Tradition says that during the Revolutionary War some German soldiers were hunting in this section and called themselves "jaeger," the German word for "hunter." "Yagger" is an approximate pronunciation of the German word.

YORK BROOK. Unknown.

YORK POND. For the York family.

ZIRCON: BROOK, LITTLE-MOUNTAIN, MOUNTAIN, MOUNT-SPRING. For zircon stones in the area.

PENOBSCOT COUNTY

ABBOTT HILL. For Moses Abbott, who had his farm here.

ACKLEY POND. For Ackley, area lumberman.

ADLEY RIDGE. For Adley, lumberman who lived on the ridge.

AIKENS RIDGE. Unknown.

ALDER: BROOK, STREAM. For alder trees.

ALLEN HILL. For the local Allen family.

ALLEN STREAM. For Joseph Allen, settler, 1802, from Salisbury, New Hampshire.

ALMANAC MOUNTAIN. Unknown.

ALTON: BOG, TOWNSHIP. For Alton, South Hampton, England.

AREY: CORNERS, flagstation. For Caroline, Roscoe, and Everett Arey, who lived in the immediate area.

ARGYLE TOWNSHIP. For Argyle, Scotland.

ARNOLD CORNER. For Henry A. Arnold, resident.

ATWOOD POND. For Atwood, a man who logged there.

AVERY BROOK. For the John Avery family, early settlers.

AYERS ISLAND. For Joshua Ayers, first owner.

BACK SETTLEMENT POND. For its isolation in the center of the township.

BAGLEY MOUNTAIN. For Moses Bagley, settler, 1825.

BAKER: BROOK (3), HILL BROOK. Brook in Kenduskeag Township, for the early Baker family who farmed. Brook in Medway Township, for the Baker family who settled in mid 1800's. Brook and Hill in the Bradley Township area, possibly for Joe Baker.

BALANCING ROCK. Descriptive.

BALD: HILL (2), MOUNTAIN. Descriptive.

BALM OF GILEAD BROOK. For balm of gilead trees.

BANGOR: EAST-, NORTH-, NORTH-STATION, WEST-, HILL, settlement, TOWNSHIP. For the hymn "Bangor," a favorite of the Reverend Seth Noble, who is supposed to have given the name.

BARKER BROOK. For the local Barker family.

BARNARD MOUNTAIN. Unknown.

BARNES BROOK. For Joseph Barnes, who owned the land where the stream rises.

BARROWS POINT. For George Barrows, father of Lewis O. Barrows, a former governor of Maine.

BARTLETT: BOG, STREAM. For James Bartlett, first settler in 1829.

BARTLETT COVE. For the local Bartlett family.

BASIN MILLS. For location at the basin where the Stillwater River meets the Penobscot River.

BATCH: BROOK, POND. For an old bachelor who said he "batched" on the pond.

BEAR: BROOK (9), LOGAN, MOUNTAIN, POND. For bears.

BEARSE BROOK. For Alexander Bearse, lumber surveyor for Springfield Township about 1845.

BEATHAM ISLAND. For Thomas Beatham, who lived on the main road near the island.

BEAVER: BROOK (3), MEADOW BROOK, POND BROOK. For beavers.

BEECH RIDGE. For beech trees.

BEN ANNIS POND. For Benjamin Annis, settler by 1784.

BERRYS CORNERS. For the local Berry family.

BIG: EDDY, ISLAND (2), ISLANDS, LOGAN. Descriptive.

BILLFISH: BROOK, MOUNTAIN, POND. For William Fish, who worked in the area.

BILLINGS HILL. For Samuel Billings, who lived on Stetson Road at the approach to the hill.

BILLY DOE BOG. For William Doe, descendant of the early Doe family.

BIRCH: EAST BRANCH-STREAM, ISLAND, ISLANDS, LITTLE-ISLAND, MOUNTAIN, POINT, STREAM (2). For birch trees.

BLACKCAP. Descriptive of a heavy growth of fir trees on the mountain.

BLACK CAT ISLAND. For a legend that says a black cat lives on the island and will bring bad luck to any camper or fisherman who disturbs him.

BLACK CAT POND. Woodsmen's name for the fisher.

BLACK: ISLAND (2), STREAM. Descriptive.

BLACKMAN BROOK. Unknown.

BLACKMAN RIDGE. A Penobscot Indian legend says that the Black Man, the warrior of death, lives here; however, since there are other "Blackman" place-names around, this might possibly be folklore.

BLACKMAN STREAM. For Bradley Blackman, early settler and namesake of Bradley Township, who operated a general store here.

BLACKWELL BOG. For the Blackwell family who owned it.

BLACK WOODS, THE. Descriptive of the coloration of fir trees at a distance.

BLOOD BROOK. For the reddish-brown color of the water.

BLUEBERRY ISLAND. For blueberries.

BOG: BROOK (6), POND, POINT. Descriptive.

BONDS CORNERS. For Winifield Bond, who lived there.

BONNIE BROOK. For the local Bonney family.

BOODY: BROOK, POND. For Shepard Boody, early lumberman.

BOOMBRIDGE BROOK. For a small lumber boom there.

BOOM ISLAND. (2). For its service as deadman for hitching lumber booms to the mainland.

BOTTLE: ISLAND, LAKE, LAKE STREAM. To make a fanciful pair with Keg Lake.

BOWDEN. Unknown.

BOWERBANK. For Bower, a lumberman who had his home on a high bank above the railroad tracks.

BOWERS. For the Benjamin J. Bowers family, settlers, 1843.

BOWERS MOUNTAIN. For Samuel Bowers, settler by 1834.

BOWLIN: BROOK, FALLS, LITTLE-BROOK, LITTLE-POND, POND. Unknown.

BOYCE COVE. For Samuel Boyce, settler from Canada, about 1850, who was originally from England.

BOYNTON BROOK. For the Boynton family who lived nearby, early 1800's.

BRADBURY BROOK. For the Bradbury family who lived in the hills at the head of the brook.

BRADFORD: CENTER, NORTH-, settlement, TOWNSHIP. For Bradford, Massachusetts.

BRADLEY: settlement, TOWNSHIP. For Bradley Blackman, one of the earlier settlers and a prominent citizen.

BRADY BROOK. For the Brady family who owned land where the brook runs.

BREEZY POINT. Descriptive.

BREWER: LAKE, NORTH-, settlement, SOUTH-, TOWNSHIP. For Colonel John Brewer, one of its first settlers, from Worcester, Massachusetts.

BRIDE ISLAND. Unknown.

BROOKS POND. For Abner Brooks, who settled nearby.

BROWN BROOK. (3). In Alton Township, for G.W. Brown, resident, 1875. In Hampden Township, for several Brown families who settled nearby. In T3R1, for Leroy Brown and his father, who settled about 1852.

BROWN HILL. For Charles, Ezekiel, and Horace Brown, settlers, 1831.

BROWN ISLAND. (2). In Winn Township, for John, Charles, and Moses Brown, who cleared land in the area. In T2R7, for Francis Brown, first owner.

BRYANT HILL. For the early Bryant family who settled on the hill.

BUCK: BROOK, HILL, POINT. For buck deer.

BULL HILL. For a man who worked the farm on the hill, using a team of bullocks.

BUNKER HILL. For Thomas Bunker, settler about 1821.

BURLINGTON: settlement, TOWNSHIP. For Burlington, Massachusetts.

BURNHAM BROOK. For Elizer Burnham, settler, 1837, from Scarborough Township.

BURNT: LITTLE- POND, POND, SWAMP. Descriptive.

BUZZELL STREAM. For Millard Buswell, who lived there.

BUZZY: BROOK, LITTLE-BROOK. For the buzzings of mosquitoes.

CALL BOG. For the local Call family.

CAMBOLASSE POND. Micmac: "chain of ponds."

CARDVILLE. For the Card family that settled there in the 1800's.

CAREY: BROOK, LAKE. For William H. Carey of Houlton, whose company cut timber in the area.

CARIBOU: BOG (2), POND. For Caribou.

CARLISLE: BROOK, SWAMP. For Carlisle, lumberman, who operated in the area.

CARMEL: settlement, TOWNSHIP. Named by the Reverend Paul Ruggles, the first settler, in honor of Elijah's experience on Mount Carmel.

CARPENTER RIDGE. Unknown.

CARR CORNER. For the local Carr family.

CARROLL: settlement, TOWNSHIP. For Daniel Carroll, signer of the Constitution.

CEDAR: BROOK, LAKE, MOUNTAIN, SWAMP, POND. For cedar trees.

CEMETERY HILL. For the cemetery located there.

CENTER POND. Descriptive of location in the center of Lincoln Township.

CHAMBERLAIN: BROOK, POND RIDGE. For the Chamberlain family.

CHAPMAN POND. For the Milton Chapman family, prominent in the area.

CHARLESTON: settlement, TOWNSHIP, WEST-. For Charleston, Massachusetts.

CHASE BOG. For the Chase famiy who owned it.

CHEMO: BOG, POND. Abnaki: "large bog." It is said that the name was transferred from the bog to the pond due to a popular song written in 1871 by James Rowe of Bangor.

CHESLEY BROOK. For Chesley, lumberman, who settled here.

CHESTER: settlement, SIDING, TOWNSHIP. Named by Samuel Chesley for his former home, Chester, New Hampshire.

CHICK HILL. For the Chick family, settlers, 1830.

CHOKECHERRY ISLAND. For chokecherries.

CHRISTIAN SPRING. One source says that a man named Christian had a lumber camp there. Another says that the name derived from baptisms being held there.

CLARK BROOK. (2). In Burlington Township, for Clark, who lived there. In Springfield Township, for the Samuel Clark family, settlers by about 1837.

CLEAVES BROOK. For Abraham Cleaves, settler between 1837-40, or Charles Cleaves.

CLEWLEVILLE CORNERS. For Isaac Clewley, first settler in area, who came May 31, 1786, with 8 men from Massachusetts.

CLIFTON: CORNERS, settlement, TOWNSHIP For the cliffs there.

COBB MOUNTAIN. For the Cobb family who lived nearby.

COBURN. For the local Coburn family.

COFFEY HILL. For the Coffey family, here before 1875.

COFFIN BROOK. (3). In Carroll Township, for the local Coffin family. In Lincoln Township, for the local Coffin family. In Drew Township, for Wes Coffin, logger.

COLD: BROOK (settlement), LITTLE-STREAM, STREAM, STREAM POND, UPPER-STREAM PONDS. Descriptive.

COLE POND. For Joseph Cole, owner.

COMSTOCK BROOK. Unknown.

CONNECTICUT RIDGE. For settlers from Connecticut.

CONTRARY: BROOK (2), BROOK BOG. For their wandering characters.

COOLIDGE CORNER. For Cornelius Coolidge, settler, summer of 1803, from Hallowell, Maine.

COPELAND HILL. For Joseph, William, and Lemuel Copeland, who came from Massachusetts, early 1800's.

CORINNA: settlement, TOWNSHIP. For Corinna, the daughter of Dr. John Warren of Boston, first proprietor.

CORINTH: EAST-, settlement, SOUTH-, TOWNSHIP, WEST-. For the ancient city of Corinth, Greece.

COSTIGAN: BROOK, flagstation. For the 3 Costigan brothers who settled on the brook.

COW ISLAND. For cows kept there.

CRAIG ISLAND. Unknown.

CRANBERRY: BROOK, COVE, ISLAND, POND (3). For cranberries.

CRANE: RIDGE, RIDGE BROOK. For cranes that nested here.

CROCKER: BROOK, -TOWN. For the numerous Crocker families.

CROCKER TURN. For the Crocker family who lived there.

CROMMETT BROOK. Unknown.

CROOKED: BROOK, POND, STREAM. Descriptive.

CROSSUNTIC STREAM. Probably Indian, but derivation unknown.

CROWFOOT RAPIDS. For a local group of Indians known as the "Crowfoots."

CRYSTAL BROOK. Descriptive.

CUMMINGS BOG. For William Comins, settler, 1802.

CUNNINGHAM LEDGE. For the Cunningham family who owned it.

CUNNINGHAM MOUNTAINS. Unknown.

CUSHMAN RIDGE. For the early settling Cushman family.

CUT: BROOK, LAKE, LAKE STREAM. For a canal cut from the lake to Hay Brook to enable logs to be driven into the Penobscot River and to Bangor to market.

DAIRY BROOK. For a dairy located near its banks.

DAMASCUS. Unknown.

DAM RIDGE. For a dam located at its foot on Number Three Pond.

DAVIDSON: BROOK, flagstation, POND. For Davidson, who ran a nearby farm.

DAVIS: BROOK (2), HILL. Hill and Brook in Charleston Township for the local Davis family. Hill in Newburgh Township, for Willard Davis and his father, who resided here on a farm. Brook in Lowell Township, unknown.

DAVIS: MOUNTAIN, POND (2), RIDGE. Pond in Eddington

Township, for Captain Samuel Davis from Charleston, Massachusetts, settler, 1800. The others for Greenleaf "Hunter" Davis, early trapper.

DEAD: BROOK (3), BROOK DEADWATER, LOWER-WATER (3), MIDDLE BRANCH-STREAM, STREAM (2), UPPER-WATER, WEST BRANCH-STREAM. Descriptive of rate of flow.

DEADMAN COVE. For a dead man found there in the 19th century.

DEAN BROOK. Unknown.

DEASEY: PONDS, MOUNTAIN. Unknown.

DEEP COVE. Descriptive.

DEER ISLAND. For deer.

DEVILS ELBOW. A sharp bend on the Aroostook River that gave river drivers trouble getting logs around it.

DEXTER: NORTH-, settlement, TOWNSHIP. For Samuel Dexter, the unsuccessful Democratic gubernatorial candidate of Massachusetts in 1816, defeated by John Brooks.

DILL: BROOK, RIDGE. For the Dill family.

DIPPER POND. Descriptive of shape.

DIXMONT: CENTER, EAST-, NORTH-, settlement, TOWNSHIP. For Dr. Elijah Dix, the principal proprietor.

DOE ISLAND. Probably for Jacob Doe, settler, 1818.

DOLBY POND. Probably for the Dolby who would not listen to advice on how to maneuver around a large rock in the river and was caught and drowned there.

DOLLAR ISLAND. (2). Descriptive of shape (round).

DOW MOUNTAIN. For the Dow family, settlers before 1829.

DRAKE PLACE. For Lloyd W. Drake, justice of the peace and town leader.

DREW TOWNSHIP. Unknown.

DRY BROOK. Descriptive.

DUCK LAKE . For ducks.

DUDLEY BROOK. For Charles Dudley, resident, 1890's.

DUFOUR LEDGE. Unknown.

DURBIN CORNER. For the Durbin family.

DUTCH ISLAND. For a lumberman resident known as "Dutch."

DWINAL POND. For Rufus Dwinal, who bought the franchise to cut timber in 1827.

EAGLE: BLUFF, POND, STREAM. For eagles.

EARNEST CORNER. For the Earnest family.

EAST: BRANCH, BRANCH LAKE. Descriptive.

EAST MILLINOCKET: settlement, TOWNSHIP. When Great Northern engineers started building the paper mill, they marked their blueprints "east of Millinocket." The "of" was later dropped when the township was organized.

EBHORSE: LITTLE-STREAM, STREAM. Unknown.

EDDINGTON: EAST-, settlement, TOWNSHIP. For Colonel Jonathan Eddy, a native of Norton, Massachusetts.

EDINBURG TOWNSHIP. Named by John Bennoch, roadbuilder, for Edinburg, Scotland.

EGG POND. (2). For bird eggs.

EIGHTEEN BOG. For its location on square mile lot 18.

ELBOW LAKE. Descriptive of shape.

ELEVEN BROOK. For its location on square mile lot 11.

ELLEN WOOD RIDGE. For Ellingwood, local surveyor. Others say that he was a lumberman.

ELLIOT LANDING. Owned by the Elliot family.

ELLIS CORNER. For the local Ellis family.

EMERSON RUNAROUND. Probably for Moses Emerson, settler, 1824.

ENDLESS LAKE. Descriptive of a long lake.

ENFIELD: HORSEBACK, settlement, STATION, TOWNSHIP, WEST-. For John Wood, settler, who made a settlement at the south end of the town, the "end field." Or, more likely, for Enfield, England.

EPHRAIM BROOK. For Ephraim Spencer, resident, 1875.

ESKUTASSIS: LITTLE-POND, STREAM, POND. Abnaki: "brook-trout" or "small trout."

ETNA: BOG, CENTER, POND, settlement, TOWNSHIP. For Mount Aetna in Sicily, supposedly by Benjamin Friend, who selected it from Webster's "Blue Backed Speller."

EXETER: CENTER, CORNERS, EAST-, MILLS, settlement, SOUTH-, TOWNSHIP. For Exeter, New Hampshire, former home of some of the settlers.

FAIRDALE HILL. Unknown.

FAY SCOTT BOG. For the Fay Scott Machine Corporation, founded in 1884.

FELTS BROOK. For Jonathan Felt, landholder by 1785.

FERGUSON LAKE. For Hardy Ferguson, engineer who helped design this man-made lake for the Great Northern Paper Company.

FIDDLER ISLAND. Unknown.

FIELDS POND. For its location on the Fields family property.

FIRST: LAKE, POND. Descriptive.

FISH HILL. For Ira Fish, early mill builder.

FITZ BOG. Unknown.

FIVE BOG. For its location on square mile lot number 5.

FIVE ISLAND RAPIDS. Descriptive.

FLATIRON POND. Descriptive of shape.

FLEMMING BROOK. Unknown.

FLOWERS BROOK. For the early Flowers family.

FOGG BROOK. For Greenleaf M. Fogg, farmer, 1833.

FOLSOM BROOK. For its location on Folsom family land.

FOLSOM: POND, RIDGE. For Samuel Folsom, early settler.

FOOTMAN BROOK. For the Footman family.

FORBES BROOK. For the early Forbes family.

FOSTER ISLAND. For the William Foster family, settlers, 1815.

FREESE ISLAND. For George and John Freese, early settlers.

FRENCH: MILL, STREAM. For the early French family who ran the mill.

FRENCH SETTLEMENT. For a settlement of French-Canadians.

FROG, THE. Descriptive of a piece of land extending into Horseshoe Lake that is shaped like the "frog", or soft part of a horse's hoof.

GAGNON FLAT. For Paul Gagnon, who logged in the area in 1916.

GANTNERS LANDING. For Gantner, lumberman who set up a fur trading post here.

GARDNER POND. For a lumberman named Gardner.

GARLAND: POND, settlement, TOWNSHIP, WEST-POND. For Joseph Garland, first settler of the township, in 1802.

GATES HILL. For the local Gates family.

GATES MEADOWS. Cartographical error for Cates Meadows, for the local Cates family.

GEORGE POND. (2). In Herman Township, for William George, settler, 1704. In Holden Township, for Thomas George, early settler.

GERRY. For O. Garey, resident, 1859.

GETCHELL: BROOK, MOUNTAIN. For the local Getchell family.

GILMORE MEADOWS. For Rufus, Apollos, and David Gilmore.

GLENBURN: CENTER, settlement, TOWNSHIP, WEST-. A descriptive Scottish word meaning "a small stream in a narrow valley," probably the Kenduskeag.

GLIDDEN HILL. For the George Glidden family, settlers, 1836.

GODFREY PITCH. Unknown.

GOODALE CORNER. For Ephraim Goodale, settler, 1803.

GOODWIN BROOK. For Silas Goodwin, settler, about 1839.

GORDON: BROOK (2), FALLS, flagstation, LITTLE-BROOK. Brook, flagstation, Falls, and Little-Brook in Mattawamkeag Township area, for John Gordon, who had a mill on the brook. One source says for a Gordon who drowned there — possibly, if true, the same man. Brook in T1R7, for a lumberman named Gordon who lived there.

GORDON CORNER. For Moses Gordon, who was born in New Hampshire in 1870 and settled here in 1895.

GORDON ISLAND. Unknown.

GOTT BROOK. For John Gott, justice of the peace, resident about 1836.

GOULD LEDGE. For the Gould family.

GOULD POND. For the J.H. Gould family.

GRAND: FALLS (2), TOWNSHIP. Descriptive of the falls.

GRAND LAKE MATAGAMON. Abnaki: "far on the other side."

GRAND PITCH. (2). Descriptive of large rapids.

GRANITE RIDGE. Descriptive.

GRANT: BROOK, BROOK DEADWATER. Unknown.

GRASS ISLAND. Descriptive.

GRAY LEDGE DEADWATER. Unknown.

GRAYS HILL. For Oscar W. Gray, early settler.

GREAT WORKS. At this place Dwinal, Sawyer, & Company erected a huge double mill in 1833. In 1834-35 more mills were built; this constituted a "great works."

GREENBUSH: settlement, SWAMP, TOWNSHIP. For the green woods.

GREENFIELD: settlement, TOWNSHIP. For the extensive green fields. More likely for Greenfield, Massachusetts, former home of some of the settlers.

GREEN: ISLAND, MOUNTAIN, MOUNTAIN POND. For a logger named Green.

GREENLAND BROOK. Descriptive of the color of the area.

GREEN POND. For William Green and his father, whose land bordered on the pond.

GRINDSTONE: FALLS, settlement, TOWNSHIP. This is where boatmen used to grind their axes.

GRISTMILL POND. For a gristmill located there.

GUILFORD. Unknown.

HALFWAY BROOK. (2). In Milford Township, for location halfway between Milford and Greenville, via Costigan. In T2R8, for location halfway between Seboeis and the East Branch Penobscot River.

HALL HILL. For W.H. Hall, resident, 1875.

HALL POND. For Hall, resident logger.

HAMMOND POND. For Henry Hammond, owner.

HAMMOND RIDGE. For Joseph Hammond, early settler.

HAMPDEN: CENTER, EAST-, HIGHLANDS, settlement, STATION, TOWNSHIP, WEST-. For John Hampden, 17th century English patriot.

HARDY BROOK. For Hardy Pond in Lake View Township, Piscataquis County.

HARDY HILL. Possibly for Joshua Harding, settler, 1787.

HARTS CORNERS. For Jacob Hart, early settler.

HARVEYS POND. For the H. Harvey mill located there in 1875.

HARVEY STREAM. For the Harvey family who lived in the area in 1875.

HARWOOD ISLAND. For the local Harwood family.

HASELTINE CORNER. For Joseph M. Hazeltine, settler from Portland, New Hampshire, 1820.

HASKELL: DEADWATER, ROCK PITCH. For Haskell, a river driver who was drowned at the pitch and whose body was found snagged near the rock.

HASTY CORNER. For the Hasty family who settled in the early 1800's.

HATCH HILL. For the Hatch family.

HATHAM BOG. For Hatham, local lumberman.

HATHAWAY RIDGE. For the early Hathaway family.

HATHORN: LITTLE-POND, MOUNTAIN, POND, Unknown.

HAY: BROOK (3), BROOK (settlement), BROOK MOUNTAIN, LAKE, LITTLE-BROOK, MOUNTAIN, POND. For an abundance of hay.

HAYDEN COVE. For Samuel Harden, first settler at the cove. The difference in spelling reflects a dialect pronunciation.

HAYNES POINT. For Guy Haynes, who had a camp there.

HAYNES RIDGE. For Haynes, a man who worked for a Bangor woods company late in the 19th century.

HAZELTON BROOK. For its location on Hazelton family land.

HEMLOCK ISLAND. This name is a translation of the Abnaki: "Kussus-cook," which means "hemlock," for the trees there.

HERMAN POINT. Unknown.

HERMON: BOG, CENTER, HILL, NORTH-, POND (2), settlement, TOWNSHIP. For the biblical Mount Hermon.

HERSEY HILL. For the local Hersey family.

HERSEY ISLAND. For William R. Hersey, settler and prominent citizen, 1832.

HERSEYTOWN TOWNSHIP. Unknown.

HICKS CORNER. For the Hicks family.

HIGGINSVILLE. For a Higgins who built and operated a sawmill here in the early days.

HIGH CUT. Descriptive of a high hill with a road cut through a portion of it.

HIGH LANDING. Descriptive.

HILL BROOK. For G. Hill, resident, 1859.

HINKLEY HILL. For Eben Cobb Hinkley, who settled here about 1806.

HOBART: BROOK, DEADWATER, POND. Unknown.

HOCTOR POND. Unknown.

HODGESON BROOK. Unknown.

HOG HILL. Descriptive of its contour.

HOG ISLAND. Hogs were kept there.

HOLBROOK: POND, settlement. For the Calvin Holbrook family, early settlers.

HOLDEN: CENTER, EAST-, settlement, STATION, TOWNSHIP. For either Holden, Massachusetts, or a Dr. Holden.

HOLLAND POND. Unknown.

HOLT POND. For John L. Holt, owner, about 1839.

HOPKINS ACADEMY GRANT: EAST TOWNSHIP, WEST TOWNSHIP. For Hopkins Academy.

HOPKINS POND. Unknown.

HORSEBACK: POND, ridge. Descriptive.

HORSE ISLAND. For horses kept there.

HORSE MOUNTAIN. (2). In T6R8, unknown. In Hermon Township, formerly known as Ass Mountain for its resemblance to a horse's posterior. The cartographers and polite society made it less descriptive.

HORSESHOE LAKE. Descriptive of shape.

HOT BROOK. Because it seldom freezes.

HOUSE POND. For the House family.

HOUSTON: BROOK, ISLAND. For a steamboat named the "Sam Houston," which ran in the area before 1849.

HOWLAND: settlement, TOWNSHIP. For John Howland, who was washed overboard on the "Mayflower" crossing. He later signed the Mayflower Compact.

HOWS CORNERS. For William Hows, resident butcher.

HOYT: BROOK, -VILLE HORSEBACK. For the N. Hoyt & Company shingle mill.

HUB HALL COVE. For Hub Hall, who camped here.

HUDSON: BROOK, HILL, RIDGE, settlement, TOWNSHIP. For Hudson, Massachusetts.

HUISE CORNERS. Formerly known as Hearse House Corner, for a hearse house there. The discrepancy in spelling reflects local pronunciation.

HUNT COVE. Unknown.

HUNTINGTON MILL. For Ernest and William Huntington, brothers who ran a mill as late as 1875.

HUNT MOUNTAIN. For the Hunt family who ran a farm nearby.

INDIAN: ISLAND, POINT ISLAND, PURCHASE T3 TOWNSHIP, PURCHASE T4 TOWNSHIP. For the Penobscot Indians.

INGALLS SIDING. Unknown.

INMAN BOG. Unknown.

INTERVALE BROOK. Descriptive.

IRELAND POND. Unknown.

ISLAND SWAMP. Descriptive of high ground in the center of the swamp.

ISTHMUS: BROOK, POND. Descriptive of the brook, which was like an isthmus, connecting two bodies of water.

JACKSON BROOK. For Godfrey Jackson, mill builder about 1827.

JEFFERSON MOUNTAIN. For Jefferson Mallett, owner.

JERRY: BROOK (2), POND. Pond and Brook in T5R7, for Jerry, a logger. Brook in TAR7, unknown.

JOHNNY AYRES BROOK. For the son of Sam Ayres, who owned the land that the brook crossed.

JOHNSON BROOK. For the early Johnson family.

JO-MARY: MIDDLE -LAKE, UPPER-STREAM. For Jo-Mary Lake in Piscataquis County.

JONES: BROOK, POND. For Thomas Jones, early settler and logger.

JORDAN BROOK. For the Jordan River in Israel, because of the many baptisms which took place here.

JORDAN MILLS. For Harvey Jordan, who built a lumber and shingle mill there in 1879.

JUDKINS BROOK. For H.C. Judkins, millowner, 1875.

JUNIOR: LAKE, MOUNTAIN, STREAM. Unknown.

KATAHDIN: BROOK, LAKE. For Mount Katahdin, Piscataquis County.

KATEN CORNER. For 3 generations of Katens who lived here.

KEENE BOG. For the local Keene family.

KEG LAKE. For the Abnaki affix "keag," which has been shortened.

KELLOCH MOUNTAIN. Probably for Cornelius Kelloch, resident in Orrington Township who explored throughout the area.

KELLY BOG. For the Kelly family who lived on a nearby hill.

KELLY HILL. For the early Kelly family.

KENDUSKEAG: settlement, STREAM, TOWNSHIP. Abnaki: "eel weir place."

KIDDER BROOK. For Jonathon and Rebecca Kidder, who lived there.

KIMBALL: BROOK, POND. For Kimball, area logger.

KIMBALL HILL. For Samuel Kimball, who had a farm there.

KIMBLE HILL. For a Kimball who settled here and cleared the land.

KING ISLAND. For the King family.

KINGMAN: settlement, TOWNSHIP. For R.S. Kingman, junior member of the firm Shaw & Kingman, an extensive sole-leather tannery, predecessors of F. Shaw & Brothers.

KINGS MOUNTAIN. For the King family.

KIRKLAND RIDGE. Unknown.

KNIGHT CORNER. For Zebulon Knight, settler, 1825.

KNOX HILL CORNER. For the local Knox family.

LAGRANGE: settlement, SOUTH-, TOWNSHIP. For La Grange, the estate of LaFayette.

LAKESIDE LEDGE. Descriptive.

LAKEVILLE TOWNSHIP. Descriptive.

LAKE WASSOOKEAG. Abnaki: "shining fishing place," or "at the whitefish place," or "fishing by torchlight."

LAMBS HILL. For the Lamb family.

LANCASTER BROOK. (2). In Passadumkeag Township, for the Lancaster family who had land bordering the brook. In Glenburn Township, for the Jonathon Lancaster family, who settled February 29, 1852, in a meadow traversed by the brook.

LANE: BROOK, BROOK HILLS, BROOK MEADOWS, BROOK POND. Unknown.

LARD POND. A lumber camp was operated on the shore of the pond where the men claimed the company cook used so much lard in his cooking that it ran out of his biscuits.

LAWLER RIDGE. For the Lawler family who owned it.

LEATHERS CORNERS. For J.W. Leathers, resident, 1875.

LEDGE: BROOK, FALLS, THE-. Descriptive.

LEDGE CUT BROOK. Because the construction crews of the Bangor & Aroostook Railroad had to cut through a ledge to divert the brook.

LEE: settlement, TOWNSHIP. For Stephen Lee, early settler.

LEVANT: settlement, SOUTH-, TOWNSHIP, WEST-. Probably for French settlers from the Levant Plateau region in Nova Scotia.

LIBBY CORNER. For Libby, a wheelwright who lived there and died in the Civil War.

LIBBY HILL. For Richard Libby, who owned part of the hill.

LILY POND. For lilies.

LINCOLN: CENTER, NORTH-, settlement, SOUTH-, TOWNSHIP. For Enoch Lincoln, landholder and sixth governor of Maine.

LINCOLN: COVE, POND, RIDGE. For the early Lincoln family.

LINCOLN MILLS. For Harry Lincoln.

LINDSEY: BOG, BROOK. For the local Lindsey family.

LITTLE ISLAND. Descriptive.

LOGAN BROOK. For the local Logan family, according to one source; however, "logan" also frequently means "a deadwater."

LOMBARD: LAKE, MOUNTAIN, STREAM. For the family of Alvin Orlando Lombard, who invented the Lombard chainsaw.

LONG A: OLD-SIDING, TOWNSHIP. Descriptive of the length and its township designation.

LONG: COVE, ISLAND, LOGAN, MOUNTAIN, POND, POINT, RIDGE. Descriptive.

LOOKOUT MOUNTAIN. (2). Descriptive of a tall mountain.

LOON ISLAND. For loons.

LORD: LOWER-BROOK, MOUNTAIN, UPPER-BROOK. For the Lord family, settlers, early 1800's.

LOST POND. (4). For their isolation.

LOWELL: BROOK, ISLAND. Unknown.

LOWELL: EAST-, settlement, TOWNSHIP. For Lowell Hayden, first male child born there, son of Alpheus Hayden.

LOWELL LAKE. For the local Lowell family.

LUCKY LEDGE. A good place to fish.

MACK HILL. For the McLauglin family.

MADAGASCAL: LITTLE-POND, POND, STREAM. Abnaki: "meadows at the mouth."

MADDEN HILL. For O. Madden, who lived there.

MAGS LEDGE. For Mag, an Indian woman who swam from this ledge to the shore of Pushaw Lake.

MAHOCKKANOCK ISLAND. Abnaki: possibly "hole in the river."

MANN HILL. For David Mann, one of the first 8 men who came to the area on May 31, 1786.

MANSELL POND. For A. Mansell, resident, 1859.

MANSFIELD LEDGE. For the Mansfield family.

MANTON POND. Unknown.

MARBLE POND. Because of a U.S. geologist's statement that there was much marble in the area.

MARDEN POND. For Joshua Marden, who had a camp here.

MARSH CREEK. Although there were Marsh families in the area early, the name is probably descriptive.

MARSH ISLAND. For John Marsh, settler, 1774.

MARTIN BOG. For the Martin family, there before 1875.

MARTIN STREAM. For Thomas Martin, old logger who loved the area.

MATTAGODUS: STREAM, WEST BRANCH-STREAM. Abnaki: "bad sliding (a rocky bottom bad for a canoe landing)."

MATTAKEUNK: EAST BRANCH-STREAM, POND, STREAM. Abnaki: "at the end of the swift stream."

MATTAMISCONTIS: LAKE, LITTLE-LAKE, LITTLE-MOUN-TAIN, MOUNTAIN, SOUTH BRANCH-STREAM, STREAM, TOWNSHIP. Abnaki: "alewife stream."

MATTANAWCOOK: ISLAND, POND, STREAM. Abnaki: "at the end of the gravel bar."

MATTAWAMKEAG: settlement, STREAM, TOWNSHIP. If Abnaki: "fishing place beyond a gravel bar." If Malecite: "rapids at mouth." If Micmac: "on a sand bar."

MAXFIELD TOWNSHIP. For Joseph McIntosh of Hingham, Massachusetts. He was the second settler, and his farm became known as "Mac's Field." The present spelling followed the pronunciation.

MAXY BROOK. For its location in Maxfield, and the McIntosh family.

McGILVREY POND. For Hugh McGilvrey, who cut logs there in the 1860's.

McGOON POND. For the local McGoon family.

McGREGOR MILL. For the McGregor family who owned it.

McKINNEY POINT. Unknown.

MEADOW: BROOK (6), BROOK RIPS, LITTLE-BROOK, -VILLE. Descriptive.

MEDUNKEUNK: LAKE, SOUTH BRANCH-STREAM, STREAM. Abnaki: "blocked up by sand."

MEDWAY: settlement, TOWNSHIP. For its location midway between Bangor and the north line of the county.

MERRILL: BROOK (2), POND. Brook and Pond in Howland Township, for James Merrill, settler, 1824. Brook in T3R1, for Charles Merrill and/or his ancestor James Merrill, who lived in Lee Township.

MERRIMAN BROOK. Unknown.

MESSER: LITTLE-POND, POND. Unknown.

MILES CORNER. Probably for Francis **Miles.**

MILFORD: settlement, TOWNSHIP. Named for Milford, Massachusetts, by settlers from there.

MILL: BROOK, POND, PRIVILEGE BROOK, PRIVILEGE LAKE. For mills.

MILLER: BOG, RIDGE. Unknown.

MILLIMAGASSETT: LAKE, RIDGE, STREAM. Abnaki: "where duckhawks abound."

MILLINOCKET: FALLS LAKE, RIDGE, settlement, STREAM (2), TOWNSHIP. Abnaki: "this place is admirable."

MINER BROOK. (2). Unknown.

MINK ISLAND. For mink.

MOHAWK: ISLAND, RAPIDS, STREAM. Abnaki: "cannibal," their term for the Mohawks.

MOLUNKUS: STREAM, WEST BRANCH-STREAM. Abnaki: "deep valley stream."

MOODY. For the local Moody family.

MOODY BROOK. Unknown.

MOOSEHORN CROSSING. Unknown.

MOOSE: ISLAND, MOUNTAIN, POND (2). For moose.

MOOSELEUK: LITTLE-STREAM, STREAM. Abnaki: "moose place."

MORGAN BEACH. For Harry Morgan, who rented the beach and built an amusement park, about 1925.

MORRELL POND. Unknown.

MORSE CORNERS. For the local Morse family.

MOUNTAIN BROOK. (2). Descriptive.

MOUNTAIN: CATCHER POND, LITTLE-CATCHER POND. For the reflection of the mountains in the water of the lake.

MOUNT CHASE: mountain, TOWNSHIP. For Chase, an agent of the state who was engaged in apprehending timber thieves on the public lands and burning hay that they had cut. A forest fire broke out, and he fled to this mountain where he was saved.

MOUNT HARRIS. For Thaddeus Mason Harris, secretary of Dr. Elijah Dix, the proprietor of Dixfield Township.

MOUSE ISLAND. Descriptive of its size.

MOWER POND. For the local Mower family.

MUD: BIG-BROOK, BROOK (4), BROOK FLOWAGE, COVE, EAST BRANCH-BROOK, LITTLE-BROOK, LITTLE-POND, POND (5), WEST BRANCH-BROOK. Descriptive.

MURCH RIDGE. Unknown.

NARROWS: ISLAND, THE -(3). Descriptive.

NASON POINT. For Eugene Nason, who ran a sporting camp here about 1945.

NEALEYS CORNER. For Eugene and Franklin Nealey.

NEALLY BROOK. For the Neally family who owned the land traversed by the brook.

NEGRO HILL. For a Negro family who lived there in the 19th century.

NELSON ISLAND. Probably for the Jeremy Nelson family, settlers, 1824.

NEWBURGH: CENTER, NORTH-, settlement, SOUTH-, TOWNSHIP, VILLAGE. For its meaning of "new town."

NEWMAN HILL. For the Newman family.

NEWPORT: EAST-, NORTH-, settlement, TOWNSHIP. For an Indian portage between the Penobscot River tributaries and the Sebasticook River, known as the "new portage" or "new port."

NICATOU ISLAND. Abnaki: "the river fork," descriptive of where the Penobscot is made up from its east and west branches.

NICKERSON ISLAND. For the local Nickerson family.

NICOLAR ISLAND. For Captain Nicolar, a sub chief who married Chief Joseph Orono's daughter and lived on the island.

NINE: MEADOW BROOK, MEADOW RIDGE. For its location on square mile lot 9 of the township.

NOLLESEMIC: LAKE, STREAM. Abnaki: "resting place at the falls above the long stretch. "

NORCROSS. For Nick Norcross, early lumberman reputed to have been the first to drive logs through Ripogenus Gorge, at which time he furnished all his men with life preservers.

NORTHERN MAINE JUNCTION. Descriptive of the rail junction for northern Maine.

NORTHWEST INLET. Descriptive.

NORWAY LAKE. For Norway pines.

NUMBER: SIXTEEN SWAMP, THIRTY-TWO SWAMP, THREE POND, TWENTY-SIX SWAMP. For location on their respective square mile lots of the townships.

OAK: HILL, ISLAND, KNOLL, KNOLL BROOK, KNOLL BROOK DEADWATER, MOUNTAIN. For oak trees.

OAKS: BOG, BOG BROOK. For oak trees.

OLAMON: ISLAND, NORTH BRANCH-STREAM, POND, settlement. Abnaki: "red paint."

OLD TOWN: LEDGE, settlement, TOWNSHIP, WEST-, Because it has been an Indian settlement since at least 1669.

OLIVER BROOK. For the Oliver family who owned the land where the brook ran.

OLIVER: HILL, HILL CORNER. For the Oliver family who settled in the early 1800's.

ONEMILE BROOK. For its location one mile from the Penobscot River.

ORIN FALLS. Unknown.

ORONO: ISLAND, settlement, TOWNSHIP. For Chief Joseph Orono of the Penobscot Indians.

ORRINGTON: CENTER, EAST-, NORTH-, settlement, SOUTH-, TOWNSHIP. One derivation is that Parson Noble misspelled the selected name of Orangetown on the bill of incorporation. Another is that an agent of the General Court of Massachusetts accidentally ran into the name in a book and liked it.

ORSON ISLAND. For Chief Orson of the Penobscot Indians, 1793.

OTTER: BROOK (3), CHAIN PONDS, STREAM. For otters.

OWEN BROOK. Unknown.

OWLS HEAD. Descriptive of shape.

OXBOW, THE. (2). Descriptive of a bend in the river.

PARKER MEADOW BROOK. For the Parker family who owned the meadow where the brook runs.

PARK POND. For a trotting park that used to be around the pond.

PARKS: POND, POND BLUFF, POND BROOK. For the Parks family, settlers by the mid 1800's.

PARTRIDGE: BROOK, BROOK FLOWAGE, COVE. For the Partridge family.

PASSADUMKEAG: EAST BRANCH-RIVER, MOUNTAIN, RIVER, settlement, TOWNSHIP, WEST BRANCH-RIVER. Abnaki: "rapids over gravel beds."

PATTAGUMPUS: LITTLE-STREAM, STREAM. Malecite: "sandy, round cove," or "gravelly bed."

PATTEN: settlement, TOWNSHIP. For Amos Patten, who bought the township about 1830.

PATTEN POND. For the Patten family who owned it.

PATTERSON BOG. For Patterson, a man lost in the bog while working in a lumber camp.

PEA COVE. Unknown.

PEAKED: LITTLE-MOUNTAIN, MOUNTAIN. Descriptive.

PEANUT ISLAND. Descriptive of shape.

PEA RIDGE. For a large group of Tash families who were very poor and always planted a lot of peas for food.

PEASELEY HILL. For the Moses Peaseley family, settlers, 1825.

PEASLEY BROOK. For Old Man Peasley, who lived and drove logs there.

PENOBSCOT: BALD MOUNTAIN, COUNTY, EAST BRANCH-RIVER, RIVER, WEST BRANCH-RIVER. Abnaki? Malecite? "at the descending rocks, or at the extended ledges." Penobscot Indians were located throughout the area.

PERROW POINT. For Tom Perrow, who built a camp there.

PETES ISLAND. For Pete Lola, an Indian.

PICKARD HILL. For R. Pickard, resident, 1875.

PICKEREL: POINT POND (2). For pickerel fish.

PICKETT: MOUNTAIN, MOUNTAIN POND. For Pickett, a logger.

PIERRE PAUL BROOK. For Pierre Paul, an Indian who settled here after losing the girl he loved to another.

PISCATAQUIS RIVER. Abnaki: "at the river branch," or "at the little divided stream."

PISGAH MOUNTAIN. A number of Pisgah mountains and hills in Maine are attributed to the biblical Mount Pisgah, as this one may well be too; however, it could be Abnaki: "dark," or Mahican: "muddy." Due to the large number of Indian place-names in the county, this may also be Indian.

PLEASANT: LAKE (2), VALE CORNER. Descriptive.

PLYMOUTH: BOG, POND, settlement, TOWNSHIP. For Plymouth, Massachusetts.

POLLACK BROOK. For the Pollack family who owned land on which the brook ran.

POLLARD: BROOK (2), BROOK (flagstation). Brook and flag-station in Lincoln Township, for Pollard, who fished here frequently. Brook in Edinburg Township, unknown.

POND: FALLS ISLAND, PITCH, RIPS. Descriptive.

POOL BROOK. For the Pool family who owned land traversed by the brook.

POPLAR BROOK. For poplar trees.

PORCUPINE: MOUNTAIN, RIDGE. For porcupines.

POTTER BROOK. Unknown.

POTTER HILL. For George Potter and his 3 sons, who lived there.

POTTER POND. For Old Man Potter, local character, who owned the pond.

POWERS POINT. For Powers, the first man to claim it.

PREBLE: CORNER, HILL. Possibly for Preble, one of the first county attorneys in Penobscot County, or his family.

PRENTISS: settlement, TOWNSHIP. For the Honorable Henry E. Prentiss of Bangor, owner of much of the township.

PRESCOTT BROOK. For John Prescott, settler, 1840.

PRIEST LOGAN. Unknown.

PUFFERS POND. For the Puffer family who ran a sawmill here.

PUG: BROOK, HOLE, HOLE BROOK, LAKE, LOWER-LAKE, LOWER-STREAM, POND (2), UPPER-LAKE, UPPER-STREAM. Descriptive of a small, shallow hole.

PUSHAW: LAKE, LITTLE-POND, STREAM. For the Pushaw family, not Indian.

QUAKISH: BOG, BROOK, LAKE, SIDING. Micmac: "rough strewn," or Abnaki: "flooded place."

RAGGED: BROOK, EAST-BROOK, LOWER EAST-POND, LOWER WEST-POND, MOUNTAIN, UPPER EAST-POND, UPPER WEST-POND, WEST-BROOK. Descriptive.

RANDALL RIDGE. For the early settling Randall family.

RAND HILL. For the local Rand family.

RAWLINS BROOK. Unknown.

RAY ISLAND, Unknown.

REBEL HILL. Unknown.

REED ISLAND. Unknown.

REEDS BROOK. For the Martin Reed family and other Reed families.

RICKER SIDING. For Fred Ricker, who shipped lumber from this siding.

RIDER BLUFF. For Elisha Rider, one of 8 men who arrived May 31, 1786.

RING BROOK. For the local Ring family.

ROARING BROOK. Descriptive.

ROBAR: BIG-POND, BROOK, POND. Unknown.

ROBERTS MOUNTAIN. For Roberts, first man to log the mountain.

ROBYVILLE. For numerous Robys.

ROCKABEMA STREAM. Abnaki: "a woodpecker."

ROCKY: BOG, BROOK (3), BROOK SWAMP, POND, RIPS. Descriptive.

ROGAN BROOK. A source said that "rogan" is a term that means a stretch of water which runs slower than the rest. This is also meaning of the term "logan." It is unknown if "rogan" might be a dialectal variant of "logan."

ROLLINS: BROOK, MILL. For the local Rollins family who ran the mill.

ROLLINS MILLS. Unknown.

ROLLINS MOUNTAIN. For the Rollins family.

ROUND: LITTLE-POND, POND (3). Descriptive.

ROUNDY RIDGE. For the early Roundy family.

ROWE BROOK. For the Rowe family.

ROWE CORNER. For Aretus, Jesse, and Edward Rowe, settlers from Brentwood, New Hampshire, 1809.

RUSH BROOK. For C. Rush, resident, 1875.

RUSH POND. For the rushes growing there.

SADDLEBACK BROOK. Descriptive of shape of a ridge.

SALLY AYERS BROOK. For the wife or daughter of Sam Ayers, who owned much of the surrounding land.

SALMON: LITTLE-STREAM, STREAM (2), STREAM LAKE. For salmon fish.

SAM AYERS: DEADWATER, STREAM. For Sam Ayers of Old Town, who owned a large acreage in the area.

SAM ROWE RIDGE. For Sam Rowe, lumberman who cut timber there.

SAND: -BANK STREAM, BEACH BROOK, COVE (2). Descriptive.

SANDY: BROOK (2), BEACH. Descriptive.

SAPONAC: POND, settlement. Abnaki: "the great outlet," or "big opening."

SARGEANT BOG. For J. and S.L. Sargeant, residents, 1875.

SARGEANT BROOK. For Lewis Sargeant, first to farm near the brook.

SAVAGE BROOK. For George Savage, who owned the land.

SAWTELLE: BROOK (2), DEADWATER, FALLS, LITTLE-POND, POND, WEST BRANCH-BROOK, WEST BRANCH-POND. Unknown.

SCHOODIC: DEADWATER, RIDGE, STREAM. Abnaki or Malecite: "trout place," or "point of land."

SCOTTS CORNER. For J.C. and William H. Scott, settlers, 1843.

SCRAGGLY: BROOK, LAKE (2). Descriptive.

SEBASTICOOK: EAST BRANCH-RIVER, LAKE, RIVER. Penobscot-Abnaki: "the shortest route."

SEBOEIS: DEADWATER, EAST BRANCH-STREAM, LAKE, RIVER, settlement, STREAM, TOWNSHIP, WEST BRANCH-STREAM, WEST-. Abnaki: "little stream."

SEBONIBUS RAPIDS. Abnaki: probably "little stream."

SEDGEUNKEDUNK STREAM. Abnaki: "rapids at the mouth."

SHAD POND. For shad fish.

SHAW LAKE RIDGE. For Shaw Lake, Washington County.

SHEEPSKIN RIDGE. Unknown.

SHERMAN STATION. For Sherman Township, Aroostook County.

SHIN: BROOK (2), FALLS, LOWER-POND, POND (settlement), UPPER-POND. Named for Shin, local lumberman.

SHOCK HILL. A misspelling of Shack Hill, for the first settlers who lived in temporary shacks there.

SIBERIA. Named by a group of Bangor & Aroostook Railroad construction workers who said that it could not be colder in Siberia, Russia, than it was there.

SIBLEY BROOK. For the Sibley family.

SIDE CHANNEL. Descriptive.

SILVERS MILLS. For the Silver family who owned the lumber mill.

SIMMONS HILL. Unknown.

SIMPSON CORNERS. For William and Mary Simpson.

SIX MILE FALLS. For location on Kenduskeag Stream approximately 6 miles from where the Kenduskeag meets the Penobscot River.

SIXTEEN RIDGE. For its location on square mile lot number 16 of the township.

SKINNER BOG. A former pond, named for William Skinner, this has been filled in with debris.

SKUNK: HILL, POND. For skunks.

SLATE QUARRY BROOK. For a bordering slate quarry.

SMART BROOK. For the Smart family who owned the surrounding land.

SMELT BROOK. For smelts.

SMITH: BROOK (3), DEADWATER, LITTLE-BROOK, LITTLE-POND, POND. Brook, Deadwater, Little-Brook, Little-Pond, Pond in TAT3 area, for Smith, old settler and lumberman. Brook in Lincoln Township, possibly for the Josiah Smith family, settlers, 1825. In Prentiss Township, the brook was named for a Smith family who lived on its banks.

SMITH LEDGE. Probably for Thomas Smith, who signed the petition of incorporation of Orrington Township.

SNAKE POINT. For snakes.

SNOW CORNER. Unknown.

SNOW ISLAND. For the local Snow family.

SNOWSHOE: LAKE, MOUNTAIN. Descriptive of the shape of the lake.

SOCKS ISLAND. For the Abnaki pronunciation of "Jaques," an old Indian who lived there in 1750.

SOCS ISLAND. For the Abnaki pronunciation of "Jaques." It also means in Abnaki: "round, sandy cove."

SOLDIER: LITTLE-POND, POND, -TOWN TOWNSHIP. One source says for soldiers who passed through here going to the Aroostook War. Another says it was set aside as a soldiers' grant.

SOPER: BROOK, LOGAN. Unknown.

SOUADABSCOOK: settlement, STREAM, WEST BRANCH-STREAM. Abnaki: "at the place of sloping ledges," or "smooth, sloping, rocky banks."

SOULE: POND, RIDGE. Unknown.

SOUTH: BRANCH BROOK, BRANCH LAKE. Descriptive.

SOUTH GATE BROOK. For the Gates family.

SPAULDING BROOK. For Christopher C. Spaulding, who assisted in the incorporation of the township.

SPAULDING POND. For Sam Spaulding, Civil War veteran.

SPECTACLE ISLANDS. Descriptive of eye-glass shape.

SPENCER BROOK. For the James Spencer family, who settled from England before 1900.

SPENCER MEADOW. For the early Spencer family.

SPENCER RIPS. For the logging Spencer family.

SPOONERS MILL. For the Spooner family who owned the sawmill.

SPRAGUES MILL. For Ollie Sprague, who had the sawmill there.

SPRING: BIG-BROOK, BROOK, ISLAND, LITTLE-BROOK, LIT-TLE-BROOK MOUNTAIN, LOGAN, POND. For springs.

SPRINGFIELD: settlement, SOUTH-, TOWNSHIP. For fields with springs. Also for Springfield, Massachusetts. Due to the large number of transferred Massachusetts place-names in Maine, the last statement is likely correct.

SPRINGY: LOWER-POND, MIDDLE-POND, UPPER-POND. Descriptive.

SPRUCE BROOK. For spruce trees.

SQUIRREL: BROOK, ISLAND. For squirrels.

STACYVILLE: settlement, TOWNSHIP. For the first settler, James Stacy.

STAFFORD HILL. For the early Stafford family.

STAIR FALLS. Descriptive of shape.

STATE ISLAND. Unknown.

STETSON: settlement, STREAM, TOWNSHIP. For Amasa Stetson of Dedham, Massachusetts, who on October 24, 1801, bought a parcel of land from Moses and Susanna Gill for $30,000.

STEVENS BROOK. For the early Stevens family.

STILLWATER: RIVER, settlement. Because the water of the river moves slower than that of the Penobscot.

STINK BROOK. Descriptive.

STINKING BOG. Descriptive.

STONY BROOK. Descriptive.

STORES CORNER. For R.G. Stores, resident, 1875.

STUBBS CORNER. For the resident Stubbs family.

STUMP POND. Descriptive of tree stumps there.

SUCKER BROOK. (2). For sucker fish.

SUGAR ISLAND. For the Indians who made sugar from maple syrup there. They called the island "Soogah-la-manahn," "soogah" being an early English loanword; "sugar" therefore, the present name, is a simple translation of the Indian word.

SUGARLOAF MOUNTAIN. Descriptive of shape.

SUMMIT MOUNTAIN. Descriptive.

SUNKEN BOG BROOK. Descriptive.

SUNKHAZE: MEADOWS, STREAM. This word is said by some not to be Indian but an English phrase given by the Indians who hid their canoes in the stream (the area land is low and sunken) during the early morning haze and fog. This might be true, but it is probably folk etymology. Undoubtedly, it is Abnaki: "concealed outlet."

SWEAT: BOG, BOG BROOK. For the Sweat family who owned it.

SWETT RIDGE. For Thomas Swett, first homesteader there.

SWETTS POND. For Solomon Swett and family.

SWIFT: BROOK, EAST BRANCH-BROOK, MIDDLE BRANCH-BROOK, WEST BRANCH-BROOK. Descriptive of the flow.

SYSLADOBSIS: UPPER-LAKE, UPPER-STREAM. Malecite: "rock shaped like a shark or dogfish."

TACK POND. Unknown.

TAR RIDGE. For a man who was tarred and feathered there about 1850.

TARBOX ISLAND. For R.B. Tarbox, settler before 1833.

TATE BROOK. For the Tate family who owned the surrounding land.

TAYLOR: BROOK, LITTLE-BROOK. For Taylor, who drove logs on the brook.

TENMILE BROOK. Probably because it runs into Birch Stream approximately 10 miles from where Birch Stream runs into the Stillwater River.

THOMPSON BROOK. For J. Thompson, resident, 1875.

THOMPSON CORNERS. For Frank and William Thompson, who lived there about 1905.

THOROUGHFARE ISLAND. (2). Descriptive.

THOUSAND ACRE: BOG, HEATH. Because they cover a large amount of land.

THURLOW BROOK. Probably for Charles Thurlow, who lived nearby, 1875.

TOBIN BROOK. For the nearby Tobin family.

TOLMAN: BROOK, DEADWATER, hill. For the local Tolman family.

TOLMAN: BROOK, DEADWATER, HILL. For the local Tolman family.

TOMAR ISLAND. For the minor Abnaki Chief Tomah. The "r" is intrusive in the Maine dialect.

TORRIE BROOK. Unknown.

TOWN HOUSE HILL. For the location of the Lowell-Burlington Meeting House there, built in 1837, when President Andrew Jackson divided up surplus tax money among the states.

TRACY POND. For the Tracy family, who settled in the early 1800's.

TRAPPER BROOK. For the camp of an old trapper located there.

TRAVELER BROOK. For Traveler Mountain in Piscataquis County.

TREDWELL HILL. For Tredwell, early lumberman.

TRIBOU BROOK. For the Tribou family.

TIGER RIPS. For being fast and mean like a tiger.

TROUT: BROOK (2), EAST BRANCH-BROOK, POND (4). For trout fish.

TUCKER RIDGE. For the Tucker family who used to give barn dances here.

TURKEY TAIL: ISLAND, LAKE. Descriptive of the shape.

TURKLOIN BROOK. Unknown.

TURNER: EAST-MOUNTAIN, SOUTH-BROOK. For the Turner place-names in Piscataquis County.

TURNER LOGAN. Unknown.

TWIN BROOK: (settlement). Probably for Burnham Brook and Kenduskeag Stream.

TWIN: ISLAND (3), NORTH-LAKE, NORTH-RIDGE, POND BROOK. Descriptive.

TWOMBLY: LITTLE-RIDGE, RIDGE. For Isaac Twombly, born here, 1838.

UMCULCUS: DEADWATER, EAST BRANCH-STREAM, WEST BRANCH-STREAM. Abnaki: "a whistling duck."

UPPER POND. Descriptive.

VARNEY HILL. For Jedediah Varney, settler, 1825.

VEAZIE: GORE, settlement, TOWNSHIP. For General Samuel Veazie, local businessman.

VILLA VAUGHN. For Vaughn, a recreational area and dance pavilion owner.

VINEGAR HILL. (2). In Carroll Township, for people who once thought that if beech trees were tapped, one could get vinegar. There are beech trees on the hill. In Lowell Township, for apple orchards there, vinegar being made from the apples.

WADLEIGH BOG. Unknown.

WADLEIGH: BROOK, POND. For Wadleigh, lumberman.

WADLEIGH DEADWATER. For Samuel Wadleigh, prominent Old Town resident who owned land in the area.

WALLIS BROOK. For Wallis, local lumberman.

WARD STREAM. For George Ward and his father, who lived nearby.

WARDSWORTH MOUNTAIN. Unknown.

WASSATAQUOIK: MOUNTAIN, STREAM. Abnaki: "a clear, shining lake," possibly where fish are speared by torchlight.

WEATHERBEE HILL. For Washington Weatherbee, who had a small store there.

WEBB BROOK. For Joshua Webb, who settled there in 1901.

WEBB COVE. Unknown.

WEBB HILL. For Webb, the contractor who built the military road through there.

WEBSTER. For the Webster family.

WEBSTER: POND, TOWNSHIP. Unknown.

WEEKS BROOK. (2). In Patten Township, for the Weeks family, local settlers and farmers. In T7R6, unknown.

WEIR POND. For weirs, or fish traps.

WEST BROOK. Descriptive.

WEYMOUTH BROOK. For Tom Weymouth, whose land it crossed.

WEYMOUTH POND. For the Weymouth family.

WHEELER BROOK. For Gus Wheeler.

WHEELER STREAM. For David Wheeler, settler by 1784.

WHETSTONE: FALLS, MOUNTAIN, STREAM. Because the rocks in the stream resemble whetstones.

WHIPPLE: BOG, POND. Unknown.

WHITE HORSE: LAKE, RIPS. Unknown.

WHITE SQUAW ISLAND. For a halfbreed Indian girl whose father was a white priest who spent a winter in the area in the 18th century. She married Susep and had 7 or 8 sons.

WHITNEY BROOK. For J.B. Whitney, resident, 1875.

WHITNEY RIDGE. For the Whitney family, first settlers on the ridge.

WHITTEN BOG. Probably a cartographical error for Whitcomb Bog, for J. Whitcomb, who lived nearby in 1859.

WHITTEN: BROOK, LITTLE-BROOK. For Benjamin Whitten from Littlefield, a timber contractor who sawed the lumber for the Mattawamkeag bridge.

WIDDEN BROOK. Unknown.

WILEY· POND. For Wiley, French-Canadian lumberman who lived nearby.

WILLETT BROOK. For two Willett families who lived there.

WILLETT EDDY. For Willett, a logger.

WILSON HILL. For Dr. Wilson, who lived there.

WINN: EAST-, settlement, TOWNSHIP. For John M. Winn from Massachusetts, who was the bookkeeper for John Fish & Bridge, who owned much area land. Winn later fell heir to it.

WITHERELL ISLAND. For the Witherell family who established the first paper in Dexter in 1856.

WOODARD. Unknown.

WOODCHUCK HILL. For woodchucks.

WOODLOT RIDGE. For a number of woodlots here, owned by Joshua Grey.

WOODMAN BROOK. For the Woodman family.
WOODVILLE: settlement, SOUTH, TOWNSHIP. Named by some-
one of the Benjamin Stanwood family for the area woods.
WRIGHTS MILL STREAM. For Colonel Rufus S. Wright, who ran a
gristmill there.
WYMAN: BROOK, BROOK RIDGE. Unknown.

PISCATAQUIS COUNTY

ABBEE POND. For S.G. Abbee, resident, 1882.

ABBOTT: settlement, TOWNSHIP, UPPER-, VILLAGE, VILLAGE STATION. For Professor John Abbott, treasurer of Bowdoin College.

ABOL: DEADWATER, FALLS, MOUNTAIN, POND, STREAM. For Abnaki: "Aboljackarnegassic," shortened by the whites to "Abol": "bare, devoid of trees."

ACORN HILL. For oak trees and their acorns.

ADAMS. Unknown.

ALDER: BROOK (3), STREAM (2). For alder trees.

ALLAGASH: EAST BRANCH-STREAM, LITTLE-FALLS, LAKE, MIDDLE-STREAM, MOUNTAIN, POND, RIVER, SOUTH BRANCH-STREAM, STREAM, WEST BRANCH-STREAM. Abnaki: "birch bark shelter."

ALLEN MOUNTAIN. Unknown.

ALLIGATOR POND. Descriptive of shape.

AMBAJEJUS: FALLS, LAKE, POINT. Abnaki: "two currents, one on either side."

AMBEJACKMOCKAMUS: BIG-FALLS, LITTLE-FALLS. Abnaki: "slantwise of the regular route."

ANNIS BROOK. Unknown.

AROOSTOOK BROOK. Micmac: "beautiful or shining river."

ASHWORTH BROOK. Unknown.

ATKINS: BROOK, EAST BRANCH-BROOK, POND, WEST BRANCH-BROOK. Unknown.

ATKINSON: CORNERS, MILLS, TOWNSHIP. For Judge Atkinson, who owned much of the area.

AUSTIN BOG. For Blanchard and Ichabod Austin.

AVALANCHE BROOK. For nearby Avalanche Slide (unlisted on the map).

AVERY: BROOK, POND. Unknown.

AYERS BROOK. For the Ayers family who settled before 1880.

BABBLE: BROOK, BROOK DEADWATER. Descriptive.

BABEL BROOK. Cartographical error for "Babble" Brook. Descriptive.

BADGER: BROOK (2), POND. For the early Badger family.

BAILEY HILL. For A. Bailey, resident, 1882.

BAIT POND. Descriptive of a pond where fishermen caught bait for fishing in the larger ponds and lakes.

BAKER: BROOK, MOUNTAIN, MOUNTAIN BROOK, POND. Unknown.

BALD: MOUNTAIN (2), MOUNTAIN STREAM. Descriptive.

BARNARD: CORNER, settlement, TOWNSHIP. For Moses Barnard, proprietor.

BARRELL RIDGE. For a molasses hogshead placed in a hemlock tree to notify teamsters to put chains on their runners because of ice.

BARREN: LEDGES, MOUNTAIN (2), SLIDE. Descriptive.

BARTLETT: BROOK, MOUNTAIN, POND. Unknown.

BASIN PONDS. Descriptive.

BAXTER PEAK. For Percival P. Baxter, Governor of Maine, who donated the Baxter State Park area.

BEAN: BROOK, POND, PONDS. Possibly for a Lieutenant Bean, a member of Captain Harmon and Captain Moulton's Indian expedition.

BEAN HILL. For the early Bean family.

BEAN: HOLE MOUNTAIN, HOLE POND. Unknown.

BEAN POT POND. Descriptive of shape.

BEAR: BROOK (9), BROOK BOG, BROOK COVE (2), MOUN-
TAIN, POND (7), POND BROOK (2), LEDGE. For bears.
BEAVER: BIG-POND (2), BOGS, BROOK (6), COVE, CREEK,
LITTLE-POND (2), POND (4), POND RIDGE, PONDS. For
beavers.
BEETHAM SWALE. Unknown.
BEETLE MOUNTAIN. Descriptive of shape.
BELL POND. (2). Unknown.
BEN CHASE HILL. Unknown.
BENNETT: BIG-POND, BROOK (3), LITTLE-BROOK, LITTLE-
POND, POND. Little-Pond, Big-Pond and Brook in Guilford and
Willimantic Townships, for Oscar Bennett, resident about 1900.
Pond in Parkman Township, for O.M. Bennett, resident, 1882, or
his ancestors. Brook in Sebec Township, for the early Bennett
family. Brook in Blanchard Township and Little-Brook in Shirley
Township, unknown.
BENSON: BIG-POND, BROOK, flagstation, LITTLE-POND,
MOUNTAIN. Unknown.
BERRY COVE. For the Berry family who owned a large farm that
bordered on the lake.
BERRY: LITTLE-POND, POND. Unknown.
BIG: DRY POINT, EDDY, ISLAND (2), SPRING (lake). Descrip-
tive.
BIGNEY COVE. For Benjamin Bigney.
BIG NIAGARA FALLS. For its fanciful resemblance to Niagara
Falls.
B: INLET BROOK, POND. For location in a B designated township.
BIRCH: ISLAND, MOUNTAIN, POINT (3), RIDGE, PONDS. For
birch trees.
BLACK: BOG, BROOK(5), BROOK MOUNTAINS, CAP MOUN-

TAIN, ISLAND (2) PINNACLE, POINT (2), PONDS (2), SAND
ISLAND, SPRUCE BOG, SPRUCE POND, STREAM. Descriptive.
BLACK CAT MOUNTAIN. (2). For the woodsmen's name for the
fisher.
BLACKMORE POND. Unknown.
BLACKSTONE BROOK. For Charles Blackstone, who farmed
nearby.
BLAIR HILL. For Lyman Blair, settler from Chicago.
BLANCHARD: settlement, TOWNSHIP. For Charles Blanchard of
Portland, co-owner of the township.
BLOOD POND. Possibly for the later family of Abiel Blood, settler,
1797.
BLUE: RIDGE, TOP. Descriptive of coloration of spruce trees from
a distance.
BLUFFER: BROOK, LITTLE-BROOK, LITTLE-POND, POND,
RIDGE, UPPER-POND. Unknown.
BLUFF: MOUNTAIN, POND. Descriptive.
BLUNDER POND. Unknown.
BOARDMAN: BIG-MOUNTAIN, LITTLE-MOUNTAIN. For J.H.
Boardman of Milo Township and his relatives, one of whom was
area surveyor in the 1800's.
BOARDWAY PONDS. For the Boardman Mountains above.
BOARSTONE MOUNTAIN. For its resemblance to a boar's testicles.
BOAT POND. Descriptive of shape.
BODFISH: flagstation, INTERVALE. For S.G. Bodfish, settler,
1826.
BOG: BROOK (6), LITTLE-BROOK, POND (2). Descriptive.
BOLT HILL. Unknown.
BOODY BROOK. Unknown.
BOOM HOUSE, THE. For the lumber boom on Ambajejus Lake.

BOTTLE: BROOK, POND. Unknown.

BOUCHER BROOK. Unknown.

BOULDER ISLAND. Descriptive.

BOWDOIN COLLEGE GRANT: EAST TOWNSHIP, WEST TOWN-
SHIP. For Bowdoin College.

BOWERBANK: settlement, TOWNSHIP. For Bowerbank, London
merchant who was the second owner of the township.

BOYD: LAKE, LAKE (settlement). For General J.P. Boyd, owner
and settler, 1805.

BRACKETT: BROOK, POND. Unknown.

BRANDY: BROOK, POND. Descriptive of the color of the water.

BRANNS MILL POND. For the Brann family who owned a mill
there in the 1800's.

BRAYLEY: BROOK, NORTH BRANCH-BROOK, POND, SOUTH
BRANCH-BROOK. Unknown.

BREAKNECK RIDGE. Descriptive of its steepness.

BREWSTER BROOK. For William Brewster, settler, early 1800's.

BRICE BROOK. Unknown.

BRIGHTON DEADWATER. Unknown.

BROTHERS, THE. Fanciful name for two mountains.

BROWN BOG. For Cotton Brown, settler, early 1800's.

BROWN: BROOK (4), BROOK POND, HILL (2), POND (2). Brook
in Atkinson Township, for E.J. Brown, who ran the first mill on
the stream. Brook and Hill in Abbott Township, for the Brown
family. Hill in Brownsville Township, for the Francis Brown
family, who built a mill in 1806. The others, unknown.

BROWNVILLE: JUNCTION, settlement, TOWNSHIP. For Francis
Brown, who built a mill and settled there by 1812.

BUCK HILL. (2). For the Buck families who settled before 1880.

BUCKLEY: BROOK, POND. Unknown.

BUCKS COVE. For Mr. Buck, owner of a slate quarry.

BUKER MOUNTAIN. For the early Buker family.

BUNKER: PONDS, STREAM. For the early Bunker family.

BURDEN POND. Unknown.

BURDIN CORNER. For Elbridge Burdin, who ran a store there.

BURGESS BROOK. For W.E. Burgess, blacksmith in Sebec Township, early 1900's.

BURNHAM: BROOK, POND. Unknown.

BURNT: ISLAND, MOUNTAIN. Descriptive.

BURNT JACKET: MOUNTAIN, POINT. Possibly for the same
reason as Burnt Coat Island and Burnt Jacket Channel on the
coast. If it is not simply a name transferred from the coast, it
could be folk etymology for the French "brule cote'," "burned
coast," which would apply here, then a variation of the "coat"
("jacket").

BUTTERMILK: BROOK, FIRST-POND, POND, SECOND-POND.
For a hermit who lived on the pond and periodically went to
Bowerbank for buttermilk; hence, he became known as "Old
Buttermilk," and the name was transferred to his homesite.

BUZZELL BROOK. For A. Bussell, resident, 1882.

CAMPBELL HILL. For Roland Campbell, resident.

CAMP POND. For people who have made camp on it.

CARIBOU: BIG-POND, BOG, BROOK (2), DEADWATER, LAKE,
LITTLE-POND, POINT (2), RIDGE, SPRING, STREAM (2). For
caribou.

CARLTON BROOK. Unknown.

CARLTON POINT. Possibly for H.M. Carlton.

CARLTON STREAM. (2). In Parkman Township, probably for
Henry Carlton, early settler in the area. In Sangerville Township,
for Guy Carlton, who had a mill there.

CARPENTER: MOUNTAIN, POND. Unknown.

CARRY: BOG, BROOK. For the carry from Mud Pond to Umbazooksus Lake.

CARRY POND. For the carry from West Branch Penobscot River to Chesuncook Pond.

CASSIDY DEADWATER. Unknown.

CAUCOMGOMAC: LAKE, MOUNTAIN, STREAM. Abnaki: "lake abounding with gulls."

CEDAR: BROOK (2), MOUNTAIN, POND (2). For cedar trees.

CELIA POND. Unknown.

CENTER: ISLAND, MOUNTAIN, POND (2), RIDGE. Descriptive.

CHAIRBACK: EAST-POND, MOUNTAIN, WEST-POND. Descriptive.

CHAMBERLAIN: ARM OF-, LAKE. Some say that the lake was named for the Chamberlain family farm located there, while others say that the farm was named for the lake.

CHANDLER: BROOK, BROOK DEADWATER, POND. For the logging Chandler family.

CHASE: BROOK (2), CARRY, COVE, LAKE. Unknown.

CHEMQUASABAMTICOOK: LAKE, STREAM. Abnaki: "where there is a large lake together with a river."

CHESUNCOOK: DAM (settlement), LAKE, POND, STREAM, TOWNSHIP, VILLAGE. Abnaki: "at the place of the principal outlet."

CHICKEN COVE. For some chicken bones found here years ago, the remains of an early picnic.

CHIMNEY: PEAK, POND. Descriptive.

CHURCHILL: BROOK, DEPOT, LAKE, LITTLE-POND, RIDGE. In the early 1800's, William Harford, William Churchill, and one each of their sons were moose hunting here. While the men were gone, the boys rowed out in the lake, and the canoe tipped over, drowning the Churchill boy. He was buried on the shore.

CHURCH POND. For J.H. Church, superintendent of schools in Shirley Township, 1905.

CISS: LITTLE-STREAM, STREAM. Unknown.

CITRON HILL. For citron trees.

CLARKSON POND. Unknown.

CLAW: BIG-, LITTLE-. For being arms of Lobster Lake.

CLEAR: LAKE, LAKE MOUNTAIN. Descriptive.

CLIFF: LAKE, RIDGE. Descriptive.

CLIFFORD POND. Unknown.

CLOUD: POND, POND BROOK. One source says that it is descriptive of its elevation.

COFFEE HOUSE STREAM. For a coffee house built there, where stagecoaches used to stop to rest the horses, and travelers got coffee.

COFFEELOS: LITTLE-POND, POND. A humorous name to make a pair with Telos (tea-los) Pond.

COLD STREAM. Descriptive.

COLE CORNER. For Herman Cole.

COLUMBUS MOUNTAIN. Unknown.

COMPASS POND. Woodsmen set their compasses by this pond.

COOK: BOG, BROOK. Unknown.

COOK ISLAND. For the family of Alice Cook.

COOPER: BROOK, BROOK DEADWATER, MOUNTAIN, POND. Unknown.

COWAN: BROOK, COVE. Unknown.

COW: BROOK, POND. Unknown.

COWETT HILL. Unknown.

CRAIG BROOK. Unknown.

CRANBERRY POND. (3). For cranberries.

CRATER POND. Descriptive of shape.

CRAWFORD POND. Unknown.

CRESCENT: BROOK, POND. Descriptive of shape.

CROCKETT BROOK. For Captain A.G. Crockett, resident by the 1880's.

CROCKETT HILL. For the Joel C. Crockett family, settlers by 1811.

CROCKETT: POND, RIDGE. For the local Crockett family.

CROSS RANGE, THE. Unknown.

CROW HILL. For crows.

CURABEXIS: COVE, LAKE, STREAM. Malecite: "little, swift, water."

CURRIER: BROOK, FIRST-POND, FIRST-BROOK, SECOND--POND, THIRD-POND, FOURTH-POND, FIFTH-POND, SIXTH--POND. Unknown.

DAGGETT BROOK. For Elisha Daggett, settler, early 1800's.

DAGGETT POND. Unknown.

DAICEY POND. Unknown.

DAISEY POND. Unknown.

DAM POND. Descriptive of the way it seems to be separated from Indian Pond.

DAVIS: BROOK (2), MOUNTAIN, FIRST-POND, SECOND-POND, THIRD-POND, FOURTH-POND. Brook in Guilford Township, probably for Elias Davis, early settler. The rest, for General A. Davis, proprietor.

DAYS ACADEMY TOWNSHIP. Granted to Days Academy.

DEAD MAN BROOK. For a man killed there on a log drive.

DEADMAN ROCK. For a dead man found there.

DEADWATER: BROOK, EAST BRANCH-, LOWER-, LOWER-POND, UPPER- (2), UPPER- POND. Descriptive of flowage.

DEAN ISLAND. Unknown.

DEBSCONEAG: DEADWATER, FALLS, FIRST-LAKE, SECOND-LAKE, THIRD-LAKE, FOURTH-LAKE, FIFTH-POND, SIXTH-LAKE, SEVENTH-POND, EIGHTH-POND. Abnaki: "ponds at the high place," or "ponds at the waterway."

DEEP: COVE (2), POND. Descriptive.

DEER: BROOK, HILL, ISLAND, POINT, POND (2). For deer.

DENNIN: BROOK, SWAMP. Probably for Samuel Dennen, settler, 1825.

DEPOT POND. For a woods depot formerly located there.

DERBY. When the Bangor & Aroostook Railroad shops moved there, it was called Medford Junction. Percy R. Todd, the president of the railroad, felt the name to be too awkward and difficult to send on the telegraph, so he suggested changing it to "Derby," a name of English origin.

DEXTER MILL POND. For S. Dexter, resident, 1882.

DOE: HILL, POND. For doe deer.

DOLLAR ISLAND. (2). Descriptive of shape (round).

DORR HILL. For Harrison Dorr, resident, 1882.

DOTTLE BROOK. Unknown.

DOUBLETOP MOUNTAIN. Descriptive.

DOUGHNUT: COVE, POND. Descriptive.

DOUGHTY: BOG, HILL, PONDS. For George Doughty, one of the earliest settlers in 1816.

DOVER: EAST-, settlement, SOUTH MILLS, SOUTH-, WEST-. For Dover, England, former home of one of the proprietors, Charles Vaughn.

DOVER-FOXCROFT TOWNSHIP. For the combination of the former townships of Dover and Foxcroft.

DOW POND. For W. Downes, resident, 1882. The spelling discrepancy is supposedly a cartographical error.

DRAPER POND. (2). Unknown.

DRUMMOND COVE. Unknown.

DRY: BROOK, GORGE, POND. Descriptive.

DUCK: BIG-COVE, BIG-POND, BROOK (2), COVE, LITTLE-COVE, LITTLE-POND, POND (5). For ducks.

DUDLEY RIPS. Unknown.

DUNHAM: BROOK, POND. For the local Dunham family.

DUNHAM CORNER. Unknown.

DUNPHY RIDGE. For Dunphy, owner of much area land.

DURAN BROOK. Unknown.

DWELLEY: BROOK, POND. Dwelly, a hide hunter, was the first white to trap in this area.

EAGLE: LAKE, LAKE TOWNSHIP. For an eagle spotted there by an expedition.

EAGLE STREAM. For eagles.

EARLEY LANDING. For William Earley, who ran sporting camps there about 1905.

EAST BRANCH: POND, RIDGE. Descriptive.

EAST MIDDLESEX CANAL GRANT TOWNSHIP. Unknown.

EAST OUTLET KENNEBEC RIVER. Abnaki: "long quiet water."

EBEEMEE: LAKE, LAKE EAST POND, LOWER-POND, MOUNTAIN, UPPER-LAKE. If Indian, Abnaki: "extended" or "berries."

ECHO: BROOK, LAKE, RIDGE. Descriptive.

EDES: BROOK, CORNER. For Albion Edes, resident about 1890.

EGG POND. For eggs the Indians gathered there.

EIGHTEEN: POND, POND BROOK, QUARRY POND. For location on Lot 18 of the township.

ELBOW: LOWER-POND, MIDDLE-POND, MOUNTAIN, POND, UPPER-POND. Descriptive of shape.

ELEPHANT MOUNTAIN. Descriptive of shape.

ELLIOTSVILLE: settlement, TOWNSHIP. For Elliot G. Vaughn, owner of the township.

ELLIS: BOG, BROOK, LOWER-POND, POND, UPPER-POND. For Old Ellis, local trapper and hunter.

ERVIN POND. Unknown.

ESSLER BROOK. For G. Essler, resident, 1882.

FAIRBROTHER BOG. For Morris Fairbrothers, resident by 1879.

FARM BROOK. For its nearness to Deer Head Farm.

FARM ISLAND. (2). For farms located there.

FARRAR: BROOK, MOUNTAIN. Unknown.

FAUNCE HILL. For Ira Faunce, early settler.

FEMALE: LITTLE-POND, MOUNTAIN, POND. Unknown.

FERGUSON BROOK. Unknown.

FINN HALL. Formerly a schoolhouse, it was purchased by the Finnish Farmers Club for a meeting place.

FIRST RIDGE. Descriptive.

FISHER: BIG-POND, BROOK, LITTLE-POND. For fishers.

FLANDERS HILL. For E.G. Flanders, resident, 1882.

FOGG POND. For Josiah Fogg, early lumberman.

FOOL BROOK. Unknown.

FORK POND. Descriptive.

FORT MOUNTAIN. Unknown.

FOSS AND KNOWLTON: BROOK, POND. For Foss & Knowlton, who had a large timber operation, with the base camp in this area.

FOSS: MOUNTAIN, POND. For A. & S. Foss, who owned the nearby land in 1882.

FOURMILE BROOK. For being 4 miles from Big Pine Pond.

FOURTH LAKE. Descriptive.

FOURTH MOUNTAIN. For being the fourth in a range with Chairback, Columbus, and Third.

FOURTH POND BOG. For Fourth Davis Pond.

FOWLER: BROOK, LITTLE-POND, LOWER-POND, MIDDLE-POND, POND. For the Fowler family from near Millinocket who made their living by trapping.

FOX: BROOK, POND. For foxes.

FOXCROFT. For Colonel J.E. Foxcroft, who explored and bought the area.

FREESE BOG. Unknown.

FRENCH HILL. For Simon French, settler, early 1800's.

FRENCH MILLS BROOK. For L. French, who had a mill there by 1882.

FROG POND. For frogs.

FROST: LITTLE-POND, POND (2). Unknown.

FROZEN OCEAN. Unknown.

GALES BROOK. For the William Gales family.

GALUSHA COVE. For W.H. Galusha, Greenville road commissioner, 1905-06.

GANNETT BROOK. Unknown.

GARCOCK: HILL, POND. Unknown.

GARLAND POND. For its location on land owned jointly by Garland and Dunphy, 1882.

GATEWAY, THE. Descriptive.

GAUNTLET: BROOK, FALLS, POND. Descriptive of running fast water in a canoe.

GERO ISLAND. Unknown.

GERRISH COVE. Unknown.

GERRISH HILL. For H. Gerrish, resident, 1882.

GIBRALTER LEDGE. By Sidney Davidson, lawyer from New York who had a camp nearby. He said it resembled the Rock of Gibraltar.

GIFFORD BROOK. For the Gifford family who took water from this brook.

GILBERT BROOK. Unknown.

GILBERT POND. For the Gilbert family who settled in the area in the 1800's.

GILLMAN BROOK. For the early Gillman family.

GILMAN CORNER. For M. Gilman, resident, 1882.

GILMAN SWAMP. For the father of William Gilman, who lived there in 1869.

GLASS HILL. For Consider Glass, Revolutionary War veteran.

GOFF BROOK. For C.L. Goff, resident, 1882.

GOFFS CORNER. For E.G. Goff, who owned a large farm there.

GOODELL BROOK. For Deacon Abel Goodell, settler, 1818.

GOODELL CORNER. For Claudius Goodell, who lived here about 1880.

GOULD: BROOK, POND. Unknown.

GRAND: FALLS, PITCH. Descriptive.

GRANITE MOUNTAIN. Descriptive.

GRANT BROOK. Unknown.

GRAPEVINE: BIG-POND, LITTLE-POND, RIDGE, STREAM. For grapevines.

GRASS POND. Descriptive.

GRASSY POND. (4). Descriptive.

GRAVEYARD POINT. For a cemetery located there by 1882.

GRAY HILL. For P.C. Gray, resident, 1882.

GREAT BASIN . Descriptive.

GREELEY LANDING. For Eben S. Greeley, settler about 1822.

GREEN: ISLAND (2), POINT. Descriptive.

GREENLEAF POND. For Moses Greenleaf, early Maine cartographer and area surveyor.

GREENVILLE: JUNCTION, settlement, TOWNSHIP. Descriptive of the wooded country.

GREENWOOD: BIG-POND, BROOK, LITTLE-POND, MOUNTAIN, POND. For Alexander Greenwood, who surveyed many of the area townships and was killed while on a log drive nearby.

GRENELL POND. For George Gardner Grenell, New York sportsman who visited the area in the 1870's and '80's.

GREY BOG. For the Gray family who owned a nearby sawmill.

GRINDSTONE: BROOK, POND. For rocks that could be used to sharpen axes and other tools.

GUERNSEY BROOK. Unknown.

GUILFORD: CENTER, MOUNTAIN, NORTH-, settlement, TOWNSHIP. In 1816, after attempting to get the township's name changed from Low to Fluvanna and failing, the inhabitants had it named for the first male child born there, Moses Guilford Low, the son of Robert Low.

GULF HAGAS: BROOK, MOUNTAIN. Unknown.

GULF STREAM. Descriptive of a deep depression.

GULLIVER BROOK. Unknown.

GULLY BROOK. Descriptive.

HALE POND. For Edward E. Hale, settler, early 1800's.

HALFWAY BROOK. Descriptive of location halfway between Lobster Lake and Moosehead Lake.

HALL BROOK. For R. Hall, resident, 1882.

HAMLIN: PEAK, RIDGE. For Professor C.E. Hamlin, who wrote about Mount Katahdin and made the first model of the area.

HAMMER ISLAND. Descriptive of shape along with Tack Island.

HAMMOND BROOK. For A. Hammond, resident, 1882.

HAMPSHIRE MOUNTAIN. By early settlers for their former home, New Hampshire.

HANSON BROOK. For the Hanson family, residents, 1882.

HAPPY CORNER. Descriptive.

HARDWOOD HILL. For hardwood trees.

HARDY: flagstop, POND. Unknown.

HARFORDS: POINT, POINT TOWNSHIP. For William Harford, who, with William Churchill, camped here before 1800. They built a campfire that got out of hand and burned over most of the point.

HARLOW POND. For Lewis Harlow.

HARRIMAN POND. For Silas Harriman, early settler.

HARRINGTON: LAKE, POND. Unknown.

HARRIS COVE. Unknown.

HARROW: BROOK, LAKE, LITTLE-LAKE, MOUNTAIN. Unknown.

HARVEY RIDGE. For Professor Leroy H. Harvey, who wrote about Mount Katahdin.

HASKELL SWAMP. For Nathaniel Haskell, who purchased the Thornton Academy Grant about 1820.

HATCH FALLS. Unknown.

HATHAWAY BROOK. For Hiram Hathaway, who had a farm there about 1900.

HATHORN BROOK. Unknown.

HAWTHORNE MEADOW. For D.F. Hawthorne, resident, 1882.

HAY: BROOK (3), BROOK LOGAN, MOUNTAIN, POND. For hay.

HAYMOCK: LAKE, MOUNTAIN. For the last two syllables of the Abnaki name of the lake, "Pongokwahemook" — "woodpecker place."

HEDGEHOG: MOUNTAIN (2), POND (3). For hedgehogs (porcupines).

HENDERSON: BROOK, POND. Unknown.

HERMITAGE, THE. Unknown.

HERON LAKE. For herons.

HERRICK ISLAND. For N.C. Herrick, area resident, 1882.

HIGGINS BROOK. Unknown.

HIGHLANDS, THE. Descriptive.

HIGH POND. Descriptive.

HILTON PONDS. For William S. and Leonard Hilton, who ran nearby mills.

HINCKLEY: BROOK (2), COVE. Unknown.

HOGBACK ISLAND. Descriptive of a ridge.

HOG ISLAND. For hogs kept there.

HOLBROOK: LITTLE-POND, POND. Unknown.

HOLMES HOLE. Unknown.

HOMER HILL. For Wallace Homer, who changed his name from Hore. The story is told that his wife exclaimed when she heard that he was going to change his name, "I'm a Hore, I've always been a Hore, and I'll always be a Hore!" Others say for William Homer.

HOMES BROOK. Unknown.

HORSEBACK. Descriptive of a ridge.

HORSERACE: BROOK, fast water, PONDS. For fast water because running it is like being in a horserace.

HORSESHOE: BOG, POND (3). Descriptive of shape.

HOUSE BOG. Unknown.

HOUSTON: BROOK, LITTLE-POND, MOUNTAIN, POND. Unknown.

HOWARD BROOK. For the local Howard family.

HOWARD CORNER. For C.A. Howard, resident, 1882.

HOWE: BROOK, PEAK. For Louis Howe, explorer, early 1800's.

HUBBARD POINT. Unknown.

HUDSON: BIG-BROOK, BROOK, LITTLE-BROOK, LITTLE-POND, LOWER-POND, MOUNTAIN, POND. Unknown.

HUFF: CORNER, MOUNTAIN. For Israel, E.W., John, and M. Huff, residents, 1882.

HUNGRY BROOK. Unknown.

HURD: BIG-POND, BROOK, CORNER, LITTLE-POND (2), MOUNTAIN, POND, POND STREAM. Corner in Dover-Foxcroft, for E.G. Hurd, resident, 1882. Little-Pond, Pond, and Pond Stream in T2R10, possibly for Josiah Hurd, farmer. The others are unknown.

HUSSEY: BROOK, POND. For the Hussey family who lived here about 1882.

HUTCHINS CORNER. For Isaac Hutchings, settler, 1821.

HUTCHINSON POND. For Forest Hutchinson, constable of Sangerville Township, 1905.

HYDE ISLAND. Unknown.

ICE CAVE BROOK. Named for its running through caves which contain ice for much of the summer.

IMLOS POND. Unknown.

INDIAN: BIG-POND, CARRY, HILL, LITTLE-POND, MOUNTAIN, PITCH, POND (3), STREAM (3). For Indians.

INLET BROOK. Descriptive.

INLET, THE. Descriptive.

INSCRIPTION ROCK. For Indian inscriptions there.

INTAKE POND. For feeding Squaw Brook.

INTERVALE BROOK. Descriptive.

IRA BOG. Unknown.

ISLAND: POND, POND BROOK, UPPER-POND. For an island located in the pond.

ITALIAN COVE. Unknown.

JACK POND. Unknown.

JACKSON BROOK. Unknown.

JACKSON: COVE, POND (2). For C.T. Jackson, state geologist, 1837.

JAMES BROOK. Unknown.

JAQUITH POND. Unknown.

JENKS BROOK. For the E.A. Jenks family, early settlers.

JEWETT: BROOK, COVE, POND. Unknown.

JOHNSON: BROOK (2), LITTLE-POND, POND (2). Brook in Willimantic Township, for James Johnson, a settler in 1826. The others, unknown.

JO-MARY: ISLAND, LOWER-STREAM, MOUNTAIN, POND. For Jo-Mary, Indian chief renowned for his hunting and swimming abilities.

JORDAN BROOK. Unknown.

JORDAN ISLAND. For Jordan, who owned this island and operated a tenting area.

JUNIPER: KNEE BOG, KNEE POND, SWAMP BROOK. Descriptive.

KATAHDIN: IRON WORKS, MOUNT-, STREAM. Abnaki: "the principal mountain." It seems that the Indians felt that a spirit dwelled in each mountain, and Katahdin was the one who lived here.

KEEP RIDGE. For Reverend Marcus R. Keep, who blazed a trail on Mount Katahdin in 1846 and was the first to climb the east spur.

KELLOGG BROOK. Unknown.

KELLY: LITTLE-POND, POND. For the early Kelly family, lumbermen.

KENNEDY: BOG, BROOK. Unknown.

KIDNEY: BROOK, POND (2). Descriptive of shape.

KIMBLE BROOK. Unknown.

KINEO: COVE, ISLAND, LITTLE-MOUNTAIN, MOUNT-, TOWN-SHIP. For Chief Kineo, a legendary wicked Indian who was exiled by his tribe and lived on the mountain. Some Indians claim that the mountain is the petrified body of a moose killed by Glooskap, an Indian demon. The word in Abnaki: "sharp peak."

KING BROOK. Unknown.

KINGSBURY: POND, settlement, STREAM, TOWNSHIP. For Judge Sanford Kingsbury of Gardiner Township, proprietor.

KLONDIKE, THE. Fanciful name for a cold valley.

KNIFE EDGE. Descriptive of a sharp ridge.

KNIGHTS LANDING. Unknown.

KOKADJO. Abnaki: "kettle mountain." The Indians say that Glooskap, an Indian demon, was hunting at Moosehead Lake and killed a moose which changed into Mount Kineo. He then pursued the moose's calf, and in order to lighten his load, he threw away his kettle, which landed upside down and became "Kokadjo," or Kettle Mountain.

KYLE POND. (2). Unknown.

LADD BROOK. For the N. Ladd family, settlers, early 1800's.

LAGOON BROOK. Descriptive.

LAKE HEBRON. For its location in a part of Monson Township which was granted to Hebron Academy of Monson, Mass.

LAKER POINT. Unknown.

LAKE VIEW: settlement, TOWNSHIP. Descriptive.

LAMBERT ISLAND. Unknown.

LAMBS COVE. For Lamb, farmer at the cove in 1882.

LAMONT PONDS. For the Lamont family, early settlers.

LAWS BRIDGE. (settlement). For Robert Law, Jr., settler, 1804.

LAZY TOM: LITTLE-STREAM, POND, STREAM. For Tom, a lazy

Indian lumberman. Another source says that it was named for "Lazy Tom," a brand of tobacco sold in Greenville. The storekeeper, it was contended, bought bulk tobacco and split it, putting some in certain bags labeled "Lazy Tom" and some in a bag with a different label. When the woodsmen became tired of one brand they switched to the other.

LEADBETTER: BROOK, LITTLE-POND, POND (2). Unknown.

LEAVITT POND. Unknown.

LEDGE: FALLS (2). HILL, HILL BROOK, ISLAND. Descriptive.

LEEMAN BROOK. For Thomas Leeman, resident.

LEONARD POND. Unknown.

LEVANSALLER HILL. For the Levansaller family, residents, 1882.

LEWIS POND. Unknown.

LEYFORD ISLAND. Unknown.

LIBBY: ISLAND, PINNACLE. Unknown.

LILY: BAY, BAY BROOK, BAY MOUNTAIN, BAY TOWNSHIP, BOG, PAD POND, POND (2). For lilies.

LINE: POND, POND MOUNTAIN. For a surveying range line going through the pond.

LITTLEFIELD: BROOK, POND. Unknown.

LITTLE POND. (2). Descriptive.

LLOYD POND. Unknown.

LOBSTER: LAKE, LITTLE-LAKE, LITTLE-STREAM, MOUNTAIN, STREAM. Descriptive of the shape of the lake.

LOGAN: BOG, BROOK (2), PONDS. Descriptive of a stretch of still water. Brook in T5R12, supposedly for, according to one source, a Logan who tried to farm in the area but was a failure.

LONE PINE POINT. Descriptive.

LONG: BOG (4), BOG BROOK, POND (4), POND STREAM, RIDGE. Descriptive.

LONGLEY: BROOK, LITTLE-BROOK, LITTLE-POND, LITTLE-STREAM, POND, STREAM. Unknown.

LOON: LAKE, POND, STREAM. For loons.

LORD MOUNTAIN. Unknown.

LOST: BROOK, POND (5). For being isolated and easily confused with other ponds.

LOUGEE BOG. For J. Lougee, resident, 1882.

LOWELL BOG. For A. and J. Lowell, residents, 1882.

LOWELL BROOK. For the local Lowell family.

LUCIA POND. Unknown.

LUCKY: BROOK, POINT, POND. Unknown.

LYFORD COVE. For James and Jonathon Lyford, settlers, 1803.

LYFORD: LITTLE-PONDS, POND. For George D. Lyford, who was on the Atkinson Township board of health in 1906.

LYFORD SWAMP. Unknown.

MAGUIRE HILL. For J.D. Maguire, resident, 1882.

MAHAR POND. If Indian, Mahican: "the one who gathers them together." Others say for the Mahar family.

MANHANOCK POND. Abnaki: "at the place of the island," or "shelter island."

MANSELL BROOK. For John Mansell, area guide about 1900.

MAPLE RIDGE. For maple trees.

MARBLE: BROOK, POND. For Eben and David Marble, who moved to the area about 1824.

MARR POND. For the Marr family who moved here about 1800.

MARSH: LITTLE- POND. Descriptive.

MARTIN COVE. Unknown.

MARTIN PONDS. For the Martin family who lived in the area.

MASTERMAN ISLAND. For F. Masterman and family, residents, 1882.

MATHEWS COVE. For the Mathews family.

MATTHEWS POND. Unknown.

MAXFIELD BROOK. (2). In Guilford Township, for the local Maxfield family. In TXR14, unknown.

MAY: BROOK, POND. Unknown.

McCARTY MOUNTAIN. Unknown.

McCLUSKEY BROOK. For the logging McCluskey family.

McCULLER ISLAND. Unknown.

McDOUGALL POND. Unknown.

McGOOSEKEY POND. Unknown.

McKENNA POND. Unknown.

McLELLAN POND. Unknown.

McMANUS POND. Unknown.

McPHERSON: BROOK, POND. Unknown.

MEADOW: BROOK (4), POND. Descriptive.

MEDFORD: CENTER, settlement, TOWNSHIP. Descriptive of being the "mid ford" on the Piscataquis River.

MERRILL: BROOK (2), HILL. Brook in Guilford Township, for the local Merrill family. Brook and Hill in T6R8, for A.H. Merrill, who operated a slate quarry in the 1880's.

MIDDAY POND. For its location between Sunrise and Sunset ponds.

MIDDLE: BRANCH-POND, BRANCH THOROUGHFARE BROOK, BROOK (3), BROOK MOUNTAIN, BROOK POND. Descriptive.

MIDNIGHT: BROOK, POND. Unknown.

MILE: BROOK, POND. For location about one mile from Allagash Lake.

MILL: BROOK (3), BROOK (flagstation), BROOK POND. For mills. Specifically in Bowerbank Township, for a sawmill built there about 1826 by Charles Vaughn.

MILLINOCKET: LAKE (2), LITTLE-LAKE, RIDGE. Abnaki: "this place is admirable."

MILLS BROOK. For the logging Mills family.

MILO: settlement, TOWNSHIP. Named by Theophilus Sargent, one of the earliest settlers, for the Greek athlete, Milo of Crotona.

MINISTER: BIG-POND, COVE, LITTLE-POND. Unknown.

MINK: BROOK, POND. For mink.

MINNOW POND. For minnows.

MIRROR POND. Descriptive.

MONKEY POND. Unknown.

MONSON: JUNCTION, POND, settlement, STREAM, TOWNSHIP. The area was granted to Hebron Academy, which was located in Monson, Massachusetts.

MOODY: EAST-ISLAND, WEST-ISLAND. Unknown.

MOORE BOG. Unknown.

MOORES POND. For L. Moore, resident, 1882.

MOORESVILLE: BROOK, settlement. For Abraham Moore, who built a sawmill on the south side of the Piscataquis River and marked the spot for the village.

MOOSE: BROOK, BROOK ISLAND, COVE (2), ISLAND (2), POND (4), UPPER-POND. For moose.

MOOSEHEAD: LAKE, NORTH BAY OF-LAKE, settlement. Some say that from Mount Kineo, the lake resembles a moose's head. Others say named for many moosehorns found there. Still others say that from the lake Mount Kineo resembles a crouching moose. It is quite likely that the name is connected with the Mount Kineo-Glooskap Indian legend.

MOOSEHORN. For Joseph Bearce, the first settler, who found a set of moosehorns and set them up in a tree to mark a branch in the road.

MOOSEHORN BROOK. For moosehorns.

MOOSELEUK: LAKE, MOUNTAIN, STREAM. Abnaki: "moose place."

MORKILL. Unknown.

MORRISON BROOK. For the Morrison family who settled in the 1800's.

MORSE MOUNTAIN. For Morse, early explorer.

MOULTON HILL. For the early Moulton family.

MOUNTAIN: BROOK (2), BROOK POND, POND (3), VIEW POND. Descriptive.

MOUNT COE. For E.S. Coe, area landholder.

MOUNT MISERY. Unknown.

MOUNT O-J-I. For slides on the face of the mountain that appeared to form the letters "O-J-I."

MOUNT VETO. Unknown.

MUD: BROOK (4), COVE (2), GAUNTLET BROOK, GAUNTLET DEAD WATER, GAUNTLET FALLS, GREENWOOD POND, LITTLE-POND (2), POND (13), POND BROOK, POND RIDGE. Descriptive.

MULE: BROOK, BROOK MOUNTAIN, BROOK MOUNTAINS. For a mule used there in timber operations.

MULLEN: BROOK, MOUNTAIN. Unknown.

MUNSUNGAN: BROOK, FALLS, LAKE, LITTLE-LAKE, LITTLE-STREAM, RIDGE, STREAM. Abnaki: "humped up island."

MURPHY: BROOK, POND, PONDS. Unknown.

MUSQUACOOK: FOURTH-LAKE, FIFTH-LAKE. Abnaki: "birch bark place," or "muskrat place."

MUSQUASH: FIRST-POND, SECOND-POND, THIRD-POND. Abnaki: "reddish-brown animal (muskrat)."

NAHMAKANTA: LAKE, STREAM. Abnaki: "plenty of fish."

NARROW: BROOK, POND, RIDGE. Descriptive.

NARROWS: FIRST-, SECOND-, THE- (3). Descriptive.

NESOWADNEHUNK: DEADWATER, FALLS, LAKE, LITTLE-LAKE, LITTLE-STREAM, STREAM. Abnaki: "swift stream between mountains."

NESUNTABUNT: MOUNTAIN, settlement. Abnaki: "three heads," descriptive of the mountains.

NEW CITY. To distinguish from Old City.

NEWELL COVE. Unknown.

NICKS GUT. Unknown.

NORCROSS: MOUNTAIN, POINT. Unknown.

NORTH: BASIN, BROOK (3), BRANCH, -EAST COVE, INLET, POND, POND BROOK, RIDGE-WEST BASIN, -WEST COVE, -WEST PLATEAU, -WEST POND. Descriptive.

NORTH BROTHER. For the most northerly of two mountains fancifully named The Brothers.

NORTH EAST CARRY. For a carry from Moosehead Lake to the West Branch Penobscot River.

NORTON COVE. For Sam Norton.

NORTON POND. Unknown.

NORWAY: BLUFF, BROOK, FALLS, POINT, POND. For Norway pines.

NOTCH: BIG-POND, LITTLE-POND, POND, THE-. Descriptive.

NUMBER FOUR MOUNTAIN. Unknown.

OAK: BROOK, HILL (2), HILL POND, RIDGE. For oak trees.

OAKES BOG. For the early Oakes family.

OGDEN POINT. Unknown.

OLD BALDFACE. Descriptive.

OLD CITY. Fanciful name for an early camp site.

ONAWA: LAKE, settlement. Chippawa: "awaken." Legend says

that an Indian girl, Onawa, committed suicide at the lake site and is buried there. Others say that it was arbitrarily selected from Longfellow's poem "Hiawatha."

ONE THOUSAND ACRE BOG. Descriptive of size.

ORDWAY: BROOK, LITTLE-POND, POND. For the early Ordway family.

ORE MOUNTAIN. For iron ore.

ORNEVILLE TOWNSHIP. For Henry Orne of Boston, who married the niece of General Boyd, original owner.

ORSON: BOG, BROOK. Unknown.

OTTER: BROOK (2), POND (4). For otters.

OWL, THE. Descriptive of shape.

OXBOW BROOK. Descriptive of shape.

PACKARD: BROOK (2), LANDING. Brook in Parkman Township, for Arthur Packard. Landing in Willimantic Township, for Burton M. Packard, who had a hotel and camp there about 1900. Brook in Lakeview Township, unknown.

PACKARDS. Unknown.

PAGE BROOK. Unknown.

PALMER MEADOW. Unknown.

PAMOLA: PEAK, POND. For Pamola, evil Indian spirit that inhabits the mountain. The Indians felt that every mountain had an Indian god in it.

PAPOOSE POND. For location near Little Squaw Pond.

PARKER POND. For J. Parker, resident, 1882.

PARKERS. For A. Parker, area landholder, 1882.

PARKMAN: settlement, TOWNSHIP. For Samuel Parkman, early owner.

PARROT. Unknown.

PARSON LANDING. For Isaac Parsons, settler, early 1800's.

PARTRIDGE: LOWER-POND, POND, UPPER-POND. For partridges.

PASSAMAGAMET: FALLS, LAKE. Abnaki? Malecite?: "at the place of many fish."

PEAKED: BIG-MOUNTAIN, LITTLE-MOUNTAIN, MOUNTAIN, MOUNTAIN POND. Descriptive.

PEARL: POND, PONDS. Descriptive of shape and appearance.

PEMADUMCOOK LAKE. Malecite: "extended sandbar place."

PENOBSCOT: EAST BRANCH-RIVER, LITTLE-POND, POND, WEST BRANCH-RIVER. Malecite? Abnaki?: "at the descending rocks," or "at the extended ledges." The Penobscot Indians lived throughout the area.

PEPPERMINT BROOK. For peppermint bushes.

PERHAM HILL. Unknown.

PICKED COVE. Unknown.

PICKEREL: BROOK, COVE (2), POND. For pickerel fish.

PILLSBURY: ISLAND, LITTLE-POND, MOUNTAIN, POND. Unknown.

PINE: BIG-POND, BROOK, ISLAND (2), KNOLL, LITTLE-STREAM, POND, STREAM, STREAM PLOWAGE. For pine trees.

PINGREE: CENTER, CENTER STREAM. For Samuel Pingree, settler about 1812.

PINNACLE RIDGE. Descriptive.

PIPER POND. For Asa Piper, settler about 1815.

PISCATAQUIS: COUNTY, EAST BRANCH-RIVER, WEST BRANCH-RIVER. Abnaki: "at the river branch."

PITMAN POND. Unknown.

PLEASANT: BIG-POND, EAST BRANCH-RIVER, LAKE, LITTLE-POND (2), MOUNTAIN, POND, RIVER, STREAM, WEST BRANCH-RIVER. Descriptive.

POCKWOCKAMUS: DEADWATER, FALLS, POND, STREAM. Abnaki: "little muddy pond."

POCO MOONSHINE BROOK. Probably an English corruption of Abnaki: "pok-wojan-i-tagook": "stumps in the brook." But possibly a mixture of English and Abnaki, "pond clear as moonshine."

POGY: BROOK, NORTH-MOUNTAIN, NOTCH, POND, SOUTH-MOUNTAIN. If Indian, Abnaki: "pond." Possibly the Indian word for "menhaden," a small fish.

POLAND: MOUNTAIN, POND. Unknown.

POLLY POND. Unknown.

POLLYWOG: POND, STREAM. For pollywogs.

POND BROOK. Descriptive.

POPLAR BROOK. For poplar trees.

PORCUPINE POINT. For porcupines.

PORTAGE: LOWER-POND, UPPER-POND. For portage from Spider Lake to Chase Lake.

PORUS: ISLAND, LITTLE-ISLAND. Unknown.

POST BROOK. Unknown.

POTAYWODJO RIDGE. Abnaki: "wind blows over mountain."

POULIN BROOK. Unknown.

POVERTY: BROOK, MOUNTAIN, POND. Descriptive of the people who tried to make a living by attempting to farm the poor land.

PRATT BROOK. For William Pratt of Foxcroft.

PRENTISS: BROOK, POND. Unknown.

PRESCOTT BROOK. (2). In Monson Township, for Seavey Prescott, resident about 1870. In Willimantic Township, for Harry and Will Prescott, brothers who lived in a camp on the bank.

PRESCOTT POND. Unknown.

PRETTY POND. Descriptive.

PRIESTLY: LAKE, MOUNTAIN. For Priestly, owner of a woods depot.

PRONG: POND, POND MOUNTAIN. Descriptive of shape.

PUDDING POND. Descriptive of muddy appearance.

PUGWASH POND. Possibly Abnaki: "pond at the end."

PUNCHBOWL: BROOK, POND. Descriptive of shape.

PYM POND. Unknown.

QUAKER BROOK. Unknown.

QUARRY BROOK. For a nearby slate quarry.

RABBIT POND. (2). For rabbits.

RAGGED: BROOK, LAKE, LITTLE-MOUNTAIN, LITTLE-POND, MOUNTAIN (2), POND, STREAM. Descriptive.

RAGMUFF: LITTLE-STREAM, STREAM. Unknown.

RAINBOW: LAKE, MOUNTAIN, STREAM, TOWN, TOWNSHIP. Descriptive of the shape of the lake.

RAM: ISLAND, ISLAND POINT. For sheep kept on this island.

RAMSELL BROOK. Unknown.

RAND COVE. Unknown.

RAPID BROOK. Descriptive.

RAT POND. For rats.

RAYS MILL POND. For the Ray family who ran a mill there..

RED: BROOK, WEST-BROOK. Descriptive of the coloration of the water.

REED: BIG-POND, BROOK, DEADWATER, LITTLE-POND, MOUNTAIN. Unknown.

RIDER BROOK. Unknown.

RIPOGENUS: GORGE, POND, STREAM. Probably Abnaki: "small rocks, gravel."

RIVER POND. Descriptive.

ROACH: FIRST-POND, SECOND-POND, THIRD-POND, FOURTH-POND, FIFTH-POND, SIXTH-POND, SEVENTH-POND, RIVER. For roach, a type of sunfish.

ROARING: BROOK (3), BROOK MOUNTAIN, BROOK POND. Descriptive.

ROBERTS ROCKY BROOK. Possibly for G.L. Roberts, area resident, 1882.

ROBINSON BOG. For Moses Robinson, settler about 1880.

ROCKY: BROOK (2), LITTLE-POND, POND (4). Descriptive.

RONCO: BROOK, COVE. For Ed Ronco, Allagash guide of the 1925 era.

ROSS: COVE, INLET, NORTH BRANCH-INLET. Unknown.

ROUND: BOG, LITTLE-POND, POND (7), TOP, -TOP MOUNTAIN. Descriptive.

ROWE: COVE, POND. Unknown.

ROWELL: BROOK, COVE. Unknown.

RUM: BROOK (2), COVE, MOUNTAIN (2), POND (2) Brook, Cove, Mountain and Pond in Greenville Township, for a group of early lumber prospectors who drained a jug of rum and left the container on the mountain. Brook, Mountain, and Pond in T2R9, unknown.

RUSSELL: BROOK, COVE, FIRST SOUTH BRANCH-POND, SECOND SOUTH BRANCH-POND, LITTLE- MOUNTAIN, LOWER-POND, MOUNTAIN (2), MIDDLE-POND, NORTH BRANCH-BROOK, POND, SOUTH BRANCH- BROOK, STREAM, UPPER-POND. Mountain and Little-Mountain in Blanchard Township, for Russell, a man who died on the mountain. Tradition says that Russell and another man went blueberrying there, and Russell got lost. His companion went back to Blanchard to get help to search for him. Russell was found dead at the bottom of a cliff. Some thought that his death was an accident, and others thought that his friend had murdered him. A variation of this story is that Russell only became sick and died of his illness there. Mountain, Stream, and Pond in T4R9, for Russell, one of the woods bosses for the lumber firm of Tracey & Love. The others are unknown.

SABLE MOUNTAIN. (2). Woodsmen's name for the martin.

SADDLEBACK: MOUNTAIN, POND. Descriptive.

SADDLE: BROOK, POND, -ROCK BROOK, SPRING. Descriptive.

ST. FRANCIS BROOK. For St. Francis Pond in Somerset County.

SALMON: ISLAND, POND (2), STREAM (3), STREAM POND. For salmon.

SAMPSON POND. Unknown.

SANBORN: BROOK, POND. Possibly for A.A. Sanborn of Atkinson, or his ancestors.

SAND: BAR ISLAND, COVE. Descriptive.

SANDY: POINT, STREAM (2), STREAM POND. Descriptive.

SANGERVILLE: EAST-, settlement, TOWNSHIP. For Colonel Calvin Sanger of Sherborn, Massachusetts, co-owner.

SAWYER POND. For Isaac Sawyer, settler about 1827.

SCAMMON RIDGE. For Edmund Scammon, settler, 1831.

SCHOODIC: LAKE, LITTLE-LAKE, MOUNTAIN, settlement, STREAM. Abnaki or Malecite: "trout place," or "point of land."

SCHOOLHOUSE BROOK. For its location near the old Guilford schoolhouse.

SCOFIELD POINT. Unknown.

SCOTT: BIG-BROOK, LITTLE-BROOK, LITTLE-DEADWATER, LITTLE-POND. Unknown.

SCREW AUGER FALLS. For the way the water comes down the falls in a zigzag fashion.

SCUTAZE STREAM. Abnaki: "trout place."

SEARLES HILL. For J. Searles, resident, 1882.

SEBEC: CORNERS, LAKE, LAKE (settlement), RIVER, settlement, STATION POST OFFICE, TOWNSHIP. Abnaki: "much water."

SEBOEIS: LAKE, WEST-STREAM. Abnaki: "small lake," or "small waterway."

SEBOOMOOK ISLAND. Abnaki: "at or near the large stream."

SECOND: LAKE, RIDGE. Descriptive.

SECRET: POND (2), POND BROOK. Descriptive of isolation.

SENTINEL MOUNTAIN. For its standing like a sentinel over the Penobscot River and Valley.

SEWALL: DEADWATER POND, POND. Pond in T3R11, for A. Frank Sewall, firewarden, early 1900's. The other is unknown.

SEYMOUR COVE. Unknown.

SHACK POND. For an old hunting camp there.

SHADOW POND. Descriptive.

SHALLOW: LAKE, LITTLE-LAKE, POND, STREAM. Descriptive.

SHANNON BROOK. For the early Shannon family.

SHANTY: BIG-MOUNTAIN, LITTLE-MOUNTAIN. Unknown.

SHAW MOUNTAIN. (2). For Milton Shaw, settler in Days Academy Township in 1841, who ran a logging business.

SHIP ISLAND. Descriptive of shape.

SHIP POND STREAM. For Ship Pond, former name of Lake Onawa, for a ship-shaped island in it.

SHIRLEY: EAST-BOG, LOWER-CORNER, MILLS, POND, settlement, TOWNSHIP, UPPER-CORNER, WEST-BOG. For Shirley, Mass., home of Joseph Kelsey, representative to the legislature.

SIBLEY ISLAND. Unknown.

SILVER LAKE. Descriptive.

SING SING POND. Unknown.

SIX PONDS. Descriptive.

SLAUGHTER: BROOK, POND. For a group of hide hunters who found a yard of moose here and slaughtered 13 on the ice of the pond.

SLY BROOK. Unknown.

SMITH: BROOK (6), BROOK BOG, BROOK POND, POND. Pond in Elliotsville Township, for the early Smith family. Brook in T4R11, for the Smith family. Brook in Sebec, for the Smith family. The others are unknown.

SNAKE: BOG, BROOK, ISLAND (2), POND. For snakes.

SNARE BROOK. For moose snares set there.

SNOW BROOK. For Aaron Snow.

SNOWSHOE: MOUNTAIN, POND. Descriptive of the shape of the pond.

SNUB PITCH. Unknown.

SOPER: BROOK (2), MOUNTAIN, MOUNTAIN TOWNSHIP, NORTH BRANCH-BROOK, POND, SOUTH BRANCH-BROOK, UPPER-POND. Unknown.

SOUBUNGE MOUNTAIN. Unknown.

SOUTH: BASIN, BRANCH, BRANCH PONDS BROOK, BROOK (4), COVE (2), COVE POINT, INLET (2), INLET BROOK, LOWER-BRANCH POND, PEAK, POND, RIDGE, UPPER-BRANCH POND. Descriptive.

SOUTH BROTHER. The southern of two mountains called "The Brothers."

SPECTACLE: POND, PONDS. Descriptive of eyeglass shape.

SPENCER: BAY, BIG-MOUNTAIN, COVE, LITTLE-MOUNTAIN, POND, STREAM. For various members of the logging Spencer family.

SPIDER LAKE. Unknown.

SPINNEY ISLAND. Unknown.

SPRING: BROOK (2), BROOK HILL, BROOK POND, POND. Descriptive.

SPUANCE POND. Unknown.

SPRUCE: BIG-MOUNTAIN, LITTLE-MOUNTAIN, MOUNTAIN BROOK, MOUNTAIN POND. For spruce trees.

SQUANKIN POND. Unknown.

SQUAW: BAY, BIG-MOUNTAIN, BIG-POND, BIG-TOWNSHIP, BROOK, BROOK (flagstation), LITTLE-BROOK, LITTLE-MOUNTAIN, LITTLE-POND, LITTLE-TOWNSHIP, MIDDLE-BROOK, POINT, UPPER-BROOK. For Maquaso, mother of the legendary wicked Indian Chief Kineo, who left him because of his wickedness and died on the mountain.

SQUIRT DAM MOUNTAIN. Unknown.

STAIR FALLS. Descriptive.

STARBIRDS. For William Starbird, who owned land at the crossing.

STEADMAN LANDING. For John Steadman, who was drowned while working on a mill flume.

STEPHENSONS LANDING. Unknown.

STEVENS POINT. Unknown.

STICKNEY HILL. For E.W. Stickney, resident, 1882.

STINKING BROOK. (3). Descriptive.

STINK POND. (2). Descriptive.

STORK ISLAND. For Colonel Harold Stork, who died shortly before it was named.

STRATTON: BROOK, POND. Unknown.

STRICKLAND MOUNTAIN. Unknown.

STRICKLIN BROOK. For the early Stricklin family.

STUBB ISLAND. For Stubb, who owned a camp there.

SUCKER: BROOK (3), BROOK POND. For sucker fish.

SUGAR ISLAND. For being a source of maple sap used in making maple sugar.

SUNDAY POND. Unknown.

SUNRISE POND. To make 3 with Midday and Sunset Ponds.

SUNSET POINT. Descriptive.

SUNSET POND. To make 3 with Midday and Sunrise Ponds.

SWEENEY BROOK. Unknown.

SWEET POTATO ISLAND. Unknown.

SWETT HILL. Probably for Captain Winborn A. Sweat, millowner, 1823.

TABLE LAND. Descriptive.

TACK ISLAND. Descriptive of shape and nearby Hammer Island.

TANNERY POND. For a tannery formerly located there.

TARBOX POND. Unknown.

TEA POND. Descriptive of the color of the water.

TEASDALE ISLAND. For J. Teasdale, sportsman.

TELOS: BROOK, LAKE MOUNTAIN, STREAM. Probably from the Greek: "far, ultimate, the end."

TIMS COVE. For Tim Pollard, area game warden about 1905-25.

THANKSGIVING POND. Unknown.

THIRD: LAKE, MOUNTAIN. Descriptive.

THIRTYFOOT FALLS. Descriptive.

THISSELL: BOG, BROOK, POND. Unknown.

THOMPSON: BROOK, POND, WEST BRANCH-BROOK. Brook in Dover-Foxcroft Township, for the early Thompson family. The others in Elliotsville Township, unknown.

THOREAU SPRING. For Henry David Thoreau, 19th century naturalist and philosopher who visited the area.

THORN BROOK. For thorn thickets.

THOROUGHFARE: BROOK, EAST BRANCH-STREAM, NORTH BRANCH-BROOK, THE-, thoroughfare, WEST BRANCH-BROOK. Descriptive of a passage.

TILLY POND. Unknown.

TOGUE: LEDGE, LOWER-POND, STREAM, UPPER-POND. For togue fish.

TOM YOUNG POND. Unknown.

TONGUE, THE. Descriptive of shape.

TOWNE: COVE, POND. For W.F. Towns, resident, 1882.

TOWN FARM HILL. For the town farm.

TOWNHOUSE BROOK. For its location near the town meeting house.

TOWNLINE BROOK. Because it enters Wassatagquoik Stream near the town line.

TRACY POND. For Foster J. Tracey, a member of the logging firm of Tracey & Love about 1883.

TRAIL BROOK. For the nearby Appalachian Trail.

TRAVELER: GAP, MOUNTAIN, NORTH-MOUNTAIN, POND, SOUTH-MOUNTAIN, THE-. Because it can be seen for a great distance, the river drivers and canoers felt that the mountain was traveling along with them.

TREASURE ISLAND. Fancifully named.

TRESTLE BROOK. For an old bridge that spanned it.

TROUT: BROOK (3), BROOK MOUNTAIN, MOUNTAIN (2), NORTH BRANCH-BROOK, POND (3), POND MOUNTAIN, SOUTH BRANCH-BROOK, STREAM. For trout fish.

TRUMBLES ROCK. Unknown.

TUMBLEDOWN DICK: POND, STREAM. Probably a descriptive and fanciful name for a nearby mountain.

TURNER: BROOK, DEADWATER, NORTH-MOUNTAIN, SOUTH-MOUNTAIN. Unknown.

TURTLE: COVE, POND, RIDGE. For turtles.

TUSSLE: BROOK, LAGOON. Unknown.

TWIN: LAKE, NORTH-BROOK, PONDS, SOUTH-BROOK. Descriptive.

TWITCHELL BROOK. Unknown.

TWOMILE ISLAND. For its location 2 miles from shore in Moosehead Lake.

UMBAZOOKSUS: LAKE, STREAM. Abnaki: "clear, gravelly outlet."

VARNEY HILL. For L. Varney, resident, 1882.

VAUGHN STREAM. For Francis Vaughn, early settler in Greenville Township, guide, trapper, and taxidermist.

VELLIEUX POND. Unknown.

WADLEIGH: BOG, BROOK, LITTLE-POND, LITTLE-STREAM, MOUNTAIN, POND (2), STREAM, VALLEY. Unknown.

WALKER HILL. For the early Walker family.

WANGAN: BROOK, BROOK DEADWATER. Abnaki: "the bend."

WARINERS LEDGES. For the Wariner family.

WASSATAQUOIK: LAKE, LITTLE-LAKE, MOUNTAIN, SOUTH BRANCH-STREAM, STREAM. Abnaki: "a clear shining lake."

WATSON HILL. For the Watson family.

WEAVER HILL. For the Weaver family, owners, 1882.

WEBSTER: BROOK, LAKE. Unknown.

WEED POND. Descriptive.

WELLINGTON: BOG, settlement, TOWNSHIP. For Arthur, Duke of Wellington.

WEST: COVE, COVE POINT, FIRST-BRANCH POND, SECOND-BRANCH POND, THIRD-BRANCH POND, FOURTH-BRANCH POND, PEAK (2), POND. Descriptive.

WEYMOUTH POINT. Unknown.

WHETSTONE: BROOK, POND. The rocks could be used for sharpening tools.

WHIDDEN PONDS. Unknown.

WHITE: BIG-BROOK, BROOK. For nearby White Cap Mountain.

WHITE CAP MOUNTAIN. For its being covered with snow until late in the spring.

WHITE HORSE ISLAND. Possibly descriptive of its color.

WHITING COVE. Unknown.

WHITTIER HILL. For James P. Whittier.

WILBUR BROOK. Unknown.

WILDER: BIG-POND, BROOK, LITTLE-POND. Unknown.

WILKIE: BIG-MOUNTAIN, LITTLE-MOUNTAIN. Unknown.

WILLARD: BROOK, MOUNTAIN, RIDGE. Unknown.

WILLIAMS BROOK. For O. Williams, resident, 1882.

WILLIAMSBURG. For the former name of a now unincorporated township, which was named for William Dodd of Boston, its owner.

WILLIAMS POND. For the Williams family who earned their living trapping and hunting.

WILLIMANTIC: settlement, TOWNSHIP. For the Willimantic Thread Company, which had a factory there in 1880.

WILLIS ISLAND. Unknown.

WINDEY: PITCH (2), PITCH POND. By area loggers, descriptive of winding rapids.

WITHAM BROOK. For A. Witham, settler, 1882.

WITHERLE RAVINE. For George H. Witherle, a man who loved the Katahdin area.

WITHEY: BOG, BROOK. For the Withey family.

WILSON: BIG-CLIFFS, BIG-STREAM, LITTLE-DEADWATER, LITTLE-FALLS, LITTLE-POND, LITTLE-STREAM, UPPER-POND. For Wilson, the man who founded the now defunct Wilson Township.

WOODMAN: BOG, BROOK, LITTLE-BOG, POND (2). Unknown.

YERXA BROOK. Unknown.

YOKE PONDS. For their likeness to two holes in an ox-yoke.

SAGADAHOC COUNTY

ABAGADASSET: POINT, RIVER. Three opinions. Micmac: "little parallel river," or "to shine (like the water)." For an Indian sagamore. For a white named Abby who killed an Indian named Dassy along this river. The last seems to be folk etymology and can probably be discounted.

AMES LEDGE. For the Ames family.

ARROWSIC: ISLAND, settlement, TOWNSHIP. Abnaki: "place of obstruction." Some say that this was the name of the Indian who professed to own the land.

ASHDALE. For ash trees.

ATKINS BAY. For Thomas Atkins, settler, 1659.

BACK COVE. Descriptive of location back from New Meadows River.

BAKER BROOK. For the early Baker family who settled there.

BALD HEAD: head, COVE, LEDGE. Descriptive.

BARENECK ISLAND. Descriptive.

BARLEY NECK. For a corruption of "Bailey," the family who lived there.

BASIN, THE. Descriptive of an enclosed cove.

BASIN POINT. For The Basin.

BATCHELDER HILL. For Captain and Mrs. Batchelder, residents, 1858.

BATH: settlement, TOWNSHIP, WEST-TOWNSHIP. Probably for Bath, England, named by Colonel Dummer Sewall.

BAY POINT. For Stage Island Bay.

BEAL ISLAND. For Jeremiah Beal, who owned it in the 1750's.

BEAR ISLAND. For bears.

BERRY ISLAND. For General Joseph Berry, boatbuilder, who lived there, early 1800's.

BIG POND. Descriptive.

BIRCH: ISLAND, POINT, -WOOD POND. For birch trees.

BLACK ROCKS, THE. Descriptive.

BLAISDELL HILL. Unknown.

BLUFF HEAD. Descriptive.

BOLD DICK ROCK. A fanciful name for a rock that stands alone.

BOWDOIN: CENTER, settlement, TOWNSHIP, WEST-. For James Bowdoin, Governor of Massachusetts, 1785-86.

BOWDOINHAM: RIDGE, settlement, TOWNSHIP. For Dr. Peter Bowdoin, early proprietor.

BOWIE HILL. For the early Bowie family.

BRADLEY POND. For the John Bradley family, who settled in 1731. Specifically for either Timothy Bradley, Jr., a Revolutionary War veteran, or Foster Bradley of the early 1800's.

BRAGDON ROCK. Unknown.

BRANCH, THE. Descriptive.

BRIDGE HILL. For a bridge located at its foot.

BRIGHAMS COVE. (settlement). For the local Brigham family,

BRIGHTWATER. Descriptive.

BROOKINGS BAY. For the Brookings family who settled here at an unknown date. One source says that the name is of recent origin, possibly the 1940's, as a Brookings family lived there then.

BURNT COAT ISLAND. For the folk etymological result of the French name applied to this island, "Brulé Cote"—"burned coast."

BURNT JACKET CHANNEL. For a humorous reference to Burnt Coat Island.

BUSHY ISLAND. Descriptive.

BUTLER: COVE, HEAD. For John Butler, settler, 1714-15.

BUTTONMOLD LEDGES. Descriptive of shape. A buttonmold is a small disk of wood which is covered by cloth or leather to make a button.

CAESAR POND. For an old Negro, Caesar, who lived on its shore.

CAMEL GROUND. For the humps of rock that show at low tide like camels' humps.

CAMPBELL COVE. For the three Campbell brothers, who settled there in the 1750's.

CAMPBELL ISLAND. For Alexander Campbell, settler of the 1750's.

CAMPBELL POND. For the local Campbell family.

CARRYING: -PLACE COVE, PLACE HEAD. Descriptive.

CASTLE ISLAND. Descriptive of shape.

CATHANCE: EAST-STREAM, RIVER, WEST BRANCH-RIVER, WEST-STREAM. Abnaki: "principal fork."

CENTERS POINT. For Samuel Center, settler, 1802.

CHOPS: CREEK, CROSSROAD, passage, POINT, WEST-POINT. For its resemblance to a passage between a pair of jaws or "chops."

CLAREYS POND. For the Edward Clarey family, owners.

CORNISH ISLAND. For the Cornish family.

COX: HEAD, LITTLE-HEAD. For William Cox, owner of headland, 1662.

COW ISLAND. Cows were grazed there.

CRAWFORD ISLAND. For John or Thomas Crawford, settlers before 1800.

CROW: ISLAND, POINT. For crows.

CUTTING CREEK. For Henry Cutting, millowner, 1815.

DAM: COVE, COVE CREEK. For a dam once built there.

DAYS FERRY. For the Day family who ran a ferry there.

DEAD RIVER. Descriptive of its rate of flow.

DENHAM STREAM. For the Thomas Denham family, settlers about 1800.

DENNY REED POINT. For S. Denny Reed, resident by 1858.

DIX ISLAND. Unknown.

DOGGARD POINT. For the Doggard family who lived there.

DOUBLING POINT. In nautical usage "doubling" means "to sail around," as one would have to do to get around this large projection of land.

DRUMMORE BAY. Named for the Irish market town of Dromore, by Irish settlers of 1730.

DRY: LEDGES, POINT. Descriptive.

DULEY POND. For any number of Dooley families in the area by 1858.

ELBOW HILL. For a sharp bend in a nearby road that resembles an elbow.

ELLINGWOOD ROCK. For John Wallace Ellingwood, early settler.

ELWELL POINT. For John Elwell, settler by the early 1800's.

EWE ISLAND. To make a fanciful pair with Ram Island.

FIDDLER REACH. Tradition says named for a man who was fiddling on the bowsprit of a ship when he fell off and drowned.

FISHER EDDY. For the Fisher family who owned a boatyard.

FISH HOUSE COVE. For a fish house formerly located there.

FIVE: ISLANDS, settlement. Descriptive.

FLAG ISLAND LEDGE. For Flag Island in Cumberland County.

FLYING POINT. For geese which flew over the point to get from one body of water to another.

FOG ISLAND. Descriptive of its frequently being shrouded in fog.

FORT BALDWIN. For Colonel Jeduthan Baldwin, a Revolutionary War engineer.

FOSTER POINT. Unknown.

FOX ISLANDS. For foxes.

FREYEE ISLAND. Unknown.

FULLER: MOUNTAIN, ROCK. Unknown.

GEORGETOWN: ISLAND, settlement, TOWNSHIP, WEST-, WEST-HILL. Some say for King George I of England. Others for Fort St. George.

GILBERT HEAD. For Captain Rawleigh Gilbert, who, on the death of George Popham, became the leader of the Popham Colony.

GILLESPIE: BROOK, LITTLE-BROOK. For Thomas Gillespie.

GILMORE HILL. For the local Gilmore family.

GOAT ISLAND. For goats kept there.

GOOSEBERRY: ISLAND, ISLAND LEDGE. For gooseberries.

GOOSE: COVE, ROCK. (2). For geese.

GOTTS COVE. For the local Gott family.

GRIFFITH HEAD. For Old Griffith, who was killed here by Indians.

HALIBUT ROCKS. For halibut fish shoaling there.

HALL BAY. For the Hall family who lived there.

HANSON BAY. For a local family.

HARBOR: ISLAND, ISLAND POINT. For Sebasco Harbor.

HARMON HARBOR. For Colonel Harmon, resident, the 1700's.

HARWARDS. For Captain Thomas Harward, shipbuilder, 1817-69.

HATCH POINT. For the Paul Hatch family, early settlers.

HATHORN HILL. For C.C. Hathorne, resident by 1858.

HEAD: BEACH, COVE. For Bald Head.

HEAL EDDY. For Peter Heald, settler, early 1700's.

HELL GATE: LITTLE-, UPPER-. For fast and dangerous water.

HEN ISLAND. Fancifully named.

HERMIT ISLAND. For Albert Moore, local old hermit.

HERON ISLAND. For herons.

HIGGINS MOUNTAIN. For Frederick Higgins.

HOCKOMOCK: BAY, POINT. Narragansett: "hook-shaped place." One source says it is an Indian word for "hell," which is possible as Upper and Lower Hell Gates are near.

HORNBEAM HILL. For hornbeam trees.

HOUGHTON POND. For the Houghton family of the early 1900's.

HUNNIWELL: BEACH, POINT. For Ambrose Hunniwell, settler before 1730.

ICEBORO. A former shipping point for ice cut on the Kennebec River.

INDIAN POINT. (2). For Indians.

ISAIAH HEAD. Unknown.

JACKKNIFE LEDGE. Descriptive of shape.

JAMISON LEDGE. Unknown.

JENNYS NUBBLE. Unknown.

KENNEBEC: POINT, RIVER, WEST BRANCH-RIVER. Abnaki: "long level water."

KETTLEBOTTOM. Descriptive of shape.

KNUBBLE: LITTLE-, projection. Descriptive.

LAMB ISLAND. Possibly for sheep kept there.

LEE ISLAND. For William Lee, Jr., given him as a wedding present by his father-in-law in 1776.

LIBBY COVE. For the local Libby family.

LINES ISLAND. Probably for Dennis Lines, settler by 1832.

LITTLE GOOD HARBOR. Descriptive.

LITTLE RIVER. (2). Descriptive.

LONG: ISLAND, ISLAND NARROWS. Descriptive.

LOWE POINT. For Francis Low, early settler.

MACMAHAN: ISLAND, settlement. For Terrence McMahan, settler of the 1700's.

MALAGA ISLAND. Abnaki: "cedar."

MALLON BROOK. For the Maloon family who settled about 1800.

MARR: ISLAND, -TOWN. For John Marr, Revolutionary War veteran and settler of the 1700's.

MAXWELL ISLAND. For Robert and his son William Kilbourne Maxwell.

MEACHAM POND. For a man of that name who ran a saw and shingle mill there.

MEADOW BROOK. (settlement). Descriptive.

MEETINGHOUSE: HILL, POND. For the Small Point Meetinghouse.

MERRITT ISLAND. For Henry Merritt.

MERRITT MOUNTAIN. Possibly for Freeman H. Merritt, local entrepreneur about 1908, or his ancestors.

MERRY COVE. Unknown.

MERRYMEETING BAY. Some say for the meeting of the water of five rivers. Others say for the meeting of two early survey crews.

MIDDLE LEDGE. Descriptive.

MIDDLE MARK ISLAND. For location between Upper and Lower Mark islands. "Mark" meant simply a place of reference in navigating.

MIDDLE POINT. For location between Bald Head and Centers Point.

MILE LEDGE. For location about one mile from Seguin Island.

MILL: COVE, ISLAND, POINT, POND. For mills located there, and specifically for one on Mill Island by the 1700's.

MONSWEAG. Abnaki: "narrow, dugout channel."

MORSE COVE. For J. Morse, resident, 1858.

MORSE: HILL, MOUNTAIN, POINT, RIVER. For the Daniel Morse family, settlers of 1750.

MOUNT ARARAT. Named for no reason, for the biblical mountain where Noah's Ark came to rest.

MUDDY RIVER: Descriptive.

MURPHY CORNER. For the Murphy family who lived there.

MUSTARD ISLAND. For John Mustard, recent owner who lived in Topsham Township.

NEQUASSET: BROOK, LAKE, settlement. Abnaki: "a pond."

NEWBURY POINT. Unknown.

NEWDICK POINT. Malecite: "at the solitary place."

NEW MEADOWS: area, RIVER. For good, new meadows located a little inland from the earliest settlements.

NEWTOWN: CREEK, HILL. At the end of King Phillip's War in 1677, all of the area inhabitants had been driven out. When they returned they settled in a different spot and called it "New Town" to distinguish it from the old settlement.

NORTH CREEK. Because it flowed from the north to Tottman Cove.

NORTHEAST POINT. Descriptive of being the northeast point of Georgetown Township.

NORTH SUGAR LOAF ISLAND. Descriptive of shape and position.

OAK ISLAND. For oak trees.

OUTER HEAD. For location farther out than Griffith Head.

OZONE MOUNTAIN. A humorous name for its fancied height.

PALACE COVE. For the main building in the Clark and Lake trading post settlement in 1676.

PARKER: FLATS, HEAD, HEAD SWAMP, settlement. For John Parker, who purchased the area from the Indians in 1659.

PASTURE: BROOK, RIDGE. Descriptive.

PEJEPSCOT. Abnaki: "extended long rapids."

PERKINS ISLAND. For the local Perkins family.

PERRY COVE. (settlement). For the local Perry family.

PERRY HILL. For the Perry family who lived there in the 1800's.

PHEBE ISLAND. Some say for an elderly lady whose first name was Phebe who lived there. Others say for an old Indian woman who lived there. They are likely the same person.

PHIPPSBURG: settlement, TOWNSHIP. For Sir William Phipps, royal governor of Massachusetts in 1692.

PHIPPS POINT. For James Phipps, a settler in the 1600's.

PITCHPINE HILL. For pitchpine trees.

PLEASANT: COVE, LITTLE-POINT, POINT, POND, UPPER-POND. Descriptive.

POND: ISLAND, ISLAND SHOAL. For a small freshwater pond located there.

POPHAM BEACH. For Fort Popham and the Popham Colony, which were named for Sir George Popham, the colony's first president.

PORK POINT. One source says the name was originally, "Port Point" and "Pork" is a corruption. Another states that during the Revolutionary War a contraband vessel loaded with pork was wrecked off the point.

PREBLE POINT. For Jonathon Preble, who built a fort there in 1716.

PURINGTON BROOK. For the Reverend Nathanial Purington and his son Albert, esteemed early inhabitants.

RAM ISLAND. (3). For their use as sheep pens.

REACH, THE. For Fiddlers Reach.

RICH HILL. For Reuben Rich.

RICHMOND: CORNER, settlement, TOWNSHIP. For Fort Richmond, named for the Duke of Richmond and built in 1719.

RIGGS COVE. For Squire Riggs, settler, 1650.

RING HILL. For the Ring family, there in 1858.

ROBINHOOD: COVE, settlement. For the English name given to an Indian sachem in 1650.

ROGERS NECK. For numerous Rogers who lived there in the 1700's.

SABINO: HEAD, settlement. For Sabino, an Abnaki sagamore.

SAGADAHOC: BAY, COUNTY. Abnaki: "the outflowing of the swift stream as it nears the sea."

SALTER ISLAND. One source says for fishermen who salted their fish· there. Another states it was for John Stevens, who evaporated seawater to get salt. (These two could overlap.) Another states for a man named Salter who was the· son-in-law of John Parker, for whom Parkers Island was named.

SAM DAY HILL. For Sam Day, the man who lived there.

SASONOA POINT. For Chief Sasonoa, who met with Champlain.

SEAL: COVE, ISLAND (2). For seals.

SEBASCO: ESTATES, HARBOR, settlement. Abnaki: "portage almost completed."

SEDGELY BROOK. For Robert Sedgely, early settler.

SEGUIN: ISLAND, LEDGES. Abnaki: "humped up," like a turtle.

SEWELL POND. For the Sewell family who owned it.

SHEEPSCOT: BAY, LITTLE-RIVER. Abnaki: "many rocky channels."

SHIPYARD POINT. For a small shipyard on Swans Island.

SILVER LAKE. Descriptive.

SISTERS POINT. For a pair of sisters living there in the 1800's, possibly the Wallace sisters.

SLOOP LEDGE. Descriptive of shape.

SMALL: CAPE-, CAPE-HARBOR, POINT, POINT (settlement), POINT BEACH, POINT HARBOR. For John Small, surveyor.

SOLDIER POINT. For the soldiers who defended the point against British ships in the War of 1812.

SPAR ISLAND. Descriptive of shape.

SPIRIT POND. For a mist that frequently covers it, giving it a ghostly appearance.

SPRAGUE HILL. For the Sprague family who owned it for years.

SPRAGUE: POND, RIVER. For Jethro Sprague, settler of the 1760's.

SQUIRREL POINT. For squirrels.

STAGE: ISLAND, ISLAND BAY. For fish drying stages located there.

STARBIRD CORNER. For the Starbird family who lived there in the 1840's and '50's.

STIPHINEN POINT. For G. Stilpen, living there in 1858.

STURGEON ISLAND. For sturgeon fishermen who camped and stored their gear here.

SWAN: ISLAND, ISLAND POINT, LITTLE-ISLAND. For Colonel James Swan, owner and Revolutionary War veteran.

SWETT MARSH. For the local Swett family.

TARRS MOUNTAIN. For Benjamin Tarr.

TATE HILL. For the local Tate family.

TEMPLE LEDGE. For Robert Temple, who led an expedition of settlers in 1750.

THEOBALD POINT. Probably for the later family of Dr. Ernest F. Theobald, a settler after the Revolution.

THORNE: HEAD, ISLAND. Probably for a Thorn that was there in 1764 who testified against the Gutch estate, which included the island.

TODD: BAY, ISLAND POINT. For George Todd, settler, 1796.

TOPSHAM: settlement, TOWNSHIP. For Topsham, England, former home of many of the settlers.

TOTTMAN COVE. For the Henry Tottman family, settlers of 1767.

TOWESIC NECK. Abnaki: "broken passage."

TRAFFTON MEADOW BROOK. For the Thomas Trafton family, settlers of 1737.

TURNIP ISLAND. Descriptive of fancied shape.

TWING POINT. For the local Twing family.

VARNEY CORNER. For the Varney family who lived there.

WADE COVE. For Robert Wade, resident by 1854.

WEASEL POINT. For weasels.

WEBBER ISLAND. For the Webber family who owned it.

WEST POINT: (point), settlement. Descriptive of being the western point of Phippsburg.

WHALEBACK: RIDGE, ROCK. Descriptive.

WHEELER HILL. For the local Wheeler family.

WHISKEAG CREEK. Abnaki: "creek runs nearby dry at low tide."

WHITTEN HILL . For the 3 or 4 Whitten families who lived there.

WILLIAMS ISLAND. For Amos and John Williams, owners.

WILMOT BROOK. Unknown.

WINNEGANCE: BAY, CREEK, settlement. Abnaki: "little portage."

WOLFE POND. Unknown.

WOOD: ISLAND (3), LITTLE-ISLAND. For timber.

WOODS ISLAND. For timber.

WOOLWICH: Settlement, TOWNSHIP. For Woolwich, England.

WYMAN BAY. For the Wyman family who settled there in 1737.

SOMERSET COUNTY

ABACOTNETIC STREAM. Abnaki: "stream opening out from between mountains."

ADDINGTON BROOK. For the Addington family.

ALDER: BROOK (4), BROOK TOWNSHIP, LITTLE-BROOK, POND (2), POND BROOK, STREAM. For alder trees.

ANSON: NORTH-, settlement, TOWNSHIP. For Lord George Anson, distinguished Englishman.

APPLETON TOWNSHIP. Unknown.

ARNOLDS LANDING. For Benedict Arnold and his army, who set up camp here on their march to Quebec.

ARNOLDS POINT. For Benedict Arnold and his army.

ATHENS: settlement, TOWNSHIP, WEST-. For Athens, Greece.

ATTEAN: FALLS, LANDING, MOUNTAIN, POND, settlement, TOWNSHIP. For Etienne Orson, settler about 1793. The Abnakis pronounce "Etienne" as "Attean."

AUSTIN: BROOK (2), LITTLE-POND, POND (2), SOUTH BRANCH-STREAM. For the large Austin family who settled in Somerset County early.

BABBITT RIDGE. Possibly for J. M. Babbitt or his family.

BAKER: BRANCH OF SAINT JOHN RIVER, BROOK, BROOK COVE, BROOK POINT, FLOWAGE, LAKE, LITTLE-BROOK, MOUNTAIN, POND (5), STREAM (3). Mountain in Moscow Township, for the Baker family who settled here in 1773; there were soon so many descendants that the town was called Bakerstown first. Ponds in Solon and Caratunk Townships, for the Baker families. The others are unknown specifically, but no doubt are named for the many Bakers who spread out from the initial family in the Moscow (Bakerstown) area.

BAKER BROOK. Unknown.

BALD: EAST INLET-MOUNTAIN POND, MOUNTAIN (2), MOUNTAIN BROOK, MOUNTAIN POND, MOUNTAIN STREAM, MOUNTAIN TOWNSHIP (2). Descriptive.

BARKER BROOK. Unknown.

BARKER POND. For Joseph Barker, one of the earliest settlers of Cornville Township.

BARRETT: BROOK, EAST BRANCH-BROOK, POND. Unknown.

BARRON CORNER. For the Barron family, local residents.

BARROWS COVE. Unknown.

BARTLEY: BIG-POND, LITTLE-POND. For the Bartley family who settled from Canada about 1850 and were reputed to be notorious outlaws.

BARTON BROOK. Unknown.

BARTON HILL. For the Barton family who lived there.

BASIN POND. Descriptive.

BASSETT BROOK. For Joseph Bassett.

BATES RIDGE. Unknown.

BEAN: BROOK, BROOK MOUNTAIN. Unknown.

BEAN POND. For the Bean family who settled before the 1880's.

BEAR: BROOK (2), LITTLE-MOUNTAIN, MOUNTAIN. POND. For bears.

BEAVER: BROOK (3), POND (2). For beavers.

BECK POND. Unknown.

BECKY INLET. For Becky Butler, whose two children drowned there. The Butler family came to the area during a minor gold rush.

BEECH: HILL, LITTLE-HILL. For beech trees.

BENJAMIN: BROOK, POND. For the profusion of benjamins, the local name for a certain wild flower, growing in the area.

BERRY: HILL, POND. For the local Berry families.

BIG BENNETT BROOK. Unknown.

BIGELOW BROOK: BIG BROOK. Possibly for Major Bigelow, one of Benedict Arnold's men, although this is unlikely, as it seems too far from their line of march.

BIGELOW HILL. For Hiram Bigelow, who lived there.

BIG ISLAND. Descriptive.

BIG TEN TOWNSHIP. For being oversize and its number designation.

BIG W TOWNSHIP. For its letter designation and larger than Little W.

BILL MORRIS POND. For Bill Morris, logger.

BILLY JACK DEPOT. Unknown.

BINGHAM: settlement, TOWNSHIP. For William Bingham, who owned much Maine land at one time.

BIRCH: ISLAND (3), POINT. For birch trees.

BITTER BROOK. Descriptive of the taste of the water due to various nearby mineral deposits.

BLACK: BROOK (6), BROOK HILL, BROOK POND (2), EAST BRANCH-STREAM, HILL, HILL POND, HILL STREAM, NARROWS, NUBBLE (4), POINT (2), STREAM, WEST BRANCH-BROOK. Descriptive.

BLACKWELL: CORNER, HILL. For Herman and Nathaniel Blackwell, twin brothers.

BLAIR. For the Blair family who had a farm nearby.

BLAKESLEE LAKE. Unknown.

BLANCHARD: BROOK, MOUNTAIN. Unknown.

BLOODSUCKER BROOK. For bloodsuckers.

BLUE RIDGE. Descriptive of its color from afar, due to the spruce trees.

BOBS POND. Unknown.

BOG: BIG-BROOK (8), CORNER, POND (2), SOUTH-STREAM, STREAM (2). Descriptive.

BOMBAZEE BROOK. For Chief Abomazine, an Abnaki leader killed at Norridgewock in 1724. The word is Abnaki; "keeper of the ceremonial fire."

BOSTON RANCH. For the owners of land near this flagstation who were from Boston.

BOULDER POND. Descriptive.

BOWDEN ISLAND. For Benjamin Bowden, settler of the 1800's who lived there.

BOWLEY POND. For the early Bowley family.

BOWTOWN TOWNSHIP. Descriptive of a bow in the Dead River where it meets the Kennebec.

BOYNTON POND. For the local Boynton family.

BRACKETT HILL. Unknown.

BRADLEY POND. Unknown.

BRAILEY BROOK. Unknown.

BRANDY: BROOK (2), POND. Descriptive of the color of the water.

BRASSUA: LAKE, LITTLE-LAKE, NORTH BRANCH-STREAM, settlement, SOUTH BRANCH-STREAM, STREAM, TOWNSHIP. For the Abnaki pronunciation of "Frank," a minor chief.

BRIGGS HILL. Unknown.

BRIGHTON: settlement, TOWNSHIP. Unknown.

BRITENELL BROOK. Unknown.

BROOKS RIDGE. For the many Brooks families who lived on the ridge in the 1800's.

BROWN BROOK. For Nicholas or Robert Brown, settlers, early 1800's.

BROWNS CORNER. For the Brown family, settlers, 1773-74.

BRYANT BOG. For James, John, and Daniel Bryant, early settlers.

BUDWORM BROOK. For budworms.

BUNKER HILL. For Francis Bunker, settler from New Hampshire, who built his home here.

BURNT: HILL (2), NUBBLE. Descriptive.

BURNT JACKET: ISLAND, MOUNTAIN. These names could have humorous reference to Brule Cote Island on the coast, which was anglicized to "Burnt Coat."

BURRILL HILL (2). In Hartland Township, for S. Burrill, the resident in 1883 whose ancestors bought the land from Squire Warren. In Norridgewock Township, for the Herod Burrill family.

BURTON CORNER. For Eben and Nathan Burton, early settlers.

BUTLER: BROOK, POND (2). Pond in T4R4, for William Butler from Industry Township, one of the earliest settlers. The others are unknown.

CALL POND. Unknown.

CAMBRIDGE: POND, settlement, TOWNSHIP. Named by the daughter of Isaac Hooper at whose house a meeting was held to select the township name in 1834, for Cambridge, England, about which she had been reading a story.

CAMERA: HILL, RIDGE. Unknown.

CAMPBELL: BROOK (2), NORTH BRANCH-BROOK, POND. Unknown.

CAMP BROOK. For camps.

CANAAN: BOG, settlement, TOWNSHIP. For the religiousness of the people and because it was as beautiful as the Promised Land.

CANADA: FALLS LAKE, LITTLE-FALLS. For Canada, which is not too far away.

CAPE HORN POND. Unknown.

CARATUNK: FALLS, settlement, TOWNSHIP. Abnaki: "forbidding or crooked stream."

CARIBOU NARROWS (2). For caribou.

CARNEY BROOK. For John Carney, who owned a large farm at the mouth of the brook.

CARRABASSETT: RIVER, STREAM. Abnaki: "small moose place."

CARRY: BROOK (3), EAST-POND, MIDDLE-POND, NORTH-BROOK, SOUTH BRANCH-BROOK, WEST-POND. For various places where canoes and boats had to be carried from one body of water to another.

CARRYING: NORTH BRANCH-PLACE STREAM, PLACE STREAM, PLACE TOWNSHIP. For where canoes had to be carried from one body of water to another. The township was named specifically for the long carry made by Benedict Arnold's men on their march to Quebec.

CARSON HILL. For the local Carson family.

CASS CORNER. For Ethan Cass, who operated a general store here.

CASTLE HARMONY. For the clubhouse of a hunting club located in Harmony Township.

CATES HILL. For the many Cates living here.

CATHEART MOUNTAIN. Unknown.

CEDAR POND. (2). For cedar trees.

CENTER POND. For its location in the center of the township.

CHAIN PONDS. Descriptive of ponds in a chain pattern.

CHANDLER HILL. (2). In Ripley Township, for the Chandler family who lived there. In T2R1, unknown.

CHAPMANS RIDGE. For the Chapman family.

CHASE: BOG, HILL, LITTLE-POND, LITTLE-STREAM MOUNTAIN, LITTLE-STREAM POND, NORTH BRANCH-STREAM,

POND (2), STREAM (2), STREAM MOUNTAIN, STREAM POND. Bog in Caratunk Township, for the Chase family. Hill in Canaan Township, for Thomas Chase, a settler by 1803. Little-Pond, Stream, and Pond in Moscow Township, for Ebezel Chase, who made cedar shingles on the pond. Pond in Solon Township, unknown. All the others in the unorganized townships, for George Chase, who drove logs here in the early 1900's.

CHENEY POND. Unknown.

CHIMES, THE. Unknown.

CHUB POND. (2). For chubs.

CHURCH BROOK. For G. Church, a resident in 1883.

CHURCH HILL. For William Church.

CHURCHILL: BROOK, STREAM, UPPER-STREAM. Unknown.

CLARK BROOK. (2). In New Portland Township, for a number of Clark families. In Smithfield Township, for LaFayette Clark, resident, 1883.

CLAYTON POND. Unknown.

CLEAR: POND, -WATER POND (2). Descriptive.

CLISH POND. Unknown.

COBURN: BROOK, MOUNTAIN, POND, RIDGE. For Abner and Philander Coburn, early surveyors and owners of much woodland.

COLD: BROOK (3), STREAM (2), STREAM MOUNTAIN, STREAM POND, WEST BRANCH-BROOK. Descriptive.

COMBER INN. For Ed Comber, who operated the inn.

COMEOUTER HILL. One source says for a family by that name. Another says that it is located near Morrel Pond which was used by the Baptist Church for immersion baptism, and the baptized would "comeouter" the pond toward the hill.

COMSTOCK: BROOK, MOUNTAIN, TOWNSHIP. Unknown.

CONCORD TOWNSHIP. For Concord, Massachusetts.

COOPER BROOK. For William and Annie Cooper, who lived nearby.

CORNER POND. For being located at the corner of two townships.

CORNISH HILL. For the Cornish family, who farmed nearby.

CORNVILLE: settlement, TOWNSHIP. For the abundance of Indian corn that could be raised there.

CORSON: BROOK, CORNER (2). Brook and Corner in Athens Township, for James Corson and his numerous descendants. Corner in Hartland Township, for the Corson family who bought land from Squire Warren.

COW MOUNTAIN. One of the early settlers lost his cows and found them on this mountain.

CRAIGIN BROOK. Unknown.

CROCKER POND. For the Crocker family.

CUNNINGHAM: BROOK, POND. Unknown.

CURRIER: BROOK, HILL. For Seth Currier, who made potash in the early 1800's and ran a store.

CYRS. For the Cyr family who operated a granite quarry nearby and shipped their product from here.

DANE CORNER. For Mary Dane, spinster, who lived nearby.

DAVIS: BROOK, POND. Unknown.

DAYMOND POND. For Fred Daymond, who lived nearby in 1910.

DEAD: BROOK, RIVER, RIVER MOUNTAIN, RIVER TOWNSHIP, STREAM, STREAM POND, -WATER BROOK. Descriptive of flow.

DECKER BROOK. For David Decker.

DECKER BOG. For Albert or Ralph Decker, settlers in the 1800's.

DEER: BOG, POND. For deer.

DEMO: BROOK, POND. Unknown.

DENNISTOWN TOWNSHIP. Unknown.

DESOLATION: BROOK, POND. For its location in a desolate, isolated area.

DETROIT: settlement, TOWNSHIP. French: "the straits," of Sebasticook River.

DEVIL: BOG, BOG BROOK. Fanciful name for a bog which is difficult to cross.

DEVILS HEAD. For a fancied resemblance.

DICKEY BROOK. For the local Dickey family.

DIMMICK: BIG-POND, LITTLE-POND, MOUNTAIN, MOUNTAIN-POND, STREAM. For the Dimmick family.

DINGLEY: LITTLE-POND, POND, UPPER-POND. Unknown.

DIPPER POND. Unknown.

DIVIDE, THE. Descriptive of a ridge between Moxie Pond and the Kennebec River.

DIXIE CORNER. For 3 families that lived here who were sympathetic to the South during the Civil War.

DIXON: MOUNTAIN, POND. Unknown.

DODLING: HILL, LITTLE-HILL. For the Dodling family who owned a granite quarry in the area.

DOGTOWN. For the many dogs which were attracted by the animal carcasses at the nearby tannery.

DOLE: BROOK, BROOK TOWNSHIP, POND. Unknown.

DORE HILL. For Joseph Dore, owner.

DORITY POND. Unknown.

DOUCIE BROOK. For Doucie, French-Canadian lumberman.

DOUGHNUT POND. Descriptive of shape.

DOUGLAS POND. Unknown.

DOW CORNER. For P. Dow, resident, 1860.

DUBOIS POND. For Dubois, French-Canadian lumberman.

DUD BROOK. Unknown.

DUNBAR HILL. For the local Dunbar family.

DUNCAN POND. Unknown.

DURGIN BROOK. For W.H. Durgin, blacksmith.

DYERVILLE. For the many Dyers who lived here.

EAGLE POND. For eagles.

EARNS HILL. For Jonathon Eames, early settler; a cartographical error.

EAST: INLET, NUBBLE. Descriptive.

EASTMAN BROOK. Unknown.

EATON HILL. For Moses and Samuel Eaton, settlers from Salisbury, Massachusetts.

EATON: MOUNTAIN, RIDGE. For the Eaton family.

EGG POND. For duck eggs.

ELBOW BOG. Descriptive of an elbow turn of Black Brook.

ELLIS CORNER. For Benjamin Ellis, early settler.

ELLIS POND. For Ellis, early lumberman.

ELM: LITTLE-POND, POND, POND MOUNTAIN, STREAM, STREAM TOWNSHIP. For elm trees.

EMBDEN: POND, settlement, TOWNSHIP. For Embden, Germany.

EMERY BROOK. For Jonathon Emery, early settler.

ENCHANTED: LITTLE-POND, LOWER-POND, LOWER-TOWNSHIP, POND, STREAM, UPPER-TOWNSHIP. Descriptive of the area before the timber was cut.

ENCHANTED. Fanciful name for an area that was very beautiful before the timber was cut over.

EVERETT POND. Unknown.

FAHI: BROOK, POND. Unknown.

FAIRFIELD: CENTER, NORTH-, settlement, TOWNSHIP. Descriptive of the beautiful surroundings.

FALL BROOK. Descriptive of the stream rising and falling quickly.

FALLS BROOK. For a small falls.

FARNHAM BROOK. For Charles Farnham, settler, 1834.

FARRAND ISLAND. For Herbert Farrand, who owned it for many years.

FELKER POND. Unknown.

FERGUSON: LITTLE-BROOK, LITTLE-STREAM, STREAM. For the early settling Ferguson family.

FERNALD POND. Unknown.

FISH: BROOK (3), LITTLE-POND (2), LITTLE-PONDS, POND (5). Brook in Fairfield Township for a number of Fish families living there in 1860. The rest, for fish.

FISHER PONDS. For fishers.

FITZGERALD POND. Unknown.

FIVE CORNERS. Descriptive of a road intersection forming 5 corners.

FLAGSTAFF: LAKE, MOUNTAIN, TOWNSHIP. For a flagstaff planted outside his tent by Benedict Arnold, while his army was marching through to attack Quebec.

FLATIRON POND. Descriptive of shape.

FLETCHER HILL. For the local Fletcher family.

FLETCHER PONDS. For Tom Fletcher Stream.

FOGG BROOK. Unknown.

FOGG POND. For the Fogg family who farmed there.

FOLEY: LITTLE-POND, OUTLET, POND. For Foley, logger.

FORD HILL. For E.L. Ford, resident, 1883.

FORKS, THE: settlement, TOWNSHIP. For where Dead River empties into the Kennebec River.

FORSYTHE: BROOK, TOWNSHIP. Unknown.

FOSS MOUNTAIN. For David Foss, who lived at the foot of the mountain.

FOSTER HILL. For the early Foster family.

FOSTER RIDGE. Unknown.

FOURMILE BROOK. (3). In T4R7, for location 4 miles from Attean Falls. In T4R4, for location one mile from Threemile Brook. In T3R6, because it runs into Moose River 4 miles from where Moose River empties into Attean Pond.

FOX HILL. For the Fox family who settled in the early 1800's.

FRENCH HILL. For Josiah French, who settled from Salisbury, Massachusetts, in 1800.

FROST: POND, POND BROOK, POND FLOWAGE. Unknown.

FRYPAN POND. Descriptive of shape.

FURBUSH HILL. For P. and P.N. Furbush, who lived there in 1883.

GAMAPE HILL. For the Gamape family who lived there.

GAMMON POND. For the A. Gammon family, residents, 1864.

GANDER: BROOK, POND. For geese.

GATES ISLAND. For B. Gage, resident in the area, 1883; a cartographical error.

GETCHELL BROOK. For Henry F. Getchell, early settler and lumberman.

GILMAN: BROOK, POND, POND MOUNTAIN. Unknown.

GILROY BROOK. Unknown.

GOLD BROOK. (2). For gold found there.

GOODRICH HILL. Unknown.

GOODWIN BROOK. For Hussey and Myra Goodwin, who owned the land where the brook rises.

GOODWIN CORNER. For the Jonathon Goodwin family.

GOODWIN HILL. (2). In Canaan Township, for Jeremiah Goodwin, settler by 1803. In Hartford Township, for C. Goodwin, resident, 1883.

GOOSE POND. For geese.

GORDON: LITTLE-POND, POND. Unknown.

GORE RAPIDS. Unknown.

GOULD CORNER. For the local Gould family.

GRACE POND. Unknown.

GRAND FALLS. Descriptive.

GRANNYS CAP. Humorously descriptive of the shape of the mountain.

GRASS: LITTLE-POND, POND (2). Descriptive.

GRAY BROOK. Unknown.

GRAY ISLAND. For the Gray family who owned it and lived there.

GREAT EDDY. Descriptive of an eddy on the Kennebec River.

GREAT WORKS. Named by John Elliot, who settled about 1800, for the many mills ("great works") he envisioned building there.

GREEN HILL. For Daddy Green, who lived on its crest in the 1800's.

GREEN MOUNTAIN. Descriptive.

GRENIER: BIG-POND, MIDDLE-POND, POND. Unknown.

GULF: EAST BRANCH-STREAM, STREAM (3), WEST BRANCH-STREAM. For their flowing through a "gulf," a depression.

GULLIVER: BROOK, EAST BRANCH-BROOK, WEST BRANCH-BROOK. Although it is not known if it applies here, the name is a frequent one for a large brook, in reference to Swift's Gulliver.

HACKETT HILL. Unknown.

HALE: BROOK, POND. Unknown.

HALEY BROOK. For R. Haley, resident, 1883.

HALFMOON POND. Descriptive of shape.

HALFWAY BROOK. (2). In Jackman Township, for location halfway between Jackman Station and Long Pond. In T3R4, for location halfway between Long Falls and Dead River Dam on Dead River.

HALFWAY POINT. For location halfway up Great Moose Lake.

HALL AND WAITE HILL. One source says for the Hall and Waite families who lived there. Another source says that this is a surveyor's mistake that refers to a logging road named "Haul and Wait Road."

HALL BROOK STREAM. For the Hall family who owned the land where the stream rose.

HALL POND. Unknown.

HAM HILL. For Samuel Ham, who settled from Harmony Township in the 1780's.

HAMMOND TOWNSHIP. Unknown.

HANCOCK: POND, STREAM. Unknown.

HANSOM BROOK. For N. Hanson, resident, 1883.

HARDSCRABBLE MOUNTAIN. Descriptive of a steep mountain that was difficult to log.

HARDWOOD MOUNTAIN. (2). For hardwood trees.

HARMONY: settlement, TOWNSHIP. Named by the wife of Deacon John Moses, for the good feeling, or "harmony," existing between the settlers.

HARRIS BROOK. Unknown.

HARRISON WHITE BROOK. For Harrison White, who owned the land traversed by the brook.

HARTLAND: settlement, TOWNSHIP. Some say for "land of the hart (deer)." Others, for "heart of the hills."

HAYDEN LANDING. Unknown.

HEALD: BROOK, LITTLE-BROOK, INLET, MOUNTAIN, POND (2), PONDS, STREAM (2). Brook, Little-Brook, Ponds, Stream in Caratunk Township, for the Heald family. The rest for Heald, a lumberman from the Anson area who logged in the neighborhood.

HEALEY BROOK. Unknown.

HEDGEHOG: HILL, MOUNTAIN (3). For hedgehogs (porcupines).

HELEN POND. Unknown.

HENHAWK LEDGE. For chickenhawks.

HICKS POND. Unknown.

HIGGINS BROOK. Unknown.

HIGHER POND. For location at a higher elevation than High Pond.

HIGHLAND TOWNSHIP. Descriptive.

HIGH POND. For location on high ground.

HILL POND. For a nearby hill.

HILTON BROOK. (2). In Mercer Township, for Allen Hilton, who married the granddaughter of Caleb Harris. In Starks Township, for Richard Hilton, a settler before 1800.

HILTON HILL. (2). In Anson Township, for Jerry Hilton, settler by 1813. In Cornville Township, for Stephen and David Hilton, settlers before 1800.

HINCKLEY. For G.W. Hinckley, who founded a school and home for boys and girls in East Fairfield. Because of the many East Fairfields in the U.S., the Postal Department asked for a name change. Due to the good name of the school and his receiving more mail than anyone else, his name was given as the name of the post office in 1900.

HINCKLEY HILL. Unknown.

HOBBSTOWN TOWNSHIP. Unknown.

HOG ISLAND. For its use as a hog pen.

HOLEB: FALLS, settlement, STREAM, TOWNSHIP. For Holeb Nichols, early trapper.

HOLLAND BROOK. Unknown.

HOLLY BROOK. For the early Holly family.

HOLWAY CORNER. For the early Holway family who settled here.

HOOD BROOK. A Mr. Hood and his dog stopped at a tavern which stood on an adjacent hill. He left his horse and wagon outside. He disappeared, and everyone felt that he was murdered and his body thrown in the brook that now bears his name.

HORN HILL. For the three Horn families who lived there.

HORSE: BROOK, POND. Unknown.

HORSESHOE POND. (6). Descriptive of shape.

HOUSTON: BROOK, LITTLE-BROOK. For the early Houston family.

HOUSTON CORNER. For the Houston family, 1883 residents.

HOWARD HILL. Unknown.

HUFF HILL. For L. Huff, resident, 1883.

HUNNEWELL BROOK. For the area Hunnewell family.

HURD CORNER. For M. Hurd, resident, 1883.

HURD HILL. For Trustrun Hurd, settler, 1796.

HURRICANE: BROOK (2), HILL, MOUNTAIN, POND. For a hurricane that knocked down much timber in the area.

HUTCHINS BROOK. For David Hutchings, first settler of New Portland Township in 1785.

HUTCHINS HILL. Unknown.

HUTCH POND. Unknown.

IKE BROOK. Unknown.

INDIAN: LITTLE-BOG, LITTLE-HILL, LITTLE-POND (3), LITTLE-STREAM, POND (3), STREAM (3), STREAM TOWNSHIP. For Indians. Stream in Mercer Township, specifically for Indians encountered here by a hunter while beaver trapping.

IRONBOUND: MOUNTAIN, POND. Descriptive of a very rocky mountain.

IRON POND. Descriptive of a rocky banked pond.

ISLAND POND. Descriptive.

JACKMAN FIELD. For William Jackman, who built a hotel here in the early 1800's.

JACKMAN: MILL, settlement, STATION, TOWNSHIP. For the Jackman family, earliest settlers.

JACKSON: BROOK, POND. For the early Jackson family.

JEROME BROOK. Unknown.

JEWELL HILL. For Enos Jewell, first settler in the area.

JEWETT: POND, STREAM. Unknown.

JIM EATON HILL. For Jim Eaton, who farmed here.

JIMMY BROOK. Unknown.

JOAQUIN BROOK. For the Joaquin family.

JOE POKUM: BOG, POND. For Joe Pokum, local Indian guide and logger.

JOES HOLE. Unknown.

JOHNS: HILL, POND. Unknown.

JOHNSON: BOG, BROOK (4), MOUNTAIN (2), MOUNTAIN TOWNSHIP. Brook and Mountain in Bingham Township, for Deremus Johnson, settler from Vermont. Brook in Pittsfield Township, for the Johnson family who farmed nearby. Mountain, Bog, and Mountain Township for Johnson, lumberman. The others, unknown.

JOHONNETT BROOK. For the early settling Johonnett family.

JONES BROOK. (2). In Madison Township, for the Jones family who lived near the brook in the early 1900's. In Norridgewock Township, for L.S. and O.L. Jones, residents in 1883.

JOSIAH BROOK. For Joshua Greenleaf, who had a farm on the brook, mid-1800's. The name has been mispronounced and changed to the present one.

JUNIPER BOG. For juniper trees.

KELLY BROOK. For the Kelly family.

KELLY MOUNTAIN. For the Kelly family who owned it.

KENNEBEC RIVER. Abnaki: "long level water without rapids," or "long quiet water."

KILGORE: POND, UPPER-POND. Unknown.

KIMBALL BROOK. (2). In Harmony Township, for David Kimball, settler, early 1800's. In Moose River Township, for the early Kimball family.

KINCAID STREAM. For the local Kincaid family.

KING: and BARTLETT LAKE, and BARTLETT MOUNTAIN, and BARTLETT TOWNSHIP, LITTLE-LAKE, LITTLE-RIVER. For King & Bartlett, the proprietors of the township.

KING POND. Unknown.

KINGSLY: BOG, FLOWAGE. Unknown.

KNIGHTS: POND, POND HILL. For Bill Knight, who lived near.

KNOWLES BROOK. For a Mr. Knowles of Fredrickton, New Brunswick, who bought the stumpage from the landowners about 1864.

LA CROIX DEPOT. French: "the cross," for a road intersection.

LADD POND. For Fred, Charles, and Dearborn Ladd, who built the dam that created the pond.

LAKE COMO. Named by workmen who built the railroad, for a lake in Italy.

LAKE GEORGE. For George, the man who built the first hotel there.

LAKEWOOD. Descriptive of its location near the woods and Wesserrunsett Lake.

LAMBERT BROOK. For Sherebiah Lambert, settler, 1786.

LAMBS COVE. For the early Lamb family.

LANE: BROOK, LITTLE-BROOK, LITTLE-POND (2), POND. Unknown.

LANE HILL. For the early Lane family.

LANG: HILL, POND. Unknown.

LARD: BROOK, POND. Unknown.

LARONE. A Mr. Emery was the owner of a roan horse, called The Roan, one of the first horses in the settlement. At a meeting to establish a post office, someone asked how were they going to get mail there, and someone else asked what were they going to name the post office. Emery said, "The Roan," in answer to the first question, and the person asking the second question replied, "What kind of a name is that?" Emery saw the confusion, but said that by changing the "the" to "La" and adding "rone" they could have a good name for the post office.

LATTY POINT. For Ed Latty, who owned a cottage there.

LEADBETTER FALLS. Unknown.

LEDGE: BROOK, ISLAND. Descriptive.

LEDGES, THE. Descriptive.

LEECH BROOK. For A. Leach, resident, 1860.

LEITH POND. Unknown.

LEMON STREAM. (2). In Harmony Township, unknown. In Starks Township, for David Leeman, an early town official, who had mills there.

LEWISTON POND. Unknown.

LEXINGTON: FLATS, TOWNSHIP. For Lexington, Massachusetts.

LILY POND. (3). For lilies.

LIMESTONE HILL. Descriptive.

LINDSEY COVE. Unknown.

LINE POND. For its location near the Maine-Quebec line.

LITTLE BIGELOW MOUNTAIN. For Bigelow Mountain in Franklin County.

LITTLE BOG. Descriptive.

LITTLE JIM POND. For Jim, an old hunter.

LITTLE W TOWNSHIP. For its letter designation and being smaller than Big W Township.

LIZZIES BOG. Unknown.

LOGAN BROOK. Descriptive of slow flowing water.

LOG LANDING POND. Descriptive.

LONG: BOG, BROOK, FALLS, POND (6), POND MOUNTAIN POND, settlement, POND TOWNSHIP. Descriptive.

LONGLEY BROOK. For the early Longley family.

LOOMIS HILL. For Dyer Loomis, Revolutionary War veteran and settler before 1806.

LOON: ISLAND, POND, STREAM, STREAM DEADWATER. For loons.

LORD BROOK. Unknown.

LORDS HILL. For the Lord family who settled there.

LOST: BROOK, POND (5), POND BROOK. Descriptive of isolation.

LOWER MILL. For its location below two other mills.

LUCE BROOK. For H. Luce, who lived there.

LUTHER: BROOK, POND. Unknown.

LYFORD CORNER. For Samuel F. Lyford.

LYSHORNES BROOK. For the Lyshorne family.

MACKAMP. For Mack's Camp, a hunting camp, located there.

MADAWASKA BROOK. Micmac: "where one river runs into another." Or Abnaki: "where there is much hay."

MADISON: EAST-, settlement, TOWNSHIP. For a bridge over the Kennebec River, called the Madison Bridge, for James Madison, fourth President of the U.S.

MAGOON BROOK. For H. McGoon, resident, 1883.

MAHONEY HILL. For Philip Mahoney and his wife who had a farm there.

MAINSTREAM: MOUNTAIN, POND, settlement, STATION. For the Main Stream Sebasticook River.

MAINSTREAM SEBASTICOOK RIVER. Penobscot-Abnaki: "shortest route."

MALBONS MILLS. For the Malbon brothers, owners.

MANSELL BROOK. Unknown.

MANSON CORNER. For R.E. Manson, resident, 1883.

MARKHAM POND. For E. Markham, lumberman.

MARSH CORNER. For E. Marsh, resident, 1883.

MARTIN CORNER. For the Martin family.

MARTIN POND. For the early Martin family.

MARTIN STREAM. (2). In Concord Township, for the Martin family, early settlers. In Fairfield Township, named by a trapper who had trapped many martins in the vicinity.

MARY PETUCHE POND. Unknown.

MAYFIELD: CORNER, POND. For the former name of T2R2, when it was incorporated.

McDONALD BROOK. Unknown.

McDOUGAL POND. For the Reverend Arthur R. McDougal.

McINTYRE HILL. For Edward McIntyre, resident, 1883.

McKAIN BROOK. Unknown.

McKENNY: BROOK (2), POND. For Patrick McKenney, settler from Ireland about 1840.

McKENNY PONDS. Unknown.

MEADOW: BIG-BOG, BROOK (3). Descriptive.

MELOON BROOK. For David Maloon, early settler.

MERCER: EAST-, settlement, TOWNSHIP. For Brigadier General Hugh Mercer, veteran of the Revolution.

MICHAEL: LITTLE-STREAM, STREAM (2). Unknown.

MIDDLE MOUNTAIN. For its location between South and Pleasant Pond Mountains.

MILLAY HILL. For Albert Millay, settler about 1869.

MILLER CORNER. For B. and I. Miller, residents, 1860.

MILLER ISLAND. For William Miller, who built the first cottage there.

MILL STREAM. (3). For mills.

MINK: BROOK (2), PONDS. For mink.

MISERY: GORE, KNOB, NORTH BRANCH-STREAM, POND, RIDGE, STREAM, TOWNSHIP, UPPER-POND, WEST BRANCH-STREAM. Unknown.

MITCHELL CORNER. For the local Mitchell family.

MOODY CORNER. For the Moody family who settled here about 1845.

MOORE BOG. For the local Moore family.

MOORE POND. Unknown.

MOORES POND. Unknown.

MOOSE: BROOK, GREAT-LAKE, POND, RIVER, RIVER (settlement), RIVER TOWNSHIP. For moose.

MORRILL POND. For the ancestors of J.B. Morrill who lived there in 1883.

MORSE POND. Unknown.

MOSCOW: settlement, TOWNSHIP. For Moscow, Russia, probably because it was surveyed in 1812, the year that the Russians defeated Napoleon.

MOSHER CORNER. For Stephen H. Mosher, Civil War veteran.

MOSQUITO: MOUNTAIN, NARROWS, POND, STREAM. For mosquitoes.

MOUNTAIN: -BROOK (2), PONDS. Descriptive.

MOUNT BETT. Unknown.

MOUNT TOM. Probably for Thomas Bigelow, who lived there in 1883.

MOXIE: BOG, EAST-TOWNSHIP, FALLS, LITTLE-BROOK, LITTLE-POND, MOUNTAIN, POND, STREAM, TOWNSHIP. Said to be Indian, "dark water".

MUCALSEA: BIG-POND, LITTLE-POND, MOUNTAIN. Unknown.

MUD: BROOK (2), POND (10), POND BROOK. Descriptive.

MULE: BROOK, POND. Unknown.

MULHERN. For the local Mulhern family.

MULHERN HILL. For the Mulhern family.

MULLEN BROOK. Unknown.

MULLIGAN STREAM. For the Mulligan family, settlers from Ireland.

MUSKRAT POND. For muskrat.

MYRON H. AVERY PEAK. For Myron H. Avery, one of Benedict Arnold's officers, who climbed the mountain to survey the marching route of the Quebec invasion army.

NARROWS: LOWER-, THE-, UPPER-. Descriptive.

NASH CORNER. For the Sam Nash family who lived there.

NEGRO BROOK. For Negro lumbermen who cut logs here.

NEGRO HILL. For a Negro family who lived there.

NELSON HILL. For John Nelson, who settled from Granada Island.

NEVIN POND. For George Nevens, who bought some land in the area in the 1930's or 40's.

NEWELL BROOK. For J.C. Newell, resident, 1860.

NEW PORTLAND: EAST-, HILL, NORTH-, settlement, TOWNSHIP. Named by settlers who had been burned out in the Indian raids on Falmouth, for Portland, Maine.

NOKOMIS POND. Abnaki: "my grandmother." Possibly taken from Longfellow's "Hiawatha."

NORRIDGEWOCK: settlement, TOWNSHIP. Abnaki: "little falls and smooth water above and below." Probably for the Abnaki chieftan Norridgewog.

NORRIS: BROOK, EAST BRANCH-BROOK, MIDDLE BRANCH-BROOK, SOUTH BRANCH-BROOK. Unknown.

NORTHEAST COVE. Description.

NORTH ONEHALF TOWNSHIP. For being the north half of Wyman Township, half of which is located in Franklin County.

NORWAYS, THE. For Norway pines.

NOTCH, THE. Descriptive.

NULHEDUS: MOUNTAIN, STREAM. Abnaki: "fall on each side."

NUMBER FIVE: BOG, MOUNTAIN. For location in T5R7 township.

NUMBER SIX: BROOK, MOUNTAIN. For location in T6R7 township.

NUMBER TWO MOUNTAIN. For its location near another unnamed mountain.

NUTTER CORNER. For James Nutter, settler, 1830's.

NYE BOG. For the Nye family.

NYES CORNER. For the many Nye families in the area.

OAK: HILL, ISLAND, STREAM. For oak trees.

OGONTY. Unknown.

OLD BLUFF MOUNTAIN. Descriptive.

OLD: POINT, POINT POND. For being the site of an ancient Indian burial ground.

OTTER: LITTLE-POND, NORTH-POND, POND (5), POND COVE, POND MOUNTAIN, POND STREAM. For otter.

OWLS HEAD. Descriptive of shape.

PACKARD POINT. For Daniel Packard.

PAGE BROOK. For John Page from Wakefield, New Hampshire, who drove here with an ox team about 1806.

PAGES POINT. Unknown.

PAINE BROOK. For the local Paine family.

PALIN POND. For the Palin family.

PALMER HILL. For J.L. Palmer, resident, 1883.

PALMER: LITTLE-POND, POND, STREAM. Unknown.

PALMYRA: settlement, TOWNSHIP, WEST-. Some say named by the son of Dr. John Warren, the proprietor, for his sister Palmyra. Another says by the wife of Dr. Warren for the ancient city.

PARKER: BOG BROOK, BOG PONDS, BROOK, POND. For the early Parker family.

PARKERS POND. Unknown.

PARKMAN HILL. For David Parkman, prominent churchman who lived there.

PARLIN: BROOK, LAKE- (settlement), MOUNTAIN, POND, POND TOWNSHIP, STREAM. Unknown.

PARLIN HILL. Probably for Jonas Parlin, settler, 1774.

PASSACONAWAY POINT. Pennacook: "bear cub." Passaconaway was the chief of the Pennacooks. As the place-name is prominent in New Hampshire, this name has probably been imported.

PATTEE BROOK. For the Pattee family, settlers between 1800-10.

PEAKED HILL. Descriptive.

PEASE BROOK. Unknown.

PEEKS HILL. Unknown.

PELTON BROOK. For the Pelton family.

PENNELL POND. For Dr. Pennell, doctor in Kingfield Township in about 1910, who had a cottage nearby.

PENOBSCOT: BROOK, LAKE, LAKE TOWN TOWNSHIP, LITTLE-BROOK, NORTH BRANCH-RIVER, WEST BRANCH-RIVER. Malecite? Abnaki?: "at the descending rocks," or "at the extended ledges." Probably named specifically for the Penobscot Indians.

PERRY POND. For the local Perry family.

PHILLIPS CORNER. For the Phillips family who lived there.

PICKED CHICKEN HILL. Descriptive of the hill after most of the timber had been cut off it.

PICKEREL POND. For pickerel fish.

PICKLE HILL. Descriptive of shape.

PIERCE HILL. For Peter Pierce and his two brothers, who settled before 1800.

PIERCE: POND, POND MOUNTAIN, POND STREAM, POND TOWNSHIP, UPPER-POND. Unknown.

PINNACLES, THE. Descriptive.

PITTSFIELD: settlement, TOWNSHIP. For William Pitts of Boston, a proprietor.

PITTSTON ACADEMY TOWNSHIP. For being granted to Pittston Academy.

PLAINS, THE. Descriptive.

PLEASANT: POND, POND (settlement), POND MOUNTAIN, POND STREAM, RIDGE, RIDGE TOWNSHIP. Descriptive.

PLUMMER CORNER. For the Plummer family, early settlers.

PLYMOUTH TOWNSHIP. For Plymouth, Massachusetts.

POMERLEAU ISLAND. For the family of Dr. Ovide Pomerleau.

POND: EAST-, EAST-BOG, STREAM. Descriptive.

POOLER BROOK. For the ancestors of Norman Pooler.

POOLER PONDS. For the Pooler family.

POPLAR: HILL, HILL FALLS, RIPS. For poplar trees.

PORCUPINE MOUNTAIN. For porcupines.

PORTER POND. Unknown.

POTTER BOG. For George Potter, settler in Wellington Township in the 1820's, who owned the lot in Brighton Township where the bog is located.

PRATT BROOK. For W. Pratt, resident, 1883.

PRATT HILL. For Micah Pratt, settler before 1790.

PRAY HILL. For Peter Pray, area landholder, 1883.

PRENTISS POND. For Prentiss, settler, mid-1800's.

PRENTISS TOWNSHIP. Unknown.

PRESCOTT POND. Unknown.

PUBLIC LOT BROOK. For running through the public lot, the lot set aside for the financing of the school.

RAILBRIDGE BROOK. For a bridge crossing it made from wooden rails.

RAINEY: BROOK, EAST BRANCH-BROOK, WEST BRANCH-BROOK. For Rainey, a lumberman.

RAM ISLAND. For its being used as a sheep pen.

RANCOURT POND. For the John Rancourt family.

RATTLING BROOK. Descriptive of the sound of the water.

RAY BROOK. For A. and I. Ray, residents, 1883.

REDMOND POND. Unknown.

REED BROOK. (2). Unknown.

RICE CORNER. For Warrin Rice, who lived there.

RIDGE: EAST-, WEST-. Descriptive.

RIFT BROOK. Descriptive of flowing through a geological rift, or fault depression.

RIPLEY: POND, STREAM, settlement, TOWNSHIP, WEST-. For General Eleazer W. Ripley, an officer in the War of 1812.

ROBBERS BOG. Unknown.

ROBBINS HILL. For the local Robbins family.

ROBERTS: BROOK, POND. For Roberts, a logger.

ROBINSON BROOK. For the local Robinson family.

ROBINSON: POND (2), POND OUTLET. Pond and Pond Outlet in Caratunk Township, for the Robinson family. Pond in T4R17, unknown.

ROCK POND. Descriptive.

ROCKWOOD: settlement, TOWNSHIP. Unknown.

RODERIQUE POND. Unknown.

ROGERS BROOK. For Daniel L. Rogers, resident, 1883.

ROSS HILL. For Sarah Ross.

ROUND: ISLAND, POND (5), -TOP MOUNTAIN. Descriptive.

ROWELL: BOG, HILL (2). Bog and Hill in Madison Township, for the Rowell brothers, residents in the area in 1883. Hill in Hartland Township, for T.B. Rowell, resident, 1883.

ROWELL: MOUNTAIN, POND. For the Rowell family.

ROWE POND. For the Rowe family who settled there before the 1880's.

RUSH POND. For rushes.

RUSSELL: BOG, LITTLE-MOUNTAIN, LITTLE-STREAM, MOUNTAIN, POND, STREAM. For Russell Mountain in Piscataquis County.

SADDLE BROOK. Descriptive of a nearby ridge.

SAFFORD BROOK. For the Safford family who settled early.

SAFFORD POND. Unknown.

ST. ALBANS: MOUNTAIN, settlement, TOWNSHIP. For St. Albans, England.

ST. FRANCIS: BROOK, LAKE. Unknown.

ST. JOHN: LOWER FIRST-POND, UPPER FIRST-POND, SECOND-POND, THIRD-POND, FOURTH-LAKE, FIFTH-POND, LITTLE-LAKE, LITTLE SOUTHWEST BRANCH-RIVER, SOUTHWEST BRANCH-RIVER. For the river being discovered on St. John the Baptist's Day in 1604, by Samuel de Champlain.

SALLY MOUNTAIN. For Sally Holden, daughter of Captain Samuel Holden, who was the first settler of the Jackman-Moose River area in 1820.

SALMON: EAST BRANCH-STREAM, STREAM. For salmon.

SANBORN CORNER. For the Sanborn family who lived there in 1883.

SAND: BAR POINT, -BAR POINT, BAR TOWNSHIP. Descriptive.

SANDWICH ACADEMY GRANT TOWNSHIP. For Sandwich Academy.

SANDY BAY: MOUNTAIN, TOWNSHIP. Descriptive.

SANDY: BIG-STREAM, EAST BRANCH-STREAM, LITTLE-STREAM, POND, RIVER, RIVER (settlement), STREAM (3), STREAM MOUNTAIN, WEST BRANCH-STREAM. Descriptive.

SAPLING TOWNSHIP. Descriptive.

SAVAGE HILL. For several Savage families who lived there.

SAVAGE ISLAND. For the Savage family who farmed the island.

SCHOOL HOUSE BROOK. For a schoolhouse nearby.

SCRIBNER BOG. (2). In Brighton Township, for Robert Scribner, who lived here in the 1830's. In T2R5, unknown.

SEARS POND. For Sears, a squatter.

SEBOOMOOK: LAKE, MOUNTAIN, POINT, settlement, TOWN-SHIP. Abnaki: "at or near the large stream."

SERPENTINE, THE. Descriptive of an irregular waterway connecting North and East Ponds.

SEVENMILE HILL. For its location 7 miles from Seboomook.

SHAW: LOWER-POND, POND. Unknown.

SHAWMUT. By a group from Boston who bought into the mills there and wanted a new name. They chose this because it was the name of the street in Boston where their offices were located.

SHEHAN BROOK. Unknown.

SHUTDOWN MOUNTAIN. Unknown.

SIBLEY POND. For the Sibley family who lived there.

SKOWHEGAN: settlement, TOWNSHIP. Abnaki: "place of waiting and watching (fish spearing place)".

SLIDEDOWN: MOUNTAIN, VALLEY. Descriptive.

SMITH BROOK. For the Smith Family who settled by 1806.

SMITHFIELD: settlement, TOWNSHIP. For Reverend Henry Smith, early citizen.

SMITH POND. (4). In Brighton Township, for Jonathon Smith, who owned a farm at the head of the pond in the 1830's. In Cornville Township, for Ithiel Smith, settler before 1800. The other two, unknown.

SNAKE POND. For snakes.

SNELL BROOK. For W.H. Snell, resident, 1883.

SNOW BROOK. Unknown.

SOCATEAN: BAY, PONDS, POINT, STREAM. Abnaki: "divided into two parts."

SOLDIERTOWN TOWNSHIP. Because of its being granted to soldiers for former military service.

SOLON: settlement, SOUTH-, TOWNSHIP. For Solon, one of the 7 sages of Greece.

SOMERSET: COUNTY, JUNCTION. For Somerset, England.

SOUTH: BRANCH BROOK, MOUNTAIN. Descriptive.

SPAN BROOK. For an old bridge on a log road.

SPAULDING POND. Unknown.

SPECTACLE POND. Descriptive of its eyeglass shape.

SPENCER: BROOK, GUT, LAKE, MOUNTAIN, POND, RIPS (2), STREAM, WEST BRANCH-STREAM. For Spencer, a lumberman.

SPLIT ROCK POND. Descriptive.

SPOTTED MOUNTAIN. Descriptive of appearance.

SPRING: LAKE, LAKE (settlement), LAKE BROOK, LAKE LANDING. For springs.

SPRUCE: BROOK, LITTLE-STREAM, NORTH BRANCH-BROOK, POND, SOUTH BRANCH-BROOK. For spruce trees.

SQUARETOWN TOWNSHIP. Descriptive of shape.

SQUIRTGUN FLOWAGE. Descriptive of a dam where pulpwood builds up behind, and when the dam is opened, the pulp and water are forced downstream.

STAFFORD BROOK. For the Stafford family, residents, 1880's.

STAFFORD: HILL, POND. For the Stafford family, residents, 1883.

STAG BROOK. For a deer killed here in the 19th century.

STARBIRD POND. For John Starbird, settler, early 1800's.

STARKS: settlement, TOWNSHIP. For General John Starks, hero of the Revolutionary War.

STEWART BROOK. Unknown.

STEWART MOUNTAIN. For M. Steward, resident, 1883.

STICKNEY HILL. For Amos Stickney, settler of about 1870.

STONY: BROOK (5), BROOK MOUNTAIN, BROOK POND. Descriptive.

STRICKLAND HILL. For Martin and Alden Strickland.

STRONGHOLD. For Rosie Strong, who lived there.

SUCKER BROOK. (2). For sucker fish.

SUGAR BERTH POND. For a maple sugar camp located there.

SUGAR HILL. For maple sugar operations there.

SUMMIT: BROOK, POND, RIDGE. Descriptive.

SUNDAY POND. Unknown.

SUNSET HILL. Descriptive.

SUPPLY: POND, STREAM. For a woods depot.

SWEENEY: BOG, BROOK. For Sweeney, a logger.

SWEETSER BROOK. Unknown.

TALBOT HILL. For the local Talbot family.

TARRATINE. For the Tarratines, a Micmac tribe from Nova Scotia, who invaded and controlled parts of Maine about 1600.

TAUNTON AND RAYNHAM TOWNSHIP. For Taunton & Raynham, proprietors.

TAYLOR. For John Taylor, who settled in 1789.

TELEPHONE HILL. For a woods telephone located there for use by stranded or lost people.

TEMPLE POND. For Elijah Temple, who created it and erected a mill there.

TENMILE SWING. For its location ten miles from Rockwood.

TEN THOUSAND ACRE POND. For its location on the Ten Thousand Acre Tract.

THOMPSON: BROOK (3), CORNER. Brooks in Attean and Jackman Townships, for Moses Thompson, an early cattle drover. Brook and Corner in Hartland Township, for P.W. Thompson, resident, 1883.

THOMPSON POINT. For being owned by the Thompson brothers in 1883.

THORNDIKE TOWNSHIP. Unknown.

THOROUGHFARE. Descriptive.

THREEMILE BROOK. For its location about one mile from McKain Brook which is located about two miles from Campbell Brook.

THREE PINE ISLAND. Descriptive.

THREE SLIDE MOUNTAIN. Descriptive.

THREE STREAMS. Descriptive for location where 3 streams converge.

THURSTON HILL. For Stephen Thurston, first settler of Madison Township.

TIBBETTS HILL. For J. Tibbitts, resident, 1883.

TIBBETTS POND. For the local Tibbetts family.

TILTON CORNER. For Alfred Tilton, settler, 1822.

TOBEY: BROOK (2), POND (2), PONDS. Brook in Norridgewock

Township, for E.N. and J.M. Tobey, residents, 1883. The others, for Tobey, local lumberman.

TOE OF THE BOOT. Descriptive of a point in Moosehead Lake.

TOM FLETCHER STREAM. For Tom Fletcher, who came with his father, William, from Concord in September 1773, and settled at Norridgewock.

TOMHEGAN: COVE, POINT, POND STREAM (2), TOWNSHIP. Abnaki: "a hatchet."

TORRY ISLAND. For Torry, owner.

TOULOUSE CORNER. For the Toulouse family — a rather recent place-name.

TOWER STREAM. Unknown.

TRICKEY: BLUFFS, PONDS. Unknown.

TROUT: BROOK (3), -DALE, POND, STREAM. For trout fish.

TRUESDALE: MOUNTAIN, POND. For Truesdale, lumberman.

TUCKER: EAST BRANCH-STREAM, STREAM. For the Tucker family.

TUMBLEDOWN MOUNTAIN. Descriptive of a mountain that has had slides in the past.

TURNER: BROOK (3), LITTLE-POND, POND (2). Unknown.

TUTTLE: BROOK, HILL. For the local Tuttle families.

TWELVE CORNERS. For a road intersection forming 12 corners.

TWELVEMILE BOG. For location 12 miles from Jackman Mills.

TWOMILE BROOK. It crosses Route 201 two miles from Parlin Pond settlement.

TWO PINE ISLAND. Descriptive of a small island.

UNKNOWN POND. For having no name.

USHER INLET. Unknown.

VARNEY HILL. For J.W. Varney, resident, 1883.

VEAZY RIDGE. Supposedly for General Samuel Veazie, of Veazie Township, who owned land in the area.

VILES BROOK. (2). For the Viles family, settlers quite early.

WAITE HILL. For L. Waite, resident, 1883.

WALTONS MILL. For the Walton family who owned the mill.

WARD HILL. For the Ward family, settlers by 1808.

WAVERLEY. For the Waverley Mill, built by the Dobsen family, of Scottish descent.

WEEKS BASIN. Unknown.

WEEKS CORNER. For Eugene and Isaac Weeks.

WELMAN POND. Unknown.

WENTWORTH POND. For the local Wentworth family.

WESSERRUNSETT: EAST BRANCH-STREAM, LAKE STREAM, WEST BRANCH-STREAM. Abnaki: "bitter water place."

WEST FORKS TOWNSHIP. For location between Kennebec and Dead Rivers. Dead River makes up the west fork of the Kennebec.

WEST MIDDLESEX CANAL GRANT TOWNSHIP. Unknown.

WESTON ISLAND. For Deacon Benjamin Weston, farmer, 1786.

WEST: OUTLET, PEAK. Descriptive.

WHIPPLE HILL. For Eleazer Whipple, settler before 1784.

WHIPPLE POND. Unknown.

WHIT BROOK. Unknown.

WHITCOMB BROOK. For the local Whitcomb family.

WHITE DEER POND. For an albino deer sighted here.

WHITEHOUSE BROOK. For several Whitehouse families living here.

WHITE SCHOOL CORNER. For a white country school located at the corner, now a dwelling.

WHITES POND. For the White family who lived in the area in 1860.

WHITMAN BOG. For the Whitman family who lived there in 1883.

WHITTEMORE HILL. For Nathan Whittemore, veteran of the War of 1812.

WHITTEN BROOK. For the Whitten family who had a ground bark
     mill and tannery here.
WILCOX HILL. For the local Wilcox family — not an old name.
WILD BROOK. Descriptive of its flow.
WILDER HILL. For Lucius Wilder, resident, 1883.
WILDWOOD. Descriptive.
WILLIAMS: BROOK (2), MOUNTAIN, POND. Unknown.
WILSON: HILL, HILL POND, LITTLE-HILL POND. Unknown.
WITHAM BROOK. (2). In Cornville Township, for the ancestors of
     Frank Witham. In Norridgewock Township, for the early Witham
     family.
WITHAM CORNER. For the large Witham family, early settlers.
WITHAM MOUNTAIN. Unknown.
WITHEE BROOK. For the Ezra Withee family, settlers about 1800.
WITHEE POND. Unknown.
WOOD: LITTLE BIG-POND, NORTH BRANCH-STREAM, POND,
     STREAM. For woody area.
WOUNDED DEER POND. Unknown.
WYMAN LAKE. For Walter Wyman, president of Central Maine
     Power Company.
WYMAN POND. For Josiah Wyman, who owned land near the pond
     in the 1830's.

WALDO COUNTY

ABORN HILL. For the early settling Aborn family who lived there for generations.

ALDER BROOK. For alder trees.

ALGER POND. For Alger Perkins, who, with Fred Perkins, created the pond for ice harvesting.

AMES COVE. For the Reverend Thomas Ames, settler, 1770.

APPLETON RIDGE. For the ridge extending into Appleton Township.

BACON BROOK. For Levi Bacon, early settler and farmer.

BALD: HILL COVE, ROCK MOUNTAIN. Descriptive.

BARTLETT HILL. For the Bartlett family, early settlers.

BARTLETT STREAM. For John Bartlett, settler, 1805 or '06.

BASIN POND. Descriptive.

BATTLE RIDGE BROOK. Unknown.

BAYSIDE. Descriptive.

BEANS CORNER. For the early settler John Bean and his sons Walter, Edgar, and John, Jr.

BEAR: HILL, POND. For bears.

BEARTRAP BROOK. For a falls where bears caught fish as they struggled upstream.

BEAVER RIDGE. For beavers.

BEECH: HILL, POND. For beech trees.

BELDEN POND. For the Stephen Beldens, early settlers.

BELFAST: BAY, RESERVOIR, settlement, TOWNSHIP. For Belfast, Ireland, former home of many of the settlers.

BELMONT: CENTER-, CORNER, TOWNSHIP. Named by George Watson, who aided in securing incorporation, for the French "belle" (beautiful) "mont" (mountain).

BIRD HILL. For Samuel Bird, settler before 1776.

BITHERS BROOK. For Elisha Bither, local millowner.

BLACK BROOK. (2). Descriptive.

BLAKE POND. For the Blake family who cleared the land and settled nearby.

BLANCHARD HILL. For Samuel Blanchard, early settler.

BOG BROOK. Descriptive.

BOLEN HILL. For William Bolen who lived at its edge.

BOUNTY COVE. Legend says that this is where Captain Kidd buried some of his treasure. The treasure was supposedly found in the 1860's and carried away in a ship. The find was a "bounty" for its discoverers.

BOWDEN POINT. For the Bowden family who cleared the land and settled here in 1800.

BOWLER POND. For Bowler, owner of some shore property.

BRANCH POND. For the West Branch Sheepscot River.

BROAD COVE. Descriptive.

BROOKS: settlement, TOWNSHIP. For Governor John Brooks of Massachusetts.

BROWN CORNER. For the Brown family, settlers, 1820's.

BROWNS HEAD. For the H. Brown family, residents, 1859.

BRYANTS CORNER. For the Bryant family who lived there for generations.

BURNHAM: settlement, TOWNSHIP. For Rufus Burnham, M.D., settler, early 1800's.

BUTLERS CORNER. For the early Butler family.

CAIN POND. For the Cain family.

CAMERON: CORNER, MOUNTAIN. For the local Cameron family.

CAPE JELLISON. Unknown.

CARGILL POND. For the Cargill family, settlers in the 1800's.

CARLEY BROOK. For the early Carley family.

CARLTON: BOG, POND, STREAM. For the early Carlton family.

CARRS CORNER. For the Carr family who lived there for generations.

CARVERS CORNER. For the Carver family.

CHAIN MEADOWS. Descriptive of meadows in a chain-like design.

CHASE STREAM. For Thomas Chase.

CHICKS HILL. For the early Chicks family.

CHISHOLM POND. For the early Chisholm family.

CITY POINT. For a small settlement there.

CLARK BROOK. For the early Clark family.

CLARKS CORNER. For J. Clark, resident, 1859.

CLEMENT HILL. For the early Clement family.

CLEMENTS BROOK. For the family of Basil Clement, schoolteacher.

COLBY: BROOK, POND. For its location on Ebeneezer Colby's land.

COLEMAN POND. For Ed Coleman.

COLES CORNER. For George E., Fred, John, and Fairfield Cole.

COLSON STREAM. For a number of early Colson families.

COMMON HILL. For the town common.

CONNORS CORNER. For Deacon Connors, early settler.

COOK BROOK. For E. Cook, resident, 1859.

COOMBS: COVE, POINT. For Hosea, Peter, and Fields Coombs, settlers between 1768-1800.

COON: HILL, MOUNTAIN, For raccoons.

COVE BROOK. Descriptive.

CROCKETT BROOK. For the Crockett family, seafaring people.

CROSBY BROOK. For the Crosby family.

CROSS POND. For Nathaniel Cross, of 1800.

CROW COVE. For crows.

CROXFORD MOUNTAIN. For the early settling Croxford family.

DARK: HARBOR, HARBOR (settlement). "Dark" in 19th Century nautical usage meant "obscure, easily passed without seeing."

DEAD: BROOK (2), -WATER SLOUGH. Descriptive of its flow.

DEANTOWN CORNER. For J., J., Jr., E., and C. Dean, residents in 1859.

DELAWARE MOUNTAIN. One source says for the local Delaware family.

DERRY MOUNTAIN. For I. Derry, resident, 1859.

DODGE CORNER. (2). In Burnham Township, for Dodge, who homesteaded after returning from the Colorado gold rush. In Searsport Township, for the local Dodge family.

DOG ISLAND CORNER. Unknown.

DOLLIFF POND. For Noah Dolliff, settler, 1798.

DOLLOFF HILL. For the Dolloff family, early settlers.

DOWE POND. For the Dowe family, settlers before 1809.

DOWNS HILL. Called "West Hill" until a Downs married into the family; the name was then changed to his.

DRAKE CORNER. For A. Drake, resident, 1859.

DRAKE POND. Unknown.

DUCKTRAP: HARBOR, MOUNTAIN, RIVER, settlement. Because Indians trapped ducks there when they were molting and couldn't fly.

DUTCH MOUNTAIN. For the early German settlers who called themselves "the Deutsch," which the English mispronounced as "Dutch."

DUTTON POND. For the Dutton family.

ELLINGWOOD CORNER. For the ancestors of Horace Ellingwood.

ELLIS POND. For the Ellis family who lived there.

ENSIGN ISLAND. For Jonathon Pendleton, who was appointed an ensign in the military and took possession of it by squatter's rights.

ERSKING HILL. For the Ersking family.

EVANS CORNER. For the ancestors of Ester Evans.

FANG, THE. Descriptive of shape.

FARWELLS CORNER. For Henry Farwell, millowner, 1788.

FERNALDS NECK. For Nathaniel Fernald, settler about 1810.

FILES HILL. For Samuel, George, and Joseph Files, brothers who settled there.

FISH: BROOK, TURN. For the Fish family, early settlers.

FLAT ISLAND. Descriptive.

FLETCHER HILL. For the Fletcher family.

FLY BROOK. For the early settling Fly family.

FORT KNOX. For General Knox, commander of the fort when built in the early 1800's.

FORT: POINT, POINT COVE. For Fort Pownal located there. The fort was named for Thomas Pownal, Governor of Massachusetts.

FOSTER POND. For the Foster family who cleared the area around the pond and farmed.

FOSTERS CORNER. For W. Foster, resident, 1859.

FOWLER BOG. For Thomas Fowler, early settler.

FRANKFORT: settlement, TOWNSHIP. One source states that it was for Frankfurt, Germany, because many of the early settlers were from Old Pownalborough, the former name of which was "Frankfort." Another says as a compliment to Count Henri Ehrenfield Luther, Aulic Councillor of the state of Frankfort on the Main, one of the foreign proprietors.

FRED LOW HILL. For Fred Lowe, resident, early 1900's.

FREEDOM: settlement, TOWNSHIP. Because it was incorporated in 1813 when feeling against England was high. They were going to retain their "freedom."

FROHOCKS MOUNTAIN. Probably for Jonathon Frohock, early settler.

GAREY MOUNTAIN. For the Garey family who settled on the west side of the mountain.

GENTNERS CORNERS. For Lenn Gentner, who ran an early hotel, liquor store, stable, and gambling house.

GERRISH CORNER. For Charles Gerrish, Jr., settler between 1801-13.

GHENT. For Ghent, Belgium.

GILKEY HARBOR. For John Gilkey, settler, 1772.

GOODWIN HILL. For the early settling Goodwin family who lived there.

GOOSEBERRY POINT. For gooseberries.

GOOSE RIDGE. A shortened form of "Goosepicker" and "Goosepecker Ridge." A family living there made their living by raising geese and picking their feathers to sell.

GOOSE RIVER. Named by an early settler of Belfast who saw numerous goose eggs while surveying along the river.

GOULD HILL. For Noah Gould.

GRANGE CORNER. For the Grange hall being located there.

GREAT BROOK. Descriptive.

GREAT FARM BROOK. For the thousand-acre farm of Israel Thorndike, called the "Great Farm."

GREELEY CORNER. For Jacob Greeley, settler before 1801.

GREEN ISLAND. Descriptive.

GREENLAWS CORNER. For 3 generations of Greenlaws who lived there.

GREENS CORNER. For the Green family who lived at the corners.

GREERS BOG. For Alonson Greer, settler, early 1800's.

GREERS CORNER. For James Greer, settler, early 1800's.

GREGORYS CORNER. For the Gregory family who settled here in the early 1800's.

GRINDEL POINT. For William Grinnel, settler between 1768-1800.

HACKMATACK POND. For hackmatack (juniper) trees.

HALES CORNER. For the early Heald family who lived here.

HALFMOON: POND (2), STREAM (3). Descriptive of shape.

HALL BROOK. For Abraham Hall, early settler.

HALL CORNER. For the Hall family who lived here.

HALLDALE. For the numerous Halls living in the area.

HASKELL HILL. For the Haskell family who settled on the hill early.

HAWES STREAM. For the Hawes family.

HAYFORD BOG. Unknown.

HAYFORD CORNER. For the Hayford family who lived in the area in the 1850's.

HAYSTACK MOUNTAIN. Descriptive of shape.

HEAD OF THE TIDE. Descriptive of location.

HEAGAN MOUNTAIN. Possibly Pennacook: "a dwelling." Possibly for Chief Sampson Heagan, 1698.

HEALS: CORNER, NECK.

HEDGEHOG: HILL (2), MOUNTAIN. For hedgehogs (porcupines).

HERRICKS: BOG, CORNER. For J. Herrick, resident, 1859.

HEWES POINT. For Elihu Hewe, settler between 1768-1800.

HILLS CORNER. For Jason Hill.

HOGBACK: LEDGE, MOUNTAIN. Descriptive of shape.

HOLMES MILL. For the Holmes family who owned the mill in the early 1800's.

HOUSTUS HILL. For the Hustis family who lived there.

HUBBARD BROOK. For the early Hubbard family.

HURDS CORNER. For J. and D. Hurd, residents, 1859.

HURDS POND. For W. and O. Hurd, residents, 1859.

HUSSEY BROOK. For Omar Hussey, Quaker.

HUTCHINS CORNER. For the Hutchens family, early settlers.

HUTCHINS ISLAND. For John Hutchins, settler, 1798.

IDE HILL. For the Ide family who settled here from Winterport.

IRISH HILL. For the Irish family, one of the first Catholic families to settle in Monroe Township.

ISLESBORO: HARBOR, ISLAND, NORTH-, settlement, TOWNSHIP. For its location on an island.

JACKSON: CORNERS, settlement, TOWNSHIP. Named by General Henry Knox, for General Henry Jackson, veteran of the Revolution.

JACKSON HILL. For a family of 14 Jacksons who lived there.

JACKSON MEADOW. For the Jackson family, early settlers.

JAMES BROOK. Unknown.

JOB ISLAND. One source says for Job Pendleton, settler, 1800's. Another source, for Job Philbrook, settler, 1700's, but since Pendleton Point is nearby, it is probably named for Job Pendleton.

JONES BOG. For the early Jones family.

JONES CORNER. For Cushman Jones, who operated a general store there.

JOSE: LITTLE-POND, POND. For Josiah Blake, resident, mid 1800's.

JUMP POND. For a steep cliff that lies on the northwest edge of the pond, called "The Jump" on old maps.

KANOKLUS BOG. For Kanokolus, an Indian who lived here.

KEDEARS HILL. For the Kidder family.

KELLER POINT. For the James Keller family, settlers by 1810.

KELLY ISLAND. For George E. Kelly of Rockland, Massachusetts, a resident in the later 1800's.

KENDALL BROOK. For T. Kendall, resident, 1859.

KENDALLS CORNER. For the early Kendall family.

KIDDER POINT. For the Kidder family.

KINGDOM, THE: area, BOG. For Muskingum, England, by an early settler. It was changed to The Kingdom by folk etymology.

KNIGHT POND. For Rena Knight, early settler.

KNIGHTS CORNER. For many generations of the Knight family who have lived there.

KNOWLTON HILL. For Stephen and John Knowlton.

KNOX: CENTER, CORNER, EAST-, LEDGE CORNER, settlement, STATION, TOWNSHIP. For General Henry Knox, commander of artillery in the Continental Army and Secretary of War.

LANE BROOK. For the early settling Lane family.

LAWRY POND. For Lawry, who owned part of the shore property.

LEDGE: HILL, POND. Descriptive.

LEVEL HILL. Descriptive.

LEVENSELLER: MOUNTAIN, POND. For the H. Levenseller family, residents, 1859.

LEVETTS CORNER. (2). In Lincolnville Township, for R.M. Levitt, resident, 1859. In Waldo Township, for the ancestors of John Levett.

LIBERTY: settlement, SOUTH-, TOWNSHIP. Named to show the people's love of liberty.

LINCOLNVILLE: CENTER, settlement, SOUTH-, TOWNSHIP. For General Benjamin Lincoln, a proprietor.

LILY POND. For lilies.

LINSCOTT BRANCH. For the early Linscott family.

LITTLEFIELD BROOK. For Oscar Littlefield.

LITTLE: HARBOR, POND (2), RIVER. Descriptive of size.

LONG: COVE, COVE BROOK. Descriptive.

MACK MOUNTAIN. Named "McMahon Mountain" and later shortened to "Mack."

MACK POINT. A source says for the Mack family.

MAIN STREAM. Descriptive.

MAPLE MEADOW. For trees.

MARDEN HILL. For Marden, who owned the hill.

MARRINERS BROOK. For the Marriner family who owned land in the area.

MARRINERS CORNER. For the I. Marriner family, residents, 1859.

MARSHALL POINT. For the Marshall family who settled between 1768-1800.

MARSH: BAY, NORTH BRANCH-RIVER, NORTH BRANCH-STREAM, SOUTH BRANCH-RIVER, STREAM. Descriptive.

MARSH FORK. For the Marsh family.

MASON HILL. For the early Mason family.

MASON: POND, UPPER-POND. For H. Mason, resident, 1859.

McCLURE POND. For the McClure family who lived nearby.

McDONALD HILL. For the early McDonald family.

McFARLANDS CORNER. For the Reverend Moses McFarland, settler, 1799.

MEADOW: BROOK (3), POND. Descriptive.

MEGUNTICOOK LAKE. Micmac or Malecite: "big mountain harbor."

MERRILL POINT. Unknown.

MESERVEY BROOK. For James Allen Meservey.

MIDDLE ISLAND. For location between Job and Minot Islands.

MILL: BROOK, COVE. For mills located there.

MILLSTONE ISLAND. Descriptive of shape.

MINNOW BROOK. For minnows.

MINOT ISLAND. For the Minot family who lived there.

MITCHELL CORNER. For the early Mitchell family.

MIXER POND. For the Mixer family who owned the pond, early 1800's.

MONROE: CENTER, NORTH-, TOWNSHIP. For James Monroe, fifth President of the U.S.

MONTVILLE: SOUTH-, TOWNSHIP, WEST-. For French "mont" (mountain) and "ville" (town). Descriptive.

MOODY: MOUNTAIN, POND, settlement. For the ancestors of J. Moody, resident, 1859.

MOOSE POINT. For moose.

MOREY HILL. For John Morey, settler, 1813.

MORRILL: settlement, TOWNSHIP. For Anson P. Morrill, Governor of Maine 1855-58.

MORROW BROOK. For the local Morrow family.

MOSQUITO MOUNTAIN. For mosquitoes.

MOUNT EPHRAIM. Unknown.

MOUNT PERCIVAL. Unknown.

MOUNT TUCK. If Indian, possibly Eastern Niantic: "lookout place," or Abnaki: "a tree."

MOUNT WALDO. Named by A. Jones in 1811 for being highest point in Waldo County.

MUD POND. (2). Descriptive.

MULLIN BOG. Unknown.

MUSSEY BROOK. For Edmund Mussey, early settler.

MUZZY RIDGE. For Joseph Muzzy, early settler of 1804.

NARROWS: ISLAND, THE. Descriptive.

NEALS CORNER. Unknown.

NICHOLS POND. Unknown.

NICKERSON MILLS. For Aaron Nickerson, early settler.

NORTHERN POND. Descriptive of location.

NORTHPORT: EAST-, settlement, TOWNSHIP. For its location in the north part of old Ducktrap Plantation.

NORTON HILL. For the Norton family who homesteaded there.

NORTON POND. For Bial Norton, early settler.

NUTTER POND. For Christopher Nutter, settler after 1809.

OAK: HILL (2), -LAND, POINT. For oak trees.

OLNEY BROOK. For the early Olney family.

PAGE HILL. For Edward Page.

PALERMO: EAST-, NORTH-, settlement, TOWNSHIP. For Palermo, Italy.

PARKER COVE. For the Parker family who settled between 1768 and 1800.

PARKER HILL. For the early Parker family.

PARK HILL. For the Park family who settled in the early 1800's.

PARTRIDGE HILL. One source says for the Partridge family. Another, for partridges.

PASSAGASSAWAKEAG: LAKE-, RIVER. Malecite: "place for spearing sturgeon by torchlight."

PATTEE CORNER. For the early Pattee family.

PATTERSON: HILL, POINT. For James and Nathaniel Patterson, brothers who settled in 1769.

PAULS CORNER. For A.K. Paul, who bought a large tract of land there and started a model farm employing many workers.

PENDLETON: COVE, POINT. For William Pendleton, first settler of Islesboro, 1760.

PENDLETON HILL. Unknown.

PENNY BROOK. Unknown.

PERKINS BROOK. For the early Perkins family.

PHILBRICKS CORNER. For the Philbrick family who lived there.

PHILBROOK COVE. For William and Job Philbrook, settlers before 1800.

PIPER BROOK. For the early Piper family.

PIPER STREAM. For the Piper family who settled in the early 1800's.

PITCHER POND. For Lewis Pitcher, settler before 1797.

PLUMMER HILL. For the early Plummer family.

POLAND STREAM. For Moses Poland, settler about 1800.

POLANDS CORNER. For Sumner Poland, and his sons, who lived and ran a store there.

POND HILL. Because one slope of the hill trails into Sanborn Pond.

POORS MILL. For J.T. Poor, resident, 1859.

PRATT ISLAND. For Dr. Pratt, who bought the island in the late 1800's and built a cabin there.

PRESCOTT POND. For the Prescott family, early settlers.

PRIEST HILL. For J. Priest, resident, 1859.

PRIPET. Some sources say the name is an Indian word, meaning unknown. Others say for the name of a Russian town in the news when the post office was established, and it was chosen because it fit the post office stamp.

PROSPECT: FERRY, settlement, TOWNSHIP. For the beautiful view from the higher elevation in the center of the township.

PUNCHBOWL HILL. A descriptive name for a hill with a large crater in the top.

QUAKER HILL. For the large number of Quakers who settled in Freedom Township.

QUANTABACOOK POND. Abnaki: "plenty of game animals."

QUARRY HILL. For a quarry located there.

RAM ISLAND. For sheep kept there.

RAY CORNER. For Ray, who settled at a sharp bend in the road about 1840.

REYNOLDS CORNER. For Charles Reynolds, early settler who had a general store there.

ROBERTS HILL. For the early Roberts family.

ROBERTSON HILL. For the Robertson family who lived there for generations.

ROBERTSON MOUNTAIN. For the early Robertson family.

ROGERS CORNERS. For the Rogers family.

ROWE HILL. For Ephraim Rowe, settler, early 1800's.

RUFFINGHAM MEADOW. For its location near the former small settlement of Ruffingham.

RYDER. For Benjamin Ryder, settler, mid-1800's.

SABAN POND. For Tom Saban, who cleared the land and settled here before 1800.

SABBATHDAY HARBOR. Named by the Penobscot Bay fishermen who anchored here to rest on Sundays.

ST. GEORGE LAKE. For the St. George River in Knox County.

SANBORN POND. For the A. Sanborn family, who owned much shore property.

SANDY: POINT, POINT (settlement), POND, STREAM. Descriptive.

SANFORD HILL. For the early Sanford family.

SATURDAY COVE. For being entered by mistake in the fog by the first settler in Belfast Township, James Miller, in 1769. When the fog cleared he saw that he had misjudged his position and named the cove for the day the error was committed.

SEAL: HARBOR, ISLAND. For seals.

SEARS: ISLAND, -MONT (settlement), -MONT TOWNSHIP, NORTH-MONT, NORTH-PORT, -PORT HARBOR, -PORT (settlement), -PORT STATION, -PORT TOWNSHIP, WEST-MONT. For David Sears, holder of much land.

SEBASTICOOK RIVER. Penobscot - Abnaki: "the shortest route."

SEVEN HUNDRED ACRE ISLAND. Descriptive.

SHAW BROOK. (2). In Northport Township, for Benjamin Shaw, settler before 1776. In Troy Township, for the Shaw family.

SHEEP ISLAND. For sheep kept there.

SHEEPSCOT: POND, RIVER, WEST BRANCH-RIVER. Abnaki: "many rocky channels."

SHERMAN POINT. For Valentine Sherman, settler between 1768-1800.

SHERMANS CORNER. (2). In Belfast Township, for the Sherman family who moved to the Belfast area in 1829. In Liberty Township, for Abiel Sherman, settler, 1829, probably of the same family as that in Belfast.

SIBLEY CORNER. For William Sibley, early settler.

SIMMONS BROOK. Unknown.

SIMPSONS CORNER. For the Simpson family who settled in the early 1800's.

SKYSCRAPER HILL. Descriptive.

SLAB CITY. (2). For sawmills where there were large stacks of slabs (outside cuts of lumber which contain bark).

SMITH HILL. For the early Smith family.

SMITH POND. For G. Smith, resident, 1859.

SMITHS: MILL BOG, MILL POND. For Benjamin Smith, millowner about 1800.

SMITHTON. A shortened version of the former Smithtown, for Stephen Smith, first settler in 1794.

SNOW MOUNTAIN. Unknown.

SPRAGUE COVE. For the Sprague family who settled between 1768-1800.

SPRING BROOK. For springs.

SPRUCE: HEAD, GREAT-HEAD, ISLAND, POINT. For spruce trees.

SQUAW: HEAD, POINT. Some say for its shape. Others, because Indians camped there.

STANTIAL: BOG, BROOK. For the early Stantial family.

STEARNS BROOK. Unknown.

STEVENS CORNER. For the Stevens family who lived at the corner.

STEVENSON HILL. For the early Stevenson family.

STEVENS POND. For Ebenezer Stevens, one of the earliest settlers.

STOCKTON SPRINGS: settlement, TOWNSHIP. Named by N.G. Hichborn for Stockton on Lees, a seaport town in Durham, England. The "Springs" was added because it was believed a local spring might prove of commercial value.

STOWERS MEADOWS. For the Stower family.

SUCKER BROOK. For sucker fish.

SWAN: LAKE (settlement), -VILLE · -VILLE TOWNSHIP. For the numerous people named Swan there.

TAGGETT HILL. For the Taggett family, early settlers.

TEMPLE HEIGHTS. For the location of the temple and camp-ground of the Spiritual Church.

THISTLE POND. For its location near the boundary line of the Thistle homestead.

THOMPSON BROOK. For the Thompson family, settlers by 1820.

THORNDIKE: EAST-, settlement, TOWNSHIP. For Israel Thorndike, one of the principal proprietors.

THRUMCAP ISLAND. Descriptive of shape like a thrumcap, a sailor's cap made from rope.

THURLOW: BROOK, HILL. For the Thurlow family.

THURSTONS CORNER. For the Thurston family, early settlers there.

TILDEN: CORNER, POND. For Nathaniel Tilden, early settler.

TODDY POND. Unknown.

TOWER BROOK. For Elisha Tower.

TOWN FARM HILL. For the location of the town farm.

TOWNHOUSE CORNERS. (2). For the location of the town house.

TREAT POINT. For Joshua Treat, one of the first settlers.

TROY: CENTER, EAST-, settlement, TOWNSHIP. For the classical city of Troy.

TRUES POND. For Ezekiel True, who bought land containing the pond in 1805.

TUCKER BROOK. For J.D. Tucker, resident, 1859.

TURNER BRANCH. For Turner Pond in Lincoln County.

TURNPIKE, THE. For a turnpike built by Bill Barrett to shorten the distance from Youngtown to Camden, but the settlers would not support it and continued to go the long way.

TURTLE: HEAD, HEAD COVE. A descriptive name given by Governor Pownal.

TWENTY-FIVE MILE STREAM. Because where it empties into the Sebasticook River is 25 miles from where the Sebasticook meets the Kennebec River.

TWITCHELL CORNER. For the early settling Twitchell family.

TWITCHELL HILL. For the Twitchell family.

TWOMBLEY MOUNTAIN. For the Twombley family.

UNITY: POND, settlement, TOWNSHIP. For a "union in political sentiment," at that time Democrat.

VICKERYS CORNER. For the Vickery family who lived there.

WALDO: COUNTY, settlement, TOWNSHIP. For Samuel Waldo, owner of the Waldo Patent.

WALKER CORNER. For Timothy Walker, who had a farm there.

WARREN ISLAND. For Samuel Warren, its early owner.

WARRENS BROOK. For Albert P. Warren, settler before 1838.

WEBBER HILL. For the early Webber family.

WEBSTERS BROOK. For the ancestors of Ada Webster Gurney.

WESCOTT STREAM. For Wescott, who built a sawmill there.

WHITCOMBS CORNER. For Eben Whitcomb, early settler.

WHITE BROOK. For the White family.

WHITES CORNER. (2). In Montville Township, for the White family there. In Winterport Township, for Ira White, postmaster in 1915.

WHITNEY BOG. Unknown.

WHITTEN HILL. For the early Whitten family.

WILDE HILL. For the Wilde family.

WILEY: BROOK, CORNER, NECK. For the Wiley family.

WILSON BROOK. Unknown.

WINDMERE. Named by Eliza J. Perley, for the surrounding country reminded her of the Windmere Lake region of England.

WING BROOK. For Benjamin Wing, who settled here.

WINNECOOK. Abnaki: "at the portage."

WINSLOW BROOK. For the Winslow family who built a home on the banks, early 1800's.

WINTERPORT: settlement, STATION, TOWNSHIP, WEST-. For its fine harbor at the head of winter navigation on the Penobscot River.

WITCHER SWAMP. Unknown.

WOOD ISLAND. Descriptive.

WOODMANS MILLS. For Adams and Moody Woodman, who built the earliest mill there.

YORK PONDS. For their location on the York family property.

YORKS CORNER. Unknown.
YOUNGS NECK. For three Young brothers who lived there.
YOUNGTOWN. For the many Youngs who lived in the area.

WASHINGTON COUNTY

ABBOTT ISLAND. Unknown.

ABRAQUIDASSAT POINT. Micmac: "little parallel river." One source says that it was the name of an Indian sachem in the 1600's, but he quite possibly took his name from the point.

ACKLEY POND. For Oliver Ackley, who owned the land surrounding it.

ADDISON: settlement, SOUTH-, TOWNSHIP. For Joseph Addison, 18th century English writer.

ALDER: BROOK (2), BROOK SWAMP. For alder trees.

ALEXANDER: settlement, TOWNSHIP. For Alexander Baring, Lord Ashburton, son-in-law of William Bingham, major landholder in Maine. Ashburton and Daniel Webster settled the Northeastern Boundary Dispute. He is also remembered in the name of Baring Township.

ALLAN: BIG-MOUNTAIN, LITTLE-MOUNTAIN. For Allan, a woods boss.

ALLEN: BROOK, HEATH. For Horace Allen of Columbia Falls, who had a camp on the brook.

ALLEN STREAM. For Colonel Allen, who came from Nova Scotia during the Revolution and was active in pacifying the Indians.

ALLEYS: BAY, ISLAND, POINT. For Captain John Alley, who settled in the area.

ALMORE COVE. Unknown.

AMAZON: BROOK, LAKE, MOUNTAIN, WEST BRANCH-BROOK. Unknown.

AMERICAN COVE. For its location on the U.S. side of the St. Croix River. A cove across the river is called English Cove.

ANDERSON BROOK. For the early Anderson family who settled near the brook.

ANDY MOUNTAIN. Unknown.

ANGUILLA ISLAND. Possibly for Anguilla Island in the British West Indies. "Anguilla," however, means "eel shaped," and the island does vaguely have this shape.

ANT ISLAND. Descriptive of being small and shaped like an ant hill.

ANVIL MEADOW. Descriptive of its shape, for it forms a point in Baskehegan Stream.

ARM: EAST-, EASTERN-, THE-, WEST- Descriptive of branches of various lakes.

ARNA MEADOW BROOK. For the Arna family who owned the meadow through which the brook ran.

AVERS: JUNCTION, POST OFFICE. For the local Ayers family who formerly owned the land where the junction is located. The spelling discrepancy is a dialectal change.

AVERY ROCK. For Captain Robert Avery, who was the first Englishman killed in the first naval battle of the Revolutionary War. He served aboard the "Margaretta" and was shot by a moose hunter named Knight.

AYERS RIPS. For Ayers, area lumberman who had a base camp there.

BACK BAY. Descriptive.

BACON RIDGE. For Ebenezer Bacon, who lived there.

BAGLEY BROOK. For J. Bagley, who lived nearby, 1881.

BAILEY BROOK. For Thomas Bailey, early settler.

BAILEYS: LEDGE, MISTAKE. Captain Bailey was sailing for the Lubec Narrows in heavy fog when he misjudged his position. Turning into this shallow cove, he destroyed his ships on the rocks. Later the Captain settled at this cove, possibly to always remind himself of his "mistake."

BAILEYVILLE TOWNSHIP. One source says for Thomas Bailey, one of the early settlers in Topsfield Township. Another source says that it was named for two Bailey brothers who were early settlers and cleared some land there. One day one of the brothers returned to the camp to find the other stabbed to death. Another similar version is that this Bailey was killed by Indians to whom he had given too much liquor. The site of his death was first called Bailey Kill, later Bailey Hill, then Baileyville.

BAKER BROOK. Unknown.

BAKER: COVE, POINT. For Lemuel Baker, early settler.

BALCH HEAD. For the Balch family, settlers after 1790.

BALD: HEAD, LEDGE, MOUNTAIN. Descriptive.

BALDWIN BROOK. For the Baldwin family, first settlers in the area.

BALDWIN HEAD. Unknown.

BALLAST: ISLAND, ISLAND LEDGE. For small round stones that sailing ships used for ballast.

BARE: COVE, ISLAND, POINT. Descriptive.

BAR HARBOR. The way to it was barred by Nips and Moose Island.

BARING: settlement, TOWNSHIP. See ALEXANDER TOWNSHIP, page 217.

BAR: ISLAND (6), LEDGE. Descriptive of shape and because they barred the way to various harbors and waterways.

BARNARD BROOK. For the Barnard family who lived along the brook.

BARNEY POINT. For Barney Beal, son of Manwaring Beal, first settler on Beals Island.

BARNEYS LITTLE ISLAND. See BARNEY POINT.

BARREN: POND, POND BROOK, WEST-. Descriptive.

BARROWS LAKE. A mispronunciation of Baring Lake, named for Alexander Baring, the namesake of Alexander and Baring Townships.

BARTER BROOK. Unknown.

BARTON LEDGE. Unknown.

BASIN, THE. (2). Descriptive.

BASKAHEGAN: LAKE, STREAM. Abnaki: "branch downstream," or "branch stream that turns downcurrent."

BASSETT CREEK. Unknown.

BATSON LEDGES. For the local Batson family.

BAY: LEDGE (2), LEDGES. Descriptive.

BEALS: HARBOR, ISLAND, ISLAND TOWNSHIP, settlement. For Manwaring Beal, first settler on the island.

BEAR: BROOK (2), ISLAND (2), MOUNTAIN. For bears.

BEAR TRAP LANDING. Unknown.

BEAVER: BROOK (3), -DAM STREAM, LAKE, NORTH-DAM LAKE, MEADOW BROOK, POND (2), SOUTH-DAM LAKE. For beavers.

BEDDINGTON: LAKE, LOWER-, settlement, TOWNSHIP. Named by the English and Scotch agents of William Bingham, for Beddington, Surrey, England.

BEECH: HILL, HILL BROOK, HILL HEATH. For beech trees.

BELLIER COVE. For a Mr. Belyea who lived there.

BELLS MOUNTAIN. For Little Bell, an early settler friendly with the Indians.

BELMONT POINT. Unknown.

BENNETT RIDGE. For the Bennett family who lived there.

BEN TUCKER MOUNTAIN. For Ben Tucker, who lumbered the mountain and had a base camp there.

BERRY: BROOK, BROOK FLOWAGE. Unknown.

BERRY HEATH. For the local Berry family.

BICKFORD POINT. For the Bickford family who settled here early.

BIG BEN. Unknown.

BIG: BROOK, FALLS, HEAD, HILL, ISLAND (2), LAKE, LEDGE, POND. Descriptive.

BILLINGS BROOK. For the Billings family who settled here.

BILL SMITH BROOK. For Bill Smith, who logged and had a camp there.

BINGO. Made up on the spot by a Mr. Ripley. After saying he had better get home, someone asked him where he lived. For no reason, he answered, "Bingo."

BIRCHES, THE. For birch trees.

BIRCH: HEAD, HILL, ISLAND (4), ISLANDS (2), LOWER-ISLAND, MOUNTAIN, POINT (6), POINT LEDGES, UPPER-ISLAND. For birch trees.

BLACK BIRD ISLAND. For blackbirds.

BLACK: BROOK, BROOK PONDS, COVE, ISLAND, LEDGE, LEDGES (2), POINT (3), POINT BROOK, POINT COVE, ROCK. Descriptive.

BLACK CAT: ISLAND, RIPS. For blackcats, woodsmen's name for the fisher.

BLACK DUCK COVE. For black ducks.

BLACK HEAD (2). In Jonesport Township, descriptive. In Lubec Township, for the Black family who lived there in 1881.

BLANCHARD CORNER. For David Blanchard, who settled here in 1821. He was the husband of Charlotte Blanchard, for whom Charlotte Township was named.

BLASKET POINT. Unknown.

BLOOD BROOK. Unknown.

BLOOD COVE. For a battle between the Abnaki and Mohawk Indians where the water was red with the blood of the slain.

BLUEBERRY BARRENS. For blueberries.

BOARD POINT. For the boards there from a nearby tidewater mill.

BOBBYS CREEK. Unknown.

BOBCAT BROOK. For bobcats.

BOBS COVE. (2). Unknown.

BOBSLED RIPS. For being fast, like a bobsled ride.

BOG: BIG-, BROOK (3), BROOK COVE, LAKE, STREAM (2). Descriptive.

BOIS BUBERT: ISLAND, LITTLE-HARBOR, LITTLE-ISLAND. Unknown.

BONNEY: BROOK LAKE, SWAMP. For Moses Bonney, settler in the area about 1817.

BONNEY POINT. For Joel Bonney, who was hired in 1763 by the settlers in Machias to build a sawmill.

BONNY CHESS LEDGE. "Chess" is a kind of grass and "bonny" means "pretty," but it is unknown if this has any relation to the naming of the ledge.

BOOMING GROUND. Descriptive of a location where logs were boomed.

BOOT: COVE, HEAD. A shortened version of the original Boatmans Cove.

BOTHER BROOK. For its frequently rising and causing a "bother" to woodsmen attempting to cross it.

BOUNDARY LEDGES. For their location near the Roque Bluffs and Jonesport Townships boundary line.

BOWLES LAKE. Unknown.

BOYDEN: LAKE, STREAM. For the Delphia Boyden family who settled nearby.

BRADFORD VALLEY. For Bradford, a lumberman who had logging camps there.

BRANDY HEATH. Descriptive of the color of the water in the marshy areas.

BRAY POINT. For the early settling Bray family.

BREAKING LEDGE; BIG-, LITTLE-. Descriptive.

BREAKNECK: HILL, MOUNTAIN. Descriptive of a steep hill or mountain.

BREEZY POINT. Descriptive.

BREWSTER CORNER. For the Brewster family who settled here.

BRIDGHAM SWAMP. For Bridgham, who ran a nearby lumber camp.

BRIGHT ISLAND. Descriptive of its shimmer from far off, for it is covered with bright green grass in the summer.

BRIM COVE. Descriptive of the tide filling cove to the brim. Another source says that fishermen would rest here after a good haul and fill their mugs to the brim with rum.

BROAD COVE. (2). Descriptive.

BROOKS AND WALDEN BROOK. For Brooks & Walden, lumbermen.

BROOKS: BLUFF, COVE. For Abiel Brooks, settler, 1810.

BROOKTON: settlement, TOWNSHIP. A shortened form of its earlier name, Jackson Brook.

BROTHERS: PASSAGE, THE-. Fanciful name for two islands.

BROWN COVE. For any of the numerous Brown family, who were in the area from 1811 on.

BROWNEY: ISLAND, ISLAND LEDGES. For its coloration most of the year.

BROWN POINT. For the second settler of Plantation Twenty-One, Samuel Brown, about 1816.

BROWN RIFFLES. Possibly for Captain David Brown.

BRYANT BROOK. For the local Bryant family.

BRYANT CORNERS. For Andrew Bryant, early settler.

BUCKMAN HEAD. For Benjamin and Seward Bucknam, merchants who lived there by 1802. The spelling variation is accounted for by metathesis.

BUCKMAN ISLAND. Unknown.

BUCK MOUNTAIN: LOWER-, UPPER-. Unknown.

BUCKS: HARBOR, HARBOR (settlement), HEAD, NECK. For Captain Thomas Buck, settler from Plymouth, Massachusetts, about 1763.

BULL: BROOK, POND. For the Bull family, settlers in 1840.

BUNKER: COVE, HOLE. One source says for Jack Bunker of Norwoods Cove, who saved the people from starving by hijacking a British vessel of her stores and cargo. Others say for a Captain Bunker, who stayed there with his vessel to keep away from the British who were impressing seamen.

BUNKER: LEDGE, REEF. For any of the very numerous Bunker sailing family, who were in the area early.

BUNKER POINT. For Dr. Bunker, a surgeon who lived there.

BURBE COVE. Unknown.

BURBEE BROOK. Unknown.

BURIAL ISLAND. Unknown.

BURKE HILL. For the Burke family who lived there.

BURKE MOUNTAIN. Unknown.

BURN, THE. Descriptive of an area which had been burned over.

BURNHAM BROOK. Unknown.

BURNT: COVE, COVE BROOK, ISLAND (3), POINT. Descriptive.

BURROUGHS BROOK. For Burroughs, a logger.

BUTCHER LAKE. Unknown.

BUTLER ISLAND. Unknown.

BUTTERFIELD: BROOK, COVE. For the Butterfield family who lived nearby.

CALAIS: settlement, TOWNSHIP. For Calais, France. As the French city lies opposite Dover, England, across the English Channel, the Maine city lies opposite Dover Hill across the St. Croix River. Others say it was named for Calais, France, in gratitude for French assistance in the Revolutionary War.

CALF: ISLAND (2), POINT. Island in Jonesport Township, for its location near the Cows Yard. Point and Island in Roque Bluffs Township, to make a fanciful pair with Cow Point.

CAMPBELLS SIDING. For the Campbell family, who owned the land where the siding was located late in the 19th century.

CAMP RIPS. For a camp located there.

CANAAN RIDGE. Unknown.

CANES COVE. For the Kane family who lived there.

CANOE BROOK. Unknown.

CANOOSE RIPS. Abnaki: "graves there" — Indian burial ground.

CAPE: COVE, LITTLE-POINT, THE-. Descriptive.

CAPE SPLIT: cape, HARBOR. Because it was a projection of land that split Pleasant Bay.

CAPE WASH: cape, ISLAND. Unknown.

CARD BROOK. For the Card family who settled here, early 1800's.

CARIBOU: BOG, COVE, ROCK. For caribou.

CARLOE: BROOK, POND. Unknown.

CARLOS COVE. Unknown.

CARLOW ISLAND. For Carlow, resident blacksmith.

CARLYLE MOUNTAIN. For the Carlyle family of Charlotte, Maine, who owned the mountain.

CARR HILL. For the local Carr family.

CARRYING: PLACE COVE (3), -PLACE COVE (3), -PLACE ISLAND. For various places where canoes had to be carried overland.

CARRY RIDGE. Where canoes had to be carried overland.

CARSON HEATH. For John Carson, who owned it.

CASE COVE. Unknown.

CASS COVE. For David Cass, who settled here, 1820.

CASTLE, THE. Descriptive of shape.

CATAMOUNT BROOK. The woodsmen's name for the eastern mountain lion.

CATHANCE: LAKE-, LITTLE-LAKE, STREAM. Abnaki: "principal fork."

CEDAR: GROVE RIDGE, settlement. For cedar trees.

CENTER ISLAND. For its location between Crockett and Governors points in Big Lake.

CENTERVILLE: settlement, TOWNSHIP. For its location in the center of Washington County.

CHAIN: FIRST-LAKE, SECOND-LAKE, THIRD-LAKE, ISLAND, LAKE STREAM, LOWER-LAKE. Descriptive of lakes arranged like links in a chain.

CHAIR: POND, POND HEAD. Descriptive of chair-shaped rock formation.

CHALK POND. Descriptive of chalk-like rock.

CHAMBERLY ISLAND. Unknown.

CHANCE ISLAND. Unknown.

CHANDLER BROOK. For the local Chandler family.

CHANDLER: EAST BRANCH-RIVER, RIVER. For Judah Chandler, the first settler near it.

CHANDLER ISLAND. For the Chandler family, who were local fishermen.

CHANNEL ROCK. Descriptive.

CHAPMAN MOUNTAIN. For C.B. Chapman, local dealer in wood, coal, and ice.

CHARLOTTE: settlement, TOWNSHIP. For Charlotte, wife of David Blanchard, a settler in 1821.

CHASE: MILLS, MILLS STREAM. For the Chase family, who owned a sawmill on the stream.

CHERRYFIELD: settlement, TOWNSHIP. For a cherry orchard.

CHERRY TREE RIDGE. For cherry trees.

CHIPUTNETICOOK LAKES. Abnaki: "at the place of the big hill stream."

CHITMAN POINT. For the early settling Chitman or Chipman family.

CHUB COVE. For chub fish.

CLAM: LEDGE, POINT, -SHELL COVE. For clams.

CLARK COVE. For the Clark family who located there, the first settlers of Princeton Township.

CLARK LEDGE. For D.N. Clark, who had a business located at the foot of Clark Street in 1881.

CLARK POINT. Unknown.

CLAY COVE. Descriptive.

CLEMENT POINT. For the early Clement family.

CLIFFORD: BAY, LAKE, STREAM. Unknown.

CLIFFORD BROOK. For Clifford, who camped here before Marion Township was incorporated.

COBBLE HILL. For cobblestones.

COBSCOOK: BAY, FALLS. Malecite: "rocks under water."

COCOA MOUNTAIN. For a group of hunters who brought cocoa wine with them on a hunting trip here. Some passed out on the mountain and others got lost.

CODHEAD LEDGE. Descriptive of shape.

CODYVILLE: settlement, TOWNSHIP. For Cody, first settler in the town.

COFFIN POINT. Unknown.

COFFINS: NECK, POINT. For the Coffin family who lived there, mid-1800's.

COGGINS HEAD. For J.H. Coggin, resident, 1881.

COLBETH ROCK. For a member of the Colbath family, early settlers, who went aground here.

COLEBLACK LAKE. For the Coalblack family, who lived here.

COLE CREEK. For Peter Cole, who lived near.

COLE POINT. For A. Cole, resident, 1881.

COLES LEDGE. For the Cole family, settlers before 1792.

COLLINS BRANCH. Unknown.

COLONEL BROOK. Unknown.

COLONEL POINT. For a retired colonel who lived here.

COLUMBIA: FALLS (settlement), FALLS TOWNSHIP, settlement, TOWNSHIP. By patriotic citizens, for "Columbia," synonym for America.

COLUMBUS ISLAND. Unknown.

COMMISSARY POINT. Unknown.

COMMONS, THE. For a cow pasture held in common by town residents.

COMPASS ROCK. For large direction marks hunters carved there to aid others who might get lost.

COMSTOCK POINT. For Colonel G. Comstock, who had a business there in 1881.

CONANT HILL. For Thunnias Conant.

CONE ISLAND. Descriptive of shape.

CONIC: LAKE, STREAM. Abnaki: "spearing place."

CONNER HILL. For the Conner family who lived there.

COOK COVE. For G. Cook, resident, 1881.

COOK MEADOW BROOK. Unknown.

COOPER: HILL, ISLAND, settlement, TOWNSHIP. For General John Cooper, proprietor and sheriff of Washington County.

CORLISS POINT. For the early Corliss family.

COTHELL MEADOW BROOK. For Daniel and Mary Cothell, owners of the meadow.

COTTAGE COVE. For a cottage located there.

COTTONTAIL HILL. For cottontail rabbits.

COW BROOK. Unknown.

COWEN COVE. For Asa Cowen, first settler there.

COW: ISLAND, POINT. For its use as a pasture for cattle.

COWS YARD, THE. One source says for being a well-sheltered harbor and that ships riding out storms there looked like cows in a yard. Another source says that the large number of rocks and ledges look like the backs of cows.

CRABTREE BOG. For the Crabtree family.

CRANBERRY: BROOK, ISLAND, LAKE RIDGE, LOWER-LAKE, MOUNTAIN, POND (2), STREAM, UPPER-LAKE. For cranberries.

CRANE: BROOK, MEADOW BROOK. For the local Crane families.

CRAWFORD: LAKE, TOWNSHIP. For William Harris Crawford, former Secretary of the Treasury.

CREAMER BROOK. For the early Creamer family.

CREBO: BROOK, FLAT. For Crebo, a lumberman.

CROCKER BROOK. Probably for John Crocker, settler about 1770.

CROCKER POINT . For C. Crocker and a number of other Crocker families who lived there in 1881.

CROCKETT POINT. For the early Crockett family.

CROOKED: BROOK, BROOK FLOWAGE, BROOK LAKE, PITCH, NORTH-BROOK (2), SOUTH-BROOK. Descriptive.

CROSS: ISLAND, ISLAND HEAD, ISLAND NARROWS. Tradition says that the explorer de Monte carved a cross on the back side of the island and reported it to the King of France. Another source says, however, that the English translation of the Indian word for the island is "a passage," meaning that the Indians carried their canoes across the island to avoid the open sea. The settlers, doing the same, named the island "Cross."

CROTCH, THE. Descriptive of shape.

CROTCH CAMP BROOK. Descriptive of a camp located in the "crotch," or branches of a stream.

CROTCHED MEADOWS. Descriptive of shape.

CROW: BROOK, ISLAND (3), NECK POINT. For crows.

CROWLEY ISLAND. For Green Crowley, retired sea captain.

CRUMPLE ISLAND. Descriptive of shape.

CUMMINGS: HEAD, LEDGE. For the Francis Cummings family, settlers in 1772.

CUNNINGHAM MOUNTAIN. Probably for the William Cunningham family, among the earliest settlers.

CURLEW ROCK. For curlews, shore birds.

CURRANT ISLAND. For wild grapes.

CURRY BROOK. For the local Curry family.

CURTIS CREEK. For Captain J.F. and P. Curtis, residents, 1881.

CUTLER: NORTH-, settlement, TOWNSHIP. For Joseph Cutler of Newburyport, Massachusetts, proprietor.

DALOTS. For the Dalot family who ran a nearby granite business.

DANFORTH: settlement, TOWNSHIP. For Thomas Danforth, principal proprietor.

DAN HILL BROOK. (2). For Daniel Hill, one of the original 16 settlers in the Centerville area.

DANIELS ISLAND. Unknown.

DARK: COVE (3), COVE MOUNTAIN, POINT. A nautical word meaning "difficult to see."

DAUGHERTY RIDGE. Unknown.

DAVIS BEACH. For J. Davis, resident, 1881.

DAWN MARIE BEACH. Unknown.

DAY COVE. For the local Day family.

DAYS HEAD. Unknown.

DEAD: BROOK (2), MEADOW STREAM, POND, STREAM (3), -WATER BROOK. Descriptive of slow-moving water.

DEADMAN: BOG, STREAM. Unknown.

DEADMAN RIDGE. For a dead man found there by J.J. Butterfield and Arthur Schillinger about 1870 while they assisted in building a road that is now Route 169. The man had been employed at a woods camp and had started home after complaining of being ill. His family at home did not know that he had left the camp, and the woods boss did not know that he did not arrive home. When the roadbuilders attempted to remove the valise on which the head was resting, the head fell off the body.

DEBLOIS: settlement, TOWNSHIP. For T.A. Deblois, president of the City Bank of Portland, who owned much of the town.

DEEP: COVE (4), HOLE POINT. Descriptive.

DEER: BROOK, BROOK COVE, ISLAND. For deer.

DEMOCRAT RIDGE. For four large families who always voted for the Democrats while most of their neighbors voted for the Republicans.

DENBOW HEATH. For the local Denbow family.

DENBOW: ISLAND, NECK, POINT. For the Denbow family, settlers in the 1880's.

DENNISON POINT. For Lucius and Ellen Dennison, who owned the point.

DENNISON PORTAGE. For Dennison, who lived at the porgtage.

DENNYS: RIVER, -VILLE SETTLEMENT, -VILLE STATION, -VILLE TOWNSHIP. For an Indian, John Denny, who had his hunting grounds in the area. Another source says for Nicholas Denys, pioneer historian and lieutenant governor of Acadia.

DESPAIR ISLAND. Possibly to make a pair with nearby Hope Island.

DEVILS HEAD. Although some say for its shape, one source says it is a linguistic change of "d'Orville's Head." d'Orville was a friend of Champlain and de Monts.

DIANA LEDGE. Unknown.

DICK, THE. For tumbledown Dick Head.

DICK ALLEN COVE. For Dick Allen, resident fisherman.

DILL HILL. For the local Dill family.

DINNER ISLAND. An island where many sportsmen stopped to eat their lunch.

DOE BROOK. For doe deer.

DOG BROOK. (2). For the many dogs that ranged there.

DOG FALLS. Unknown.

DOGFISH ROCKS. For dogfish.

DOG ISLAND. Descriptive of its shape.

DOG TOWN. (2). For the many dogs kept by the settlers.

DOLLY HEAD. Unknown.

DONOVAN COVE. For the early Donovan family.

DORMAN. For Jabez Doeman, who settled there in 1771.

DORMAN ISLAND. For Israel Dorman, an early settler.

DOUBLESHOT ISLAND. (2). A common name descriptive of two small islands side by side.

DOUGHERTY: COVE, POINT. For J. Dority, settler before 1880.

DOUGLAS: ISLANDS, ISLANDS HARBOR. Unknown.

DOYLE ISLAND. For the Doyle family, owners.

DRAKE LAKE. Unknown.

DRAM: ISLAND, LITTLE-ISLAND. Descriptive of size.

DRISKO: ISLAND, LITTLE-ISLAND. For the Joseph Drisko family, settlers by 1778.

DRISKO LEDGE. (2). For the numerous Drisko family.

DROWN BOYS LEDGES. For two drowned boys, possibly the Lairey brothers, found there.

DRY: BROOK, LEDGE. Descriptive.

DUCK: COVE, HARBOR, POND. For ducks.

DUDLEY: BROOK, ISLAND. For the Dudley families who lived nearby.

DUNGFORK POINTS. For three parallel points on Baskahegan Lake that resemble the points of a dungfork.

DUNNING BROOK. Unknown.

DUNN ISLAND. For the local Dunn family.

DYER: BAY, HARBOR, NECK, POINT. For Henry Dyer, who built a home here before 1769.

DYER: COVE (2), COVE POINT, COVE RIDGE. Cove in Addison Township, for the Lemuel Dyer family, who settled in 1821. The others in Grand Lake Stream Township, for the local Dyer family.

DYER ISLAND. For Captain Dyer, resident sea captain.

DYER POINT RIFFLES. For the early settling Dyer family.

DYKE BROOK. For a dike, or levee, built along it to keep it from overflowing into the hayfields.

EAGLE: HILL, ISLAND, ISLAND REEF. For eagles.

EAST: BAY, STREAM. Descriptive.

EASTERN: BAY, HARBOR, HEAD, HEAD LEDGES, ISLAND, LAKE, LEDGE, LEDGES, NUBBLE, POND, STREAM, WAY. Descriptive.

EASTMAN HILL. For the local Eastman family.

EASTON POINT. For the Easton family who owned it.

EASTPORT: settlement, TOWNSHIP. By Captain Hopley Yeaton, for its easterly location.

EATON. For Henry Eaton of the Eaton Lumber Co., the first to cut timber here.

EATON COVE. For J.M. Eaton, resident, 1881.

EDGECOMB POINT. For Fred Edgecomb, who had a fish-packing plant there.

EDMUNDS: settlement, TOWNSHIP. Named for Edmund Hobart, who was born in Hingham, England, about 1570 and came to Massachusetts about 1620 as a minister, by his great-grandson who purchased the township.

EGG: ROCK (2), WESTERN-ROCK. For seabird eggs there.

ELBOW RIPS. For rapids on an elbow of the St. Croix River.

ELIJAH BROWN HEATH. For Elijah Brown, who settled there.

ELLEN BROOK. Unknown.

ELLIOT FLATS. For W. Elliot, resident, 1881.

ELLIOT GUT. For the local Elliot family.

ELLIOTS MOUNTAIN. For Simon Elliot, early settler.

ELLIS HILL. For the Ellis family who lived there in the 1800's.

ELSEMORE LANDING. Unknown.

ELSIE POINT. Unknown.

ELWELL: BROOK, RIDGE. Unknown.

ENGLISHMAN: BAY, RIVER. For Day, an Englishman, who settled there.

ENOCH: BROOK, HILL, LAKE, WEST BRANCH-BROOK. Unknown.

EPPING. For settlers from Epping, New Hampshire.

ESTES HEAD. For Estes, who owned it and much surrounding acreage.

ESTEY MOUNTAIN. For R.E. Estey, resident, 1881.

FAIRY HEAD. Unknown.

FALKINGHAM COVE. For a Faulkingham family who settled here.

FALLS ISLAND. For Cobscook Falls.

FAN ISLAND. Possibly for its shape.

FARM: COVE (2), COVE MOUNTAIN (2). For farms.

FARRAR HILL. For J.N. Farrar, resident, 1881.

FARROW: LAKE, MOUNTAIN. For the Farrow family living nearby in 1881.

FEDERAL HARBOR. Unknown.

FELLOWS ISLAND. For Gustavus and Cornelius Fellows of Boston, two of the original grantees.

FESSENDEN LEDGE. Unknown.

FIELD POINT. Unknown.

FIFTEENTH STREAM. Unknown.

FIFTH ROCK. Descriptive.

FINNEGAN BROOK. Unknown.

FIRST LAKE. Descriptive.

FISHERMAN ISLAND. For fishermen who lived there.

FISH: ISLAND, ISLAND LEDGE, POINT. For fish weirs.

FIVE ISLANDS. Descriptive.

FLAGSTAFF MOUNTAIN. For flags surveyors put on staffs so that they could be seen from another mountain.

FLAKE POINT BAR. For fish-drying racks called "flakes."

FLAT: BAY, ISLAND, ISLAND LEDGES. Descriptive.

FLETCHER: BROOK, FIELD, PEAK (2). Unknown.

FLINT: ISLAND, ISLAND NARROWS. Where the Indians got stone for weapons.

FLIPPER CREEK. Unknown.

FLOOD: BROOK, COVE, LAKE, UPPER-LAKE. Descriptive.

FLOWED LAND PONDS. Descriptive of marshy land.

FLYING PLACE, THE. Where ducks flew over to get from one bay to another.

FLYNN: BROOK, POND. Unknown.

FOLLY, THE. Unknown.

FORD POINT. For W.H. Ford, resident, 1881.

FOREST: CITY, CITY LANDING. For its location in the forest.

FORK RIPS. Descriptive.

FORT: ISLAND, LITTLE-ISLAND. Unknown.

FORT O'BRIEN POINT. Probably for Jeremiah O'Brien of Machias, who commanded the colonial sloop "Unity" in the first naval battle of the Revolution in June 1775, in Machias Bay.

FOSS POINT. For the Foss family who settled by 1765.

FOSTER BROOK. For Foster, a lumberman who had camps there.

FOSTER: CHANNEL, ISLAND (2). Island in Harrington Township, for the early Foster family. Channel and Island in Machiasport Township, for Benjamin Foster, who built a sawmill with Ichabod Jones. Others say for Isaiah Foster, a settler from Scarborough in the fall of 1762.

FOSTER LAKE. For J. Foster, resident, 1881.

FOURMILE BROOK. For its entering Grand Lake Stream 4 miles from where Grand Lake Stream enters Big Lake.

FOURTH LAKE STREAM. For Fourth Machias Lake.

FOX: ISLAND, PASSAGE. Probably for foxes.

FOX POINT. For Fox, a lumberman.

FRED DORR BROOK. For Fred Dorr, who had a lumber camp there.

FREDS ISLAND. Unknown.

FREEMAN ROCK. For Freeman Beal, a relative of Manwaring Beal, first settler on Beals Island.

FRENCH HOUSE ISLAND. For a house built there very early by a French settler.

FRENCH RIDGE. For French, a man who lived there.

FRIAR ROAD. For a rock on Campobello Island that resembles a friar.

FROST: COVE, HEAD, ISLAND, LEDGE. For Samuel and John Frost, settlers by 1790.

FULTON LAKE. For the Fulton family, owners.

GANGWAY: ledge, LEDGE. Descriptive.

GARDNER BROOK. Unknown.

GARDNER LAKE. For Laban Gardner, settler before 1790.

GARDNER RIPS. For Gardner, a lumberman who had a camp there.

GARNET POINT. For Captain Garnet, owner.

GAY HILL. For the local Gay family.

GENTNER COVE. Unknown.

GEORGE BROOK. Unknown.

GETCHEL LAKES. Unknown.

GETCHELL RIFFLES. For the early Getchell family.

GIBBS ISLAND. For the Gibbs family who owned the island.

GILCHRIST ROCK. Unknown.

GILMAN BROOK. For the local Gilman family.

GILMAN HILL. For Richard E. Gilman.

GIN COVE. Where liquor was smuggled into the county.

GLEASON: COVE, POINT. For Gleason, very early settler.

GOOCH BROOK. For the Gooch family sawmill located there.

GOODS POINT. For Captain John Good.

GOOSEBERRY: ISLAND, NUBBLE. For gooseberries.

GOOSE: INNER-ISLAND, ISLAND (2), ISLANDS, OUTER-ISLAND, POND. For geese.

GORDON ISLAND. For John Gordon, a settler about 1812.

GOULDING LAKE. For the Goulding family who settled along the shore.

GOULD: LANDING, MEADOW BROOK. Unknown.

GOVE POINT. For C., M., L., and A. Gove, residents, 1881.

GOVERNORS POINT. Unknown.

GRAND: FALLS, FALLS FLOWAGE, LAKE BROOK, LAKE STREAM, LAKE STREAM TOWNSHIP, WEST-LAKE. Descriptive.

GRASSEY: ISLAND, POINT (2), POND (2). Descriptive.

GRASS POND. Descriptive..

GRAVEL POINT. Descriptive.

GRAY COVE. For Gray, a lumberman.

GRAY POND. Unknown.

GRAYS: BEACH, ROCK. Unknown.

GRAYS: BROOK, COVE. For the Gray family who fished the cove.

GREAT: BAR, BROOK, BROOK LAKE, COVE, FALLS, FALLS BRANCH, HEAD (2), MEADOW, MEADOW RIFFLES, PINE POINT, POND, RIDGE, SPRUCE ISLAND, SPRUCE LEDGES. Descriptive.

GREAT WASS ISLAND. For Wilmot Wass, Sr., settler, 1763.

GREAT WORKS POND. For hopes that the area would become a great milling center.

GREEN: HILL, ISLAND (5), ISLAND LEDGE. Descriptive of color.

GREENLAND: BIG-LAKE, BROOK, COVE (2), LITTLE-LAKE, MOUNTAIN, POINT, RIDGE. Possibly descriptive.

GREENLAW: CHOPPING LANDING, ISLAND. Probably for the later family of Solomon Greenlaw.

GREEN SPRING. Possibly descriptive.

GREY MOUNTAIN. Unknown.

GROVE. Descriptive of a grove of trees.

GROVER LAKE. Unknown.

GUARD POINT. For its use as a lookout for British ships during the Revolution.

GULL ROCK. (2). For seagulls.

GUT, THE. Descriptive of a passage.

HACKMATACK BOG. Local name for juniper trees.

HADLEY: BROOK, LAKE, LAKES. For numerous Hadley families.

HALEY POINT. For the early Haley family.

HALFMOON COVE. Descriptive of shape.

HALFTIDE LEDGE. (3). Descriptive.

HALIFAX ISLAND. A British ship was wrecked here whose name, one source feels, was the "Halifax."

HALL HILL. For John Hall, settler by 1778.

HALLOWELL ISLAND. Possibly for the Abner Hallowell family.

HALL RIDGE. Unknown.

HALLS: COVE, ISLAND, RIDGE. For various Hall families who were in the county early.

HALLS MILL. For Nelson and Peter Hall.

HALLS RIPS. For John Hall, early settler.

HAMILTON: BROOK, COVE. For B. Hamilton, resident at the cove in 1881.

HAMMOND POND. Unknown.

HANNAHS COVE. Unknown.

HANNEMAN ISLAND. Unknown.

HARBOR LEDGES. Descriptive.

HARDING: BROOK, COVE. For William Harding, first settler in the area.

HARDSCRABBLE RIVER. For the hard time that the settlers along it had in making a living.

HARDWOOD: HILL, ISLAND (4), ISLAND LEDGE, POINT (2), RIDGE. For hardwood trees.

HARDY POINT. Unknown.

HARMON: BROOK, HEATH, LAKE, MOUNTAIN (2), STREAM. Stream and Heath in Marion and Cutler Townships, for local Harmon families. Mountain in Northfield Township, probably for Benjamin Harmon, settler, 1824. The others, unknown.

HARRINGTON: BAY, RIVER, settlement, TOWNSHIP, WEST-. David Dunbar, a surveyor for the King of England, was granted a tract of land of which he named a third "Harrington," for a British noble and writer. Later, the name of this third was changed to Bristol. The discarded name "Harrington" was selected by the early settlers as a name for the present township when it was incorporated.

HARRIS COVE. For I.T. Harris, resident, 1881.

HARRISON BROOK. For the local Harrison family.

HARTHORNE LEDGE. Unknown.

HARWOOD ISLAND: INNER-, MIDDLE-. Cartographical mistake for "Hardwood Island," for hardwood trees.

HASTY COVE. Unknown.

HAUNTED BROOK. Unknown.

HAWKINS BROOK. For the Harkins family.

HAWKINS RIDGE. (2). Unknown.

HAWKS MOUNTAIN. For Josiah Hawks, who was born in 1868.

HAYCOCK: BOG, HARBOR. Unknown.

HAY: CREEK, LEDGE. For hay.

HAYES BROOK. Unknown.

HAYS BOG. Unknown.

HAYWOOD ISLAND. Unknown.

HEAD: HARBOR, HARBOR CREEK, HARBOR ISLAND. For being at the head of Moosabec Reach and Chandler Bay.

HEATH: BIG-(2), BROOK, SOUTH BRANCH-BROOK. Descriptive.

HEDGEHOG: ISLAND, POINT. For hedgehogs (porcupines).

HELL RAPIDS. Fast and dangerous rapids on Baskahegan Stream.

HEMLOCK: HILL, ISLAND. For hemlock trees.

HEN ISLAND. Fanciful, or for hen lobsters.

HERRING: LOWER-COVE, UPPER-COVE. For herring.

HERSEY: COVE, NECK, POINT, UPPER LEDGE. For a large number of Hersey families living there.

HICKS CREEK. For the Hicks family who owned the land where the creek runs.

HIGGINS BROOK. For James Higgins.

HIGH: HEAD, HILL, THE-BLUFFS, THE-LANDS. Descriptive.

HILL BROOK. For A. Hill, on whose property it rose.

HINCKLEY POINT. For Hinckley, who bought it from Wilson Mayhew or his heirs.

HINTON POINT. For the local Hinton family.

HOBART: BOG, LAKE, MEADOW MOUNTAIN, STREAM (2). Stream in Edmunds Township, for Edmund Hobart, for whom the township is named. The others, unknown.

HOG ISLAND. (4). For their use as hog pens.

HOLLY: BIG-COVE, LITTLE-COVE, POINT. For the local Holly family.

HOLMES: BAY, POINT. Probably for Joseph Holmes, millwright, and his family, settlers in 1765.

HOLMES: BROOK, FALLS. Unknown.

HOLMES: COVE, COVE BROOK. For Holmes, local lobster fisherman.

HOLMES: POND, STREAM. For the Holmes family, residents, 1881.

HOLWAYS POINT. Probably for John Holway, shipbuilder and lumberman.

HONEYMOON BROOK. Unknown.

HOOPER POINT. For Hoopers living there in 1881.

HOPE ISLAND. Possibly fancifully named, for there is a nearby Despair Island.

HOPKINS POINT. For Clement Hopkins, who settled here and opened a business in 1826.

HORAN HEAD. For A. Horan, resident, 1881.

HORSEBACK, THE. Descriptive of a ridge.

HORSE COVE. A shortened form of its previous name "Horseshoe Cove," for its shape.

HORSE: HILL, HILL BROOK, LEDGE, RIPS. Unknown.

HORSESHOE: COVE, LAKE (2), LITTLE-POND, POND. Descriptive of shape.

HOSEA PUG LAKE. Unknown.

HOT: BROOK, EAST BRANCH-BROOK, LOWER-BROOK LAKE, UPPER-BROOK LAKE, WEST BRANCH-BROOK. Descriptive of a brook that seldom freezes.

HOUND: BROOK, BROOK LAKE. For dogs that ran there.

HOUSE COVE. For a house located there.

HOWARD: COVE, MOUNTAIN, POINT. Unknown.

HOWARD LAKE. For Captain William Howard, who settled in the area.

HOWARD RIDGE. For Ernest Howard, who camped here in 1900 or 1910.

HOWE BROOK. For the Howe family.

HOYTTOWN. For the Hoyt family, one of the first two groups of settlers in the area.

HUCKINS: ISLAND, LEDGE. For Clement Huckins, owner of one of the original Lubec lots.

HUGHES BROOK. Unknown.

HUNTLEY: BROOK (3), BROOK FLOWAGE, LITTLE-BROOK, RIDGE, WEST BRANCH-BROOK. Brook in Wesley Township, for J.S. Huntley, resident, 1881. Brook, Little-Brook, and Ridge in Plantation Twenty-One, for the local Huntley family. The others, unknown.

HUNTLEY CREEK. For J.R. and H. Huntley, residents, 1881.

HUNTLEY MOUNTAIN. For E. and Fred Huntley, late 19th century residents.

HUNT RIDGE. Unknown.

HURLEY POINT. For the William Hurley family, settlers by 1799.

ICE HOUSE POINT. For a lumber company that had a large icehouse here.

IDLE ISLAND. Fancifully named.

IKES HILL. For Isaac Farnsworth.

INDIAN: COVE, CHANNEL, HEAD, LAKE (2), LANDING, POINT, RIDGE, RIVER, SOUTHWEST BRANCH-RIVER, STREAM, TOWNSHIP. For Indians.

INGALLS BROOK. Unknown.

INGERSOLL POINT. For William Ingersoll, settler, 1798.

INGLEY COVE. Unknown.

INLET: BIG-, COVE, LITTLE-, NORTHERN-, SOUTHERN-. Descriptive.

IRISH SETTLEMENT. For the Kinney, McCluskey, and McGrave families, settlers from Ireland.

IRONWORKS MOUNTAIN. For an ironworks here years ago.

ISAAC LEDGE. Unknown.

JACKSON: BROOK, BROOK LAKE. For the maiden name of Dorcus, wife of James J. Dudley, innkeeper, surveyor, and influential citizen.

JACKSONVILLE. For President Andrew Jackson. The people here who backed him were called Jacksonites, and the name for the settlement followed.

JAMESON COVE. For the Jameson family.

JAMES POND. For Lin James, born in 1852.

JASPER HEAD. Unknown.

JENKINS BROOK. For Jenkins, lumberman who operated there.

JERRY LEDGE. Unknown.

JIM BROWN BROOK. For Jim Brown, who drowned there.

JIMMEY MOUNTAIN. Unknown.

JIMMY LIBBY COVE. For Jimmy Libby, one of the earliest settlers.

JIMS HEAD. Unknown.

JIM WOOD RIDGE. For Jim Wood, who lived on the ridge in the latter part of the 1800's.

JOE DYER POINT. For Joseph Dyer, son of an early settler.

JOE GEORGES RIPS. For Joe Georges, early settler.

JOE HANSCOM HEATH. For Joe Hanscom, owner.

JOE: HILL BROOK, MEADOW BROOK. For Joe Hill, one of the first 16 settlers in the Centerville area.

JOHNSON BAY. For the Johnson family living there about 1800. One day the wife of the family was abducted by a man from a ship anchored nearby. The husband pursued, but finally gave up the chase. He said that the captor was his wife's former husband, and they were later heard of in Halifax. The bay was named for the incident.

JOHNSON: COVE (2), MOUNTAIN. Cove in Eastport Township, for the Paul Johnson family of 1789. Cove and Mountain in Roque Bluffs Township, for the early Johnson family.

JOHN WHITE ISLAND. For the John White family who owned it.

JONESBORO: settlement, STATION, TOWNSHIP. For John Coffin Jones, grantee of the area in 1789.

JONESPORT: settlement, TOWNSHIP, WEST-. For John Coffin Jones, grantee of the area in 1789. The name was retained when Jonesport was separated from Jonesboro.

JORDAN BEACH. For the Jordan family.

JORDANS: DELIGHT, DELIGHT LEDGE. For the Jordan family. The significance of "delight" is unknown.

JOSH POND. Unknown.

JOYS COVE. For Samuel Joy.

JULIAS COVE. Unknown.

JUMBO LANDING. Unknown.

JUMPER LEDGE. Unknown.

JUNIOR: BAY, LAKE. Unknown.

KANE RIDGE. For W.H. Cain.

KAYLOR BROOK. For many Calers living along it in 1881.

KEELEY LAKE. Unknown.

KEENE LAKE. For Jarius Keene, shipbuilder.

KELLEY POINT. For the Thomas Kelley family, settlers about 1773.

KELLYLAND. For B.F. Kelly, who owned the land when the St. Croix Paper Co. built a hydro-electric station here.

KELLY POINT. For the early Kelly family.

KELP LEDGE. For kelp, or seaweed.

KENDALL HEAD. For Kendall, who farmed here.

KENDALL MOUNTAIN. For Kendall, a man who lived there.

KENNEBEC: BROOK, EAST BRANCH LITTLE-BAY, LITTLE-BAY, settlement, WEST BRANCH LITTLE-BAY. Abnaki: "long level water without rapids."

KENNISTON MOUNTAIN. For G.H. Kenniston, resident, 1881.

KENT COVE. Unknown.

KEROSENE POND. Unknown.

KERWIN BROOK. Unknown.

KILTON: MOUNTAIN, POINT. For the Kilton family who lived here in 1881.

KIMBALL POINT. For the local Kimball family.

KING BROOK. Unknown.

KING DAVID HILL. By religious people, for the biblical king.

KINNEY COVE. (2). For the Martin Kinney family.

KINNEY: BILL-COVE, NATION. For Bill Kinney, who had extensive holdings in the area.

KITCHEN: COVE, COVE POINT. Unknown.

KITTERY ISLAND. Probably for Kittery, Maine, but for an unknown reason.

KNIGHT ISLAND. For the Knight family who settled after 1776.

KNIGHTS POINT. For Captain Jonathon Knight, settler, 1790.

KNOWLES BROOK. For the Knowles family, settlers there by 1778.

KNOWNOTHING COVE. By boys who fished there and never caught anything. There were no fish, "no nothing," there.

KNOX HILL. One source says for General Henry Knox.

KNOX: LAKE, MOUNTAIN. Unknown.

KOLE KILL ISLAND. Unknown.

LA COUTE: LAKE, POINT. For several Indian families named Lacoute who lived there in the late 1890's and early 1900's.

LADLE: EASTERN-LEDGE, THE-, WESTERN-LEDGE. Descriptive of shape.

LAKE: BROOK, RIPS. Descriptive.

LAKEMAN: ISLAND, HARBOR, POINT. For the local Lakeman family.

LAMB COVE. (2). In Robbinston Township, for James Lamb, who settled at the cove. In T27ED, unknown.

LAMBERT: LAKE, LAKE (settlement), LAKE TOWNSHIP. For Sheribiah and Robert Lambert from New Hampshire, who settled here in 1754.

LAMB PLACE. For P.C. Lamb, resident farmer, 1880's.

LAMBS DEADWATER. For Natty Lamb, lumber contractor for the Todd Lumber Co. of Calais, who drove logs there.

LAMSEN BROOK. For the local Lamsen family.

LAPSTONE LEDGE. For a variety of polishing stone found there.

LARRABEE: COVE, settlement. For the Larrabee family.

LARRY BROOK. Unknown.

LATHROP HEATH. For O.F. and F.A. Lathrop, residents, 1881.

LEACH POINT. For numerous Leech families in the area.

LEADURNY POINT. Unknown.

LEDGE POND. Descriptive.

LEIGHTON: COVE, POINT. For the Samuel Leighton family who settled about 1790.

LEIGHTON: LEDGES, NECK, ROCK. For the early Leighton family.

LENROY ISLAND. Unknown.

LEWIS COVE. For the early Lewis family.

LEWY LAKE. For the many Lewys.

LEWYS BROOK. For the many Leweys.

LIBBY BROOK. (4). In T19M9 and T36MD, for Libby, a logger. In Machias Township, for the early Libby family. In Centerville Township, unknown.

LIBBY COVE. For T.D., G., and many other Libbys there in 1881.

LIBBY HEAD. For Ezekiel Libby, settler, 1763.

LIBBY ISLAND. Unknown.

LIBERTY POINT. Where U.S. soldiers landed in the War of 1812 to liberate Robbinston from the British.

LILY: COVE, LITTLE-LAKE, LAKE (4). For lilies.

LINCOLN COVE. For Moses and Jacob Lincoln, who settled by 1790.

LINDSEY BROOK. Unknown.

LINDSEY COVE. For the early Lindsey family.

LITTLE: BAY, FALLS (4), LAKE (2), LEDGE (2), MOUNTAIN, POND BEACH, POND HEAD, RIVER (3), RIVER ISLAND (2), RIVER MOUNTAIN. Descriptive.

LITTLE DOCHET ISLAND. Probably a linguistic change of "Docear Island," name bestowed by Champlain.

LIVELY BROOK. Descriptive.

LOBSTER: COVE, ISLAND. For lobsters.

LONG: COVE (2), CREEK, ISLAND (2), ISLAND PASSAGE, LAKE (2), LAKE COVE, LAKE RIDGE, LEDGE (2), POINT (6), POINT COVE, POND. Descriptive.

LONGFELLOW BROOK. For the W. Longfellow family.

LONGFELLOW PITCH. For the Longfellow family.

LOOK: HEAD, POINT. For the Look family who settled here by 1778.

LOOKOUT MOUNTAIN. Descriptive.

LOOK POINT. For Leander Look.

LOON: BAY, LAKE, POINT. For loons.

LOONS NEST. For loons.

LORING COVE. For Peter Loring, settler by 1790.

LORING HILL. Unknown.

LOVEJOY COVE. Unknown.

LOVE: LAKE, RIDGE. For John (or Jot) Love, who settled near the lake, late 1700's.

LOWE COVE. For D.G. Lowe, resident, 1881.

LOWER RIFFLES. Descriptive.

LUBEC: NARROWS, NORTH-, settlement, SOUTH-, TOWNSHIP, WEST-. For Lubec, Germany.

MacELROY HEATH. For H. McElroy, owner, 1881.

MACHIAS: BAY, EAST-, EAST-RIVER, EAST-TOWNSHIP, EDDY, FOURTH-LAKE, LITTLE-, LITTLE-BAY, -PORT, -PORT TOWNSHIP, -PORT STATION, RIVER, SEAL ISLAND, settlement, THIRD-LAKE, TOWNSHIP, WEST BRANCH-RIVER. Abnaki: "bad little falls."

MACKEREL ROCK. For mackerel.

MACKS COVE. Unknown.

MAGAZINE BROOK. Unknown.

MAGURREWOCK: EAST BRANCH-STREAM, LAKES, MOUNTAIN, STREAM. Malecite: "at the place of the shoveler (caribou)."

MAHAR POINT. For the Mahar family who settled in the 1780's.

MAIN CHANNEL WAY. Descriptive.

MAINE RIVER. For the State of Maine.

MAINLAND COVE. Descriptive.

MAJOR ISLAND. Unknown.

MAN ISLAND. For the body of an unknown seaman in a uniform coat that was washed up here, found by fishermen, and buried on the island.

MANLEY ISLAND. For Manley, owner of the island during the early settlement of Forest City.

MANNINGS FARM. Unknown.

MANSFIELD CREEK. For the Mansfield family living there in 1881.

MARGIE ROCK. Unknown.

MARION: settlement, TOWNSHIP. For General Francis Marion, general in the American Revolution.

MARK: ISLAND, LITTLE-ISLAND. Used as a triangulation mark for finding fishing grounds.

MARKS: ISLAND, LAKE, SECOND-LAKE. Unknown.

MARSHALL POINT. Unknown.

MARSH: COVE, COVE POINT, EASTERN-BROOK, ISLAND (2), POINT, -VILLE, WESTERN-BROOK. Descriptive.

MARSHFIELD: settlement, TOWNSHIP. Descriptive.

MARST: BROOK, HEATH. A shortened form of "Marston," an early family.

MARSTON POINT. For Nathaniel Marston, surveyor, early 1800's.

MARY LOOK POINT. For Mary Look, who lived there, relative of an early settler.

MASH: HARBOR, HARBOR ISLAND, ISLAND. Descriptive. The Maine dialect pronunciation of "marsh."

MASON BAY. For the early Mason family.

MASTERS ISLAND. For the Masters family, early owners.

MATHEWS ISLAND. For the J. Mathews family, residents, 1881.

MAYBERRY COVE: BIG-, LITTLE-. Unknown.

MAYS BROOK. For numerous area Mays in 1881.

McALLSTER POINT. For the McAllister family who lived there.

McCURDY POINT. For Captain W.H. McCurdy, who lived on the point in the late 19th century.

McKEESICK ISLAND. For L. McKeesic, resident, 1881.

McLAIN MOUNTAIN. For the McLain family who settled in 1834.

MEADOW: BROOK (6), LITTLE-BROOK. Descriptive.

MEDDYBEMPS: HEATH, LAKE, settlement, TOWNSHIP. Passamaquoddy-Abnaki: "plenty of alewives."

MEETINGHOUSE RIPS. For a meetinghouse located nearby.

MERRIT: BROOK, POND. Unknown.

MERRITT POINT. For Daniel Merritt, first settler in the area.

MESERVE HEAD. For the Meserve family who lived there in 1881.

MIDDLE: BROOK, DEADWATER, GROUND (2), ISLAND, RIVER, THE-. Descriptive.

MILBRIDGE: settlement, TOWNSHIP. For a bridge built there in the 1830's and a mill of a Mr. Gardner.

MILE RIPS. Because it is approximately one mile long.

MILLBERRY: BROOK, WEST BRANCH-BROOK. Unknown.

MILL: BROOK (2), COVE, CREEK (4), POND, -POND BROOK, POINT, RIVER STREAM, -TOWN. For mills.

MILLER MOUNTAIN. For James Miller, settler by 1790.

MILLER POINT. For Miller, who bought the point from Colonel Rendolf Whidden.

MILTON MOUNTAIN. A cartographical error for Mitten Mountain, so-named because Josiah Weston lost his mittens there while hunting.

MINK ISLAND. (3). For mink.

MINX ISLAND. For mink.

MISERY LEDGE. Because a boat was grounded there.

MISTAKE: HARBOR, ISLAND. A sea captain once made a mistake in taking this passage. He wanted the channel between Steels Harbor Island and Knights Island, but ended up here instead.

MITCHELL POINT. (2). In Milbridge Township, for the Mitchell family who lived here by 1880. In Eastport, unknown.

MOLLIE COVE. For an Indian woman, Mollie Lacoute.

MONEY: COVE, ISLAND. Tradition says that pirates buried their treasure here, and much excavation has taken place, but with no success.

MONEYMAKER LAKE. For the counterfeiting of silver dollars here by Ebenezer Ball and John Hall about 1810. Ball shot and killed the officer who came to arrest them, but was later tried for the offense and became the first man legally hanged in Maine. Hall escaped.

MONHONON COVE. For the Mohannas family who lived at the cove by 1880.

MONROE: BROOK, LAKE. Unknown.

MONTEGAIL: POND, STREAM. Said to be an Indian word, but definition unknown.

MONUMENT COVE. For many large, free-standing rocks like monuments along its banks.

MOODY ISLAND. Unknown.

MOON ISLAND. Descriptive of its quarter-moon shape.

MOONS BROOK. Unknown.

MOOSABEC REACH. Abnaki: "moosehead rock."

MOOSEHORN BROOK. Descriptive of a moosehorn in its various branches and crooks.

MOOSE: ISLAND, LEDGE, LITTLE-ISLAND, NECK, RIVER, ROCK. For moose.

MOOSE SNARE COVE. For moose snares.

MOPANG: EAST BRANCH-STREAM, FIRST LAKE, LAKE, LITTLE-STREAM, SECOND LAKE, STREAM. Malecite: "solitary place."

MORONG COVE. For W. Morong, resident, 1879.

MORRISON COVE. (2). In Lubec Township, for P.M. Morrison, who lived there in 1881. In T5ND, unknown.

MORRISON POINT. For Morrison, lumberman who drowned there years ago.

MORTON LEDGE. For Captain Leander Morton.

MOUNT AETNA. Probably for Mount Etna in Sicily, but the reason is unknown.

MOUNTAIN: HEAD, POND. Descriptive.

MOUNT DELIGHT. Unknown.

MOUNT DORCUS. For Dorcus Haywood.

MOUNT MISERY. Unknown.

MOUNT SEEALL. Descriptive of a tall hill.

MOUNT TOM. For Thomas Annas.

MOUSE ISLAND. Descriptive of size.

MOWRY POINT. For Jabez Mowry, who escaped to this point from the British with his valuables and papers hidden in a grandfather's clock.

MUD: BROOK, COVE, HOLE, HOLE CHANNEL, HOLE POINT, LOWER-LAKE, LAKE (3), LANDING, UPPER-LAKE. Descriptive.

MUNCY COVE. Unknown.

MUNSON: ISLAND, LAKE, RIPS. Unknown.

MURPHY POINT. For the Murphy family.

MUSCLE SHOAL. For mussels.

MUSQUASH: BAY, BIG-STREAM, COVE, EAST BRANCH BIG-STREAM, EAST BRANCH-STREAM, EAST-LAKE, ISLAND, MOUNTAIN, POINT, WEST BIG-STREAM, WEST BRANCH-STREAM, WEST LAKE. Abnaki: "reddish-brown animal (muskrat)."

MUTTON: COVE, COVE BROOK. Unknown.

NARRAGUAGUS: BAY, RIVER, WEST BRANCH-RIVER. Abnaki: "above the boggy place."

NARROWS: ISLAND, MOUNTAIN, THE-. Descriptive.

NASH ISLAND. For Joseph, Samuel, Isaiah, and Joseph Nash, Jr., settlers in 1778.

NASH POINT. For a number of Nash families at the point in 1881.

NASHS LAKE. For Amaziah Nash, an early settler.

NASON POINT. For Nathaniel Nason, who built a camp there.

NATS ROCK. For Nathaniel Sawyer.

NATTS POINT. For Nathaniel Sawyer, who lived there.

NEAL MOUNTAIN. For the Neal family who lived there in 1881.

NEPPS POINT. If Indian, Abnaki: "water."

NEWCOMB POINT. For the Necombs, a well-to-do family who had a summer cottage there.

NEW: STREAM, WEST BRANCH-STREAM. To differentiate from Old Stream.

NIGHTCAP: ISLAND, LEDGE. Descriptive of shape.

NIPPLE. Humorous name for a rock located near Virgin Island and The Virgins Breasts.

NIPS ISLAND. Unknown.

NO. 19 TOWNSHIP. Descriptive of its township designation.

NORSE POND. Tradition says that the pond was made by Norsemen.

NORTH: -EAST BLUFF, -EAST HARBOR, -EAST HILL, -EAST COVE, -WEST COVE, WEST HARBOR, -WEST HEAD. Descriptive.

NORTHERN STREAM. Descriptive.

NORTHFIELD: settlement, TOWNSHIP. For the large fields lying north of Machias.

NORTON: ISLAND (2), ISLAND LEDGE, ISLAND REEF, LEDGE, POINT. Island, Island Ledge and Island Reef in Addison Township, for Seth Norton, a settler by 1778. Island, Ledge, and Point in Jonesport Township, for Elihu Norton, moose hunter who settled in 1785.

NORWAY: ISLAND, POINT (2). For Norway pine trees.

NOVA ROCKS. Unknown.

NUMBER NINE HILL. For the former designation of Trescott Township as Number Nine Plantation.

NUTTER COVE. Unknown.

OAK: HILL (2), POINT MEADOW, POND (2). For oak trees.

OHIO BROOK. Mohawk: "large or beautiful river."

OLD: BULL, MAN. Fancifully named islands.

OLD HOUSE POINT. For an old house that stood there and was used as a landmark by fishermen.

OLD STREAM. For being used first to drive logs.

OLIVER LORD POINT. For Oliver Lord, first person to live there.

ORANGE: LAKE, RIVER. For the former designation of Whiting Township, Orangetown.

ORIE: LAKE, LAKE STREAM. For the local Orie family.

OTTER: BROOK, ISLAND, LAKE, POND, POINT. For otters.

OVERS: COVE, POINT. For Albert Over, a Negro who lived there.

OWL MOUNTAIN. Descriptive of resemblance.

OXBOW, THE. Descriptive of a bend in Chandler River.

OXBROOK: LOWER-LAKE, STREAM, UPPER-LAKE. Unknown.

OX COVE. For an ox that strayed on to the mud flats at low tide and became mired. When the tide came in, he drowned.

PAGE HILL. For Simon Page, who lived there.

PAGE ROCK. Unknown.

PALMER BROOK. (2). For the early Palmer families.

PARKER COVE. Unknown.

PARKER HEAD. (2). In Jonesport Township, probably for the Stephen Parker family, early settlers. In Steuben Township, for Squire Jonathon D. Parker, early owner and settler.

PARKER ISLAND. For Captain James Parker and his sons, Captain Isaac and Captain J.M.

PARRIT: COVE, POINT. For Samuel Parrit, who lived there.

PARTRIDGE ISLAND. Probably for partridges.

PASSAMAQUODDY BAY. Malecite: "pollock plenty place."

PATRICK LAKE. For a man named Patrick who drowned there.

PATTANGAL COVE. For Nathan Pattangal, settler, early 1800's.

PATTEN COVE. Probably for Joseph Patten, shipbuilder.

PATTEN HILL. For the Patten family who lived there.

PATTEN POND. For the David Patten family, settlers in 1850.

PATTINGILL RIDGE. Unknown.

PEABODY: BIG-ISLAND, LITTLE-ISLAND. Unknown.

PEA ISLAND. Descriptive of size.

PEAKED: MOUNTAIN (2), MOUNTAIN POND. Descriptive.

PEASELEY CORNERS. For J. Peaseley, resident, 1881.

PECKY BROOK. For John Peck, who owned land in the area.

PEEP LAKE. Unknown.

PEMBROKE: LITTLE-BROOK, STREAM. Unknown.

PEMBROKE: settlement, TOWNSHIP, WEST-. Named by Jerry Burgin for Pembroke, Wales.

PENKNIFE: BROOK, LAKES. For their open penknife shape.

PENMAN RIPS. Possibly a corruption of an Abnaki word: "extensive area covered by maple trees."

PENNAMAQUAN: LAKE, RIVER. Abnaki: "sloping ridge of maples."

PENNAMEN BROOK. See Penman Rips.

PERIO POINT. Unknown.

PERRY: NORTH-, settlement, TOWNSHIP. For Oliver H. Perry, a War of 1812 naval hero.

PETEGROW COVE. For G. Pettegrew, resident, 1881.

PETER DANA POINT. For a former chief of the Passamaquoddy tribe.

PETIT: MANAN ISLAND, MANAN POINT, MANAN REEF. Named by Champlain, for it reminded him of Grand Manan Island.

PETTEGROVE MOUNTAIN. For the Pettegrove family who lived there in 1881.

PETTEGROVE POINT. For Thomas Pettegrove, a settler by 1790.

PICKEREL: LAKE, LITTLE-POND, POND (2). For pickerel fish.

PIERCE ISLAND. For Pierce, its owner.

PIERSON LEDGE. Unknown.

PIGEON: HILL (2), HILL COVE, HILL (settlement). For pigeons.

PIG: ISLAND, ISLAND GUT. For use as a pig pen.

PIKE COVE. For pike fish.

PINE: CORNER, COVE, ISLAND (4), LAKE, LITTLE-ISLAND, POINT. For pine trees.

PINEO: BROOK, MOUNTAIN, MOUNTAINS, POINT (2). Mountain and Point in Cooper and Harrington townships, for the Pineo families. The others, unknown.

PINEO RIDGE. For Fred Pineo and his sons, who had a sawmill and lumberyard there.

PINES, THE. (2). For pine trees.

PINKHAM: BAY, ISLAND. For Richard and Tristram Pinkham, first settlers there and builders of a tidemill.

PIRATE HILL. Unknown.

PLANTATION NUMBER: FOURTEEN, TWENTY-ONE. For their number designations.

PLEASANT: BAY, BROOK, LAKE, LAKE RIDGE, MOUNTAIN, NORTH BRANCH-RIVER, POINT, RIVER (2), RIVER LAKE, WEST BRANCH-RIVER. Descriptive.

PLUMMER: ISLAND, LEDGE. For Moses Plummer, a settler by 1778.

POCOMOONSHINE: LAKE, MOUNTAIN. Folk etymology for Abnaki: "pok-wajan-i-tagook" — "stumps in the brook." But possibly an Abnaki-English blend meaning "pond as clear as moonshine."

POCUMCUS: LAKE, NARROWS. Micmac: "at the gravelly place."

POINT OF MAIN. Descriptive as a point of the mainland.

POINT RUTH. Unknown.

POMP ISLAND. For Pompey Norton, owner.

POND: COVE, COVE ISLAND, LAKE, POINT, RIDGE, THE-. Descriptive.

POOL, THE. Descriptive.

POPES FOLLY. For Pope, who, while drunk, fell over the steep cliff to his death.

POP ISLAND. Unknown.

POPPLESTONE: BEACH, COVE, LEDGES. For popplestones (small round stones).

PORCUPINES: HILL (2), ISLAND, LEDGES, MOUNTAIN (6), PINNACLE, THE-. For porcupines.

PORK BARREL LAKE. Unknown.

PORT HARBOR. Descriptive.

POSSUM LAKE. For o'possums.

POTATO: HOLE, POINT. Tradition says for a man carrying a load of potatoes in his canoe when it upset. He gathered up what he could find and buried them there.

POT: BIG-, HEAD, ROCK. For lobster pots, or traps.

POTTLE BROOK. For J.P. Pottle, resident, 1881.

PRATT POINT. Unknown.

PRESTON BROOK. For the local Preston family.

PRETTY POND. Descriptive.

PRINCE COVE. For Captain Prince, who lived there by 1799.

PRINCETON ISLAND. Unknown.

PRINCETON: settlement, SOUTH-, TOWNSHIP, WEST-. Named by Ebenezer Rolfe, the third settler, for his former home, Princeton, Massachusetts.

PROVOST: ISLAND, POINT. For Rod Provo, a German settler who bought the adjoining land.

PRUNE ISLAND. Probably descriptive of its shape.

PUBLIC LOT RIDGE. Set aside by the settlers as a public lot.

PUDDING BROOK. Descriptive of the consistency of its muddy water.

PUG: BROOK, HEATH, -HOLE MOUNTAIN, LAKE (2). Descriptive of small, round holes.

PULPIT ROCK. Descriptive of shape.

PUMPKIN RIDGE. Probably for pumpkin pine trees.

QUAKER HEAD. Unknown.

QUODDY: ROADS, settlement, WEST-HEAD. For a shortening of "Passamaquoddy": "pollock plenty place."

RACE POINT. For the Race family.

RAFT COVE. For men who placed cattle on rafts here and crossed the bay to other towns to sell them.

RAINEY BROOK. Unknown.

RAM: ISLAND (3), ISLAND LEDGE, LITTLE-ISLAND (2), OUTER-ISLAND. For use as sheep pens.

RAMSDELL COVE. For the Ramsdell family.

RANDALL: POINT, POINT FLATS. For L. Randall, who lived there in 1881.

RAND LAKE. For the local Rand family.

RASPBERRY ISLAND. For raspberries.

RAYS POINT. For the early Ray family.

RAZOR ISLAND. Unknown.

RED: BEACH, BEACH COVE, BEACH LANDING, COVE, POINT (2). Descriptive of color.

REDINGTON ISLAND. For the Redington family who owned it about 1871.

REDOUBT HILL. (2). For fortifications there.

REEF POINT. Descriptive.

REYNOLDS: BAY, BROOK, POINT. For the local Reynolds families.

RHINE POINT. For Patrick Ryan, a settler there from Ireland.

RICHARDSON BROOK. For the early Richardson family.

RIDGE. Descriptive.

RIM, THE. Descriptive.

RIPLEY: COVE, NECK, settlement. For the Ripley families.

ROARING: BROOK, LAKE. Descriptive.

ROBB HILL. For the Robb family who settled here before 1826.

ROBBINSTON: settlement, TOWNSHIP. For Nathaniel J. and Edward H. Robbins, grantees of the township.

ROBERTSON COVE. Unknown.

ROBINSON. Unknown.

ROCK: ISLAND (2), NORTH-. Descriptive.

ROCKY: BROOK (5), COVE, LAKE (3), LAKE RIDGE, LAKE STREAM, MEADOW, MEADOW BROOK, RIPS. Descriptive.

ROGERS ISLAND. Unknown.

ROGERS POINT. (2). In Pembroke Township, for Dr. John Rogers, a Civil War veteran. In Steuben Township, for Rogers, its owner and an early settler.

ROGUE LAKE. For smugglers, or "rogues," who used it as a hideout.

ROLFE: BROOK, BROOK POND, NORTH BRANCH-BROOK, SOUTH BRANCH-BROOK. Unknown.

ROLFE COVE. For the Ebenezer Rolfe family, settlers after 1815.

ROLFORD BROOK. Unknown.

ROQUE: BLUFFS (settlement), BLUFFS TOWNSHIP, ISLAND, ISLAND HARBOR, ISLAND LEDGE. The township was named by H.P. Garner of Boston, a summer resident, for nearby Roque Island. One source says the names were given because the area was a haven for smugglers, and it was formerly called "Rogues Bluff." Another source says that Champlain named the island St. Roch, and the present name is a corruption of that.

ROUND: COVE, ISLAND, ISLAND FLATS, LAKE (2), LAKE HILLS. Descriptive of shape.

RUNAWAY BOG. Unknown.

RUSH COVE. Unknown.

RUTH POINT. Unknown.

RYAN LAKE. For the early settling Ryan family.

RYE HILL. Unknown.

SAIL ROCK. A local pronunciation of "Seal Rock."

ST. CROIX: RIVER, ISLAND, JUNCTION. By Champlain, for the bay where the St. Croix and Waweig rivers enter and form a cross.

SALLY ISLAND. Probably for the Scilly Islands of southwest England.

SALMON: BROOK, POND. For salmon fish.

SAL SEAL ISLAND. For Sally Seeley.

SALT ISLAND. For salt stored there.

SAMADE BROOK. Unknown.

SAM HILL: BARRENS, BROOK, LAKE. For Samuel Hill, one of the 16 first settlers.

SANBORN: COVE, MARSH. Probably for John and William Sanborn, settlers about 1800.

SAND: BIG-BEACH, COVE (3), COVE NORTH, INNER-ISLAND, ISLAND, LEDGE, OUTER-ISLAND, RIVER BEACH, THE -BAR. Descriptive.

SANDS, THE. Descriptive.

SANDY: BROOK, COVE (2), POINT, RIVER. Descriptive.

SANFORD COVE. Unknown.

SAWDUST ISLAND. Descriptive, as there was once a mill there.

SAWTELLE HEATH. For the local Sawtelle family.

SAWYER: COVE, ISLAND (2), ROCK. Cove, Island, and Rock in Jonesport Township, for the John Sawyer family, settlers from Limington. Island in Addison Township, unknown.

SCABBY: ISLAND, ISLAND LEDGE. Descriptive of a small, worthless island.

SCHOONER BROOK. Lumber was floated down this brook to be loaded on timber schooners in the 1850's.

SCHOONER: COVE (2), POINT. Because schooners frequently harbored in the usually ice-free coves and many were beached for repairs.

SCOTCH ISLAND. Unknown.

SCOTT ARM. For Scott, who owned the land surrounding this arm of Meddybemps Lake.

SCOTT: BROOK (3), UPPER-BROOK. Brook and Upper-Brook in the Northfield Township area, possibly for the Samuel Scott family, settlers in 1770. Brook in T1R3, for Samuel Scott, first settler. (It is unknown if these are the same man.) The other, unknown.

SCOTTS BROOK. Unknown.

SCOW POINT. Unknown.

SCRUB ISLAND. Descriptive.

SEADUCK: POINT, ROCK. For seaducks.

SEAHORSE ROCK. At low tide, descriptive of its shape of a horse lying down.

SEALAND. Descriptive.

SEAL: COVE (3), LEDGE (3), ROCK. For seals.

SEASHORE: MOUNTAIN, LEDGE. Descriptive.

SEAVEY: BROOK (3), LAKE (2), LITTLE-LAKE, STREAM. Brook, Lake, Little-Lake, and Stream in Wesley Township, for the Seavey family. Brook in Crawford Township, for Edward Seavey, a settler by 1855. Brook in Codyville Township, for the Seavey family. Lake in Machias Township, possibly for the Captain Joseph Seavey family, settlers by 1770.

SEAVEY POINT. For the Seavey family, local fishermen.

SEAVEY RIDGE. For the Edward Seavey family, who settled nearby in 1855.

SEA WALL POINT. Descriptive.

SECOND LAKE. (2). Descriptive.

SEGUIN: ISLAND, LEDGE, PASSAGE. Abnaki: "a hump."

SEWARD NECK. For Soward, brickmaker.

SHABBIT: ISLAND, ISLAND LEDGE. Misunderstanding for "Shabby Island," descriptive.

SHACKFORD: HEAD, LEDGE. For the John Shackford family, settlers by 1784.

SHAG: ISLAND, LEDGE, ROCK. For shags (cormorants).

SHATTUCK LAKE. For the Shattuck family who lived on the Calais side of the lake.

SHAW: LAKE, MEADOW. For the local Shaw families.

SHAW POINT. For Howard Shaw, early settler.

SHEDRAKE ISLAND. For sheldrakes.

SHEEP: COVE, EAST-ISLAND, ISLAND (2), LEDGE, LITTLE-ISLAND. Because they were used as sheep pens.

SHERB BROOK. A shortened form of "Sherburn," a Negro family living there by 1790.

SHINY LAKE. Descriptive.

SHIP: BIG-ISLAND, ISLAND, ISLAND HOLE, LITTLE-ISLAND. Island and Island Hole in Brookton Township, because the island had 2 tall pines like the masts of a ship. Big-Island and Little-Island in T43MD, descriptive of their shape.

SHIPSTERN ISLAND. Descriptive of shape.

SHIPYARD COVE. Because ships were built and repaired there.

SHOPPEE: ISLAND, POINT. For a Scotchman, Anthony Shoppee, who fought on both sides in the American Revolution.

SHOREY BROOK. Unknown.

SILVER PUG LAKE. Descriptive of a small sunken lake.

SIMON POND. For Simon Cross.

SIMPSON ISLAND. For the Simpson family who owned a lumber shipping outlet.

SIMQUISH: BROOK, LAKE, LITTLE-BROOK. Abnaki: "dip up a drink."

SINCLAIR BROOK. Unknown.

SIPP: BAY, BROOK. For a Negro, Scipio Dutton, nicknamed "Sipp," who drowned in the bay.

SIX MILE LAKE. For its location 6 miles from Machias.

SIXTEENTH STREAM. Unknown.

SLATE: ISLAND, ISLAND COVE. Descriptive.

SLEWGUNDY RIDGE. Unknown.

SMALLS ISLAND. For A. and H. Small, residents, 1881.

SMELT BROOK. (2). For smelt fish.

SMITH COVE. (2). In Milbridge Township, unknown. In Plantation Number Fourteen, for Smith, a lumberman.

SMITH LANDING. Probably for the Turner Smith family, settlers about 1825.

SMITH MEADOW BROOK. For Moses Smith, a settler after 1815.

SMITH MILL PITCH. For the nearby mill owned by the Smith family.

SMITH: POINT (2), ROCK. For the many area Smith families.

SNARE CREEK. For moose snares set there by Elihu Norton, a moosehunter.

SNOW MOUNTAIN. For Major Reuben Snow, prominent citizen of Danforth Township about 1830.

SNOWS ROCKS. Unknown.

SODDY MEADOW BROOK. For the Thody family who homesteaded there.

SOUTH: BAY, BROOK, MOUNTAIN, -WEST BREAKER, -WEST BROOK, -WEST BLUFF, -WEST CREEK, -WEST POND. Descriptive.

SPAR ISLAND. Descriptive of shape.

SPEARING BROOK. One source says for a Spearing family that lived there. Another says for the Indians who speared fish there.

SPECTACLE: ISLAND, ISLANDS, LAKES. Descriptive of eyeglass shape.

SPEDNICK: FALLS, MOUNTAIN. Abnaki: "visible, but shut in by mountains."

SPEDNIK LAKE. See Spednick.

SPINNEY COVE. For Horatio N. Spinney, early settler.

SPIRIT BROOK. For an incident in which a resident, many years ago, was walking by and claimed that he saw a ghost here.

SPLINTER BROOK. Descriptive of being a splinter of Dead Stream.

SPLIT HILL. Descriptive.

SPOONER POINT. For the local Spooner family.

SPRAGUE MEADOW BROOK. For Abial Sprague, settler, early 1800's.

SPRAGUE: NECK, NECK BAR. For the local Sprague family.

SPRING: BROOK, COVE. Descriptive.

SPRINGY: BIG-, LITTLE-BROOK. Descriptive.

SPRUCE: COVE, LITTLE-ISLAND, MOUNTAIN (2), MOUNTAIN COVE, MOUNTAIN LAKE, MOUNTAIN LAKE BROOK, POINT, POINT COVE. For spruce trees.

SQUAW CAP. Descriptive of shape.

SQUAW ISLAND. Unknown.

SQUIRE: POINT, POINT LEDGE. The local pronunciation of "square."

SQUIRREL POINT. For squirrels.

STANHOPE MEADOW. Unknown.

STANLEY: COVE, LEDGE, POINT. For the local Stanley families.

STAPLE RIDGE. Cartographical error for Sable Ridge, for sables, or martins.

STAPLES: COVE, MOUNTAIN. Unknown.

STARBOARD: COVE, CREEK ISLAND, ISLAND BAR, ISLAND LEDGE, settlement. A nautical term meaning "on the right."

STEAMBOAT COVE. Where a steamboat used to be seen in log-driving days.

STEELE POINT. For the local Steele family.

STEELS HARBOR ISLAND. For the Steele family.

STETSON MOUNTAIN. Probably for the Stetson family of Bangor who owned land in the area.

STEUBEN: EAST-, HARBOR, settlement, TOWNSHIP. For Baron Steuben, German officer who aided the U.S. in the Revolutionary War.

STEVENS COVE. For the local Stevens family.

STEVENS ISLAND. For Edmund Stevens, settler by 1778.

STINKING JAM RAPIDS. An area which always caused bad log jams. Because of the frustration of the drivers, they referred to the rapids as the "stinking jam."

STODDARD RIPS. For Stoddard, lumberman who camped here.

STONE HILL. For the local Stone family.

STONE: ISLAND (2), ISLAND LEDGE. Descriptive.

STONY BROOK. (2). Descriptive.

STOVERS COVE. For N. Stover, resident, 1881.

STROUT: ISLAND, ISLAND LEDGES, ISLAND NARROWS, POINT. For the early settling Strout families.

STUART BROOK. Unknown.

SUCKER: BROOK, LAKE. For sucker fish.

SUGAR HILL. For maple sugar operations there.

SUMAC HILL. For sumac.

SUNKEN: LAKE, STREAM. Descriptive.

SUSSIE HILL. For Joe Sussie.

SWEET: BROOK, CHOPPING RIDGE, COVE. For the Sweet family.

SYLVAN PARK. One source says for Sylvanus Scott, who was chosen ensign in the first Machias militia, which was founded in 1769. Others say that it is simply Latin for "woods."

TALBOT COVE. Unknown.

TALBOT RIDGE. For J. Talbot, resident, 1881.

TALMADGE TOWNSHIP. For Benjamin Talmadge, who purchased it in 1804.

TANGLE BROOK. Descriptive of the brush in the area.

TAYLOR: BROOK (3), BROOK POND. Brook and Brook Pond in T18MD, for Taylor, a lumberman. Brook in Pembroke Township, for the numerous Taylor family. Brook in Codyville Township, unknown.

TAYLOR ISLAND. Unknown.

TAYLOR POINT. For many Taylors in the area in 1881.

TENNEY BROOK. For the Tinny family, who settled by 1790.

TENNY COVE. Unknown.

THAYER LEDGES. Unknown.

THIRTY-FIVE RIDGE. For township T35MD.

THOMPSON BROOK. Unknown.

THORNTON: POINT, POINT LEDGE. For D. Thornton, resident by 1880.

THOROFARE: passage, THE-. Descriptive.

THOROUGHFARE. Descriptive.

THREE: BROOK, BROOK COVE, FALLS HARBOR, FALLS POINT. Descriptive.

TIBBETTS RIDGE. Unknown.

TIBBITTSTOWN. For the Tibbitts family who settled there by 1790 and multiplied.

TIDE MILL CREEK. For a tidemill.

TIERNEY POINT. For Tierney, a logger who died there.

TIMBER COVE. (2). Descriptive.

TIMMY POINT. Unknown.

TODD HEAD. Unknown.

TODD ISLAND. For Todd, a lumberman.

TODD POINT. For William Todd, early settler.

TOMAH: flagstation, LAKE, LITTLE-LAKE, LITTLE-STREAM, MOUNTAIN, RIDGE, STREAM. For the Abnaki chief Tomah. The word means "deep."

TOMMYS ISLAND. Unknown.

TOMS ISLAND. Unknown.

TONGUE POINT. Descriptive of a projection of land.

TOPSFIELD: settlement, TOWNSHIP. For Topsfield, Massachusetts, former home of its first settler, Nehemiah Kneeland.

TOWERS BROOK. Unknown.

TOWNSHIP ROCK. For location where the boundary lines of Cutler, Machias, and Whiting divide.

TRACY CORNERS. For John Tracy, early settler.

TRACY MOUNTAIN. For W. Tracy, resident, 1881.

TRAFTON: ISLAND, ISLAND LEDGE. For the Trafton family.

TRAFTON ROCK. Unknown.

TREASURE ISLAND. By a Mrs. Lydie, for no reason.

TREAT ISLAND. For Treat, who had a fish business here and built a homemade railroad to make the handling of his products easier.

TRESCOTT: NORTH-, SOUTH-, TOWNSHIP. For Major Lemuel Trescott, Revolutionary War veteran and prominent citizen of Washington County.

TRIMBLE MOUNTAIN. Unknown.

TROUT: BROOK (2), LAKE (2), LAKE RIDGE, LAKE STREAM. For trout fish.

TUG MOUNTAIN. Abnaki: "tree" or "river."

TUMBLEDOWN DICK HEAD. Although there are several variations of the story, the main one is that Dick Farnsworth was chasing sheep along the side of a steep cliff when he fell over the side. He died a few days later. Another variation is that a ram named Dick fell off the cliff and was killed.

TUNK STREAM. An early family invited a group of men to dinner at which they served a meat stew with soft bread dumplings called "doeboys." On the table were more doeboys as a side dish. When the meal was over, one of the men asked the host what they were going to do with the leftover doeboys. "This," he said as he hurled one at him. Soon all the men were throwing doeboys at each other, and when they missed, they hit the wall with a "tunk." Noticing the sound, when the men wanted a particular person hit, they shouted, "Tunk him." In remembrance of the battle they referred to the area as "Tunk." Naturally, this is quite possibly folk-etymology. There is a possibility that the word is Abnaki: "principal," or "large swift stream."

TUNNEL RIPS. Unknown.

TURNER: HILL, POINT. For the early Turner family.

TWENTY-EIGHT POND. For township T28MD.

TWO HOUR ROCK. For being located 2 hours from Lubec by boat in the early days.

TWO MILE CURVE. For its location about 2 miles from Danforth.

TYLER RIPS. For John Tyler.

UNCLE SAM COVE. Unknown.

UNIONVILLE. For the union of 3 roads.

UNKNOWN POND. Descriptive of a pond with no name.

UPPER LEDGE. Descriptive.

VALS POINT. Unknown.

VANCEBORO: settlement, TOWNSHIP. For William Vance, landholder in Baring Township.

VANCE MOUNTAIN. See Vanceboro.

VENTURE BROOK. A small brook, where, against the advice of others, a lumberman said he would "venture" floating logs.

VICKERY: BROOK, NORTH BRANCH-BROOK, SOUTH BRANCH-BROOK. For Vickery, a lumberman who had camps in the area.

VINING LAKE. For the Vining family.

VIRGIN ISLAND. Fancifully named.

VIRGINS BREASTS. Descriptive of two rocks near Virgin Island. Nearby is another small rock called the "Nipple."

VOSE POND. For Thomas Vose and his later family.

WABASSUS: LAKE, MOUNTAIN. Malecite: "torchlight," or "shining."

WAITE: settlement, TOWNSHIP. For Benjamin Waite, Calais lumberman.

WALKER: BROOK, COVE. For Walker, a farmer.

WALLACE COVE. For J. Wallace, resident, 1881.

WALLACE LEDGE. Unknown.

WALLACE POINT. For the local Wallace family.

WALLAMATOGUE: BIG-STREAM, LITTLE-STREAM. Abnaki: "coves in little river."

WALLS HILL. For George and Frank Walls, who cleared the hill about 1880.

WAPSACONHAGAN BROOK. Abnaki: "white rocks portage." The Indians tell a legend that implies that this was not a canoe portage, but the actual carrying of the white rocks. During the Revolution, the English would not let them go down the St. Croix River, so one night they took all the rocks out of the brook and cleared a passage to Pocomoonshine Lake, and then used the East Machias River instead of the St. Croix.

WARREN MEADOWS. Unknown.

WASHINGTON: BALD MOUNTAIN, COUNTY. For General George Washington.

WASS: LOWER-COVE, POINT (2), UPPER-COVE. Lower-Cove, Point, and Upper-Cove in Harrington Township, for Wilmot Wass, nearby resident, late 1800's. Point in Addison Township, for David Wass, settler, 1778.

WATER ISLAND. Where ships stopped for fresh water.

WATTS COVE. For the early Watts family.

WEBBER BOG. For the local Webber family.

WEBSTER BROOK. For Webster, a lumberman.

WEIR COVE. For herring weirs.

WESLEY: settlement, TOWNSHIP. For John Wesley, founder of the Methodist Church.

WESTERN: BAY, HEAD, LAKE, PASSAGE, POND, RIVER, STREAM. Descriptive.

WHALEBACK: COVE, ridge. Descriptive of a ridge or a ledge.

WHALE LEDGE. Descriptive of shape.

WHITE BIRCH ISLAND. For white birch trees.

WHITE CREEK. For the White family.

WHITEHORSE POINT. Descriptive of a white outcropping of rock.

WHITE ISLAND. For Nicholas White, who lived there before 1800.

WHITES POINT. Probably for Benjamin White, early settler.

WHITING BAY. Probably for Jonathon Whiting, a settler about 1771.

WHITING: settlement, TOWNSHIP. For Timothy Whiting, early settler.

WHITLOCKS MILL. For the Whitlock family, owners.

WHITNEY: COVE, COVE MOUNTAIN. Unknown.

WHITNEYVILLE: settlement, TOWNSHIP. For Colonel Joseph Whitney of Calais, who built a dam on the river and established a mill.

WHITTAKER PARRITT STREAM. For Whittaker Parritt, resident, 1800's.

WIDOWS LEDGE. A fanciful name for a shallow, dangerous ledge.

WIGGINS BROOK. Unknown.

WIGWAM RAPIDS. For Indian camps located there. Also Micmac: "at the head," as the Indians viewed streams in sections, and this is near the head of the Machias River.

WIGWAM RIFFLES. For Indian camps located there.

WILBER POINT. For J. Wilbur, resident, 1881.

WILBUR NECK. For the local Wilbur family.

WILLARD POINT. For Willard Ash, who drowned here.

WILLOW BROOK. For willow trees.

WILMOT COVE. For Wilmot Wass.

WILSON LEDGES. Unknown.

WILSON STREAM. For the son of Captain Robert Wilson, who fought with General Wolfe in Quebec in 1759.

WINGDAM ISLAND. For a dam that extended from the American side of the St. Croix River to the island in log-driving days. Its wing angled toward the Canadian side.

WINTER HARBOR. For log drivers who used to put out log booms during storms in the winter.

WITCHER BROOK. Unknown.

WOHOA BAY. For a cry used by fishermen lost in the fog to let other boats know their position.

WOODCOCK BROOK. For woodcocks.

WOODLAND: JUNCTION, settlement. Descriptive of their location.

WOOD: POND COVE, POINT. For woods.

WOODRUFF: COVE, MOUNTAIN. For W. Woodruff, resident, 1881.

WOODWARD POINT. For S.H. Woodward, resident, 1881.

WORMELL LEDGES. For E. and M.W. Wormell, who had adjoining property in 1880.

WRIGHT POINT. For the Wright family.

WYMAN. For the early Wyman family.

WYMAN BROOK. For Wyman, a lumberman who camped there.

YATES POINT. For the local Yates family.

YEATON: COVE, POINT. For Captain John Yeaton, who lived near the cove.

YELLOWBIRCH MOUNTAIN. For yellow birch trees.

YELLOWHEAD. Descriptive.

YOHO: CREEK, HEAD. For fishermen who yelled to give the position of their boats in the fog.

YOUNGS COVE. Probably for the transient Young family who lived there a short time.

YOUNGS POINT. Unknown.

YOUNG SIDING. For the Cyrus Young family, settlers in 1810.

YORK COUNTY

ABBOTT: BROOK, HILL. For Thomas Abbott, who built a garrison house there about 1690.

ABBOTT MOUNTAIN. For Jacob, Lorenzo, Wesley, and Horace Abbott, farmers in the area in the 1800's.

ACTON: RIDGE, settlement, SOUTH-, TOWNSHIP. For Acton, England, a town which is now a part of London.

ADAMS BROOK. Probably for Christopher Adams, settler, 1682.

ADAMS CORNER. For Nathanial Adams, schoolmaster, 1750's.

ADLINGTON: CREEK, HILL. For T. Addington, resident, 1872.

ADMIRALTY VILLAGE. For its connection with the United States sea services.

AGAMENTICUS: MOUNT-, STATION, VILLAGE. Abnaki: "the other side of the little river."

ALEWIFE: POND, settlement. For alewives.

ALFRED: MILLS, NORTH-, settlement, TOWNSHIP. For King Alfred the Great, 9th century king of England.

ALLEN HILL. For Robert Allen, who settled on 100 acres in 1743.

APPLEDORE ISLAND. For Appledore, England.

ARGO POINT. For the privateer "Argo," a ship of 18 guns, commanded by Richard Trevett, which was wrecked here.

ARUNDEL: CAPE-, settlement, SWAMP, TOWNSHIP. For Lord Arundel, Earl of Warder, of England.

BACK BAY. Descriptive of a section of a tidal flat known as "The Pool."

BACK BROOK. A shortening of its previous name "Whaleback Brook," which, in turn, was named for a nearby ridge.

BACK CREEK. For its location back from the ocean.

BADGERS ISLAND. For William Badger, who built ships there.

BALCH POND. Unknown.

BALD: HEAD, HEAD CLIFF, HILL, HILL CROSSING. Descriptive.

BANKS ROCK. For nearby property owned by Richard Banks.

BARKER POND. For a man named Barker who ran a mill there.

BAR MILLS. For a series of lumber mills set up near a land bar in the river in the 1700's.

BARN POINT. For a barn located there.

BARRELLS MILLPOND. For Jonathon Sayward Barrell, who inherited the mill there in 1793.

BARTER CREEK. For Henry Barter, resident during the late 1600's.

BARTLETT: BROOK, POND. For Benjamin Bartlett, settler, 1785.

BARTLETT HILL. Unknown.

BARTLETT MILLS. For Oliver Bartlett, who owned a gristmill there and a bakery business in Kennebunk in the 1830's.

BASKET ISLAND. For thatch gathered there by the Indians and early settlers for making baskets.

BASS ISLAND. For Peter Bass, to whom it was granted for helping settle the Indian unrest of the 1690's.

BATSON RIVER. For Stephen Batson, nearby landowner in 1642.

BAUNEG BEG: MOUNTAIN, POND. Abnaki: "at the spread out lake."

BAY VIEW. Descriptive.

BEACH ISLAND. For its location near Fortunes Rocks Beach.

BEACON CORNER. For a flashing air line beacon once placed there.

BEAR HILL. If originally "bear" for the area bears. If a corruption of "Bean Hill," for Jonathon Bean, who set up a blockhouse here in 1783.

BEAVER: DAM, DAM BROOK, DAM HEATH, DAM POND, HILL, HILL POND, POND. For beavers.

BEDELL CROSSING. For Robert Bedell, land grantee, 1641.

BEECH RIDGE. (2). For beech trees.

BELL MARSH. For Ann Bell, first wife of Sir Ferdinando Gorges.

BENNETT BROOK. For William Bennett, resident, 1872.

BENSON BROOK. For John Benson and his son James, settlers about 1780.

BERRY HILL. For Ambrose Berry, a farmer in 1636.

BERWICK: NORTH-(settlement), NORTH-TOWNSHIP, settlement, TOWNSHIP, SOUTH-(settlement), SOUTH-TOWNSHIP, TOWN-SHIP. For Berwick, Dorsetshire, England.

BIBB ROCK. For its fancied resemblance to a "bibb," or a bracket which supports the trestle trees on a ship's mast. Another source says a bibb was once found there.

BICKFORD HILL. For George Bickford, schoolteacher, 1778.

BIDDEFORD: POOL, settlement, TOWNSHIP. Named for Bideford, Devonshire, England, by early immigrants.

BIG BRIDGE HILL. For a big bridge over Josiahs River.

BIG LEDGE. Descriptive.

BIRCH KNOLL. Descriptive.

BLACKBERRY HILL. For its blackberry vines.

BLACK BROOK. For Josiah Black, a settler of the 1790's.

BLACK POND. Descriptive.

BLACKSMITH BROOK. For a blacksmith shop located nearby.

BLAISDELL CORNERS. For the Blaisdell family, one of the first group of settlers in 1746.

BLAISDELL POND. For Ralph Blaisdell, who lived in the area in the 1600's.

BLOWING CAVE. Descriptive of the noise made by the cave at high tide.

BLUFF ISLAND. Descriptive.

BOG BROOK. Descriptive.

BOLT HILL. Probably the site of a former "bolting" or gristmill.

BOND MOUNTAIN. For W. Bond, resident, 1872.

BONNEY EAGLE. Tradition says that a scotchman was crossing a bridge when he met another man. As an eagle flew over them, the Scotchman said, "See the bonnie eagle."

BOON ISLAND. Named by the men of the wrecked ship "Increase," who were said to have considered their salvation here a great "boon" from God.

BOOTHBAY PARK. For S. and S.G. Boothby, residents, 1872.

BOULTER POND. For Geroge Boulter, member of the Kittery Water District, when the pond was created in 1950.

BOYD: BROOK, CORNER. For S. Boyd, resident, 1872.

BOYD POND. For Reverend David Boyd, a prominent citizen and teacher at Limington Academy in the early 1800's and a representative to the General Court of Massachusetts.

BOYNTON BROOK. For Richard Boynton, who owned the area land in 1631.

BRACEYS SWAMP. For John Bracey, an English settler of about 1673.

BRACKETT HILL. Possibly for the Joshua Brackett family, settlers of about 1778.

BRACKETTS POINT. Unknown.

BRAEBURN. For the Braeburn Country Club of Massachusetts.

BRAGDON BROOK. For J.M. Bragdon, resident, 1872.

BRAGDON ISLAND. For the Arthur Bragdon family, early settlers.

BRANCH BROOK. (3). Descriptive.

BRAVE BOAT HARBOR. Since it is shallow and difficult to enter at low tide, it would take a "brave boat" to enter. Another source says "brave" here has the obsolete meaning of "good."

BRICKFORD ISLAND. For Samuel Brickford, owner about 1760.

BRIDGES SWAMP. For Samuel Bridges and family, settlers about 1750.

BRIGGS CORNER. For H.D. Briggs, resident, 1872.

BRILEY: BROOK, POND. For Joseph Briley, who cut ice there.

BRIMSTONE POND. This pond was formed by the merger of three other ponds, one of which was fed by a sulphur spring, or "brimstone" spring.

BRIXHAM: LOWER CORNERS, UPPER CORNERS. Named by John Frost for his former home, Brixham, England, in 1678.

BROWN BROOK. For Clement Brown, a settler by the 1790's.

BROWN HILL. For William and W. Brown, residents, 1872.

BUCKLIN ROCK. One source says the name is descriptive of its shape—corruption of "buckling."

BUFF BROOK. Unknown.

BUFFUM HILL. For the Buffam family who ran a mill nearby.

BUMPKIN ISLAND. One source says it was first called Bunker Island for a man of that name; then it was corrupted to Bucking Island, then to the present. Another source states that only a "bumpkin" would attempt to land on it.

BUNGANUT POND. Abnaki: "at the boundary mark."

BUSH BROOK. Descriptive.

BUXTON: CENTER, settlement, SOUTH-, TOWNSHIP, WEST-. Named by Dr. Paul Coffin, for his former home of Buxton, England.

CAMP ELLIS. For Thomas B. Ellis, settler of the 1800's.

CANNON HILL. Named in 1836 when cannons were part of the local artillery company. The hill served as a military lookout post.

CAPE ISLAND. For being the outermost island that forms Cape Porpoise.

CAPE NEDDICK: cape, HARBOR, NUBBLE, RIVER, settlement. Micmac: "solitary," for the nubble that stands alone.

CAPE PORPOISE: cape, HARBOR, settlement. Some say for porpoises. Another source states it could be Abnaki: "stopped up," with islands.

CAPE ROCK. For its location at Cape Porpoise.

CARLISLE BROOK. For the nearby Carlisle family homestead.

CARLL BRANCH. For S.S. Carll, resident, 1872.

CASCADE FALLS BROOK. Descriptive.

CAT MOUNTAIN. For wildcats.

CEDAR: ISLAND, MOUNTAIN. For cedar trees.

CHAMPION POND. For James Champion, settler of 1785.

CHANDLER POINT. For Thomas Chandler, settler of the 1840's.

CHARLES CHASE CORNER. One source says for Charles Chase Littlefield. Another says for Charles Chase, early settler.

CHASE POINT. For Amos Chase, who ran a nearby ferry in 1753.

CHASES: POND, settlement. For Josiah Chase, who used it as a source of power for his woolen mill in 1768.

CHAUNCEY CREEK. For Charles Chauncey, early resident.

CHELLIS BROOK. For S. Chellis, resident, 1872.

CHICKERING CREEK. For the Chickering family who lived there in 1872.

CHICKS BROOK. For Moses Chick, one of the founders of a Baptist group in 1791.

CHICOPEE. Nipmuck: "cedar trees."

CHURCHILL HILL. For Major Thomas Churchill, a settler of the 1700's.

CIDER: HILL CREEK, MILL POND. For its use as water power for making cider.

CLARK MOUNTAIN. (2). In Cornish Township, for Benjamin

Clark, a settler of the 1790's. In Limerick Township, for Pennel Clark, a settler in the early 1780's.

CLARKS ISLAND. Unknown.

CLARKS MILLS. For Aaron Clark, woolen manufacturer of the 1830's.

CLAY: HILL, HILL BROOK. For clay pits.

CLEAVES COVE. For H. Cleaves, resident, 1872.

CLOCK FARM CORNER. For a tower clock located in a barn at this corner.

COCKLE HILL. For cockles, variety of weed.

COFFIN BROOK. For E. Coffin, resident, 1872.

COLD WATER BROOK. Descriptive.

COLES HILL. For William Coles, one of the first settlers in Wells Township.

COLLOMY HILL. For the Collomy family, settlers of the 1830's.

CONANT BROOK. For C. Conant, resident 1856.

CONCORDVILLE. Major Samuel Derby's home of Concord, Massachusetts and his service at the Battle of Concord are remembered in this name.

COOKS BROOK. For Caleb Cook, early settler.

COOPERS CORNERS. For George J. Cooper, who built a garage at the corners in 1923-24 and operated it for years.

CORNISH: settlement, TOWNSHIP. For Cornwall, near Devonshire, England.

COW ISLAND. For the cows that were ferried here for grazing.

COWS BEACH POINT. For the cows that grazed here on the Norwood farm in the 1640's.

COX POND. For the early Wilcox family.

COZY CORNERS. For a restaurant by that name that was located here.

CRAMS CORNER. For E.H. Cram, resident, 1872.

CRANBERRY: MEADOW. SWAMP. For cranberry bogs.

CRESCENT: BEACH, SURF. Descriptive of shape.

CROCKETT BROOK. For Joseph Crockett, who lived nearby in the 1830's.

CROCKETTS: BROOK, NECK. For Thomas Crockett, settler in 1630.

CROW: HILL, SWAMP. For crows.

CUMMINGS HILL. For Cummings, owner of a shoe factory and workers' homes in the area.

CURTIS COVE. For William Curtis, resident, 1872.

CURTIS POND. For William Curtis, settler, 1739.

CUTTS: ISLAND, POND, RIDGE, RIDGE BROOK, settlement. For John, Robert, and Richard Cutts, brothers from Wales in the 1600's.

DANSBURY REEF. Unknown.

DAVIS BROOK. For Ichabod Davis, who lived near in 1872.

DAVIS POND. For the early Davis family.

DAY BROOK. For the Day family, early settlers.

DAY HILL. For Nathaniel, William, and Stephen Day, settlers in the 1790's.

DAYS MILLS. For C. Day, resident, 1872.

DAYTON TOWNSHIP. For Jonathon Dayton, youngest member of the Constitutional Convention and Speaker of the House of Representatives.

DEARBORN MOUNTAIN. For Jeremiah Dearborn, settler, 1794.

DEEP BROOK. Descriptive.

DEERING BROOK. For Deacon Rufus Deering, who taught school in Buxton in the 1770's, and later established a lumber business in Portland.

DEERING POND. For Gideon, John and William Deering, who owned the surrounding land.

DEERING RIDGE. For William Deering, who owned the farm here in 1770.

DEERINGS POND. For L. Deering, resident, 1872.

DEER POND. For deer.

DENNETT BROOK. (2). In South Berwick Township, for the Dennett family who lived on its banks. In Saco Township, for the descendants of the Samuel Dennett family, settlers in 1738.

DEPOT STATION. For Wells Beach Station on the Boston & Maine Railroad.

DIAMOND HILL. Unknown.

DOG BROOK. for the numerous dogs that ran there.

DOLES POND. For Loring Dole, who lived nearby in the 1890's.

DOLLAR POND. Descriptive of its round shape.

DOLLY GORDON BROOK. For the daughter of Robert Gordon.

DOVER BLUFF. For people from Dover, New Hampshire, who had cottages there.

DRAKES: ISLAND, ISLAND BEACH. For Robert Drake, owner of the island and veteran of the Revolutionary War.

DREW POND. For Elijah Drew, settler, 1780.

DRISCOLL BROOK. For the Driscoll family who lived there in 1872.

DUCK: BROOK, ISLAND, POND. For ducks.

DUNGEON BROOK. This was the place where the early settlers punished the wrongdoers of their society.

EAGLE: ISLAND, POINT. For eagles.

EASTERN ROCKS. Descriptive.

EAST OUTLET. For the east outlet of Kennebunk Pond.

EAST POINT. (2). In York Township, for being the eastern most point of York Harbor. In Biddeford, for being the easternmost point in Biddeford Township.

ELIOT: EAST-, settlement, SOUTH-, TOWNSHIP. For Robert Eliot of Kittery Township, member of the Provincial Council of New Hampshire.

ELMS. For elm trees.

EMERSON BROOK. For Captain Luther Emerson, settler, 1814.

EMERY MILLS. For Simon Emery, owner of the sawmill prior to 1775.

EMERYS BRIDGE. (settlement). For Job Emery, resident, 1694.

EMERYS CORNER. For James Emery, settler, 1783.

EMORY CORNER. For James Emery, French and Indian War soldier, who owned the land in 1757.

ESTES: BROOK, HILL. For Reverend Sumner Estes, minister and druggist in the 1870's.

ESTES LAKE. For Benjamin Estes, settler, 1780.

ETHERINGTON POND. For the Etherington family who owned it.

FACTORY ISLAND. For the Blackman mill located there in the 1800's.

FAIRFIELD HILL. For John Fairfield of Lovell's War fame.

FALLS RIVER. Descriptive.

FELCH CORNER. For the first permanent settler of Limerick Township, Abijah Felch, who came in 1771.

FENDERSON BROOK. For John Fenderson, Revolutionary War veteran and aid-de-camp to Lafayette, who settled in 1795.

FERGUSON BROOK. Probably for the Alexander Ferguson family, settlers of 1673.

FERNALD BROOK. For J. Fernald, resident, 1872.

FERNALD SHORE. (settlement). For J. Fernald, resident, 1872.

FERRY BEACH. For a former ferry that ran from here.

FISHERMANS COVE. For fishermen.

FISHING ISLAND. For fishing operations in the area.

FISHING: ROCK, LITTLE-ROCK. For good fishing there.

FIVE CORNERS. For the crossing of roads to create 5 corners.

FLETCHER NECK. For Pendleton Fletcher, settler, 1680.

FLOWAGE, THE. Descriptive of a section of the Little Ossipee River.

FOGG BROOK. For Fogg Hill in Cumberland County.

FOLSOM POND. Unknown.

FOLLY ISLAND. There were two harbors at Cape Porpoise. One was Stage Island Harbor, and it was used first by the settlers. A decision was made to use the other harbor, and some felt that this was a "folly." The island is in the harbor area. Another source says that a "make gold from seawater" scheme was operated there and shares were sold. The idea, of course, was a "folly."

FOLLY POND. For a mill built there in 1680 which proved to be a failure.

FORISTALL CORNERS. For the Foristall family who lived there in the 1600's.

FORT HILL. For Fort Mary, which was there during King William's War in the 1690's.

FORT RIDGE. For a structure, not a fort, built there to load and unload logs on a sharp turn on the ridge. It resembled a fort to the settlers.

FORTUNES: ROCKS, ROCKS BEACH, ROCKS COVE. Named as a good luck omen by the settlers.

FORTY ACRE HILL. The hill supposedly covers 40 acres.

FOSS PONDS. For Job and John Foss, who lived here by the 1790's.

FOUR CORNERS. Crossroads form 4 corners.

FOXWELL BROOK. For Richard Foxwell, settler, 1636.

FRANKFORT ISLAND. One source says at a distance the island resembles a fort. The "Frank" part of the word is unknown.

FROST BROOK. For Deacon John Frost, settler, 1784.

FROST HILL. For Nicholas Frost, chosen to lay out a boundary between York and Wells Township. Others say for Charles Frost, settler, 1675.

FULLER BROOK. Unknown.

GERRISH ISLAND. For Timothy Gerrish, who purchased it on February 10, 1709.

GERRY COVE. For the Gerry family, residents, 1872.

GERRISH MOUNTAIN. For Nathan Gerrish, a settler of the early 1800's.

GILE MOUNTAIN. For D. and S. Gile, residents, 1872.

GOAT ISLAND. While there is no record of this island being so used, settlers along the Maine coast frequently kept goats and other animals on small islands as natural pens.

GODFREYS: COVE, POND. For the wife of Edward Godfrey Anna, who owned the land.

GOFF MILL BROOK. For Colonel Edmund Goff's mill, located here by 1735.

GOOCHS BEACH. For the John Gooch family, settlers of 1663.

GOODALL BROOK. For Ernest Goodall, who developed the area as a park.

GOODRICH POINT. Unknown.

GOODWINS MILLS. For Nathaniel Goodwin, who built the first mill here in 1787.

GOOSEBERRY ISLAND. (2). For gooseberries.

GOOSE: EAST-ROCKS, POND, ROCKS BEACH, WEST-ROCKS. For geese.

GOOSEFARE: BAY, BROOK, HILL. A place where geese flocked.

GORDON POINT. For E. Gordon, resident, 1872.

GOSPORT HARBOR. For Gosport in New Hampshire.

GOULD CORNER. For Benjamin Gould, whose house was selected as a garrison in 1722.

GOULDS ROCKS. Unknown.

GRANITE POINT. For granite rocks.

GRANNY KENT POND. For an old lady of the Kent family who lived nearby before 1782.

GRANT BROOK. For James Grant, selectman, 1713.

GRANT HILL. For G.W. Grant, resident, 1872.

GRAYS CORNER. For J. Gray, resident, 1872.

GRAYS POINT. Probably for Captain John Gray and family, settlers of about 1760.

GREAT: BROOK (2), CREEK, EAST LAKE, HILL (3), POND. Descriptive.

GREAT: WORKS, WORKS RIVER. For all the factories, or "great works," built along its banks to use the water for power, but primarily for a mill containing 18 saws erected by Richard Leader in the 1600's.

GREEN BROOK. For S. Green, resident, 1872.

GREEN ISLAND. For its owner Benjamin Green, Chief Justice of the Court of Common Pleas in the 1790's.

GRIST MILL POND. For a gristmill located there.

GROUNDNUT HILL. For the orange-red lily, the bulb of which the Indians used for food.

GROVEVILLE. Unknown.

GUINEA CORNER. A trading center where many "guineas" (early coins) changed hands.

GULF HILL. One source says that the Gulf of Maine can be seen from its summit. Another says for a deep depression, or "gulf," nearby.

GUPTILL HILL. For H. Guptill, resident, 1872.

HALEY COVE. For Samuel Haley, settler about 1800.

HALEY POND. For Joseph or Banjamin Haley, early residents.

HALFTIDE: LEDGES, ROCK. Because visible at halftide.

HALL HILL. For B. Hall, resident, 1872.

HAMILTON BROOK. Unknown.

HAMLIN BROOK. For Gershom Hamblen, settler from Gorham Township in 1798.

HAMLINTON BROOK. For the Hamilton family, settlers of the 1790's. The spelling variance is a cartographical error.

HANSCOM HILL Probably for Thomas Hanscom, who had an early garrison home.

HANSEN POND. Probably for John B. Hanson, who cut a road through the township for the proprietors.

HANSON RIDGE. For the Honorable Benjamin Hanson, a Sanford blacksmith who was interested in agricultural innovations.

HARMON BROOK. For the Harmon family who have been in the area since the 1600's.

HARRIS ISLAND. For Samuel Harris, owner of the island and on the board of selectmen in 1775.

HARVEY MILL STREAM. Unknown.

HAY BROOK. Because hay was cut there.

HEATH, THE: heath (4), BROOK. Descriptive.

HENDERSON BROOK. For J.S. Henderson, resident, 1872.

HENDERSON POINT. For William Henderson, who settled there in 1700.

HICKS ROCKS. For John Hicks, resident at the Point by the late 1600's.

HIDDEN LAKE. Descriptive of location between two hills.

HIGH PASTURE. Descriptive of location near ocean cliffs.

HIGHPINE. Descriptive.

HILL CREEK. For Samuel Hill, settler, 1686.

HILLS: BEACH, BEACH (settlement). For Major Roger Hill, settler in the 1660's.

HILTON BROOK. While the Hilton family was in the area by the 1700's, it is unknown if the brook was named for this early group.

HOBBS: BROOK. CROSSING, POND. For Joseph Hobbs, who built 2 forges on the Mousam River in 1770.

HOLLIS: CENTER, NORTH-, SOUTH-, TOWNSHIP, WEST-. For the Duke of Newcastle, whose family name was Hollis, a friend of the colonists.

HOOPERS: BROOK, SWAMP. For Elder William Hooper, a Calvinist who lived in the area in the 1780's.

HORN: HILL, POND. For D. Horn, resident prior to 1872.

HORNE ISLAND. Probably for its shape.

HORNE POND. Because it is shaped like a cow's head with horns.

HORSE HILLS. For Joseph Horn, early settler. Spelling is a cartographical error.

HORSESHOE COVE. Descriptive of shape.

HOSAC MOUNTAIN. If Indian, possible Mahican: "stone place."

HOYT MOUNTAIN. For Everett Hoyt, retired schoolteacher, who settled there about 45 years ago.

HOYT NECK. For the Hoyt family, settlers of the 1770's.

HOYTS ISLAND. For Thomas Hoyt, who owned the island in the 1830's.

HUBBARD HILL. For James Hubbard, Wells resident, 1761.

HUBBARD RIDGE. For Joshua Hubbard, one of the leading proprietors, and his numerous issue.

HURD HILL. For Daniel Hurd, settler, 1779.

HUSSEY BROOK. For Paul Hussey, who ran a carding and cloth business in 1820.

HUSSEY: HILL, MOUNTAIN. Although they are located in different areas, informants said both were named for John Hussey, who settled about 1778.

HUTCHINS CREEK. For Enoch Hutchins killed by the Indians on May 9, 1698.

INDIAN POND. For a pond so-named in a local historical pageant years ago.

INNIS BROOK. For Charles H. Innes.

ISINGLASS: HILL, POND. For the mineral isinglass.

ISLES OF SHOALS, THE. For either shoals of fish or shoaling, shallow water.

ISRAELS HEAD. Unknown.

JACKS COVE. For Jackson Perkins, who lived near.

JAGGER POND. For the Jagger family who owned a large mill.

JAMAICA ISLAND. If Indian, Natick: "beaver."

JEWETT. The ancestoral home and birthplace of Sarah Orne Jewett, the novelist.

JIMMIES LEDGE. Unknown.

JOHNS SWAMP. Unknown.

JOHNSON BROOK. For James Johnson, settler, 1657.

JONES BROOK. Unknown.

JOSIAHS RIVER. For Josiah Littlefield, settler of about 1700.

JOY HILL. For S. Joy, resident, 1860's.

JUNKINS BROOK. For Elisha Junkins, farmer and early settler.

KEAY BROOK. For numerous Keay families who were in the area in 1872.

KENNARD CORNER. For Michael Kennard, settler, 1700's.

KENNEBUNK: BEACH, BEACH (settlement), LANDING, POND, -PORT RIVER, -PORT (settlement), -PORT TOWNSHIP, settlement, TOWNSHIP, WEST-. If Abnaki: "long sandbar." If Micmac: "long cut banks."

KENYON HILL. For Mrs. Hollis Kenyon, who lived there in the 1950's.

KEZAR FALLS. For George Kezar, who first set up a footbridge over the falls.

KEZAR HILL. For Abner Kezar, legislator of the 1770's. Others say for Kezar Falls.

KILLICK POND. For a Scotchman who was driving an ox team up a nearby hill, pulling a heavy mast pine. The team could pull no farther, and he was heard to remark, "Bide, mon, bide, ye hae come to a killick." "Killick" is a Scots dialect word which means "a sudden stop." The term was first applied to the hill and later to the pond.

KIMBLES CORNER. For Caleb Kimball, a settler who was granted land in the 1660's.

KINNEY SHORES. For Aaron McKinney, who owned 200 acres of land in the 1730's.

KITTERY: FORESIDE, POINT, settlement, TOWNSHIP. For the manor of Kittery Point in Kingsweare, Devon, England.

KNIGHTS: BROOK. POND. For John Knight, settler, 1780.

KNOX MOUNTAIN. For I. Knox, resident, 1872.

LAKE CAROLYN. By Mr. Vermule, who cut ice there, for his wife Caroline.

LAUDHOLM BEACH. For George C. Lord and the imposing house he built there.

LEAVITT BROOK. For the Leavitt family on its banks in 1872.

LEBANON: CENTER-, EAST-, NORTH-, SOUTH-, TOWNSHIP, WEST-. For the biblical Lebanon.

LEIGHS MILL POND. For Major Leigh, who owned mills there.

LIBBY BROOK. For David Libby, who owned property nearby in 1725.

LIBBY MOUNTAIN. For Abner Libby, settler before 1800.

LIBBYSHEARS. Unknown.

LIBBYS POINT. For Arthur Libby of Wells Township, the owner.

LILY POND. (2). For lilies.

LIMERICK: MILLS, settlement, TOWNSHIP. By James Sullivan in 1787, for his former home of Limerick, Ireland.

LIMINGTON: EAST-, NORTH-, settlement, SOUTH-, TOWNSHIP. For either Limington, Somersetshire, or Lymington, Hampshire, England.

LION HILL. For Dr. Job Lyman, a large landholder in the 1700's. Through usage the name was corrupted.

LITTLE BROOK. To distinguish it from nearby Great Brook.

LITTLEFIELD POND. For the many Littlefields in the area in 1872.

LITTLEFIELD RIVER. Location of the Littlefield Mills, owned by S. and E.H. Littlefield in 1872.

LITTLE LONG POND. Descriptive.

LITTLE RIVER. (5). For their relative sizes.

LOBSTER COVE. For the lobsters which could be caught in abundance.

LOCKE BROOK. For Caleb Lock, a settler before 1800.

LONG: BEACH, BEACH (settlement), HILL, POND(2), SWAMP, SWAMP BROOK. Descriptive.

LONG BEACH: beach, settlement, Descriptive.

LOON POND. For loons.

L POND. For its approximate shape.

LORD BROOK. For Nathan Lord, local landowner.

LORDS BROOK. For T. Lord, resident, in 1872.

LORDS POINT. For the Tobias Lord family, very early settlers.

LORDS POND. For the Lord family who settled here in the 1700's.

LOVERS BROOK. For John Love, settler, 1636.

LYMAN TOWNSHIP. For Theodore Lyman, Esq., wealthy Boston merchant who was born there.

MACINTIRE GARRISON. For the ancestors of J.M. MacIntire, who lived nearby in 1872.

MACINTIRE JUNKINS BROOK. For the brook crossing the land of A.J. MacIntire and a Mrs. Junkins in 1872.

MALAGA. Probably Abnaki: "cedar."

MALOY MOUNTAIN. For Dennis Malloy, a settler before 1792.

MANN: MOUNTAIN, POND. For Albert Mann, farmer and butcher of the 1800's.

MAPLE: SWAMP, -WOOD. For maple trees.

MARSHALL POINT. For Thomas Marshall, shipmaster who settled here in 1790.

MARSHES, THE. Descriptive.

MARSH HILL. Possibly for Reverend Christopher Marsh, but another source states for its location near a marsh.

MAST COVE. Where mast pines were rafted.

MATHEWS: HILL, MILLPOND. For C. and H.N. Mathews, who had a mill there in 1872.

MEE CORNERS. For the Mee family.

MERRIFIELD BROOK. For Levi Merrifield, early settler on the brook.

MERRILAND: RIDGE, RIVER. For settlers from Maryland.

MIDDLE BRANCH POND. For the Middle Branch Mousam River.

MIDDLE POND. For its location between Folly and Scituate Ponds.

MILDRAM HILL. For C.L. Mildram, resident, 1872.

MILL BROOK. For Milliken Mills located on it.

MILL COVE. For a former mill there.

MILLER CORNER. For E., B.W., and O.W. Miller, residents, 1872.

MILLERS CROSSING. For the John Miller family, settlers about 1670.

MILLIKEN: MILLS, POND. For Charles Milliken, who built the mills in the early 1700's.

MILTON: MILLS, POND. For Milton, New Hampshire.

MINGO ROCK. Delaware: a term applied by the Delawares to the Iroquois: "dangerous, sneaky."

MIRROR LAKE. Descriptive.

MITCHELL MOUNTAIN. For John Mitchell, settler, 1797.

MOODY: BEACH, BEACH (settlement), POINT, POINT (settlement), settlement. For Captain Samuel Moody, active in Indian affairs in the early 1700's.

MOODY MOUNTAIN. For John and Cyrus Moody, settlers in about the 1790's. Others say for Leander Moody, resident before 1850.

MOODY POND. For Clement Moody, who bought a large tract of land, including the pond, in the 18th century.

MOORS BROOK. For Wyatt Moore, member of the first church organized in the Saco Valley, about 1730.

MOOSE POND. For moose.

MOULTON BROOK. (2). In Newfield Township, for Ephraim Moulton, settler, 1780. In York Township, for G. Moulton, resident, 1872.

MOUNT HOPE. Possibly Narragansett: "montaup"–"lookout place."

MOUSAM: LAKE, MIDDLE BRANCH, RIVER. If Indian, Abnaki: "grandfather," or Old Abnaki: "a snare."

MOUSE ISLAND. Descriptive of size.

MUD POND. (2). Descriptive.

MUDDY BROOK. Descriptive.

MULLOY BROOK. Unknown.

MURRAY ROCK. Unknown.

NEGRO: ISLAND (2), ISLAND LEDGE. Probably for free Negroes who lived there in the early 1800's, as there were a number in the area.

NEOUTAQUET RIVER. Abnaki: "at the solitary river."

NESSLER POINT. For the Nessler family, settlers, early 1700's.

NEW BARN COVE. For a barn built there.

NEWFIELD: settlement, TOWNSHIP, WEST-. Descriptive, "a new field."

NISBITT POND. For the prominent Nisbitt family who lived nearby.

NOAHS POND. For Noah Weeks.

NORMAN HILL. For the Norman family who lived there.

NORTHEAST POND. (2). In Lebanon Township, for its location northeast of Milton, New Hampshire. In Waterboro Township, for its location in the northeast section of the township.

NORTHWEST LEDGES. Descriptive of being northwest of Duck Island.

NORTON BROOK. For John Norton, one of the early settlers.

NO. 1 POND. Traveling northwest of Sanford settlement, it is the first of 3 ponds.

OAK: HILL, RIDGE. For oak trees.

OAKS: FALLS POND, NECK, REEF. For Oaks, early settler on the neck.

OARWEED COVE. For oarweed.

OCEAN PARK. Descriptive.

OGUNQUIT: BEACH, RIVER, settlement. Abnaki: "place of waves." Possible Micmac: "lagoons within dunes."

OLD FISHING POND. Descriptive.

OLD ORCHARD BEACH: settlement, TOWNSHIP. For an orchard planted by Thomas Rogers in 1638.

OSSIPEE: HILL, LITTLE-POND, LITTLE-RIVER, MILLS, RIVER. Abnaki: "water on the other side."

PADDY CREEK. For Judah Paddock, wealthy manufacturer.

PAGE MOUNTAIN For Taylor and Samuel Page, subscribers of Parsonsfield Township in 1785.

PAINT HILL. For a paint mill located there in the 1800's. The Indians also used this ocher earlier and called it "red paint hill."

PARSONAGE CORNER. For a parsonage built there in 1719.

PARSONS BEACH. For Charles Parson, summer resident.

PARSONSFIELD: EAST-, NORTH-, settlement, SOUTH-, TOWNSHIP. For Thomas Parsons, Esq., proprietor.

PAYNETON. For Thomas Payne, early settler killed at the Candlemas Day Massacre in 1692.

PEASE: BROOK, MOUNTAIN. For Stephen Pease, a settler of 1790.

PENDEXTER BROOK. For S. Poindexter, resident, 1872.

PEPPERRELL COVE. For William Pepperell, prominent settler, 1680.

PERKINS: BROOK, MARSH BROOK. TOWN. For the numerous area Perkins families.

PERKINS COVE. For Mrs. Daniel Perkins, who took in boarders at the former Pennace (Penants) Cove and called her residence Cove House. Later she put up a sign, "Perkins Cove House." The name was finally adopted from the sign.

PERRYS CORNER. For James Perry, settler, 1770.

PHILIP ROCK. Possibly for William Phillips, landholder, 1660.

PHILLIPS: COVE, POND. For Norton W. Phillips, settler, 1811.

PHILLIPS ISLAND. For J.S. Phillips, area resident, 1872.

PHILLIPS SPRING. For Major William Phillips, a land grantee, 1719.

PHILPOT MOUNTAIN. For Elkanah S. and Andrew R. Philpot, who owned a shingle and sawmill in the 1780's.

PICKEREL POND. For pickerel fish.

PICKET MOUNTAIN. Unknown.

PICTURE POND. Legend says for a daughter of Peter Morrell, who in 1754 went to get material to make a broom. She was captured and decapitated by the Indians when they felt that they did not have time to scalp her. When they reached the pond, they carved her picture on a tree to commemorate the event.

PIKE HILL. For John Pike, settler, 1800's.

PINE: HILL (2), HILL BROOK, PARK. For pine trees.

PINT COVE. Eighteenth and 19th century local pronunciation of "point."

PISCATAQUIS RIVER. Pennacook: "the place where the river divides."

PLAINS, THE. Descriptive.

POND IN THE RIVER. Descriptive.

POND ROCKS. For two nearby saltwater ponds.

POOL, THE. Because it was a tidal flat enclosed by land.

POPE CREEK. For J.S. Pope, resident, 1872.

PORTSMOUTH HARBOR. For Portsmouth, New Hampshire.

POVERTY: LITTLE-POND, POND. For the people who could barely make a living farming in the area.

POWDERHOUSE HILL. For powder stored here during the War of 1812.

PREBBLES POINT. For Abram Preble, who was in charge of the Patent of York in 1653.

PRESCOTT HILL. For the Prescott family who lived there.

PROSPECT HILL. Descriptive of view.

PROVINCE: LAKE, MOUNTAIN. For its location near the Maine-New Hampshire state line, formerly called the "Province Line."

PUGSLEY BROOK. For Andrew Pugsley, early settler and promoter of the Baptist Church in the 1800's.

PUMP BOX BROOK. Unknown.

PUNKY SWAMP. For the large amount of punky—dry, decayed—wood.

QUAMHEGAN BROOK. Abnaki: "dip net."

RAITT HILL. For Oliver Raitt, landholder in the 1600's.

RAM: ISLAND, ISLAND LEDGE. For sheep raised there.

RAMSHEAD POINT. Descriptive of shape.

RANDALL MOUNTAIN. For Miles Randall, who built a garrison on this site in 1705.

RAYNES NECK. For Captain Francis Raynes, who was named a royal justice by King Charles II in 1665.

REDIN ISLAND. For John Redding, the owner in 1684.

REMICK CORNERS. For R.H. Remick, resident, 1872.

RICHARDSON BROOK. For the early settling Richardson family.

RICKER BROOK. For George and T. Ricker, residents, 1872.

RICKER HILL. For R.W. Ricker.

ROARING ROCK POINT. For the noise made by the rock in high water.

ROBERTS: CORNER (2), RIDGE. Corner and Ridge in Buxton and Waterboro townships, for the Job Roberts family, early area settlers. Corner in Parsonsfield Township, for Joshua Roberts, settler, 1811.

ROBERTS POND. For R. and S. Roberts, residents, 1872.

ROCK HAVEN LAKE. Chosen because it was a "pretty" name.

ROCKY HILLS. Descriptive of terrain.

ROGERS BROOK. For Christopher Rogers, a servant of Sir Ferdinando Gorges in the 1640's.

ROSEMARY. An area named for a rest home for mothers and children-from the Boston slums. Mrs. Hannah Shapleigh bestowed the name for no discernible reason.

ROSS CORNER. For Jonathon Ross, American Revolutionary War veteran and settler, 1782.

ROSS MOUNTAIN. For the numerous area Rosses in 1872.

ROUND: POND (4), SWAMPS, SWAMPS BROOK. Descriptive.

RUSH: SWAMP, SWAMP BROOK. For rushes.

SACO: BAY, RIVER, settlement, TOWNSHIP. Abnaki: "flowing out."

SACOPEE POND. Abnaki: "having to do with a pond outlet."

SADDLEBACK, THE. Descriptive.

SALMON: FALLS, FALLS RIVER. For salmon fish.

SAMPSON COVE. For James Sampson, resident, 1720.

SAND POND. (2). Descriptive.

SANDS, THE. Descriptive.

SANDY: BROOK, BROOK (settlement). For Walter Sandy, a Bristol merchant who owned land there in the 1630's.

SANDY COVE. Descriptive.

SANFORD: settlement, SOUTH-, TOWNSHIP. For the children of John Sanford.

SAWYER MOUNTAIN. For the family of William Sawyer, settlers of the 1790's.

SAYWARDS CORNER. For Henry Sayward, settler, 1669.

SCITUATE: POND, settlement. By Thomas Chambers, for his home, Scituate, Massachusetts.

SCOTLAND. Named by Lewis Bean and Daniel Black for the many Scots who had been banished by Cromwell and took refuge here.

SEABURY. For Seabury Allen, resident, 1886.

SEAL: HEAD POINT, ROCKS. For seals.

SEAPOINT: BEACH, settlement. Descriptive.

SEAVEY ISLAND. For the Seavey family, among the first settlers.

SECOND HILL. For its being the first hill north of Mount Agamenticus, counting the mountain as the first.

SEWALL HILL. For D. Sewall, resident, 1872.

SEWARDS: COVE, POINT. For Richard Seaward, resident, late 1790's.

SHADY NOOK. Descriptive.

SHAG ROCK. For shags (cormorants).

SHAKER: BROOK, POND. For a colony of Shakers in the area, 1782.

SHAPLEIGH: NORTH-, POND, settlement, TOWNSHIP. For the Englishman Nicholas Shapleigh, landowner at Kittery Point and principal proprietor here.

SHARPS ROCKS. Probably for the John Sharp family, settlers in 1685.

SHEPARD ISLAND. Unknown.

SHEPARDS: HILL, HILL COVE. For John Shepard, resident, early 1700's.

SHOREYS BROOK. For Samuel Shorey, a landowner in the 1600's.

SHORT POND. Descriptive.

SHORT SANDS. Descriptive of a short, sandy beach.

SHY BEAVER POND. Unknown.

SIMPSON HILL. For William Simpson, resident, 1872.

SISTER: EAST-, WEST-. Fanciful names for two rocks.

SISTERS POINT. For the East and West Sisters.

SKILLY: BROOK, HILLS. Probably for the Silly family who were in the area in the 1600's.

SLATER HILL. Unknown.

SMALLS HILL. For Joshua Small, one of the purchasers of Cornish Township.

SMARTS POND. Unknown.

SMELT BROOK. For smelt fish.

SMITH BROOK. (2). In Hollis Township, for Daniel Smith, early settler. In Kennebunkport Township, for Benjamin Smith, wealthy merchant of 1797.

SMUTTY NOSE ISLAND. Descriptive of a rocky black point projecting into the sea which contrasts with the surrounding pale gneiss.

SOKOKIS LAKE. For the Sokokis Indian tribe that inhabited the area.

SOUTH: POINT, RIVER, SIDE, SIDE BROOK. Descriptive.

SPANG MILLS. For Phillip Spang, who used this area for lumber storage.

SPAULDING POND. For the prominent Spaulding family of Rochester, New Hampshire, who were in the leather board business.

SPENCER BROOK. For the Spencer family who lived in the area by 1856.

SPICER POND. For Walter Spicer, who owned and developed the surrounding land in the mid 1930's.

SPINNEY CREEK. For Thomas Spinney, who was granted the area land in 1659.

SPRAGUE CITY. For the L. and C. Sprague families, residents in 1872.

SPRING: HILL, -VALE. For springs.

SPRINGS ISLAND. For Captain Seth Spring, who began developing the island in 1794 with his partner Captain Moses Bradbury.

SPRINGY BROOK. For springs.

SPRUCE: CREEK, POND. For spruce trees.

SQUARE POND. For its approximate shape.

SQUASH ISLAND. For its shape.

STACEY CREEK. For William Stacey, resident, 1679.

STACKPOLE CREEK. For Lieutenant John Stackpole, a chainman with a surveying crew in 1733.

STAGE: ISLAND, ISLAND HARBOR, NECK. For stages (fish drying racks) located there.

STAPLES POND. For Captain M.C. Staples, resident, 1872.

STEVENS BROOK. For Amos Stevens, who had an almshouse here in the 1770's.

STEVENS CORNER. For A.R. and N. Stevens, residents of 1872.

STONES ROCK. The local lobstermen think a boat was wrecked there which had a man named Stone as its master.

STONY BROOK. Descriptive.

STRATTON ISLAND. For John Stratton, first owner, early 1600's.

STUMP POND. Descriptive.

STURGEON CREEK. For sturgeon fish.

SUCKER BROOK. For sucker fish.

SUGARLOAF MOUNTAIN. Descriptive.

SULLIVAN POINT. For old Fort Sullivan, which was located there in the 1800's.

SUNKEN BRANCH BROOK. Descriptive.

SUNSET HILL. Descriptive.

SURFSIDE. Descriptive.

SWAN: POND (2), POND CREEK. Pond in Acton Township, unknown. Pond and Pond Creek in Limington Township area, for Lieutenant Caleb Swan, an officer in the French and Indian War and a settler in 1766.

SWASEY HILL. For the early Swasey family.

SWETTS MEADOW. For Dr. Moses E. Swett, resident, 1837.

SYMMES POND. For William and Eben Symms, settlers prior to 1780.

TARWATER POND. Descriptive of the color of the water.

TATNIC: HILL, HILLS, settlement. Abnaki: "at the shaking place (boggy)."

TATTLE CORNER. For gossip passed as horses were watered at a trough at the corner of Pool Road and Guinea Road.

TEA KETTLE CORNER. Descriptive of the curving of one road as it branches from another, like the spout of a tea kettle.

THACHER BROOK. For Judge George Thacher, settler, late 1700's.

THIRD HILL. (2). In York Township, starting with Mount Agamenticus as the first one, this hill is the third hill going north. In Eliot Township, for being one of 3 hills in the area.

THOMPSON HILL. Probably for Miles Thompson, settler, 1699.

THUNDER ISLAND. Descriptive of the sound as water rushed by.

TIMBER: ISLAND, POINT. Descriptive of huge trees found there.

TOBEYS CORNER. For James Tobey of Kittery, a resident of 1687, who was killed by the Indians.

TOGUE BROOK. For togue fish.

TORY HILL. For a group of tories living there in the 1770's.

TOWLE MOUNTAIN. For Josiah Towle, a settler in the 1770's.

TOWLES HILL. For the two Towle brothers who received a grant of land there and trapped and traded in the area.

TOWN THATCH BED. For being where thatch was gathered.

TOWN: WOODS, WOODS BROOK. A woods held in common by the town as a "fowling woods."

TRAFTON BROOK. For R., A.G., and E. Trafton, nearby farmers in 1872.

TROTT ISLAND. For John Trott, the owner in the 1600's.

TURBATS: CREEK, CREEK (settlement). For Peter Turbot, settler, 1663.

TYLER BROOK. For James Tyler, who had a mill there in 1719.

TYLERS CORNER. For James and Edith Tyler, who bought a farm there in 1899.

UNION FALLS. Descriptive of where a small brook unites with the Saco River.

UPPER LANDING. Descriptive.

VARNEY CROSSING. For I. Varney, who lived at the crossing.

VAUGHN ISLAND. For the Vaughn family who owned it in the 1800's.

WADLEIGHS HEAD. For the early Wadleigh family.

WADLEY POND. Probably for Jessie Wadleigh, who lived in the area, after Ben Lunt dammed a small brook to create the pond in 1918-19.

WALES POND. For John Whales, a squatter in the 1770's, who was half Indian.

WALKERS POINT. For Richard Walker, settler of the 1740's.

WALLINGFORD POND. For the Wallingford family, settlers of 1746.

WALNUT HILL. For walnut trees.

WANDER HILL. Probably descriptive.

WARD BROOK. For Harold Ward.

WARDS POND. Unknown.

WARREN BROOK. For Daniel Warren, veteran of the American Revolution.

WASHMAN ROCK. Unknown.

WATERBORO: EAST-, NORTH-, settlement, TOWNSHIP. For Joseph Waters, one of the proprietors.

WATSON HILL. For Nathaniel Watson, settler in the 1800's.

WEARE COVE. For Peter Weare, surveyor and landowner in 1652.

WEBHANNET RIVER. Abnaki: "at the clear stream."

WEDGWOOD BROOK. For the local Wedgwood family.

WELCH HILL. Unknown.

WELCHS POND. For Benjamin Welch, resident in the 1600's.

WELLS: BEACH, BEACH (settlement), BRANCH, settlement, TOWNSHIP. Named by Sir Ferdinando Gorges, for Wells, England.

WEST BROOK. (2). In Biddeford Township, for John West, who leased land nearby in 1638. In Wells Township, for C.H. and L. West, residents in 1872.

WESTERN POND. Descriptive.

WEST: OUTLET, POND. Descriptive.

WHALE: -BACK, -BACK REEF, ROCK LEDGE. Descriptive.

WHIPPOORWILL SWAMP. For whippoorwills.

WHITE: ISLAND, ISLAND REEF. For John White, a settler of 1654.

WHITES MARSH BROOK. For R. White, resident by 1856.

WHITTEN HILLS. Unknown.

WIGGIN MOUNTAIN. For Bradstreet and Winthrop Wiggin, settlers of the 1780's.

WILCOX POND. For the Wilcox family who used it to harvest ice there.

WILDES: CORNER, DISTRICT. For Captain Israel Wilde, who lived in the area in the early 1700's.

WILSON CREEK. Unknown.

WILSON LAKE. For Gowen Wilson, resident in the 1690's.

WINDMILL POINT. Captain Jordan owned a farm and a windmill here.

WITCHTROT HILL. For nearby Witchtrot Road. Reverend George Burroughs passed by here on his way to trial and execution at the Salem witch trials.

WOOD: ISLAND, ISLAND HARBOR. For woods.

WORSTER BROOK. For William Worster, blacksmith, 1750.

YEATON HILL. For John Yeaton, settler in the 1770's.

YORK: BEACH, CLIFFS, CORNER, COUNTY, HARBOR, HARBOR (settlement), HEIGHTS, LEDGE, POND, RIVER, settlement, TOWNSHIP, VILLAGE, WOODS. For York, England.

YOUNG HILL. For Rowland Young, English settler of the 1640's.

ZEKES MOUNTAIN. Unknown.

INFORMATION SOURCES

From Maine:

Abbott, Robert. *Madison*
Adams, Cynthia F. *Town Clerk, Perry*
Aiken, Ruth J. *President, Cushing Historical Society, South Cushing*
Allan, A. Sawyer. *Northfield*
Ames, Vonnie. *Lobsterman, Vinalhaven*
Anderson, A. Atwood. *Postmaster, Caribou*
Anderson, Florence. *Cary*
Andrews, Elliot M. *Former President Lee Historical Society, Lee*
Annas, Leo F. *Selectman, Charlotte*
Atchison, Helen K. *Librarian, Cary Free Public Library, Houlton*
Bagley, Hazel. *Liberty*
Bagley, Laurence. *Secretary, Maine Teachers' Association, Augusta*
Bardwell, Mrs. Willis. *Librarian, York Public Library, York*
Barker, Ineze. *Town Clerk, Stoneham*
Barker, Norris. *Enfield*
Barrett, Beatrice. *Librarian, Richards Library, Georgetown*
Barrows, Mrs. Lewis O. *Newport*
Barter, Mrs. Marjorie. *Newagen*
Batson, Mr. Walter. *Addison*
Bearce, Elizabeth J. *Librarian, Caribou Public Library, Caribou*
Beal, Everett. *Postmaster, Ellsworth*
Beal, Ralph. *Selectman, Addison*
Bean, Miss Eva. *Bethel*
Beckler, Mrs. Earle. *Livermore Falls*

Belanger, Nancy N. *Student, Gorham State College, Gorham*
Belden, Mrs. Madeline. *Palermo*
Belletty, Helene. *Librarian, Ellsworth City Library, Ellsworth*
Bennett, Charles W. *Postmaster, Monroe*
Benoit, Jeffrey T. *Student, Gorham State College, Gorham*
Berg, Elmer G. *Postmaster, Onawa*
Best, Gordon. *Student, Gorham State College, Gorham*
Bigelow, Gladys M.
Billings, Mrs. Marion. *Bryant Pond*
Birt, Walter A. *East Millinocket*
Biscaha, Eileen. *Student, Gorham State College, Gorham*
Blackwood, Harold F. *Retired teacher and lawyer, Pembroke*
Blake, George H. *Mount Vernon*
Blake, Orland. *Yarmouth*
Blake, Roland. *Farmer and insurance agent, Denmark*
Boddy, Nadine. *Deputy Clerk, Millinocket*
Bond, Mrs. Barbara. *Librarian, Dyer Library Association, Saco*
Bordeaux, Pearl. *Chairman, Board of Assessors, Mount Desert, Me. Township, Northeast Harbor*
Borgerson, Miss Beryl. *Owls Head*
Bowden, Bertha. *Penobscot*
Bowden, Reginald. *Public Relations Director, Gorham State College, Gorham*
Bowles, Lewis. *Whiting*
Boyce, Gilbert. *Lakeville*
Boylan, Mrs. Frank. *Newport*
Boyle, Betty Ann. *Plantation Clerk, Lakeville*
Brackett, Agnes M. *Jay*
Brackett, Betty. *Town Clerk, Springfield*
Bray, Alan. *Student, Gorham State College, Gorham*

Bray, Vivienne. *Librarian, Monson Free Public Library, Monson*
Brooks, Mrs. Chester. *Camden*
Brown, Diane. *Calais*
Brown, Edson. *Sebago*
Brown, Harold E. *Curator, Bath Marine Museum, Bath*
Brown, Hazel. *Town Clerk, Kenduskeag*
Brown, Lindy. *Calais*
Brown, M. *Town Clerk, Cherryfield*
Bubar, Verna. *Postmaster, North Amity*
Burnell, Mrs. Olive. *Old Tavern Antique Shop, West Baldwin*
Burnham, Hazel A. *Librarian, Naples Public Library, Naples*
Burns, Maurice. *Danforth*
Burton, Clara. *Librarian, Monhegan Library, Monhegan*
Butcher, Grace. *Lewiston*
Butler, Mrs. Natalie S. *Farmington*
Campbell, Susie J. *Town Clerk, Minot*
Campbell, W.H. *Postmaster, Fort Fairfield*
Carlow, Georgia S. *Town Clerk, Wesley*
Carlson, Mary Thomas. *Harrison*
Carlton, George M. *Woolwich*
Carman, Dorothy S. *Executive Secretary for Deer Isle and Stonington Historical Society, Deer Isle*
Carr, R.E. *Postmaster, Harmony*
Carroll, Ron. *Student, Continuing Education Division, University of Maine, Brunswick*
Carter, Mrs. C.W. *Etna*
Carter, Mrs. Lydia. *Librarian, Seal Harbor Library, Seal Harbor*
Carter, Pauline. *Gardiner*
Carver, Stella R. *Housemother, Phi Gamma Delta, University of Maine, Orono*
Castner, Merle S. *Waldoboro*

Chamberlain, Earle. *Brownfield*
Chase, Otta Louise. *Town Clerk, Sweden*
Chasse, Suzanne T. *Student, Gorham State College, Gorham*
Clapp, Joanne M. *Town Clerk, Veazie*
Clark, Bertram. *South Berwick*
Clark, Mrs. Herbert. *Former Town Clerk, Plymouth*
Clark, Harry M. *Retired Postmaster, Masardis*
Clark, William M. *Kennebunk*
Cleaves, Colonel Haskell. *President, Bar Harbor Historical Society, Bar Harbor*
Clifford, H.B. *East Boothbay*
Collins, Delma. *Town Clerk, Hudson*
Connor, Gary E. *Student, Gorham State College, Gorham*
Cook, Cara. *Trustee of Bridgton Public Library, Bridgton*
Coombs, Donald. *Postmaster, Stonington*
Copeland, Mary L. *Brewer*
Corey, Mrs. Thomas. *Westfield*
Costello, Mrs. Melissa. *Head, Education Dept., Gorham State College, Gorham*
Costigan, Rhonda. *Student, Gorham State College, Gorham*
Cousins, Mary. *Librarian, Stonington Public Library, Stonington*
Crandlemire, W.R. *Postmaster, Vanceboro*
Crane, Clyde. *Whiting*
Crane, Jonas R. *Author and Superintendent of the Grindstone Neck Golf Course, Winter Harbor*
Creamer, Neal. *Bucksport*
Crockett, Mrs. David N. *Raymond*
Crockett, Leon. *Camden*
Crooker, Mrs. Enid. *Librarian, B.H. Bartol Library, Freeport*
Cross, Natalie H. *Town Clerk, Brighton*
Crowley, Lois. *Corea*

Crouse, Alden C. *Crouseville*
Cummings, Catherine. *Deputy Town Clerk, East Corinth*
Cunningham, Joyce. *Secretary, Augusta Chamber of Commerce, Augusta*
Currier, Susan A. *Student, Gorham State College, Gorham*
Curtis, Helen L. *Librarian Calais Free Library, Calais*
Curtis, Ralph H. *Harrington*
Cushman, Helen. *Editor, Livermore Falls Advertiser, Mt. Vernon*
Cyr, Arlene. *Jackman*
Cyr, Claude. *Postmaster, Fort Kent*
Danforth, Avis. *Clerk, Carroll*
Davis, Mrs. B.T. *Postmaster, Georgetown*
Davis, Geraldine. *Student, Gorham State College, Gorham*
Davis, Ida F. *Librarian, Stewart Free Library, Corinna*
Davis, Luther. *Maine Forest Service, District Ranger, Cherryfield*
Davison, Ann R. *Student, Gorham State College, Gorham*
Day, Adelaide. *Kennebunkport Historical Society, Kennebunkport*
Day, Clarence. *Orono*
Day, Mrs. Faye. *Librarian, New Sharon Town Library, New Sharon*
Dean, Hazel. *Town Clerk, Barnard*
DeArmott, Miriam R. *Brick House, Fayette*
Delaware, Anna M. *Treasurer, Scarborough Society, Scarborough*
Dennison, Mrs. Arthur. *Cutler*
Dodge, Ernest W. *Guilford*
Dolley, Mira L. *Portland*
Donley, Sue. *Student, Gorham State College, Gorham*
Douglas, Sterling B. *President Franklin Historical Society, Franklin*
Dow, Doris B. *Librarian, Charles M. Bailey Public Library, Winthrop*
Dowling, Frank S. *Jacksonville*

Drew, Bertha F. *Librarian, Parsons Memorial Library, Alfred*
Drisko, Clarence H. *Columbia Falls*
Drisko, Frank. *Retired schoolteacher, Harrington*
Dudley, John M. *Princeton*
Dufresne, Sylvia E. *Student, Gorham State College, Gorham*
Dunham, Rowena. *Town Clerk, Greenwood, Locke Mills*
Duquette, Fern. *Town Clerk, Brunswick*
Durgin, Mrs. Leona E. *Librarian, D.A. Hurd Library, North Berwick*
Dyer, Leslie. *Retired seaman, Rockland*
Dyer, Winnifred D. *Eliot*
Earl, Mrs. Theodore A. *Winter Harbor*
Eaton, Harvey Doane. *Skowhegan*
Edes, Milton. *Postmaster, Sangerville*
Ellis, Alice V. *Stockton Springs*
Ellis, Mrs. Beryl. *Trustee, Harvey Memorial Library, Guilford*
Emery, Mrs. Guy. *Bryant Pond*
Emerson, Dr. Horton. *Professor of History, Gorham State College, Gorham*
Emerson, Roosevelt. *Island Falls*
Estabrook, Ralph. *Blaine*
Evans, Ora L. *Publisher of Piscataquis Observer, Dover-Foxcroft*
Fairbanks, Hayden. *Phillips*
Ferguson, Wanda. *Sandy River Plantation*
Fernald, Dorothy. *Municipal Clerk, Franklin*
Fernald, Douglas. *Detroit*
Field, Madeline H. *Vanceboro*
Finley, Josephine. *Washington*
Finn, Alan P. *Student, Gorham State College, Gorham*
Fish, Dr. Lincoln T. *Professor of Mathematics, Gorham State College, Gorham*

Fisher, Carleton. *Brigadier General, Winthrop*
Fitzpatrick, M.J. *Student, Gorham State College, Gorham*
Flanders, H. Earle. *Monmouth*
Flemming, Mrs. Edwinn. *Ludlow*
Fogg, Barbara. *Librarian, Readfield Community Library, Readfield*
Foley, Phillip. *Winterport*
Forbus, Charles R. *Wellington*
Foss, E. Velma. *Librarian, Sanford Library Association, Sanford*
Foster, Mr. *Druggist, Machias*
Foster, Marguerite. *Librarian, Fort Fairfield Public Library, Fort Fairfield*
Foster, Rosemary. *Student, Gorham State College, Gorham*
Foster, Mrs. William. *China*
Fox, Ethel W. *Librarian, Hartland Free Library, Hartland*
French, Arthur L. *Kingfield*
Fuller, Mrs. Hildred W. *Librarian, Jackman Public Library, Jackman*
Furber, Iva. *Town Clerk, Hartland*
Gagnon, Oscar A. *Forest Ranger, Greenville*
Gallant, Naida J. *Town Clerk, Glenburn, Bangor*
Gardner, Louis W. *Dennysville*
Gay, Mrs. Glenna T. *Town Clerk, South Paris*
Gifford, Walter. *North New Portland*
Gill, Eva Weston. *Belgrade*
Gilman, Mrs. Olive G. *Librarian, Kezar Falls Library, Parsonsfield*
Golding, Jane E. *Student, Gorham State College, Gorham*
Goodwin, Eula N. *Anson*
Goulet, Carol A. *Student, Gorham State College, Gorham*
Grant, Everett. *Addison*
Grant, Mr. and Mrs. Everett A. *Marion*

Grant, Reginald. *Student, Gorham State College, Gorham*
Graves, Marion N. *Librarian, Andover Public Library, Andover*
Gray, Mrs. *Chester*
Great, Mildred. *Town Clerk, Holden*
Greene, Edith L. *Wilton*
Greenleaf, Ruth N. *Norway*
Grey, Ella C. *East Holden*
Grinnell, Mary E. *Islesboro*
Gross, Clayton. *Stonington*
Guptill, Mrs. Edwin. *Portland*
Hagaman, Adaline P. *Librarian, Lebanon Area Library, East Lebanon*
Hale, Doris. *Millinocket*
Hall, Elsie R. *Librarian, Kennebunk Free Library, Kennebunk*
Hall, Harold E. *Historian, Hebron Academy, Hebron*
Hall, John H. *Kennebunk*
Hall, Mrs. Verna. *Newport*
Hamblen, Millicent. *Librarian, Bass Harbor Memorial Library, Tremont*
Hanson, Mrs. Ray G. *Director of Pejepscot Historical Society, Topsham*
Harkness, Miss Elizabeth A. *Lincolnville*
Harnois, Cheryl A. *Student, Gorham State College, Gorham*
Harriman, R.B. *Orrington*
Harris, Harriet W. *Town Clerk, Brownfield*
Harris, Harry B. *Canaan*
Hartman, Herbert. *West Forks*
Harvey, Mrs. Bessie. *Town Clerk, Magalloway Plantation*
Hatto, Fonda. *Student, Gorham State College, Gorham*
Hatton, Leta F. *Town Clerk, Charlotte*
Hawkins, Alan. *Student, Lincoln*

Haycock, Jean M. *Student, Gorham State College, Gorham*
Hicks, Mary B. *Town Clerk, East Sumner*
Higgins, Mrs. Edward D. *Pittsfield*
Hill, Mrs. Alfred. *Librarian, Owls Head Village Library, Owls Head*
Hill, George. *Gray*
Hill, Rosemarie. *Houlton*
Hilton, Brian D. *Student, Gorham State College, Gorham*
Hilton, Clarence. *Athens*
Histler, Marguerite. *Clerk, Somerville Plantation*
Hitchner, Barbara D. *Orono*
Hock, Mary T. *Readfield Depot*
Hodgkiss, Austin. *Postmaster, Temple*
Hodgkins, Sarah T. *Lamoine*
Holling, Mrs. Constance G. *Librarian, Brewer Public Library, Brewer*
Holmes, Mildred. *Secretary, Border Historical Society, Eastport*
Horseman, Allen. *Littleton*
Houghton, Susan E. *Librarian, Orrs Island Library, Orrs Island*
Houle, Mrs. Jean. *Librarian, Madison Public Library, Madison*
House, Maynard. *North Turner*
Howard, Roland. *Bluehill*
Hunt, Mrs. Donald. *Member of local historical association, Readfield*
Hunter, Dorothy. *Town Clerk, Benton*
Huntley, Annette. *Town Clerk, Sherman Station*
Huntley, Eldred. *Postmaster, East Machias*
Hupp, Daniel D. *Student, Gorham State College, Gorham*
Hurt, Lawrence. *Great Northern Paper Co., Rockwood*
Huston, Mrs. Helen. *Librarian, Lisbon Falls Community Library, Lisbon Falls*
Hutchins, Doris M. *Postmaster, Orland*

Hutchinson, Mrs. Pearl. *Town Clerk, Carthage*
Ingraham, Maynard D. *Rockport*
Irving, Welles. *Reporter, Baileyville*
Jackson, Kay. *China*
Jackson, Moses. *Bradley*
Jacobs, Bailey. *Winthrop*
Jacques, Adrian O. *Fort Kent*
Jenkins, Mrs. Evelyn L. *Librarian, Lincoln Memorial Library, Lincoln*
Jenkins, Mrs. Sue. *Milo*
Jenness, Joan M. *Student, Gorham State College, Gorham*
Jipson, Doris. *Town Clerk, Maxfield*
Johnson, Cheryl A. *Student, Gorham State.College, Gorham*
Johnson, Grace. *Appleton*
Jones, Flossie. *Anson*
Jones-Hill, Gertrude. *Pleasant Point*
Jordan, Mrs. Elizabeth. *Librarian, Bingham Union Library, Bingham*
Joy, Kenneth. *Kennebunk Historian, Kennebunk*
Joy, Lillis. *Librarian, Northeast Harbor Library, Northeast Harbor*
Judkins, Mrs. Jennie L. *Librarian, Upton*
Junkins, Stanley C. *Oxbow*
Keiser, Harry R. *Tax Assessor for the State of Maine, Brewer*
Keith, Sharon S. *Student, Gorham State College, Gorham*
Kennedy, Robert T. *Student, Gorham State College, Gorham*
Kidder, Rachel. *Librarian, Ludden Memorial Library, Dixfield*
Kimball, Amos W. *Local Historian, Newburg*
Kimball, Mr. and Mrs. Ober. *South Waterford*
Kirby, Lewis.
Knapp, Evelyn R. *Clerk, Webster Library Association, Kingfield*

Knight, Arne. *Lincolnville*
Knight, Diane. *Student, Gorham State College, Gorham*
Knox, John R. *Student, Gorham State College, Gorham*
LaGross, Leroy. *Town Clerk, Harmony*
Landon, Mrs. Ruth. *Kennebunkport*
Larrabee, Ann. *Librarian, Merrill Memorial Library, Yarmouth*
LaVarge, Mrs. Marion B. *First Selectman, Prospect*
Law, Mrs. Edward. *Washburn*
Learned, Phil M. *Andover*
Leavett, Hazel D. *Postmaster, Exeter*
Leland, Louise. *Bar Harbor*
Lewis, Clara A. *Gardiner*
Lewis, Ruth E. *Springfield*
Libby, Florence. *Town Clerk, Litchfield*
Libby, F. Wayne. *Hartland*
Liggins, Barbara. *Student, Gorham State College, Gorham*
Lincoln, Mary. *Retired teacher, Solon*
Littlehale, Mrs. Carl. *Clerk, Lincoln Plantation*
Look, Mrs. Theone F. *Town Clerk, Jonesboro*
Lovell, Mrs. Atwood. *Sangerville*
Lucas, Michael G. *Student, Gorham State College, Gorham*
Lucas, Ruth. *Town Clerk, Bradbury*
Lydie, Guy L. *Forest City*
MacArthur, Mrs. Lawrence. *Alexander*
MacDonald, Thomas L. *Eustis*
MacDonald, Mrs. Virginia. *Librarian, Isle au Haut*
MacMaster, Brian. *Editor,* Kennebec Journal, *Gardiner*
Mahar, Albert G. *Postmaster, Dennysville*

Mallory, Edna. *Town Clerk, Codyville*
Manelick, Cheryl. *Student, Gorham State College, Gorham*
Marble, Gerald C. *Former manager of Dodling Quarries, Skowhegan*
Marcho, Mrs. *Carmel*
Markay, Margaret. *Maine Forest Service, Greenville*
Marquis, John. *Student, Gorham State College, Gorham*
Marquis, Romeo. *Insurance agent, Fort Kent*
Marriner, Mrs. *President, Waterville Historical Society, Waterville*
Marston, Catharine. *Librarian, Sargentville Library, Sargentville*
Martin, Robert L. *Anson*
Martin, Tommy. *Student, Gorham State College, Gorham*
McCurda, E.E. *Newcastle*
McEwen, Mrs. Ceola B. *Bowdoinham*
McFarland, Phyllis. *Librarian, Friendship Public Library, Friendship*
McGowan, Mrs. *Town Clerk, Carmel*
McKay, Ernest A. *Town Manager, Danforth*
McKeown, Cecil E. *Crawford*
McKinnon, Leland. *Houlton*
McLeod, John E. *Calais*
McNear, Susan E. *Student, Gorham State College, Gorham*
McQuilkin, Lizzie G. *Skowhegan*
Melanson, K.R. *Postmaster, St. Francis*
Melvin, Charlotte. *Monticello*
Merill, Carolyn. *Town Clerk, Roxbury*
Merrifield, Lance. *Student, Gorham State College, Gorham*
Merrill, Hiram. *Maxfield*
Merry, Felix M. *Retired carpenter, Sherman*
Meserve, Rory M. *Carpenter, Casco*

Meyer, Carla. *Nurse, Orrington*
Michaud, Gilbert E. *Postmaster, Eagle Lake*
Milde, D. *Town Clerk, Sullivan*
Miller, George. *Retired postman, Mars Hill*
Miller, Mrs. Roger E. *Waldoboro*
Mitchell, Mrs. Verda. *Sherman*
Moholland, Clarence. *Librarian, Robbinston*
Moore, Franklin L. *Student, Gorham State College, Gorham*
Moore, Norman B. *Librarian, Waterville Public Library, Waterville*
Moore, Mrs. Pauline H. *Lovell*
Morris, Frank J. *Masardis*
Morris, Gerald. *Postmaster, Kingman*
Morrison, Clover M. *Librarian, Ellsworth City Library, Ellsworth*
Morrison, Pearl. *Saint Francis*
Mullen, Marilyn E. *Town Clerk, Levant*
Neal, Benjamin P. *Town Clerk, Talmadge*
Neal, Val. *Calais*
Newman, Gladys. *Plantation Clerk, Lake View*
Nightingale, Carroll. *New Sharon*
Norton, Lawrence B. *West Jonesport*
Noyes, Clyde. *Warden of Inland Fish and Game, Dennysville*
Noyes, George A. *Manset*
Nye, Mary E. *Librarian, Shirley Free Public Library, Shirley*
Ober, Grace M. *Woodland*
Ober, Mrs. S.E. *Baileysville*
O'Brien, F.M. *Portland*
O'Keefe, Nancy. *Student, Gorham State College, Gorham*
Oliver, Gwendolyn P. *Post office clerk, Nobleboro*

Oliver, Wesley G. *Postmaster, Nobleboro*
Olson, Helen. *Librarian, Fryeburg Public Library, Fryeburg*
Onyango, Sharon. *Student, Gorham State College, Gorham*
Packard, Vernon. *Town Clerk, Garland*
Pagus, Lora. *Patten*
Palmer, Carrie. *Moro*
Parent, Patricia. *Student, Gorham State College, Gorham*
Parsons, Larry. *Andover*
Partridge, Shirley. *Librarian, Thompson Free Library, Dover-Foxcroft*
Patchill, Fay A. *Wytopitlock*
Patrick, Ivaloo. *Town Clerk, Vinalhaven*
Paul, Mrs. Owen. *Waldo*
Pearce, Albert L. *Assistant Librarian, McArthur Public Library, Biddeford*
Pease, Rebecca. *Librarian, Bonney Memorial Library, Cornish*
Pecoraro, Camilla. *Student, Gorham State College, Gorham*
Pelletier, M.A. *Van Buren*
Perkins, Lizzie M. *Town Clerk, Cooper*
Perkins, Miss Madeline A. *Librarian, Ogunquit Memorial Library, Ogunquit*
Perkins, Vera. *Norridgewock*
Perry, Arthur. *Bath*
Philbrook, Everett. *Matinicus Island*
Philippon, Mona A. *Student, Gorham State College, Gorham*
Pierce, Cecil. *East Boothbay*
Pitman, Evelyn. *Union*
Plourde, Pauline. *Belgrade*
Plummer, Francis W. *Librarian, Lisbon Community Library Association, Lisbon*
Polk, Charles. *Vinalhaven*
Polk, Elsie. *Town Clerk, Plantation Number 21*

Porey, Mrs. Rudolph. *Member, local historical society, Readfield*
Postmaster. *Ashland*
Postmaster. *Burnham*
Postmaster. *Cambridge*
Postmaster. *Concord*
Postmaster. *East Dixfield*
Postmaster. *Embden*
Postmaster. *Frankfort*
Postmaster. *Rangeley*
Pottle, John. *Casco High School teacher, Otisfield*
Pottle, Marion. *Oxford*
Pratt, Helen. *South Paris*
Prevost, Robert. *Student, Gorham State College, Gorham*
Priest, David C. *Lincoln Center*
Prince, Armanda. *Sabattus Local member, Daughters of American Revolution*
Prosser, Capt. Albert L. *York County Historical Society, Springvale*
Purcell, Mark. *Student, Gorham State College, Gorham*
Purington, Mr. *Postmaster, Mechanic Falls*
Qualey, Edward T. *Benedicta*
Randall, Mrs. Floralee A. *Librarian, Gallison Memorial Library, Harrington*
Rather, Ernest W. *Searsmont*
Raynes, Alton. *Tenants Harbor*
Redman, Arlo L. *Lincolnville*
Reed, R. *Town Clerk, Jackman*
Reed, Ruth S. *Moose River*
Rhodes, Carl. *Goodwin's Mills*
Rich, Elizabeth. *Postmaster, Isle au Haut*
Richardson, Inez. *Town Clerk, Great Pond Plantation*

Richardson, Stanley. *Plymouth*
Rideout, Charlene, *Clerk, Mattawamkeag*
Robbinson, Harlon. *State Sealer of Weights and Measures, Gardiner*
Rogers, Aeta. *Town Clerk, Hampden Highlands*
Rogers, Mrs. Katherine. *Librarian, Patten Memorial Library, Patten*
Rogers, Lore. *Curator, Lumberman's Museum, Patten*
Rogers, William. *Employee, Lincoln County Cultural and Historical Association, Wiscasset*
Rolfe, Mrs. Katharine Moses. *Bridgton*
Rollins, Leola. *Town Clerk, Moscow*
Romanoff, Ellen J. *Student, Gorham State College, Gorham*
Rousseau, Raylene D. *Student, Gorham State College, Gorham*
Rowe, Margaret. *Sorrento*
Rowland, Mrs. Cecil V. *Bath*
Roy, Phyllis A. *Town Clerk, Freeport*
Ruth, John. *Minister, Houlton*
Sanborn, Harriet A. *Librarian, Steep Falls Library, Steep Falls*
Sand, Mrs. Verna. *Prentiss*
Sanders, Harry. *Greenville*
Savage, Ruth A. *Town Clerk, Stetson*
Sawyer, Mrs. Frank. *Retired teacher, Island Falls*
Sawyer, George C. *Forestry Agent for Dunn Timberlands, Ashland*
Schillinger, A.C. *Danforth*
Schillinger, Agnes. *Danforth*
Schillinger, Lindsay. *Danforth*
Schmidt, Frank. *Denmark*
Schmidt, Miss Henrietta. *Kennebunkport*
Scott, Elwood. *Principal, Houlton High School, Houlton*
Scribner, Mrs. *Town Clerk, Charleston*

Scribner, James W. *Student, Gorham State College, Gorham*
Scribner, Rolland. *Lee*
Seeley, Ruth. *Grove*
Sevey, Howard L. *Ripley*
Shaw, Dorothy M. *Librarian, Charles E. Thomas Memorial Library, Scarborough*
Shaw, Eunice. *Librarian, Spaulding Memorial Library, East Sebago*
Shelton, Barbara E. *Librarian, Wiscasset Public Library, Wiscasset*
Sherman, Mrs. Evelyn. *West Southport*
Sherman, Wayne. *Student, Gorham State College, Gorham*
Shirley, N.D. *District Ranger, Forest Service, Bethel*
Simmons, Carlton. *Friendship*
Sinclair, John. *Bangor*
Skinner, Ralph. *Auburn Historical Society, Auburn*
Small, Bruce Alan. *Student, Gorham State College, Gorham*
Smalley, A.J. *St. George*
Smith, Barry W. *Student, Continuing Education Division, University of Maine, Brunswick*
Smith, Mrs. Clementine Tyler. *Librarian, Hollis Center Public Library, Hollis Center*
Smith, David. *Student, Lewiston*
Smith, Earl. *Dixmont*
Smith, Mrs. Edna. *Librarian, Atkins Memorial Library, East Corinth*
Smith, Genie E. *Student, Gorham State College, Gorham*
Smith, Harold O. *Student, Farmington State College, Farmington*
Smith, Kilton. *Vinalhaven*
Smith, Mabel. *Town Clerk, Mount Vernon*
Smith, Marion S. *Hampden*
Smith, Myrtle. *Librarian, Washburn Memorial Library, Washburn*
Snow, Walter. *Chairman, Research Committee, Brooksville Historical Society, Brooksville*
Soule, Margaret. *Buxton*

Southard, Mrs. Frank. *Augusta*
Spizuoco, Frank. *President, Dexter Historical Society, Dexter*
Spruce, Wilfred L. *Postmaster, Milford*
Stanley, Leroy. *Town Clerk, Mexico*
Staples, Geneva. *Curator, Searsport Historical Society, Searsport*
Stevens, Eloise. *Guilford*
Stewart, Mrs. John. *Corea*
Stineford, Bertha. *Librarian, Oakland Public Library, Oakland*
Strout, Cynthia. *Gorham*
Strout, Gordon. *Student, Gorham State College, Gorham*
Strout, Helen L. *Clerk, New Gloucester Historical Society, New Gloucester*
Sturtevant, L.M. *North Belgrade*
Swain, Stephen. *Rangeley Plantation*
Sweetser, Harlan.
Swendson, Mary G. *Student, Gorham State College, Gorham*
Talarico, Marilyn. *Student, Gorham State College, Gorham*
Taylor, Robert. *Graduate student, Gorham State College, Gorham*
Terrill, Esther E. *Librarian, Bucksport Memorial Library, Bucksport*
Thayer, Donald S. *Searsport*
Thomas, Edwin A. *Caribou*
Thomas, Edwin. *Carlton*
Thomas, Mrs. Gertrude. *Librarian, Mexico Free Public Library, Mexico*
Thomas, Miriam S. *South Harpswell*
Thompson, Carolyn S. *Georgetown*
Thompson, Mrs. Merle. *Farmington*
Thompson, William. *Lincoln*
Thurlow, Marion W. *Weeks Mills*
Thurston, Marion H. *Librarian, Henry D. Moore Library, Steuben*

Thurston, Russell. *Chairman, Library Committee, Rockport Public Library, Rockport*
Tinker, Katherine. *Retired school teacher, Cousins Island*
Tobey, Ray. *Fairfield*
Torelley, L. *Belgrade*
Town Clerk. *Brownville*
Town Clerk. *Freedom*
Town Clerk. *Gilead*
Town Clerk. *Liberty*
Town Clerk. *Pittsfield*
Town Clerk. *Washington*
Tozier, Mrs. Prince Y. *Assistant Librarian, Lawrence Library, Fairfield*
Traves, A.R. *Auburn*
Treat, Harry. *South Portland*
True, Dorothy. *Town Clerk, Mercer*
Trundy, W.F. *Town Clerk, Stockton Springs*
Tutlis, Joseph M. *Student, Gorham State College, Gorham*
Tuttle, Riba. *Town Clerk, Corinna*
Twombly, Adela. *Postmaster, Enfield*
Upton, Jane C. *Old Town*
VanNess, Noble. *President, Vinalhaven Historical Society, Vinalhaven*
Veilleux, Marine. *Student, Gorham State College, Gorham*
Verow, Arthur C. *City Clerk, Brewer*
Vickery, James B. *Brewer*
Viles, Ruth T. *Chairman, Historical Section, Turner Public Library, Turner*
Wadleigh, Geneva. *Belgrade*
Wagg, William: *Lisbon*
Walar, Albert. *Postmaster, No. 14 Plantation area, Denneysville*
Walden, Harold. *Greenville*

Walker, Irene. *Town Clerk, Lovell*
Wallace, Kerry Sue. *Student, Gorham State College, Gorham*
Ward, Ernest E. *Harrison*
Ward, Lynda L. *Student, Gorham State College, Gorham*
Ward, Mabel. *Yarmouth*
Ware, Adelia. *Postmaster, Passadumkeag*
Waters, Henry C. *Whitefield*
Webb, Norma. *Town Clerk, West Forks*
Webber, Margaret. *Librarian, The Dr. Shaw Memorial Library, Mount Vernon*
Webber, Rosevelt A. *Madrid*
Webster, Kent D. *Student, Gorham State College, Gorham*
Welch, Merwin E. *Selectman, Chapman*
Wescott, Sharon A. *Student, Gorham State College, Gorham*
White, Alice H. *Brookton*
White, Norman R. *Forest Ranger, Greenville*
Whitehead, Vaughn E. *Student, Gorham State College, Gorham*
Whitney, Alice L. *Acting Librarian, Perley Memorial Library, Bridgton*
Wiggins, Harry. *Maine Forest Service, Greenville*
Wilbur, Robert M. *Franklin*
Wilder, John B. *Norridgewock*
Williams, Alma. *Town Clerk, Clifton*
Willis, Iva. *Postmaster and Town Clerk, Starks*
Wing, Duluth. *District Ranger, Maine Forestry Service, Eustis*
Winship, Doris. *Deputy Collector, Bradford*
Winter, Dorothy. *Librarian, Weld Memorial Library, Weld*
Winter, Florence. *Augusta*
Witham, Alfred. *Smithfield*
Withee, Karen J. *Student, Gorham State College, Gorham*

Wood, Miss Esther. *Professor of History, Gorham State College, Gorham*
Woodward, Mrs. Dean. *York*
Woodward, Homer C. *Postmaster, Newport*
Worcester, B.C. *Manset*
Yeaton, Judith A. *Student, Gorham State College, Gorham*
York, Donald. *Owner, Lobster Lane Book Shop, Spruce Head*
York, Mary S. *East Blue Hill*
York, Nancy. *Town Clerk, Caratunk*
York, Walter E. *Caratunk*
Young, Ellen. *Student, Gorham State College, Gorham*

From Other States:

Cole, Jane. *Henderson, Ky.*
Starkey, Earl, Jr. *New York City, N.Y.*
Watson, Leon E. *Largo, Florida*